HISTORIC PHOTOS OF
INDIANA

TEXT AND CAPTIONS BY SCOTT M. BUSHNELL

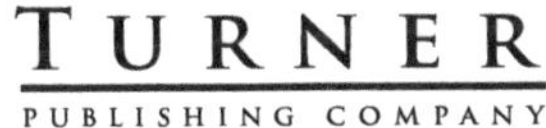
TURNER
PUBLISHING COMPANY

Madison was among Indiana's most successful communities when this photograph was taken in 1866. Its population had doubled in the 1840s because of its location on the Ohio River and the commerce it generated, and continued to grow in the next decade because of the Madison & Indianapolis Railroad, the first railroad built in the state.

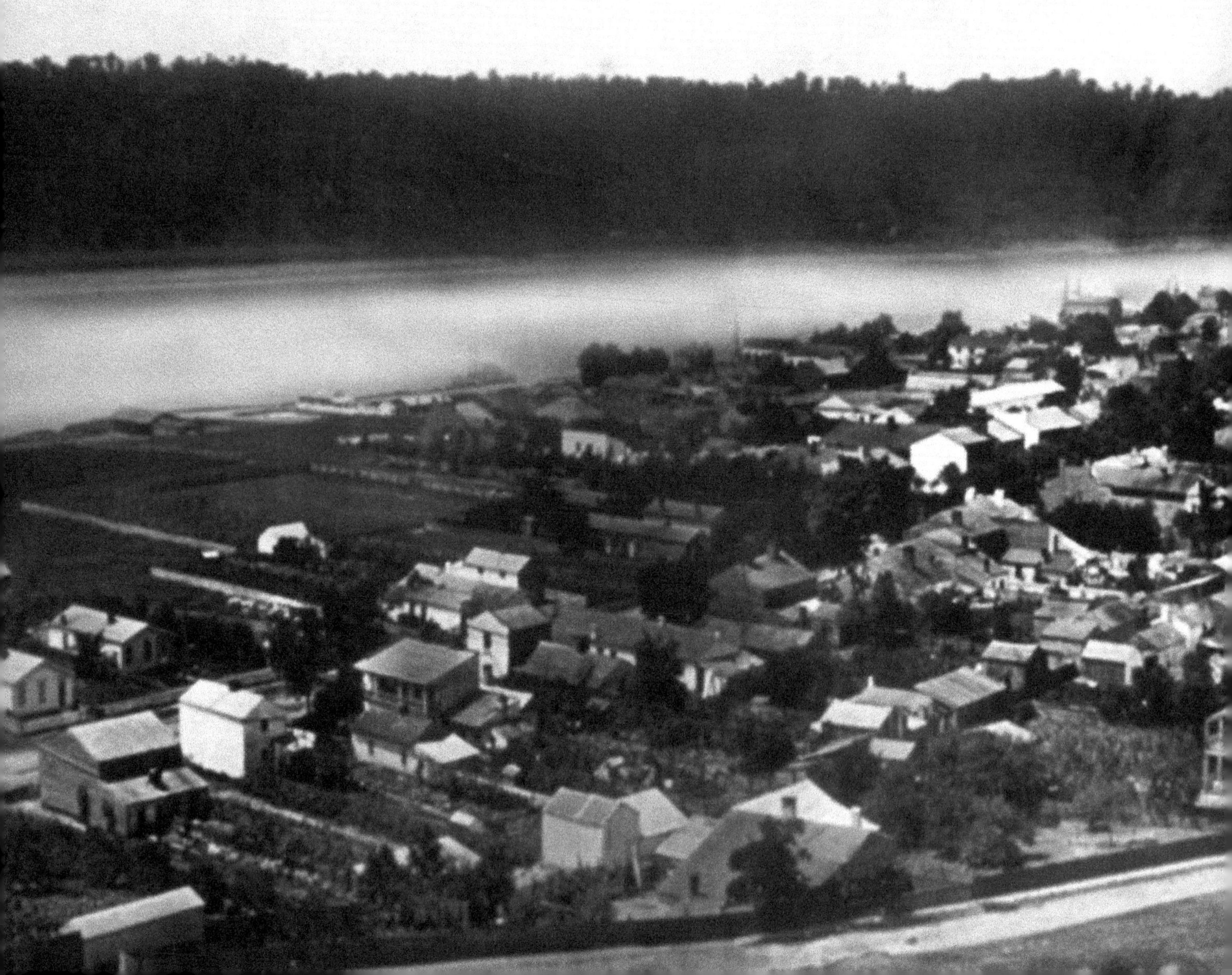

HISTORIC PHOTOS OF
INDIANA

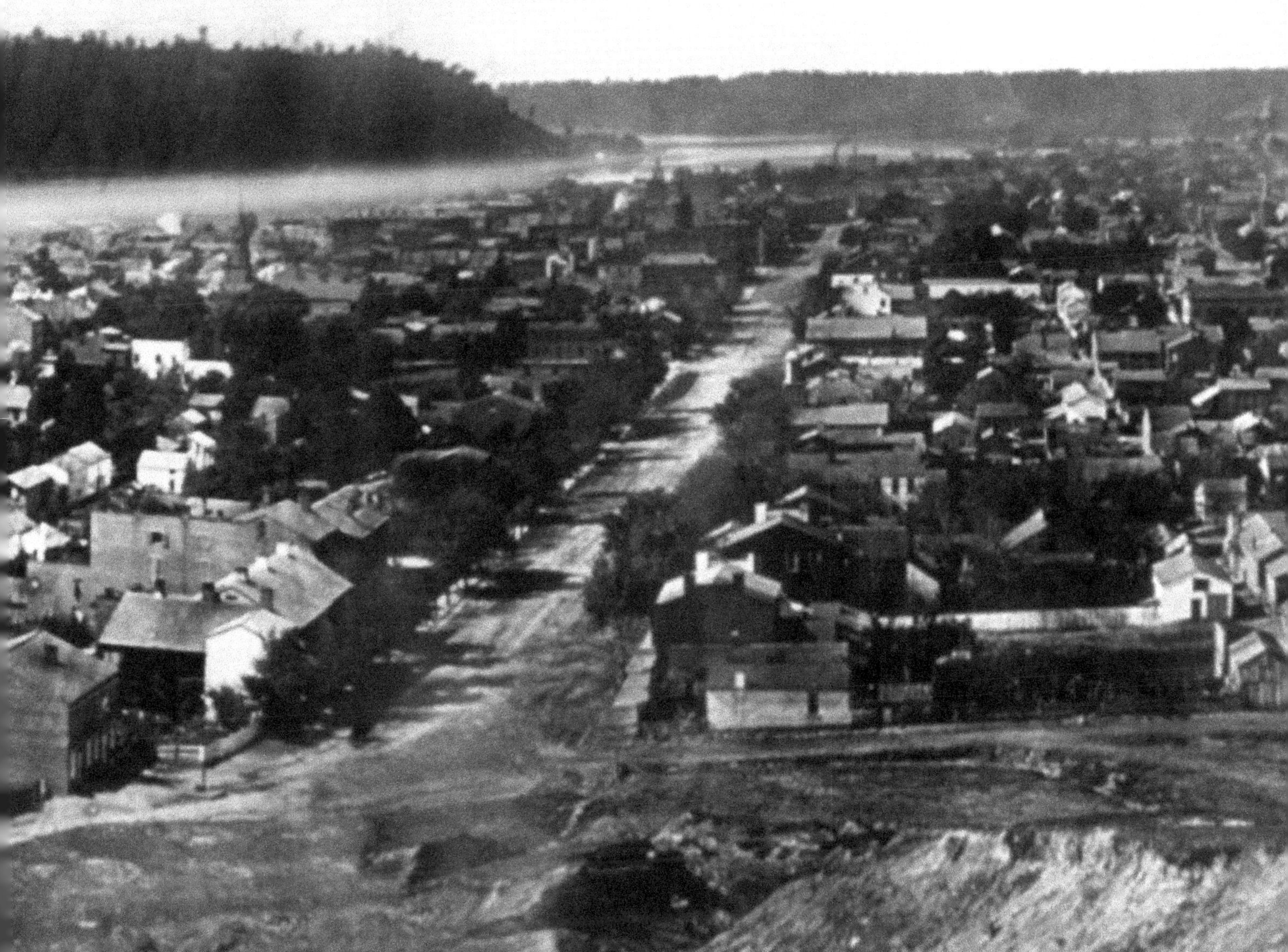

Turner Publishing Company
www.turnerpublishing.com

Historic Photos of Indiana

Library of Congress Control Number: 2009933005

ISBN: 978-1-59652-553-5

Printed in the United States of America

ISBN 978-1-68442-100-8 (hc)

Contents

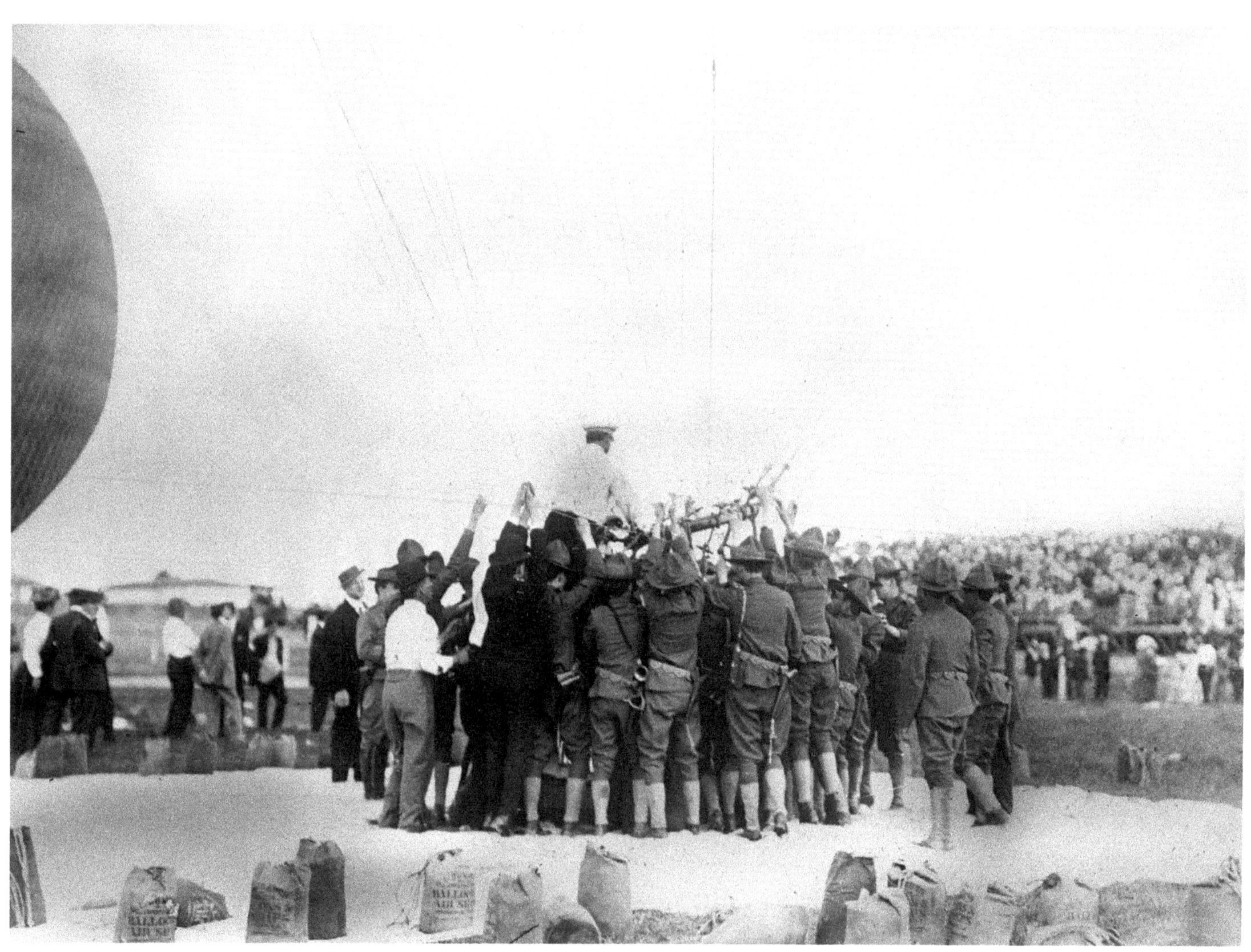

The beginning of a balloon race in 1909 was a perilous moment as the ground crew struggled to maintain control of the craft while the pilot clambered aboard. Only the ropes of the *Indiana*—one of nine hot-air balloons in this race—are visible at the nascent Indianapolis Motor Speedway.

Acknowledgments

This volume, *Historic Photos of Indiana,* is the result of the cooperation and efforts of many individuals and organizations. It is with great thanks that we acknowledge the valuable contribution of the following archives for their support, as well as the efforts of many individuals, including:

John Beatty and Curt B. Witcher of the Allen County Public Library; Thomas Castaldi, Allen County Historian; Beau Cunnygham, Tipton County Public Library; Walter Font, Curator, Allen County–Fort Wayne Historical Society; Janelle Graber, director, Eckhart Public Library, Auburn; James Harlan, director, Wayne County Historical Museum, Richmond; Jamey Hickson, Lebanon Public Library; B. Joan Keefer, director, Indiana Room, Huntington City Township Public Library; Sue King, Archivist, Morrisson-Reeves Library, Richmond; the Library of Congress; Stephen McShane, director, Calumet Regional Archives, Indiana University Northwest, Gary; Nancy Masten, archivist, Miami County Historical Society; James Rodgers, director, and Fern Schultz at La Porte County Historical Society; Jan Shupert-Arick, Lincoln Highway Association; John Martin Smith, DeKalb County Historian; Mark Vopelak, Brent Abercrombie, and Marcia Caudell, Indiana State Library; Brenda Williams, director, Princeton Public Library; Gregg Williamson, director, William H. Willennar Genealogy Center, Auburn

Steven Cox and Michael McCalip of Turner Publishing Company are due considerable gratitude for steering this book through editing and production.

My deep appreciation is due John Walls for his professional skills in recognizing and scanning old photographs as well as to E. J. Richards and Ed Breen for their work in finding rarely seen historic images. Good friends who appreciate history and the art of photography—and who are willing to drive all over the state of Indiana to find them—are a priceless commodity.

Last, none of this work could have been accomplished without the support and encouragement of my wife, Barbara, who makes each Indiana sunrise a wondrous event.

With the exception of touching up imperfections that have accrued with the passage of time and cropping where necessary, no changes have been made. The focus and clarity of many images is limited by the technology and the ability of the photographer at the time they were taken.

PREFACE

There are many images of Indiana that are common to the American mind. One imagines the Corn Belt sweeping across Indiana's torso like a shawl. Others see the great manufactories of the late nineteenth century, arising from the sweat and determination of thousands of workers, native-born and immigrants. Some point to the natural beauty of the landscape interrupted by few, if any, impediments to the panoramas that seem to sweep on without end. More cite the cities that grew from stump-pocked crossroads into major metropolitan areas in a matter of decades. A few know of the literature, art, and music produced by Indiana artists in the nineteenth and early twentieth centuries who contributed to an understanding of who we are as a nation. Those who follow agriculture recognize that Indiana is among the nation's leaders in the production of corn, soybeans, and hogs. There are car enthusiasts who will tell you that until 1905 Indianapolis had more automobile manufacturers than Detroit. Demographers will note that while Indiana is the smallest of the contiguous states west of the Appalachian Mountains, it ranks 16th in the nation's population.

To an extent Indiana has always been a checkerboard of contradictions. Slavery, for example, was outlawed in the Northwest Territory from which the state was carved, but that was not the popular sentiment. A constitutional convention in 1802 unsuccessfully tried to make slavery legal, and in 1851 the state passed a constitution that prohibited African-Americans from settling in Indiana and disfranchised those freed slaves living within its borders. Yet studies show there were probably never more than 250 slaves in the state, and when it came to the Civil War, more than 24,000 men from Indiana died for the Union cause.

The state has also played an unusual role in the nation's politics. Indiana is the only state with a grandfather and grandson to both serve as President, although neither William Henry Harrison nor Benjamin Harrison were born in Indiana. The elder Harrison was the first president to die in office, after contracting pneumonia during his hour-long inaugural that featured his lengthy address. Benjamin Harrison, too, holds an unusual distinction in the nation's line of presidents: He was preceded and succeeded by the same man, Grover Cleveland. Harrison defeated the incumbent in the election of 1888 to become the nation's 23rd president; however, in part because of the economy and in part because Harrison refused to leave the bedside of his dying wife, Cassie, in order to campaign, he lost to Cleveland in 1892. Indiana is also sometimes referred to as the State of Vice-presidents because of the number of residents to hold the office. Five men have served as vice-president of the nation: Schuyler Colfax, Thomas A. Hendricks, Charles W. Fairbanks, Thomas Marshall, and J. Danforth Quayle. Three of the men—Hendricks, Fairbanks, and Quayle—were also unsuccessful candidates for the presidency. Three other men were also unsuccessful: George W. Julian, William Hayden English, and John W. Kern. The reason for so many Indiana candidates was simple: In the middle 1800s, Indiana was among a handful of states to hold presidential elections in October. The outcomes were considered a good indicator for the presidential vote in the rest of the nation in November. A strong campaign with a "homegrown" vice-presidential candidate was viewed as a way of winning the election in Indiana and influencing November voters. By way of comparison, only one Indiana man has been named to the U.S. Supreme Court. Sherman Minton served as a justice from 1949 to 1956.

Then there is the issue of Indiana's nickname. Despite the years of searching by professional historians and just plain curious folks, no one really knows the origin, or meaning, of the word "Hoosier." A heroic effort at research by Jeffrey Graf of the Herman B. Wells Library at Indiana University uncovered different spellings for the term and its derivation. The definitions ranged from "Who's here?" to an Indian word for corn. Some believe there is a connection with a man named Hoosier or Howsier who built a canal near Louisville and whose workers were known as "Hoosier's men." Others, like James Whitcomb Riley, maintained its origins lay with the ornery proclivities of early settlers, who were said to bite off noses and ears during a fight. Some of these stories end with the victor wearing the loser's ears on his belt, to which someone asks, "Whose ears?"

Wherever you land on this issue, permit me the temerity to speak for my adopted state and offer the point of view once attributed to nineteenth-century writer Maurice Thompson: "Say Hoosier, if you like, but say it with admiration." This is a state with a history that many historical museums, genealogy societies, and libraries have preserved. This volume of photographs, I hope, will demonstrate that their effort has not been in vain.

—Scott M. Bushnell

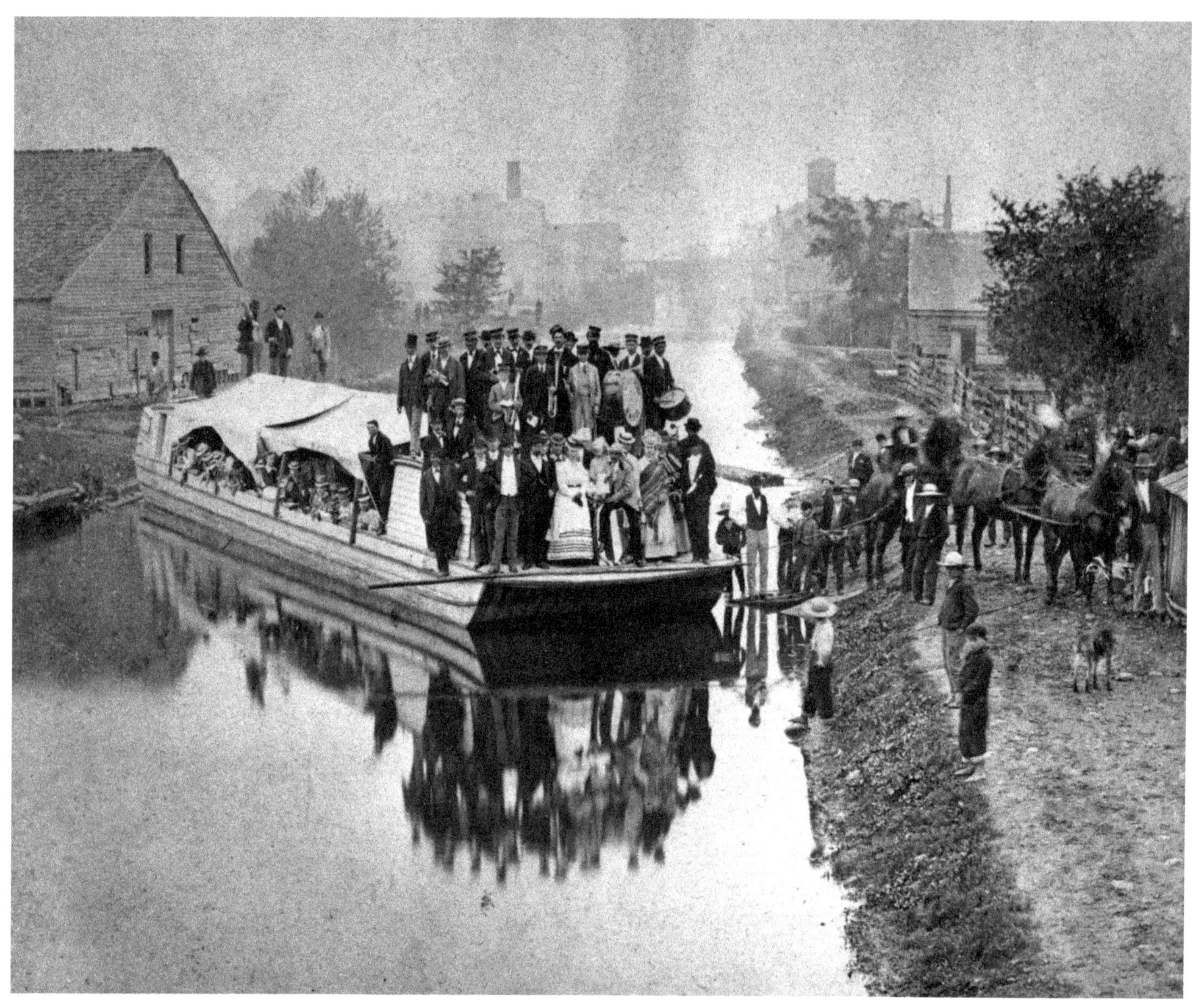

There has been a good deal of nostalgia about the Wabash and Erie Canal since its construction from Lake Erie to the Ohio River at Evansville during the years 1832 to 1853. Few reminiscences could be so romantic, though, as this image showing a wedding party aboard an old canal barge—complete with band and well-wishers—in the town of Attica on May 16, 1872.

Roads to Prosperity

(1850–1889)

By the 1850s Indiana was recovering from the nightmare of being on the brink of bankruptcy a decade earlier. The state had made two mistakes in 1834: One was to use public funds to undertake a massive program to build canals and turnpikes; the second was to discount the role that railroads could play in efforts to improve transportation. By 1840, expenditures were higher than expected and revenues were falling short, leaving Indiana all but bankrupt. The idea of state-owned enterprises was dead.

One aspect of the program, however, showed promise. The state's pioneer railroad, the Madison & Indianapolis, was a success by 1850. Its concept was simple and provided valuable lessons for future railroads: Indianapolis would serve as a hub for the collection of produce to be shipped by rail to Madison, where it would be loaded onto steamboats for delivery to cities along the Ohio River. It was an elegant idea and Madison's population doubled in a decade.

Growth was experienced throughout the state during this period, especially in the northern counties. Indiana's population rose from 988,000 in the 1850 census to 1,978,000 in 1880. Immigration was a leading factor—in 1870 nearly 10 percent of the state population was European-born. Interesting from a geographical point of view, most of the new native-born citizens came from Ohio rather than the South as had been the case previously.

The toll of the Civil War and ensuing economic recession cannot be overestimated. By some accounts, more than 70 percent of all eligible Indiana men served in the Union army or paid a fee to be exempt from service. This was the second-highest percentage of any state in the Union. The war effort deprived families, farms, and communities of the manpower needed for day-to-day living. The financial collapse after the war was cruel, too, particularly on farmers whose trade had been with the South before 1861.

Yet the war and the railroads brought commercial development and transformed many small towns into profitable cities. Prior to the Civil War, there were only 4 communities with more than 10,000 residents. In 1880 there were 9, and ten years later there were 14, with Indianapolis' population exceeding 100,000. The businesses once located along the canals and rivers were now found along the rails.

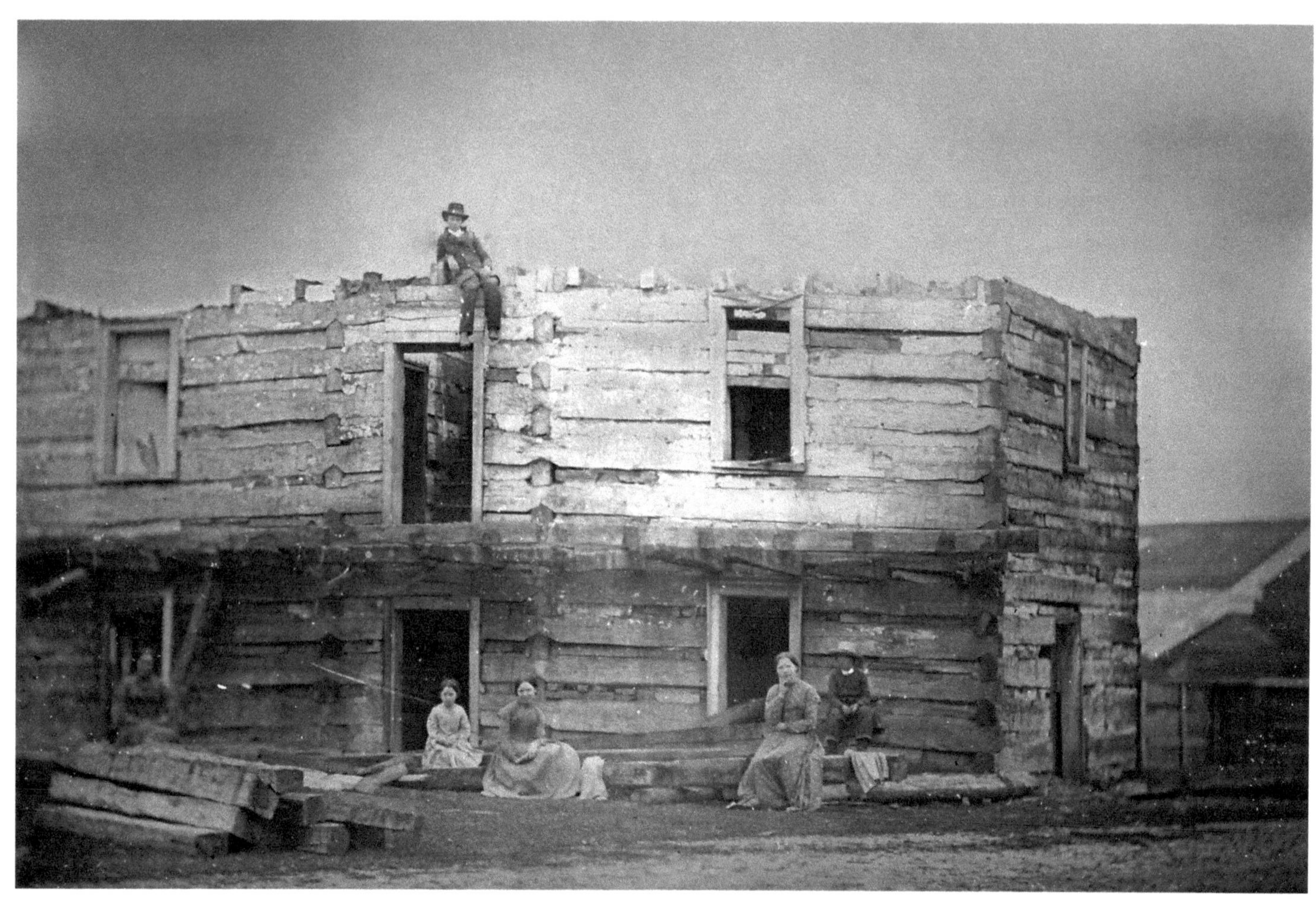

A group of Fort Wayne citizens recognized a historic moment and posed in the ruined blockhouse of the American fort shortly before it was demolished in 1852. Built in 1816 by Major John Whistler, it was the last of five forts in the city built during the conflict between early Americans and European settlers.

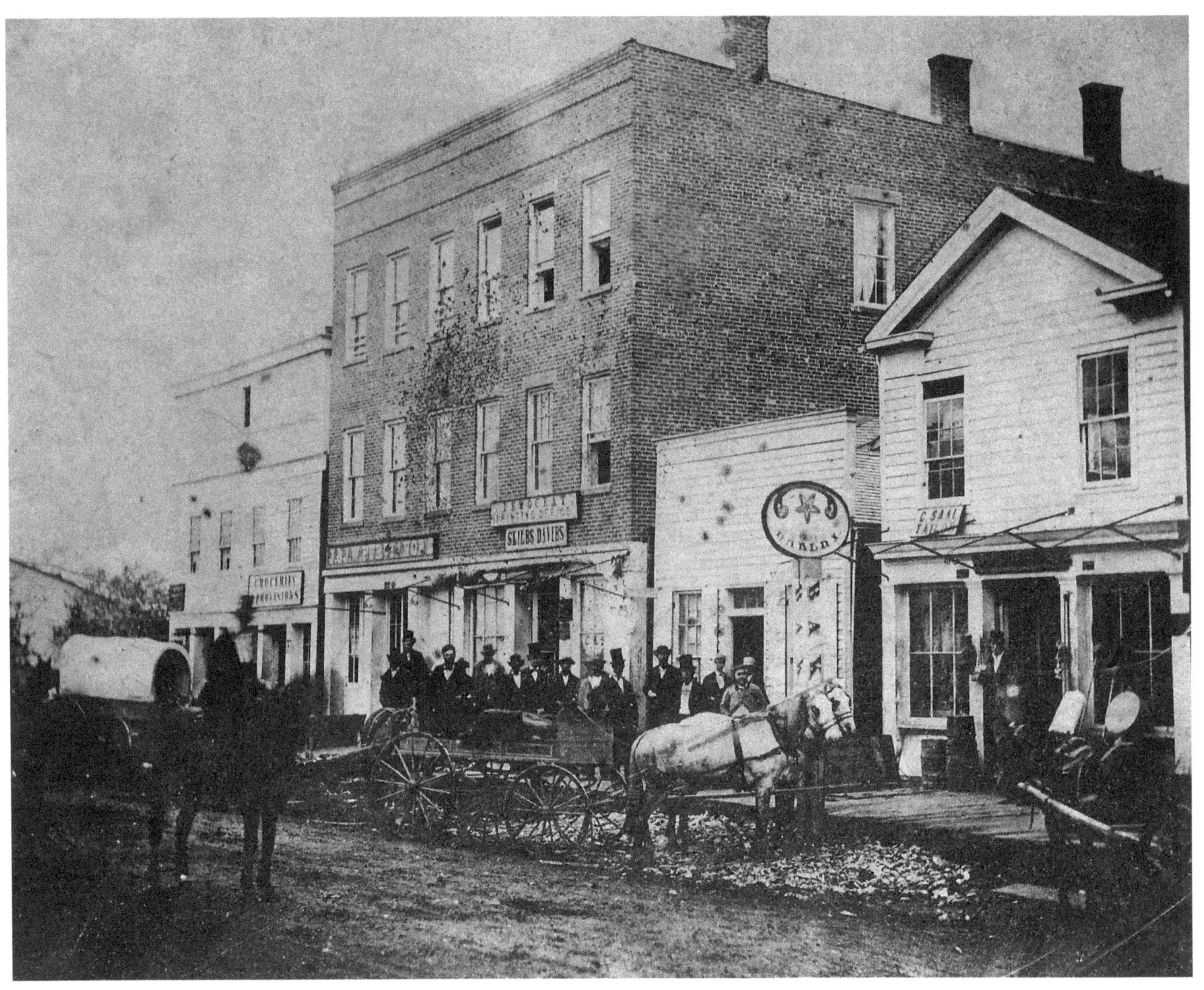

The principal business district of Huntington—with its muddy streets and plank sidewalk—was the subject of this photograph taken in 1860. On the horse at left is the town physician, Dr. F. S. C. Grayston, who was said to make his house calls on horseback because he believed buggies were a luxury. Early photography could not freeze objects in motion; the doctor and his horse, in motion when the exposure was taken, thus appear blurred in the image.

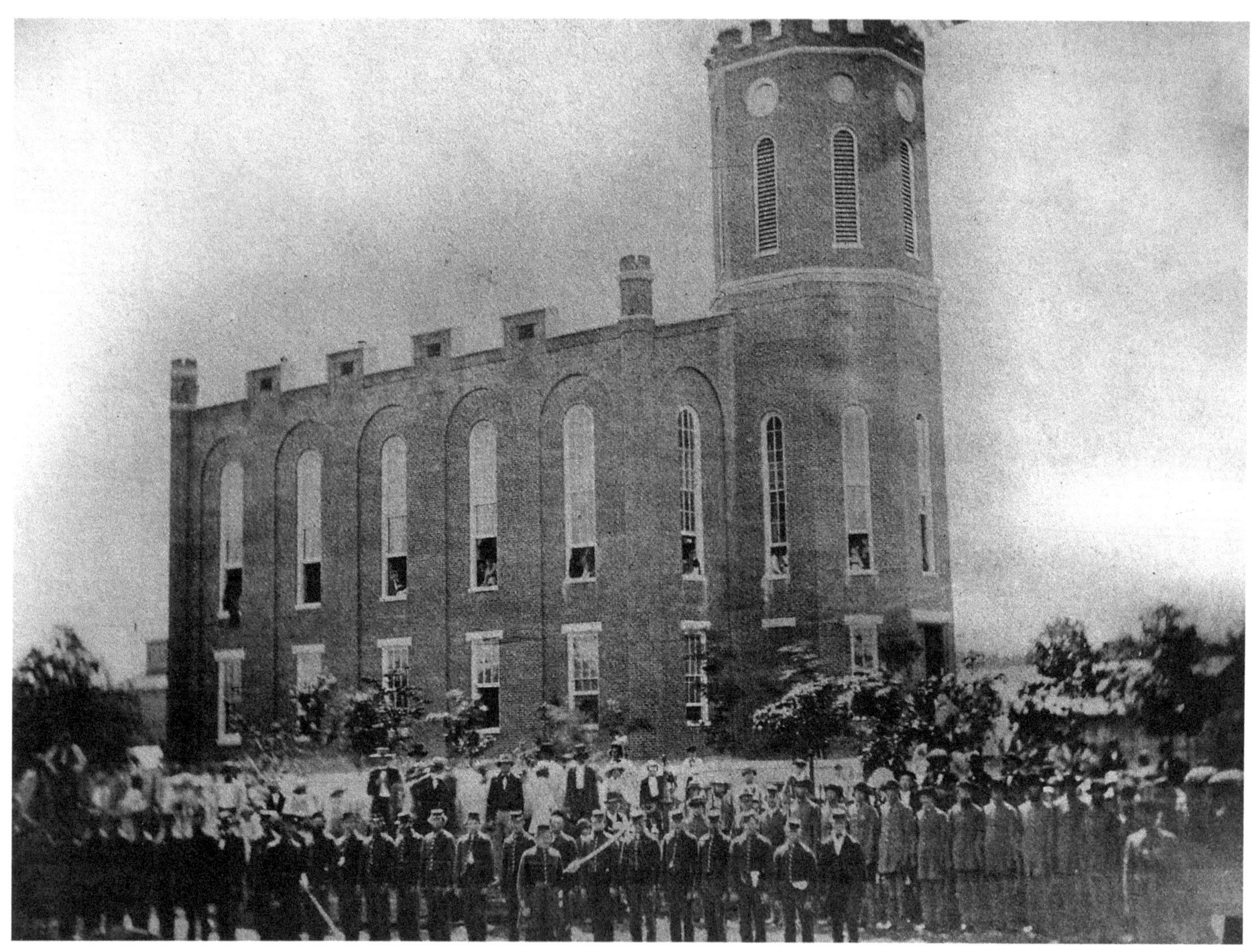

Two companies of soldiers muster outside the Huntington County Courthouse in 1861, the first year of the Civil War. The courthouse, featuring an octagonal tower, was built in 1858 and demolished in 1904.

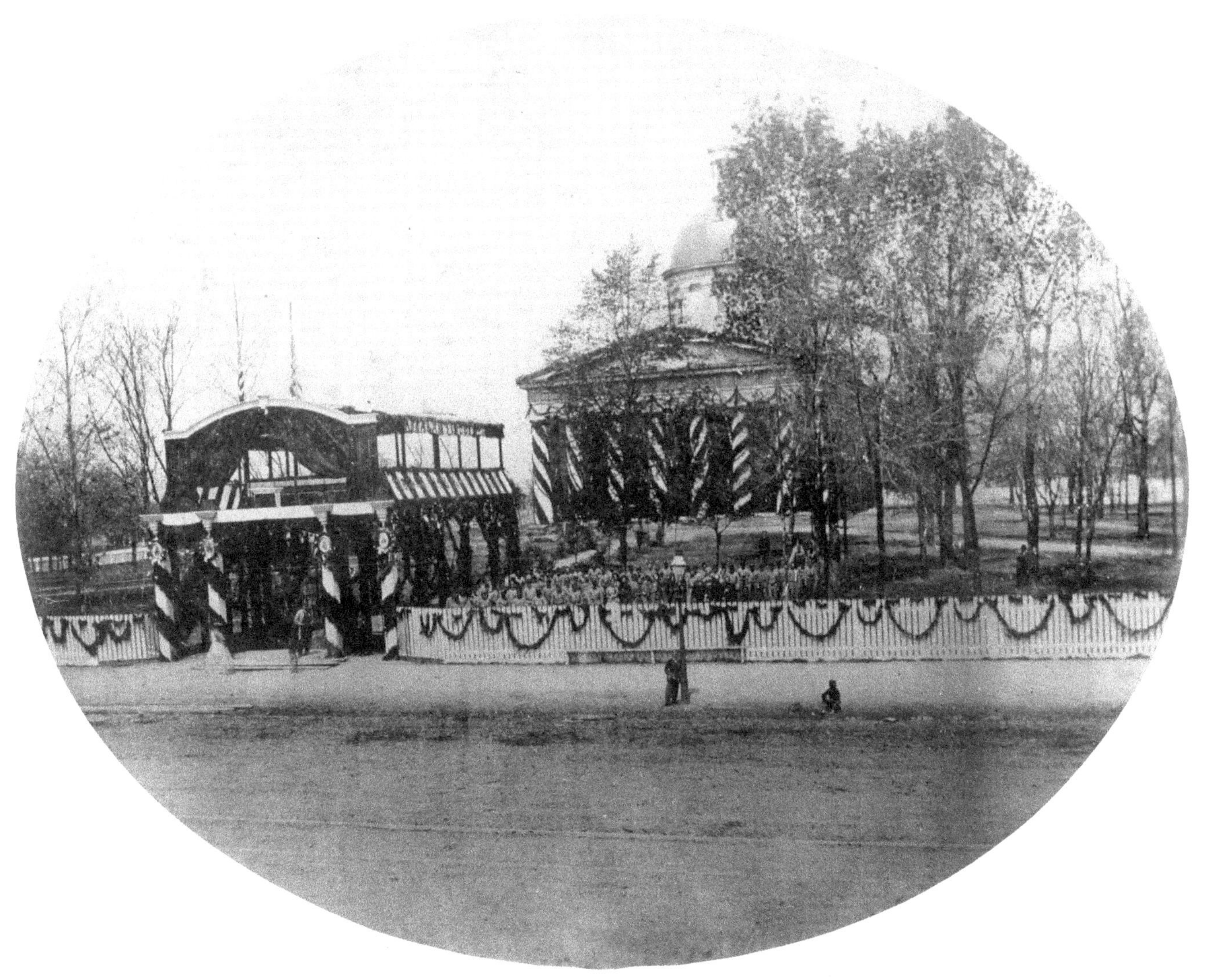

Indianapolis was one of many cities where the funeral train of President Abraham Lincoln stopped for a processional and public viewing in April 1865. Heavy rains, however, canceled the march in Indianapolis and thousands crowded into the Capitol, draped for mourning, to view the president's body. This photograph was one of several images taken the following day. Lincoln had spent many boyhood days in the state.

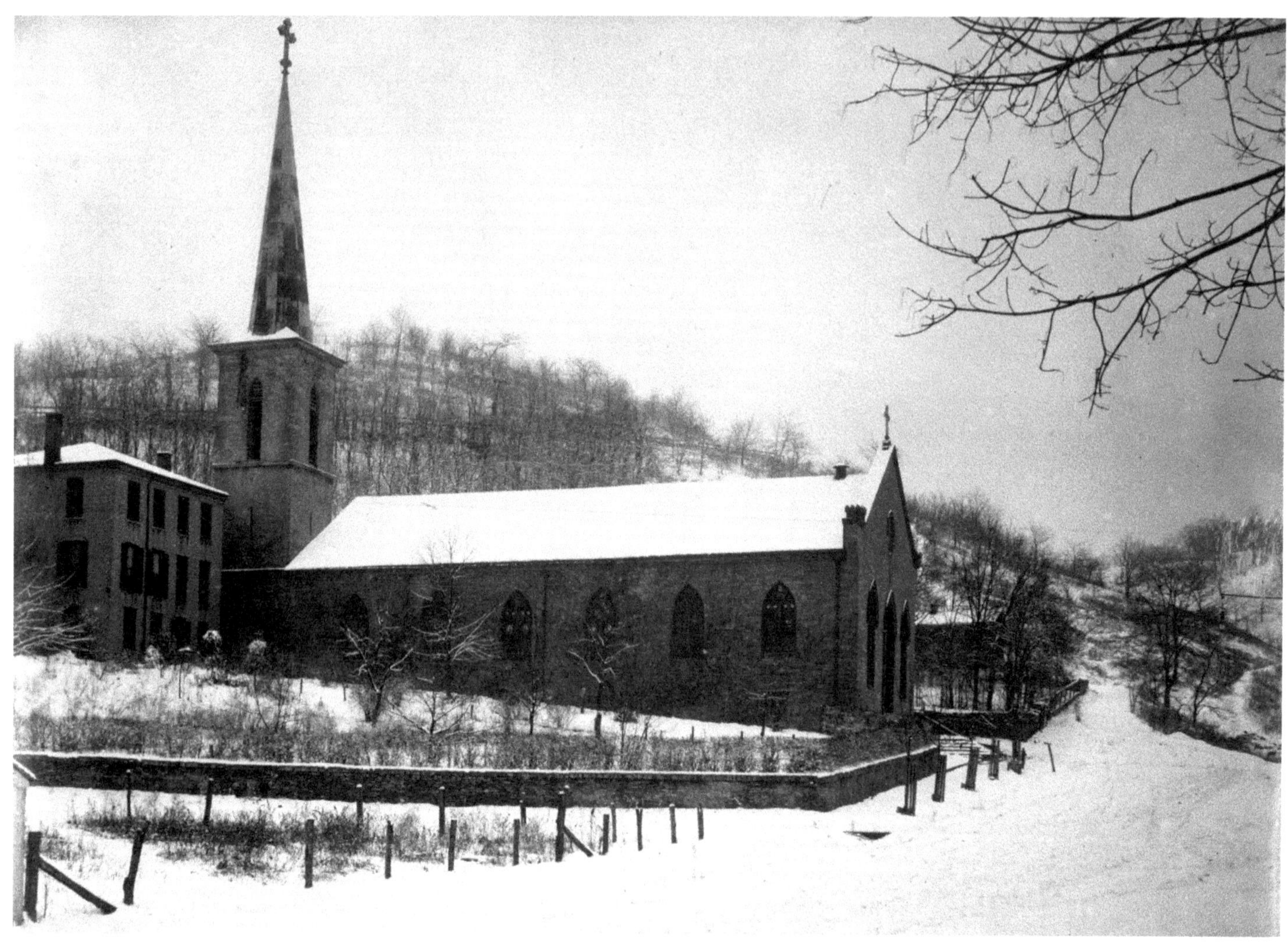

St. Michael the Archangel Church had been serving the Madison community for about 30 years when this photograph was taken after the Civil War. Built by Irish immigrants who worked on the Madison & Indianapolis Railroad, the church served the community for more than a century before becoming a site for cultural and special events rather than religious services.

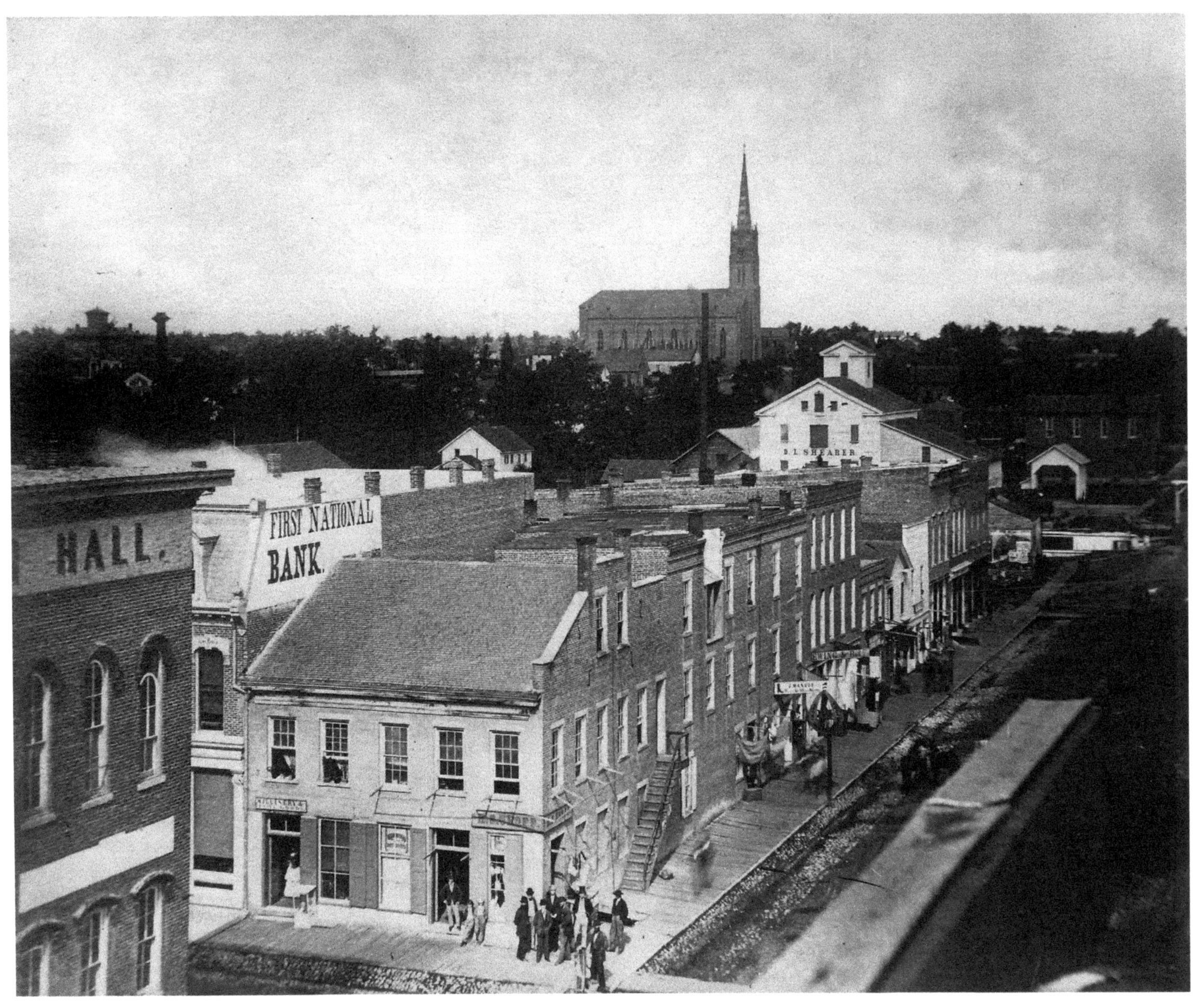

With the spire of Saints Peter and Paul Church looming over the town of Huntington in northern Indiana, the mayor and councilmen pose in the foreground for the camera, mounted on a rooftop, sometime in the 1860s or 1870s. The horizontal white object at far-right may be a Wabash and Erie Canal boat plying its way southwest toward Wabash.

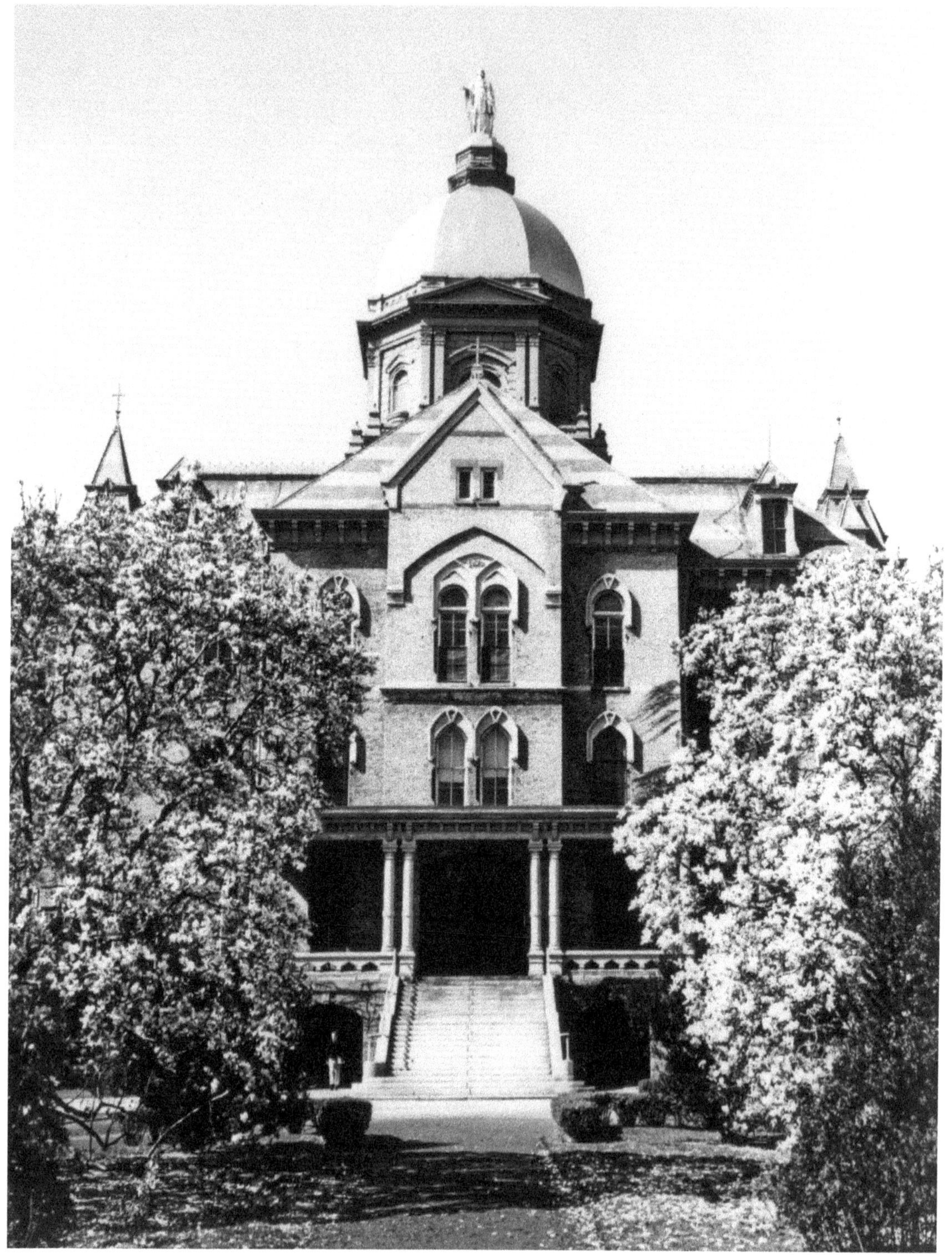

The "Golden Dome" or the "Main Building" at the University of Notre Dame actually houses the president's and other administrative offices in South Bend. It was built in 1879 after its predecessor burned, and the dome was a gift from the sisters of St. Mary's.

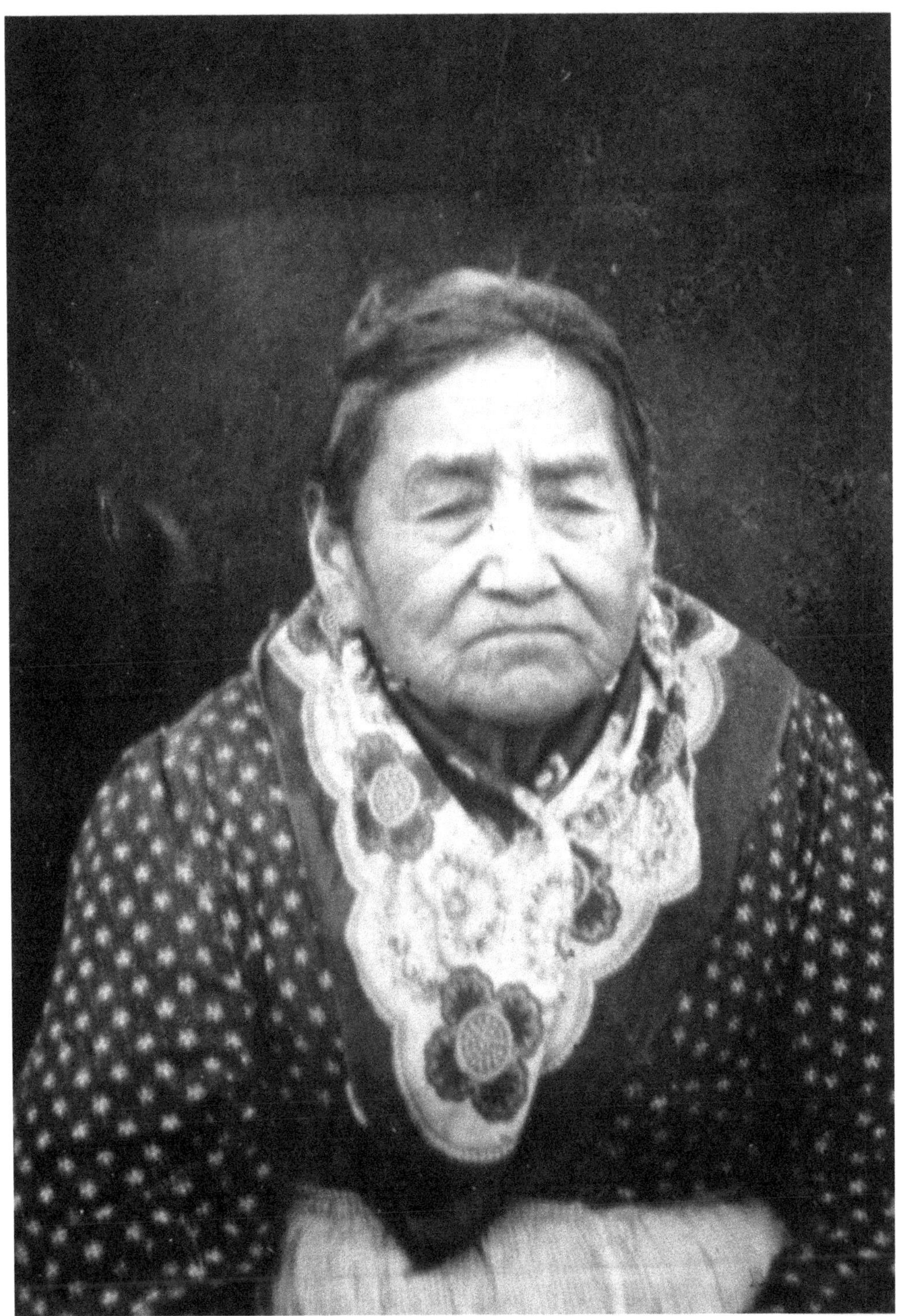

Kil-so-quah was the last full-blooded Miami to live in northeastern Indiana. The granddaughter of Chief Little Turtle, Kil-so-quah (1810–1915) resided in Roanoke, Indiana, in her later years, living in a teepee in the summer and a house in the winter. She knew little English and relied on her grandson as interpreter to share much of what is known about the Miami.

Four trains on four tracks at one intersection seem to pose an issue worth discussing by several bystanders here in the 1880s or a bit later. One of the locomotives at idle was apparently owned by the Jeffersonville, Madison and Indianapolis Railroad. For bystanders deeply puzzled by the issue, the Y Saloon at trackside offered Indianapolis beer on tap.

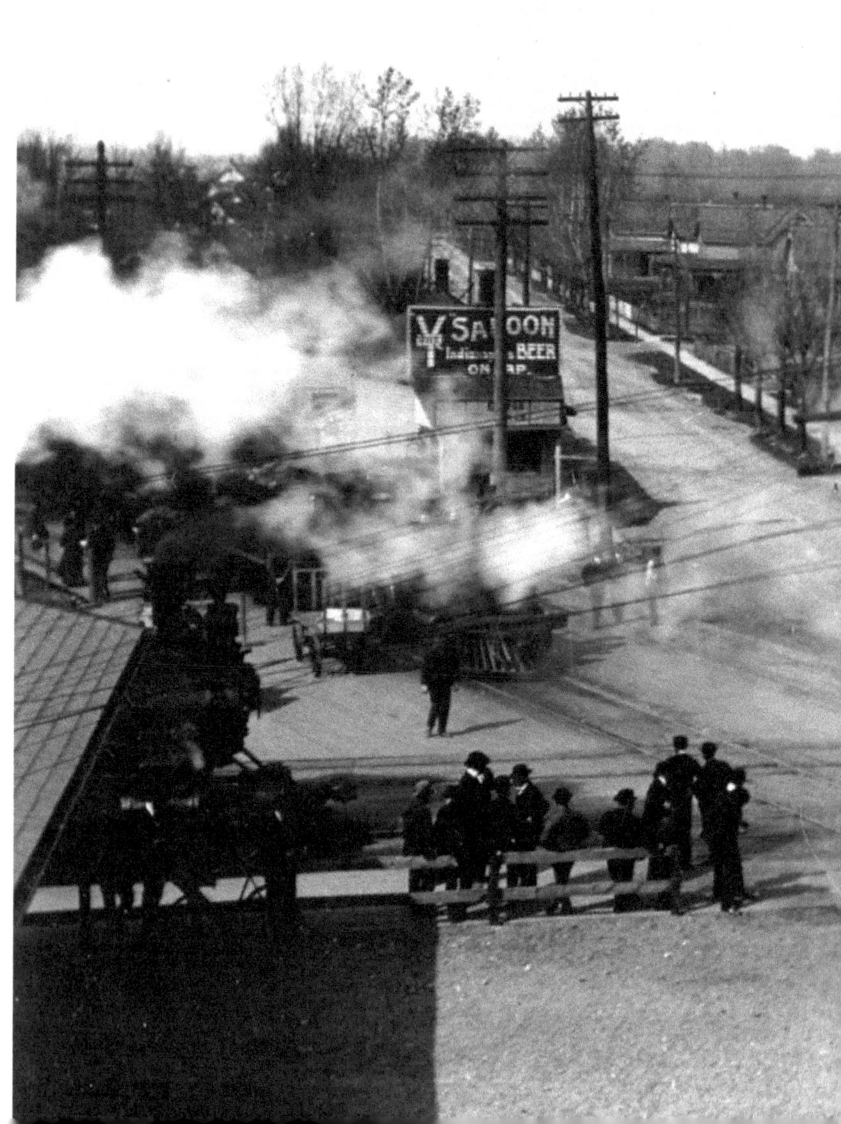

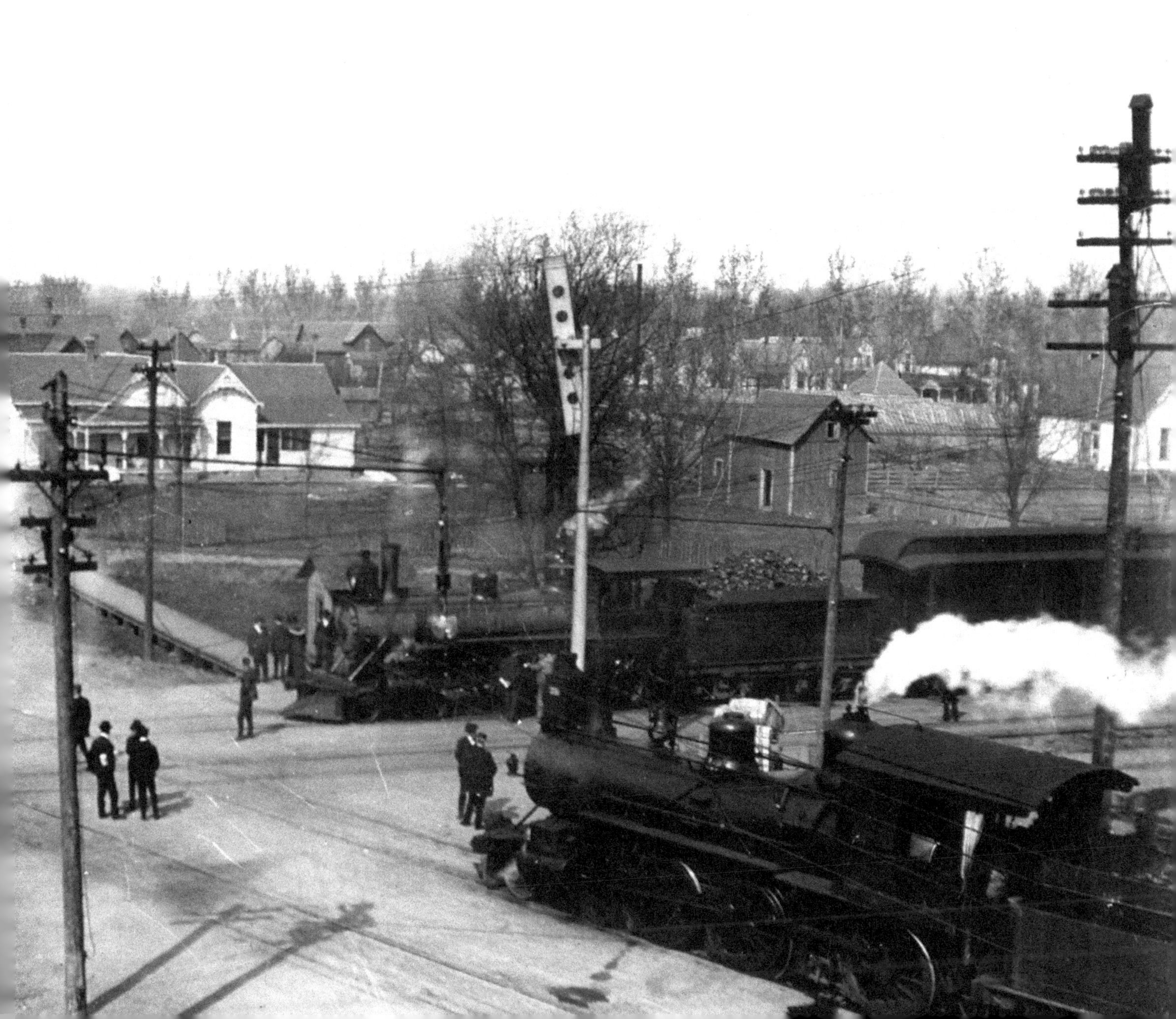

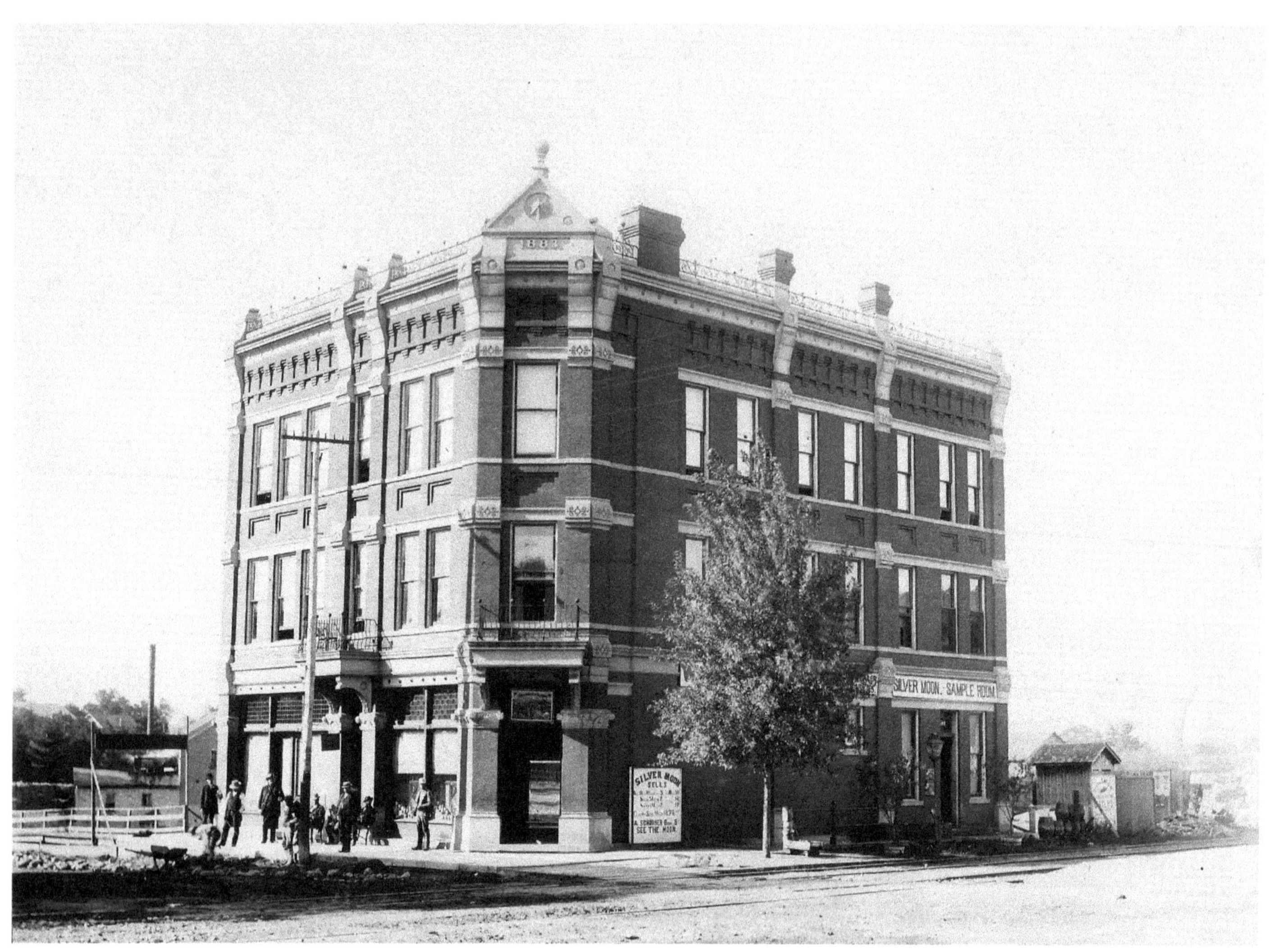

Lambdin Milligan, who built this structure in Huntington with his son in 1883, was among the most controversial figures of the Civil War. He and four others were convicted by a military tribunal of treason for their outspoken opposition to the Union cause. The Supreme Court overturned Milligan's conviction, however, because he was not tried by a civilian court.

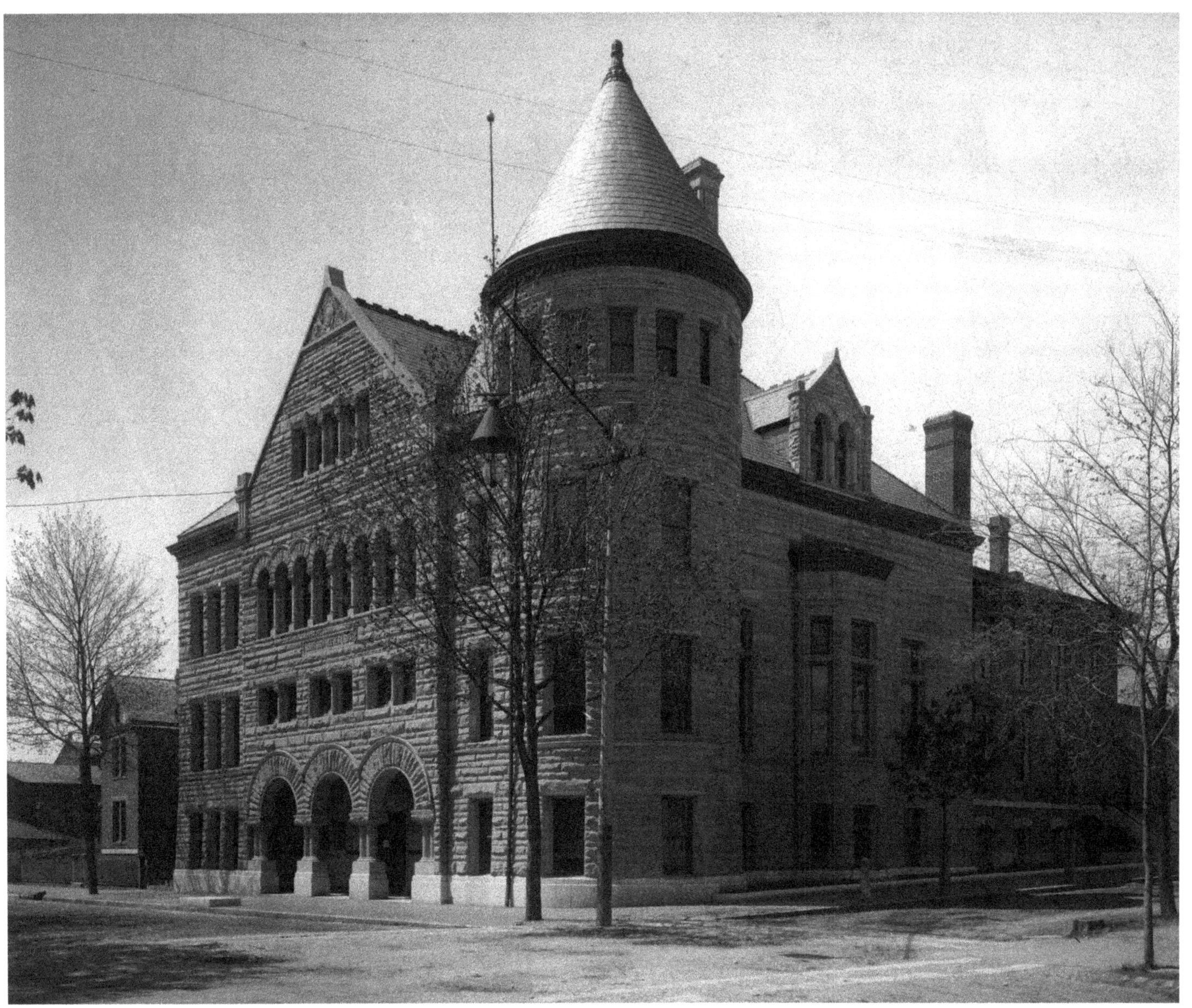

When the first Richmond patrons walked past the Morrisson Library tower and through its archways when it opened in 1864, the building housed 6,000 volumes in the care of one librarian. Some years later, Caroline Morrisson Reeves financed a major renovation and addition to the library.

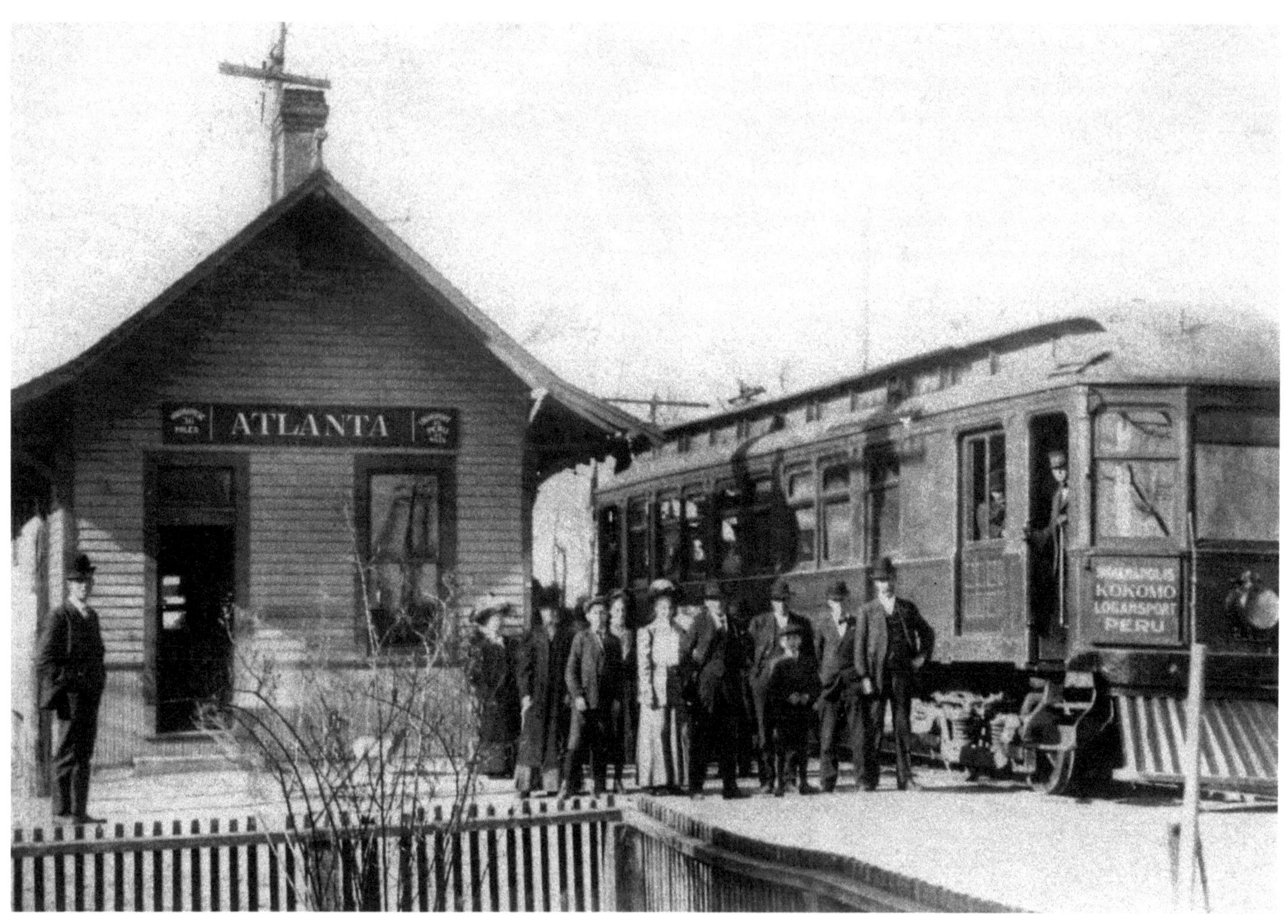

It was 20 years after the Civil War that Shielsville, or sometimes Shielville, was renamed Atlanta in an apparent reference to the city in Georgia. The interurban was the preferred means of travel for outings from the Hamilton County town.

Progress into a New Century

(1890–1920)

Great changes took place in Indiana during this period, not least of which was the introduction of mechanized farm equipment. As the nineteenth century came to a close and the twentieth century dawned, other businesses grew as well. Farming remained the state's primary economic engine, and flour and grist mills were number two. There were also more than 10,000 workers employed in the lumber industry, as Indiana's forests of black walnut trees became a popular resource for furniture prized throughout the nation. But with the advent of the automobile, all of this would change.

The 1880 census showed that the carriage and wagon business constituted the fourth-largest industry in Indiana when measured by number of firms and workers. Businesses that made wagons, buggies, and surreys prospered. It was probably inevitable that entrepreneurs like Elwood Haynes of Kokomo would begin wondering if a gasoline-powered vehicle could be built. His success with a motorized car helped spark automobile manufacturing in Indiana that became second only to Michigan's share of the industry. In 1910, 67 automobile manufacturers operated in the state, employing more than 6,700 workers. Names that are legendary in automotive history—like Stutz, Studebaker, Marmon, Auburn, and Overland—enjoyed their heyday in Indiana. Rubber tire manufacturers and other ancillary businesses spurred more growth in the state. It was only because Michigan companies wound up turning out lower-cost, mass-produced automobiles that Detroit prevailed in the marketplace. The number of Indiana manufacturers would ultimately dwindle, although companies like Auburn, Cord, Duesenberg, and especially Studebaker remained prominent for decades to come.

There was another aspect of transportation that flowered during this period—the interurban. Convenient, fast, and reliable, the interurban originated from an 1861 law allowing street railway companies to incorporate. Soon horse-drawn lines were ubiquitous, replaced with electric power by the 1890s. Then around 1900, the Anderson Street Railway's owner proposed extending his lines to neighboring cities. Within a decade Indiana had more than 2,000 miles of intercity routes. Some cities became hubs for many interurban lines. Five lines served Muncie by 1913, and residents could travel as far as Chicago or Buffalo. The interurban replaced steam railroads for local travel because the lines were cheaper, safer, and stopped in small, rural towns.

Born in 1869 in Reelsville along the National Road, Paul Pickett was a teacher, poet, artist, fisherman, and friend of future governor George Craig. Pickett sits for a photograph with his wife, Grace, and first of ten children, Leland, in the 1890s. His prolific album of verse holds many memorable lines, including a rhapsody to his beloved home state, in the requisite Hoosier dialect:

Ye kin smell perfume uv Heaven
When ye pass a pawpaw patch,
Sich a scent 'at no man livin'
Ever foun' fer hit a match.

. . . .

Ye kin look, er ye kin lissen,
Er jest use yer nose, By Granny!
An' ye'll find haint NOTHIN' missin'
When it's Fall in Indianny!

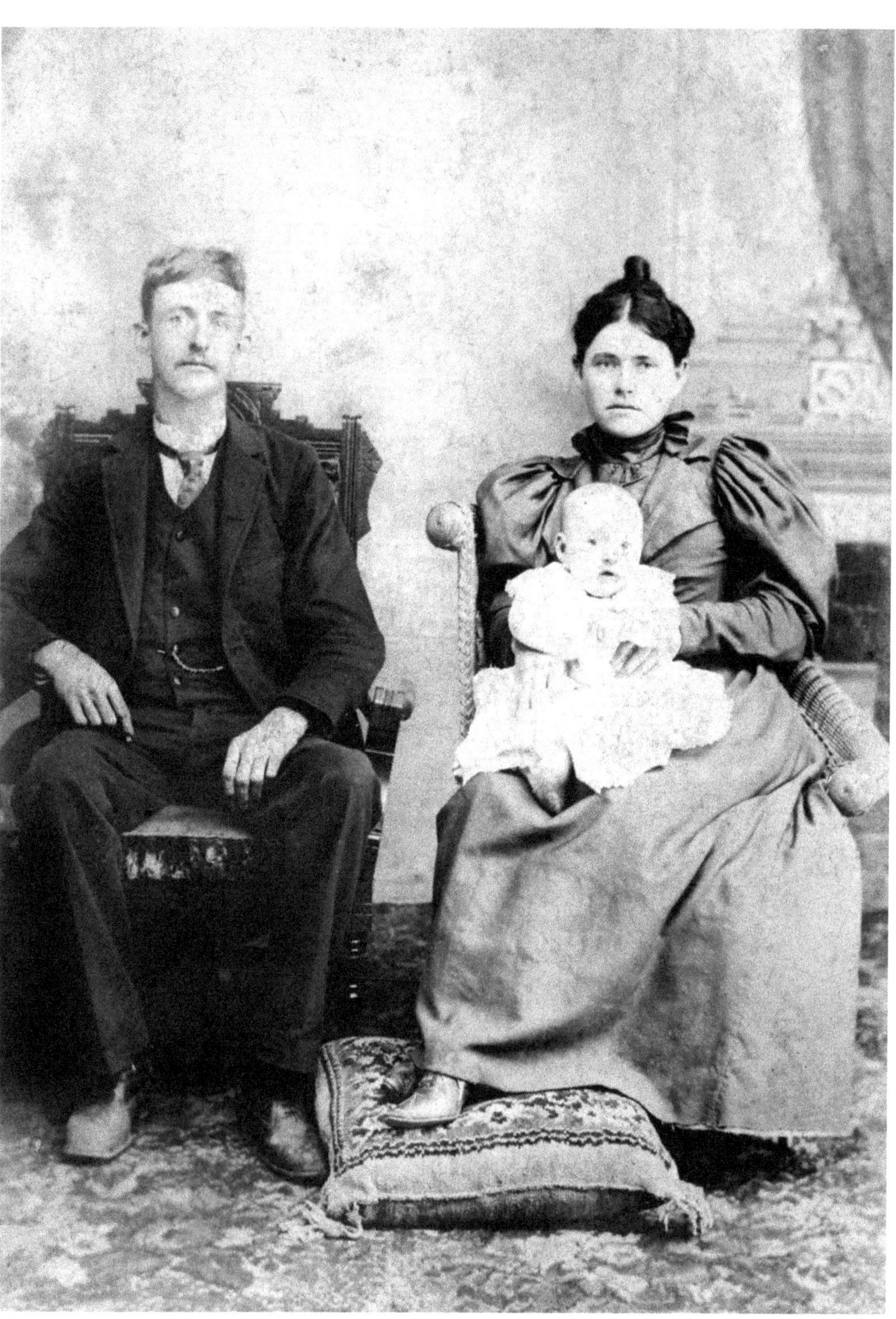

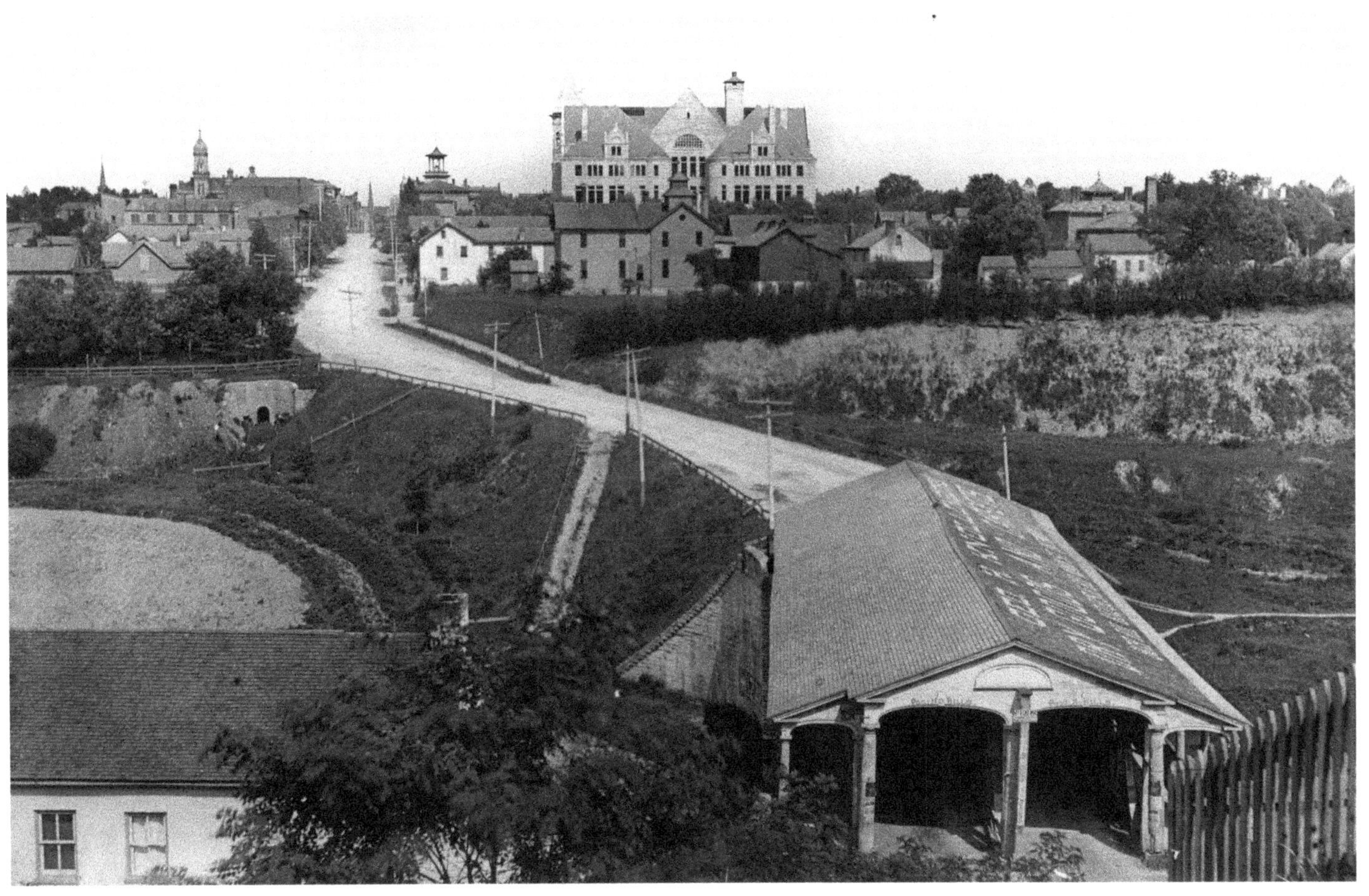

Historic covered bridges are treasured as relics of Indiana's past, and the annual Parke County covered bridge festival is always a favorite. The covered bridge that carried travelers across the Whitewater River in Richmond on the National Road was considered among the nation's finest. Authorized by President Jefferson in 1806, the National Road itself would become one of the nation's first true highways, its route through the state intended to link Richmond, Indianapolis, Terre Haute, and other communities to points east and west. The road would serve as a gateway to the West for great numbers of settlers. This photograph was taken in 1893 as the Wayne County Courthouse—the large structure in the distance—was being built. To its left are the spire of the 1873 courthouse and, farther left, Richmond's 1886 city hall.

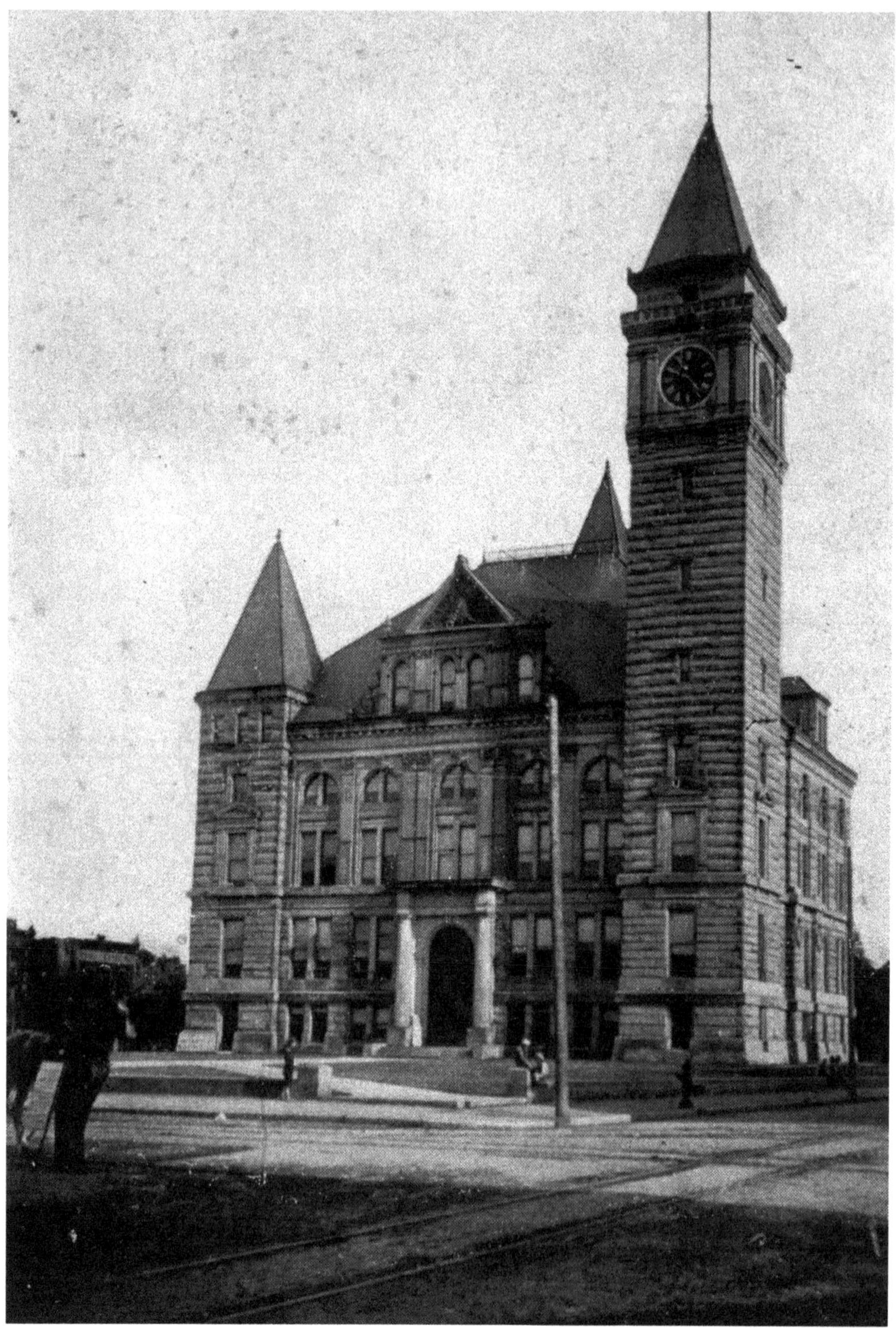

County courthouses arose over the Indiana landscape in the late nineteenth century like sentinels. With its 208-foot-tall tower rising above the rest of the sandstone structure, the Romanesque Tipton County Courthouse was among the most impressive when it was completed in 1894. Its architect, Adolph Scherrer, had completed the state's Capitol in Indianapolis in 1888.

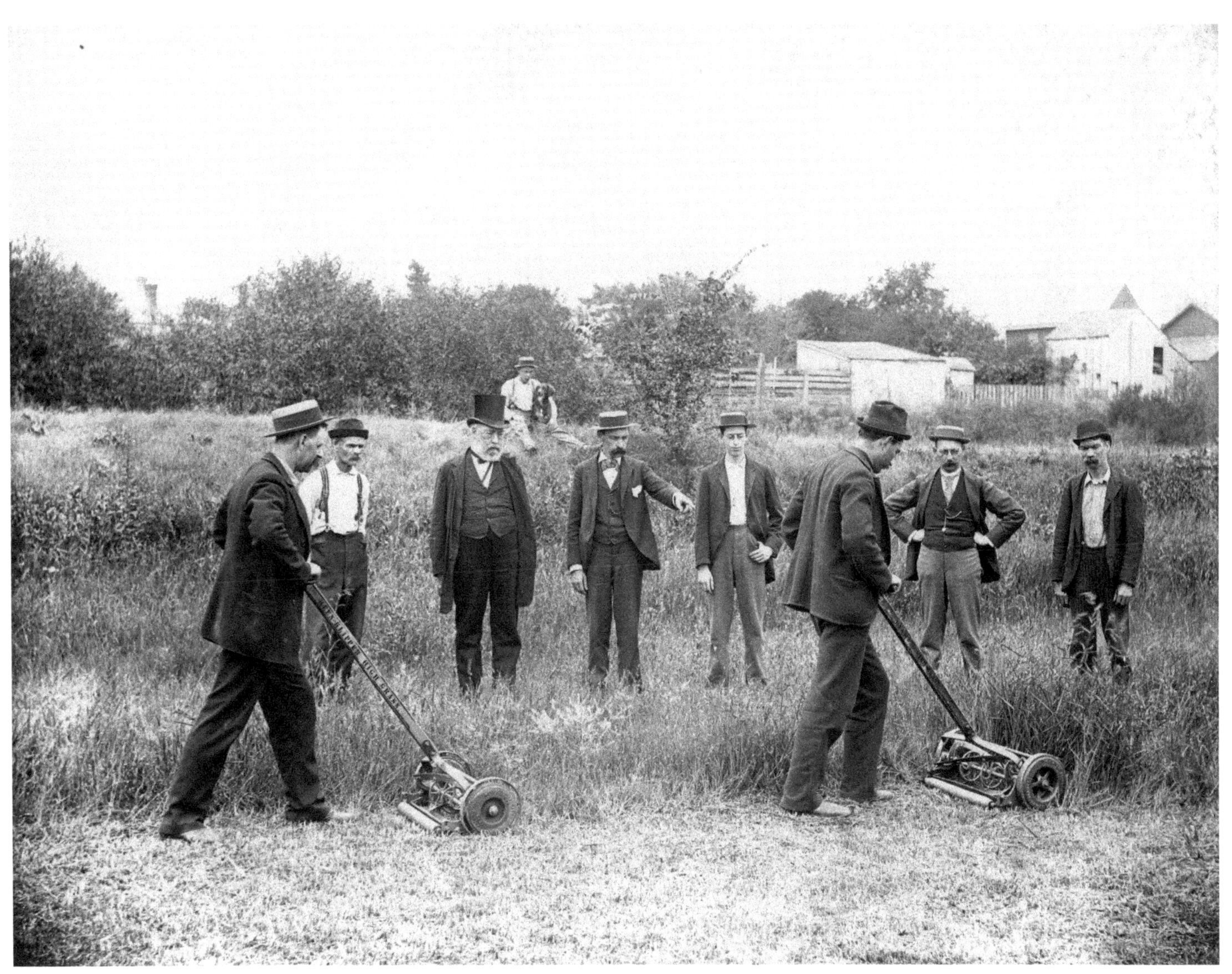

Elwood W. McGuire made the first lawn mower in the United States in 1874, introducing the concept of a nicely cut lawn first to the Midwest and then to the rest of the nation and the world. At its peak after World War II, Dille and McGuire was making 2,100 hand mowers a day. With company officials looking on, the company's Keen Klipper for high grass undergoes a stern field test in 1892.

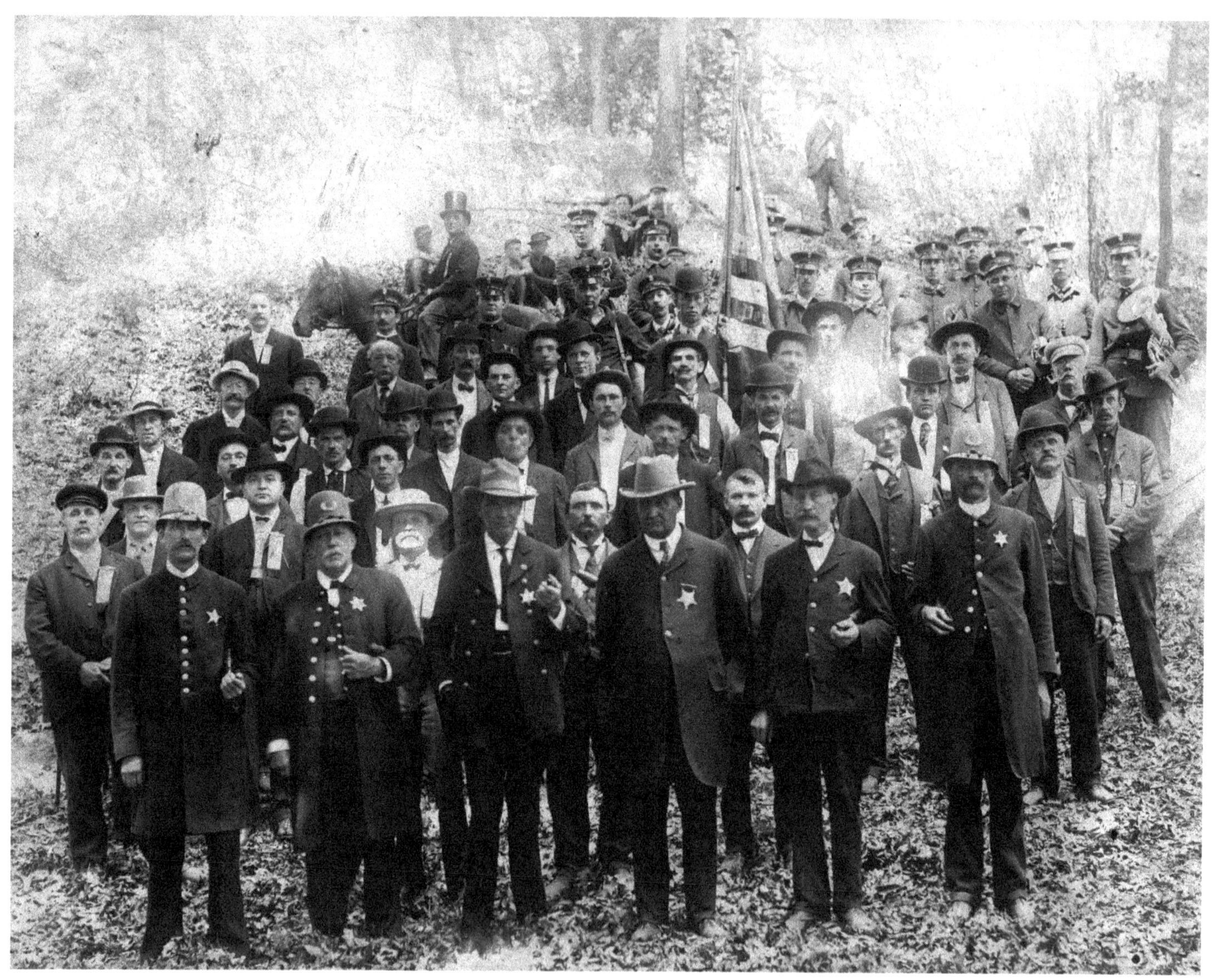

Sheriff W. John Volpert, second from right in the front row, poses with his sworn deputies (those with badges) and what is ostensibly the Miami County Horse Thief Detective Association, around 1900. The legislature had granted police powers to such vigilante groups in the nineteenth century.

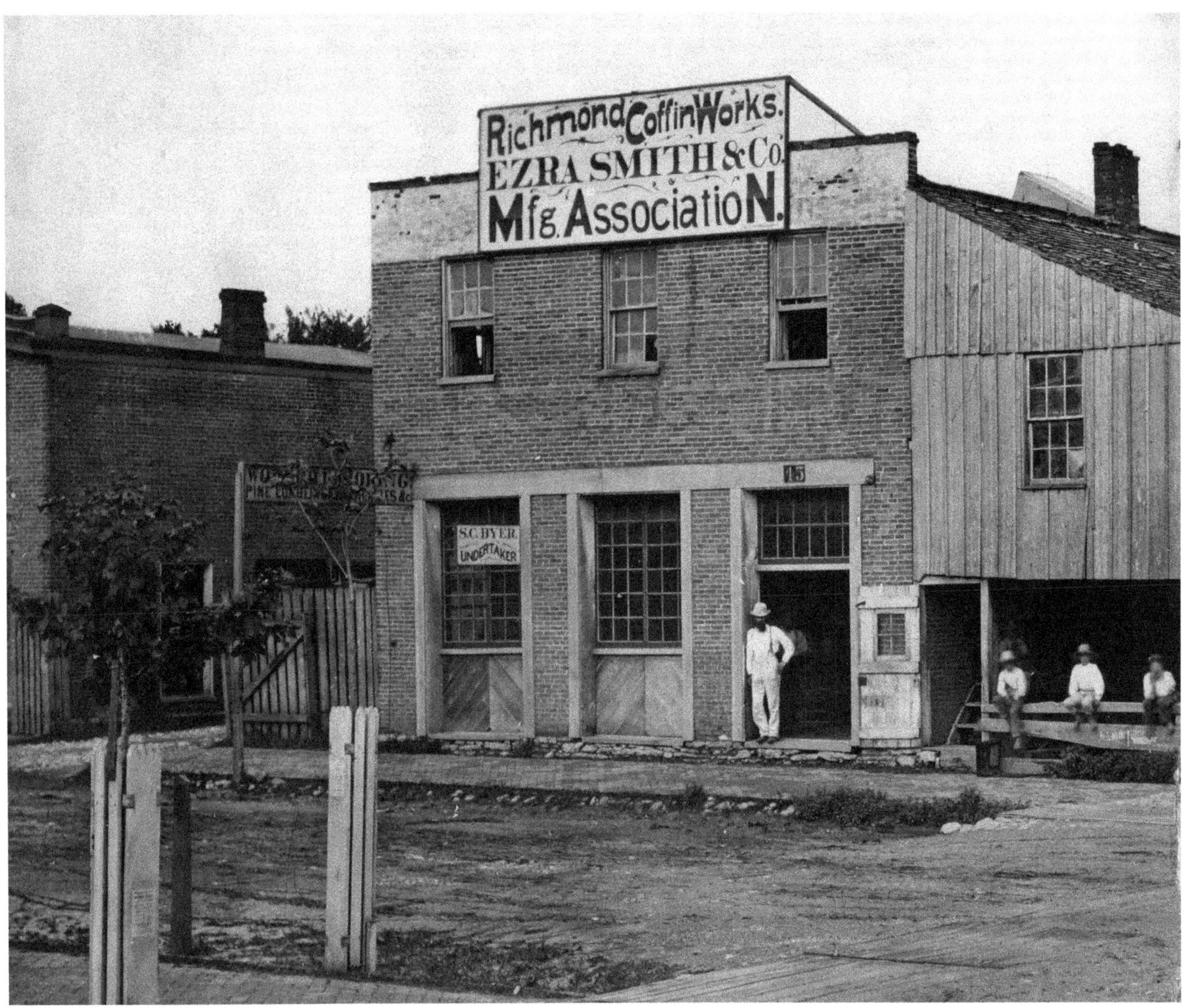

Coffin-makers were a vital part of any community of size in the nineteenth century, but they often had to double as furniture builders to stay in business. The manufactory of Ezra Smith & Company in this image is sizable, while its Richmond Coffin Works business receives smaller billing in the signage.

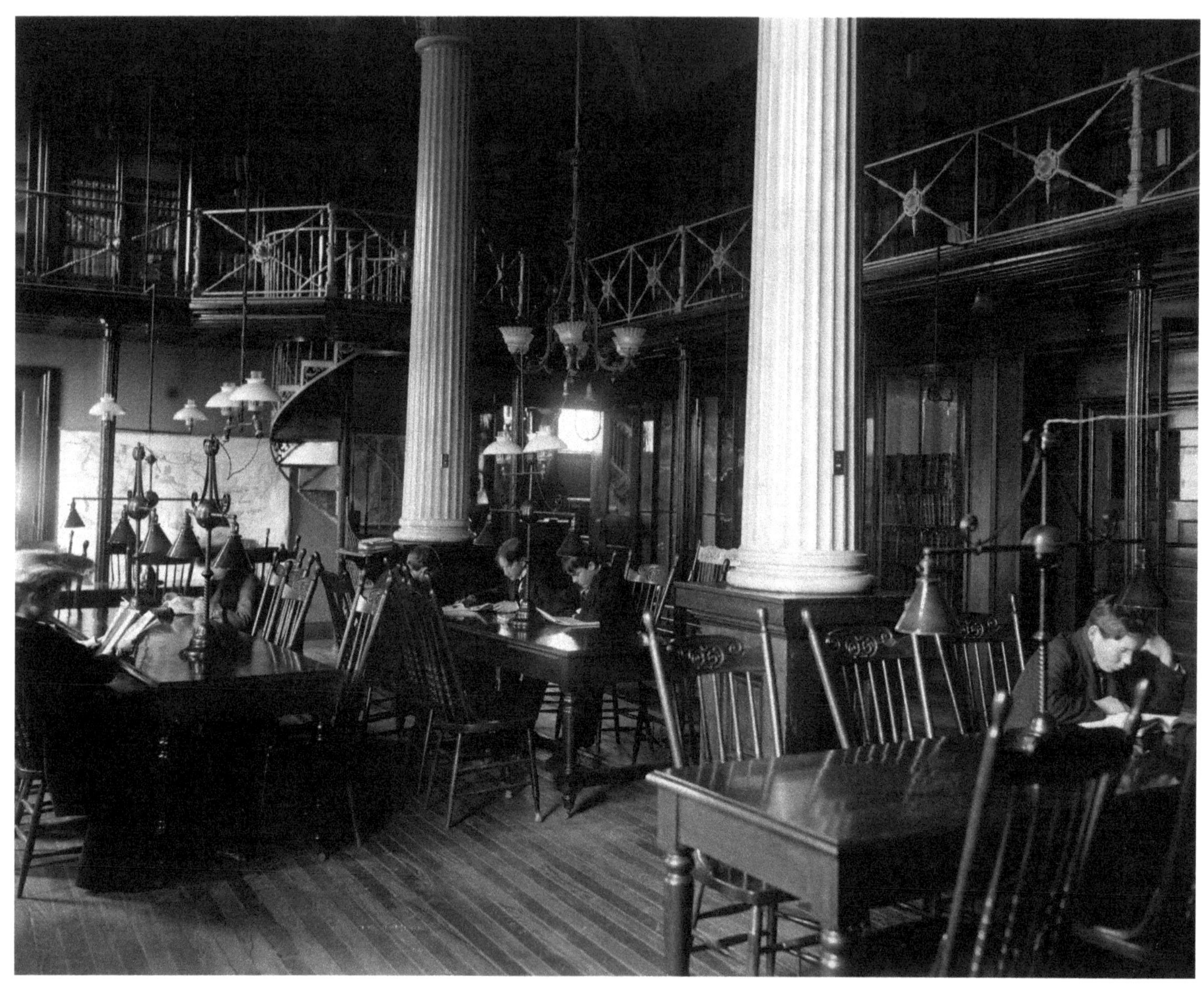

The reading room of the Morrisson-Reeves Library in Richmond was an architectural treasure beyond its volumes. When a new structure was built in 1975, several features adorning the old library—including the spiral staircase, wood columns, and glass cupboards—were preserved.

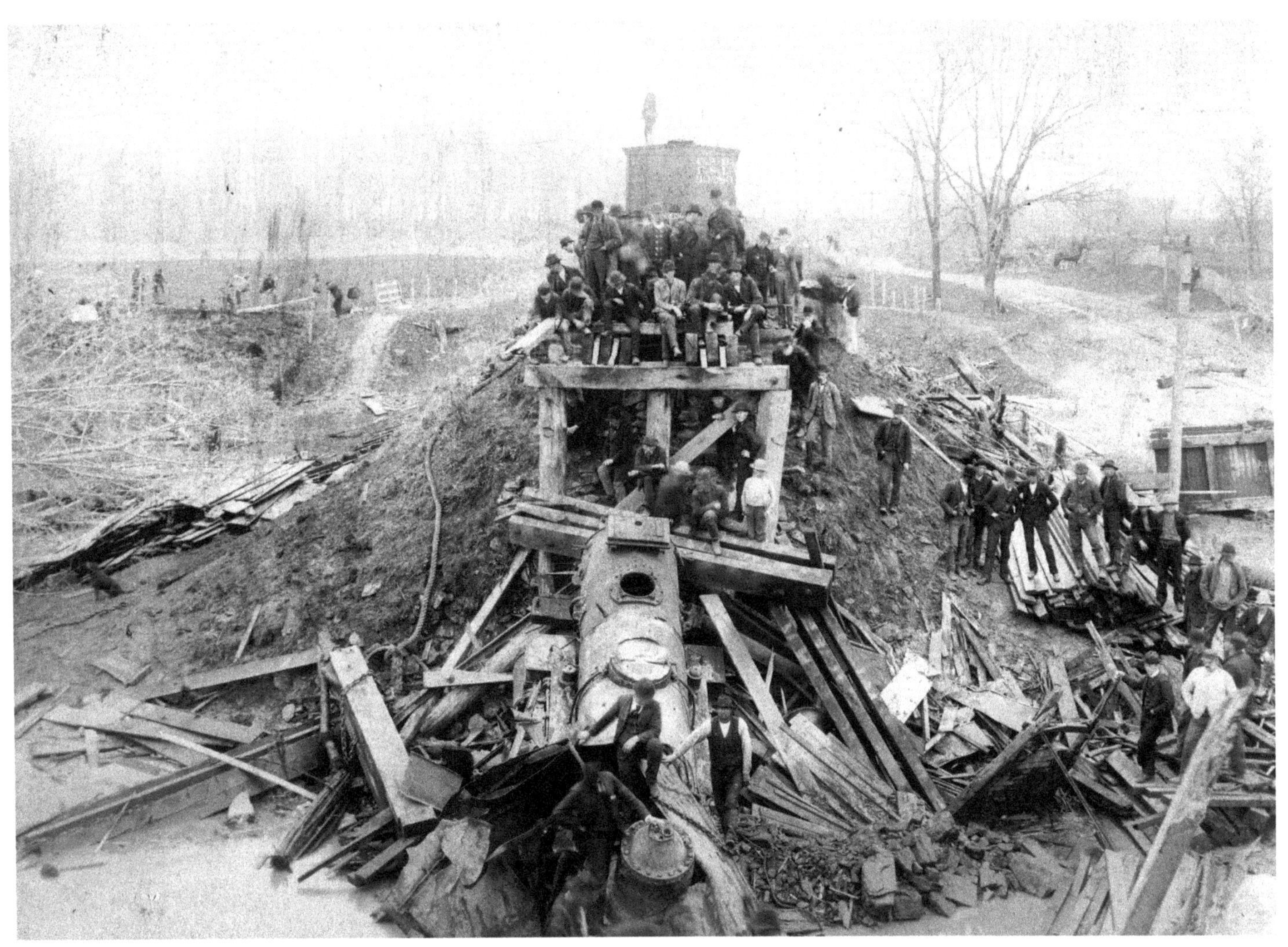

Kibitzers crowd onto the scene of a railroad trestle collapse over the Little Calumet River in Otis, Indiana, in early May 1892. A survey of the wreckage is under way in the foreground, no doubt led by inspectors for the Monon Railroad.

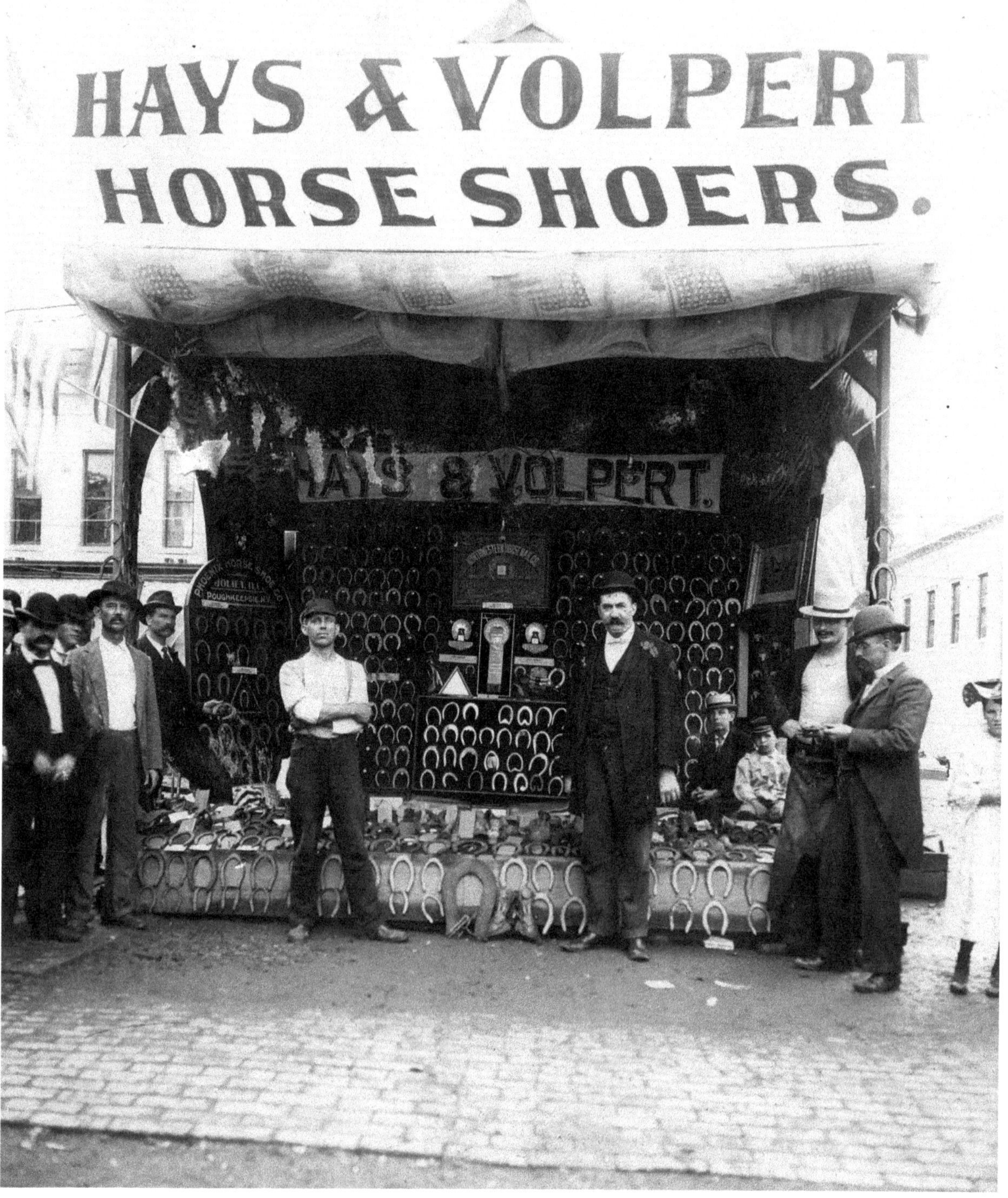

Peru's 1894 "Street Fair Days" brought to the attention of the buying public purveyors of goods and services of many kinds—including Hays & Volpert farriers and their vast array of horseshoes. Local accounts claimed that Street Fair Days was the first such event in Indiana history.

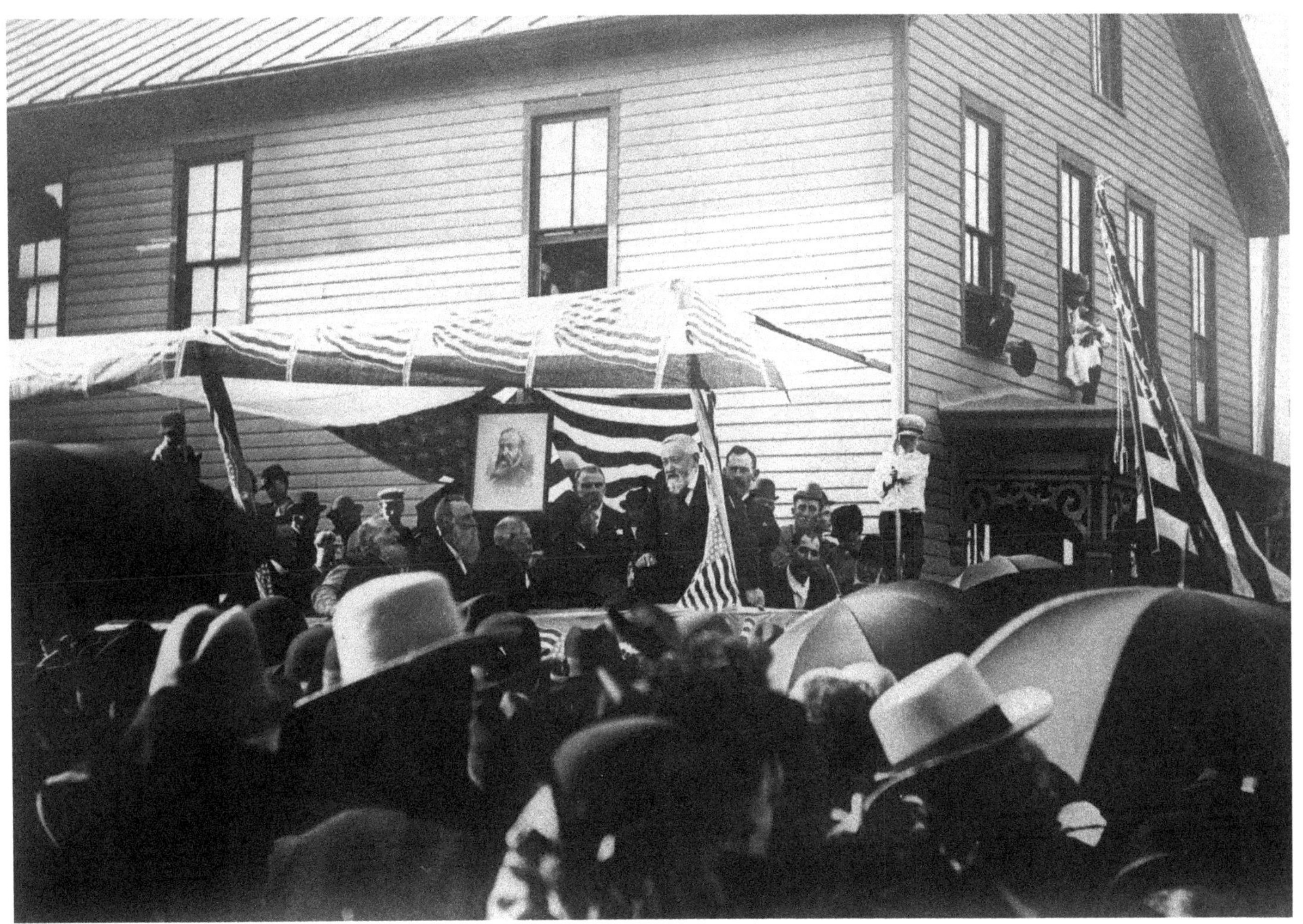

A noticeably aging former President Benjamin Harrison speaks to a large, friendly audience in Peru in 1894, two years after the death of his wife, Caroline, and his unsuccessful bid for reelection. Harrison's speeches were seen as the best of his time for their thoughtful and cogent content.

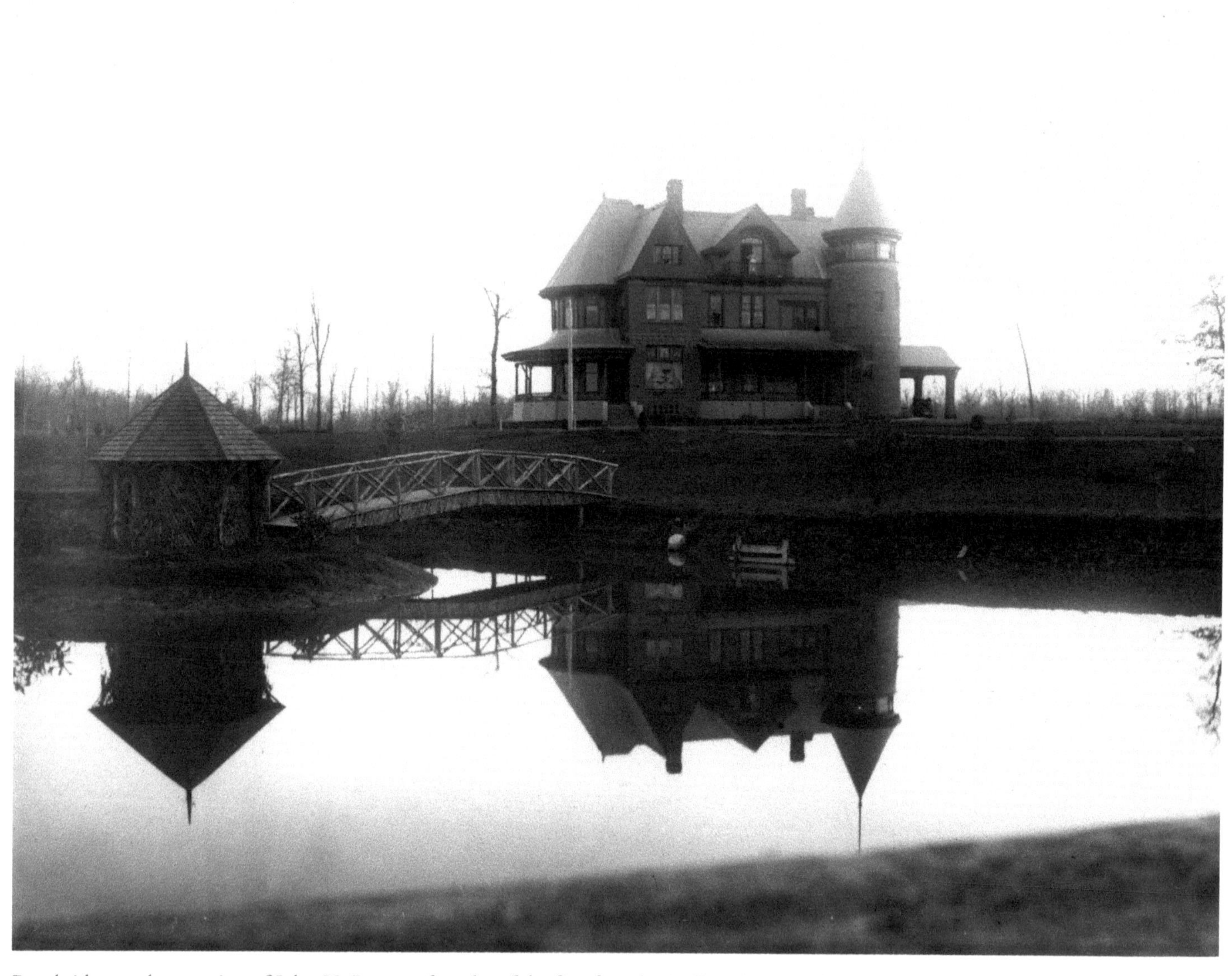

Brookside was the mansion of John H. Bass, co-founder of the first foundry in Fort Wayne, a leading manufacturer of railroad wheels and axles. The mansion, which sported a ballroom, gilt ceilings, and frescoes, later became the home of the University of St. Francis.

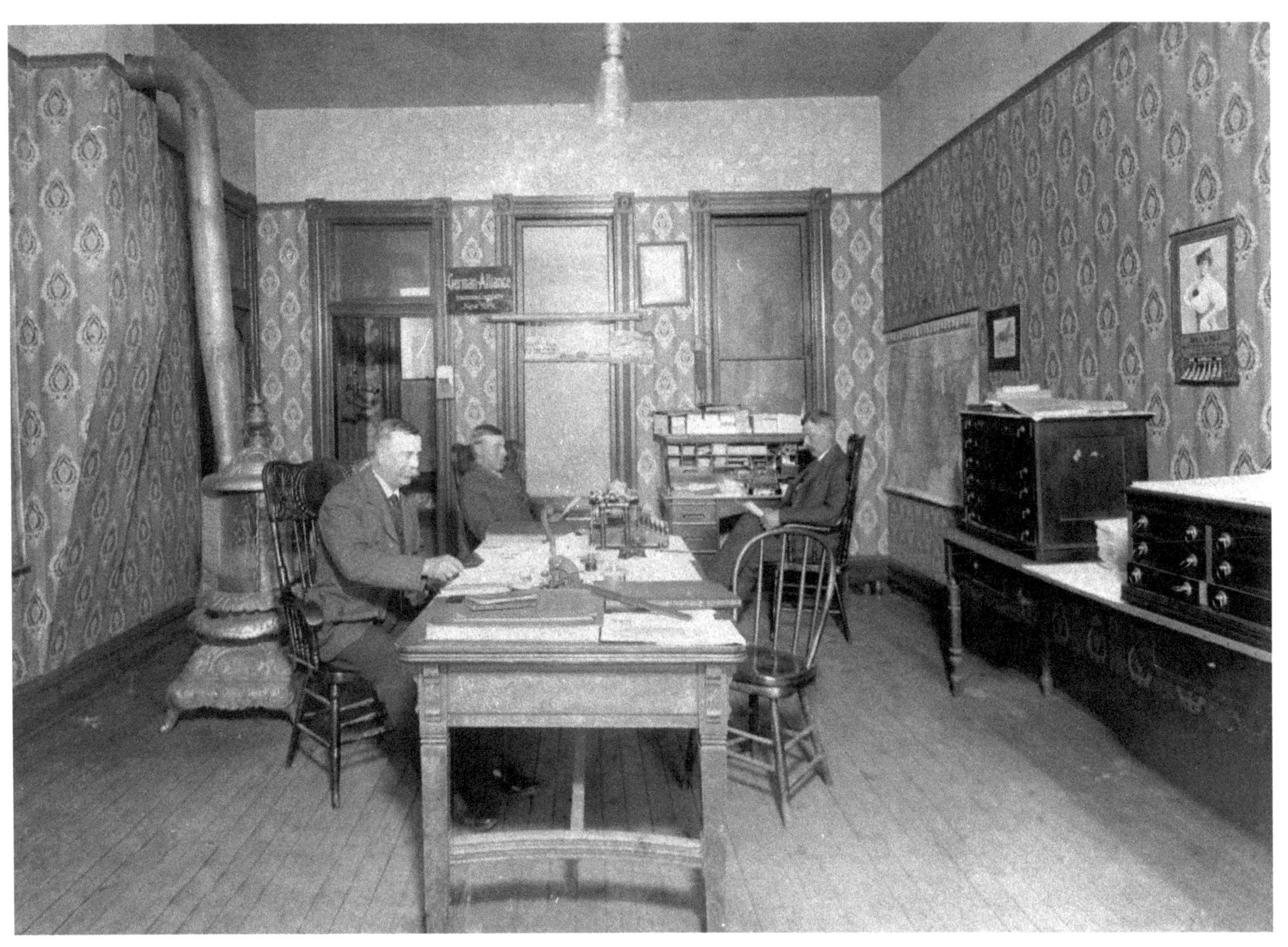

Amid heavily ornate Victorian-era decor, it is all business in the office of Tipton mayor Solomon D. Rouls. The first Republican ever to be elected city clerk, Rouls was elected mayor in 1892 and served one term.

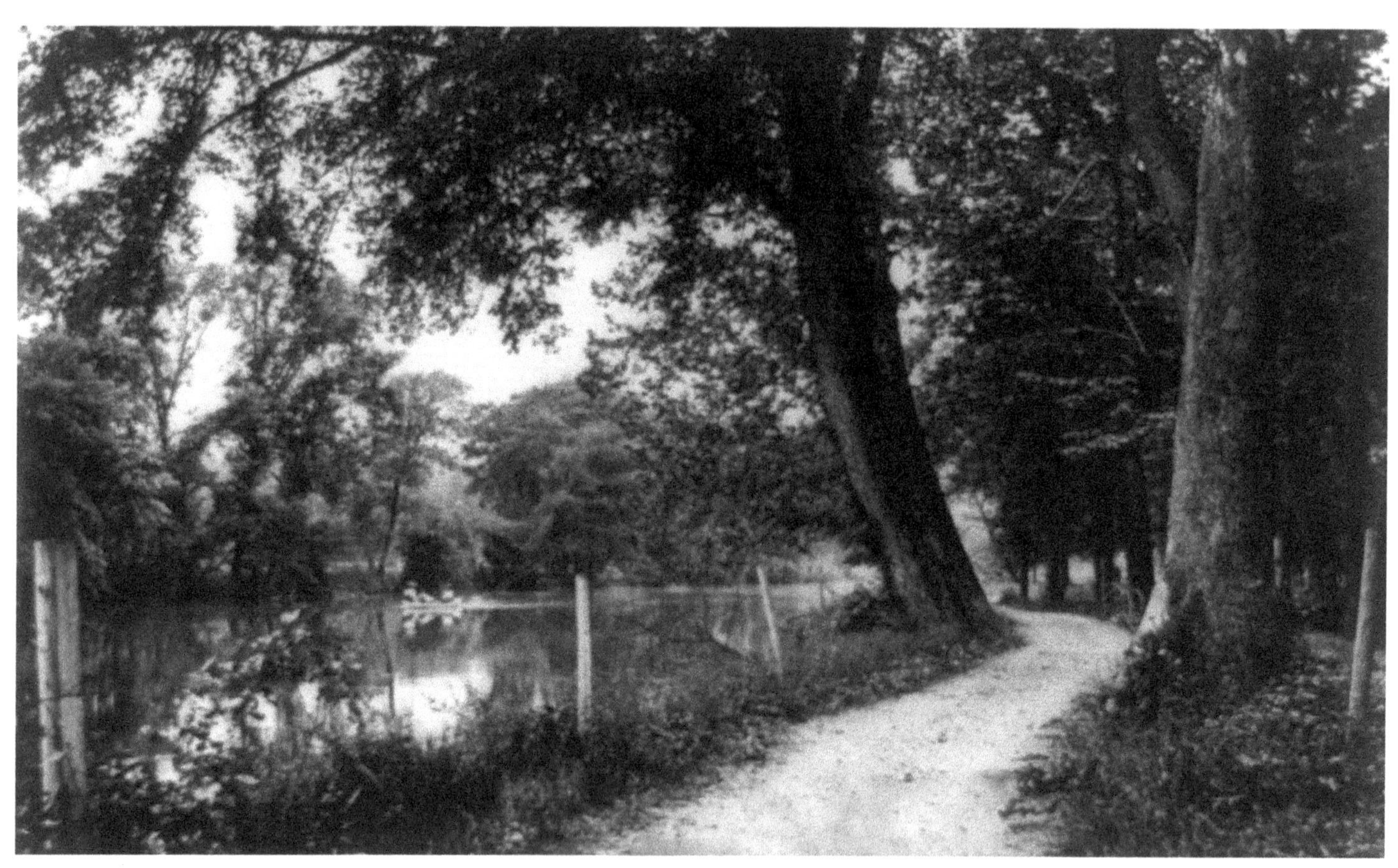

As substantial urban growth in the Midwest unfolded in the late nineteenth century, cities like Indianapolis began beautification programs. Pastoral settings began to be valued for activities like bicycling, walking, and canoeing, and parks were included in city planning.

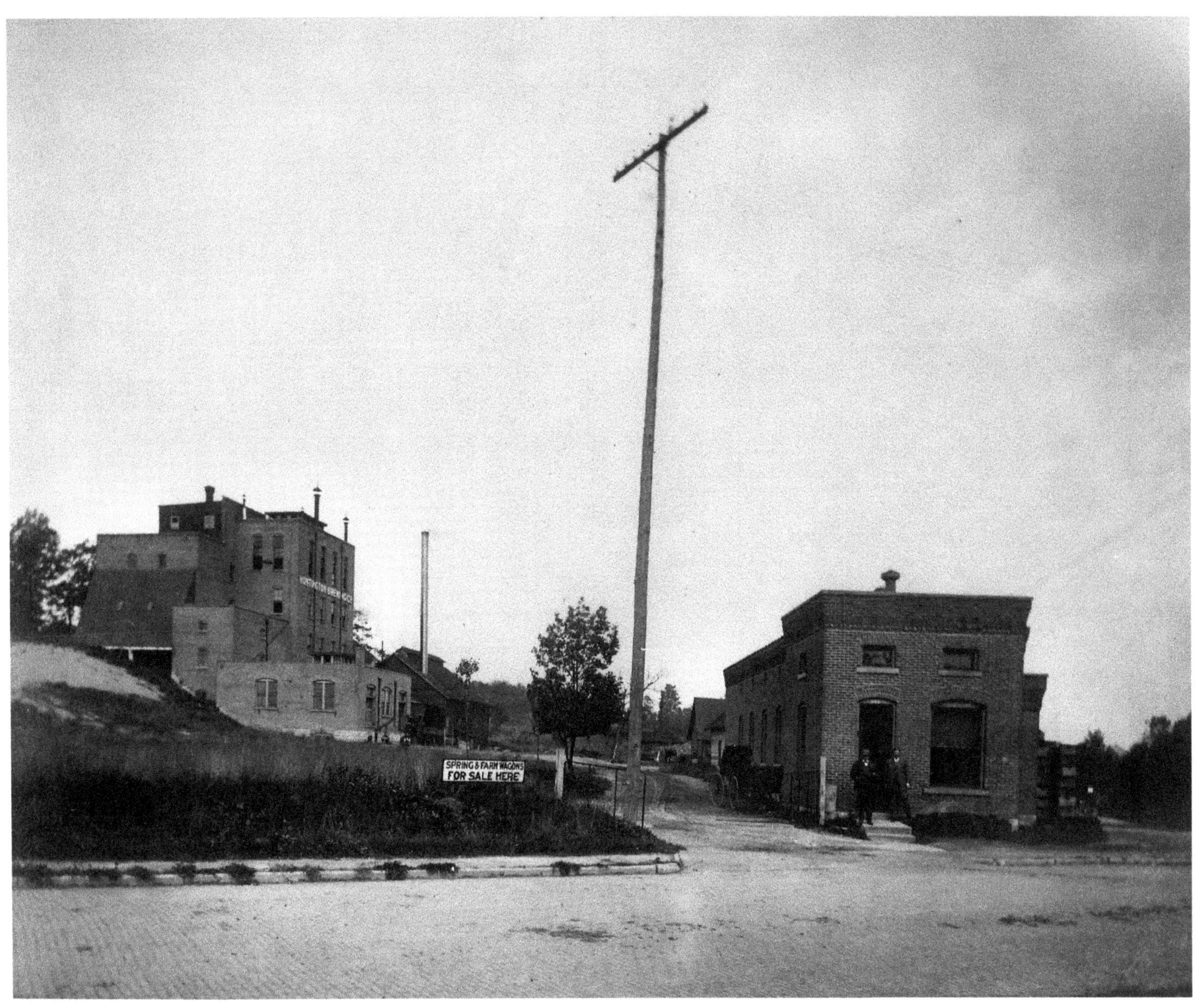

Many cities in Indiana had breweries, and with few exceptions they resembled the Huntington Brewery. Begun shortly after the Civil War to serve the local market and without grandiose facilities, the brewery, shown here on the hill to the left with an icehouse below it, produced around 1,000 barrels of beer and ale annually. The brewery burned in 1900.

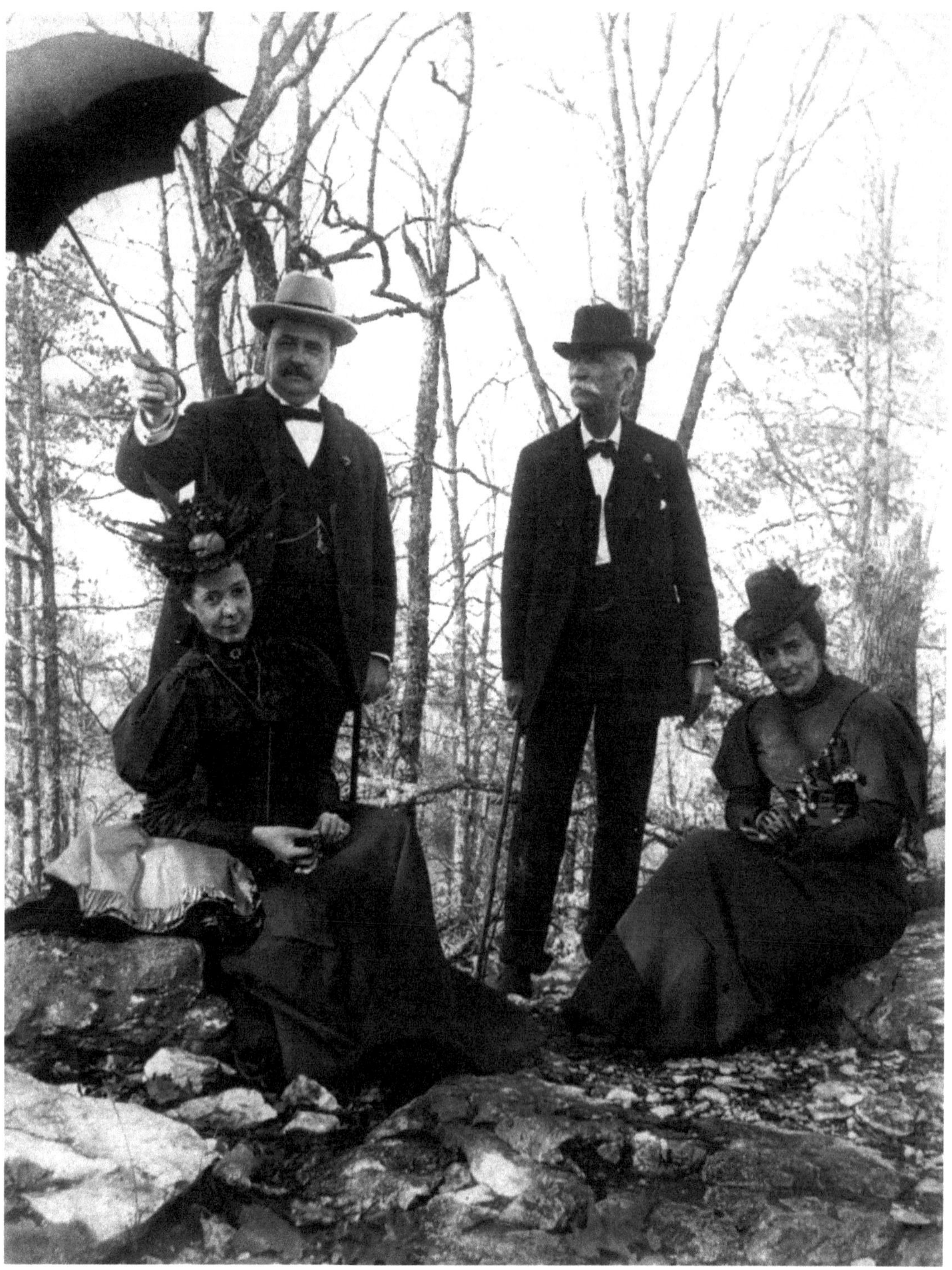

Crawfordsville native Joseph Marshall Graham (at left with umbrella) went to work for the railroads in 1873, becoming chief engineer of the Baltimore & Ohio by 1891 and vice-president of the Erie Railroad thereafter. Heralded for his efficiency and efficacy, Graham was reportedly tapped by Panama Canal Commission chairman Theodore Shonts to serve as chief engineer for Teddy Roosevelt's monumental project but declined the offer. Graham is shown here with his wife, Evalyn, and companions sometime before his death in 1909 at the age of 56.

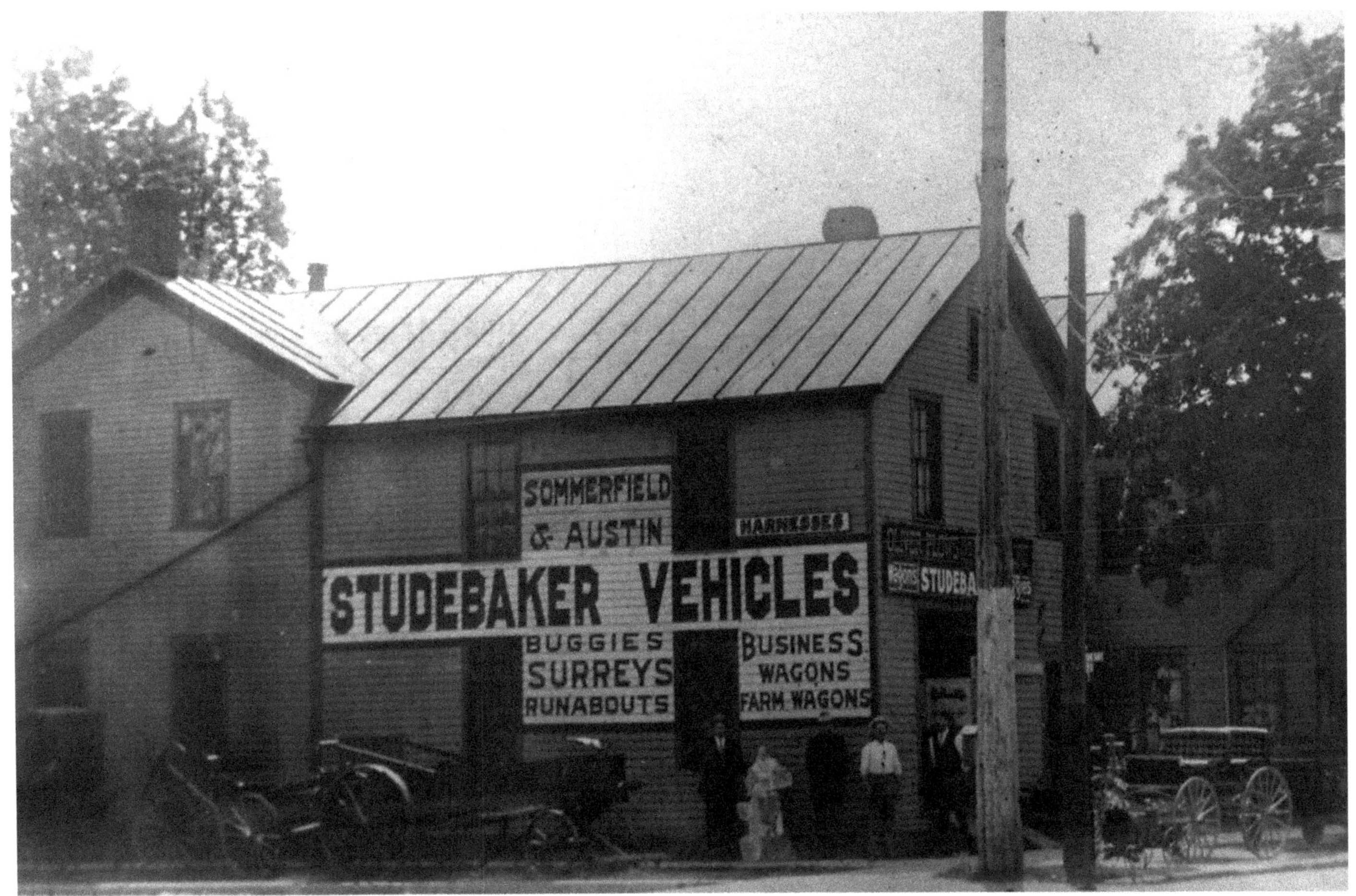

Long before it became nationally synonymous with automobiles, the Studebaker brand was highly regarded for its buggies, surreys, runabouts, business wagons, and farm wagons, as the sign on the La Porte livery advertises. The owners, Abram Sommerfield and Henry Austin, pose for the camera outside the business.

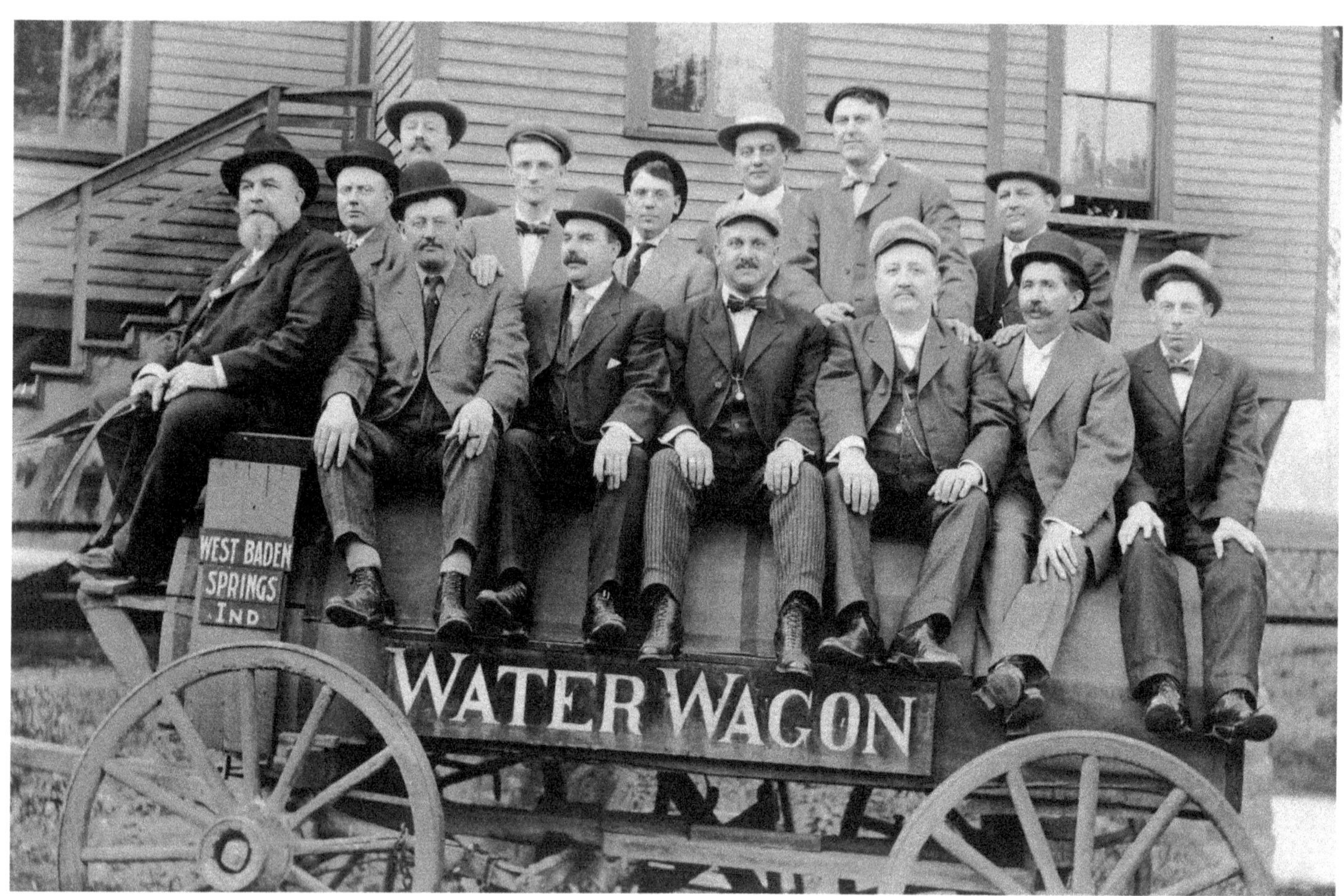

There was a double entendre to the name on the means of transportation to the grand hotel at West Baden Springs. The waters from four sulphur springs there were said to have curative powers for a wide variety of ailments—offering in particular a sobering experience for some high livers. Mineral water baths of the kind were popular retreats during the era, visited by Americans far and wide for the cures they were thought to offer.

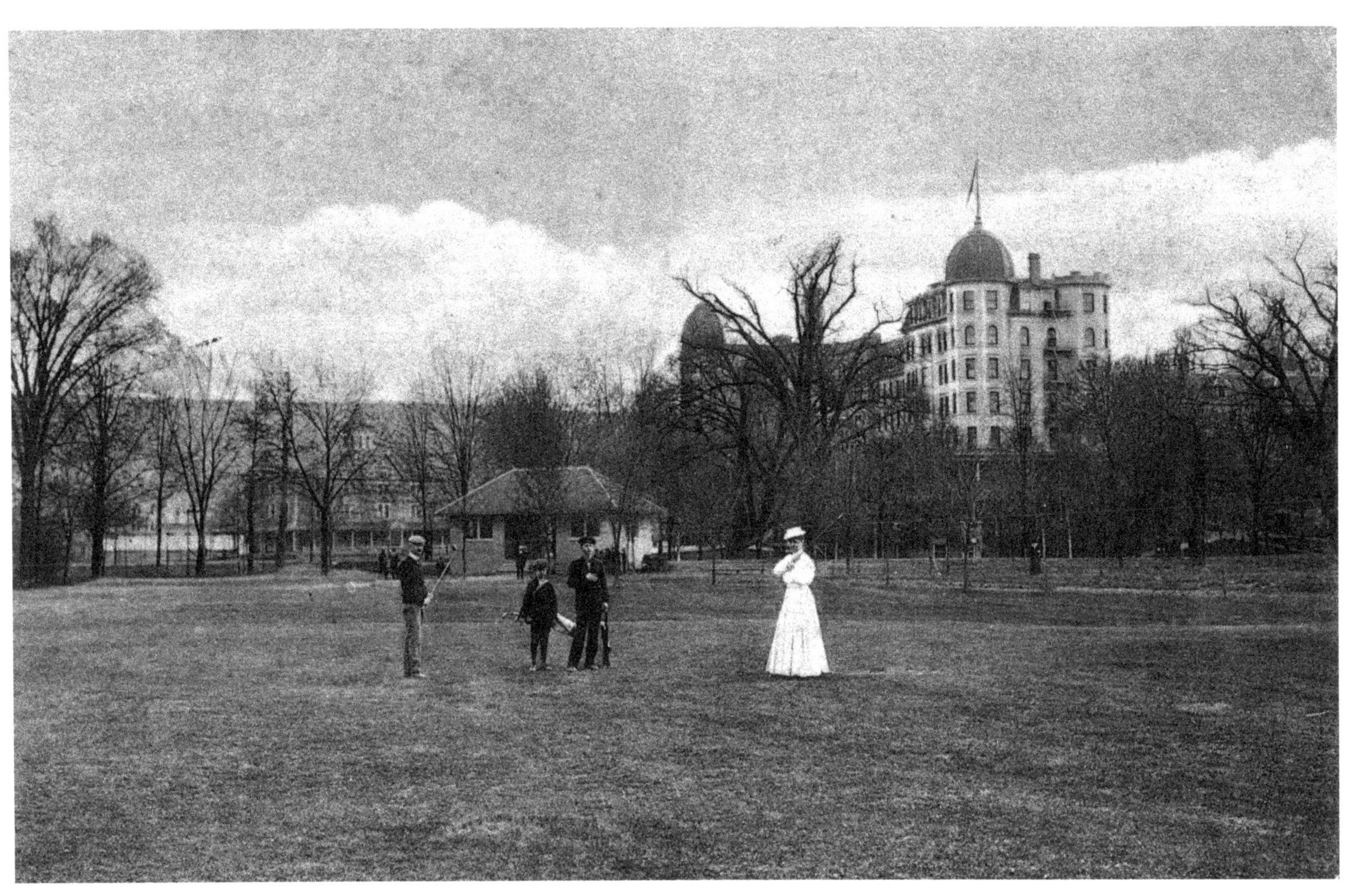

The hotel at French Lick Springs was renowned not only for its luxurious accommodations and healthful spas, but also for its lush gardens and grounds. Americans at leisure found, too, that they could partake of that wonderful new game of golf which was then overtaking the nation's fancy.

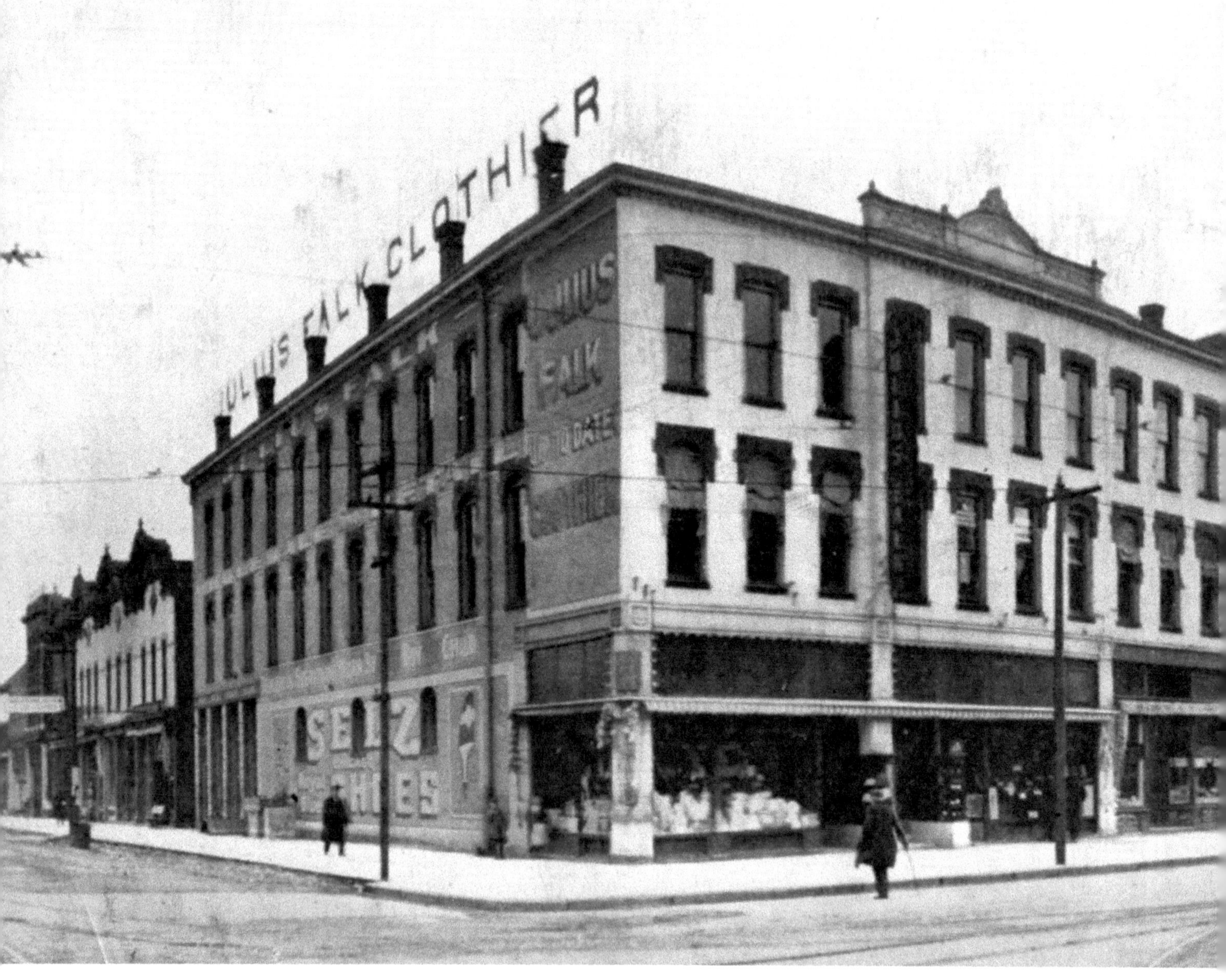

This image of downtown Peru was printed as a postcard, which could be mailed flat or rolled. In the space designated for postage, it was noted that mailing would cost 1 cent with no writing and 2 cents with writing. The cost of basic postage would remain unchanged for generations, from the introduction of the first postage stamps in 1847 to the first decades of the twentieth century.

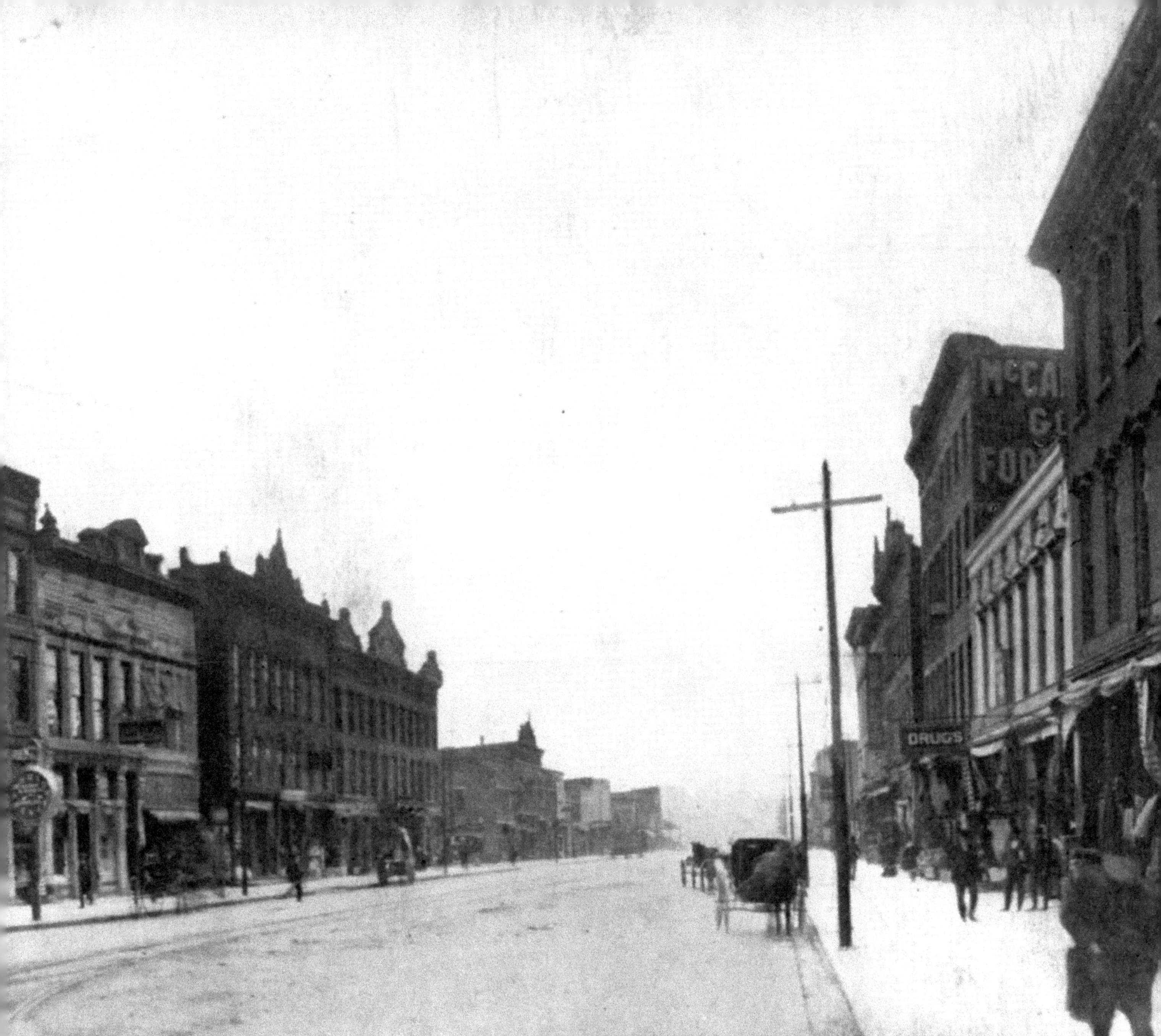
DRUGS

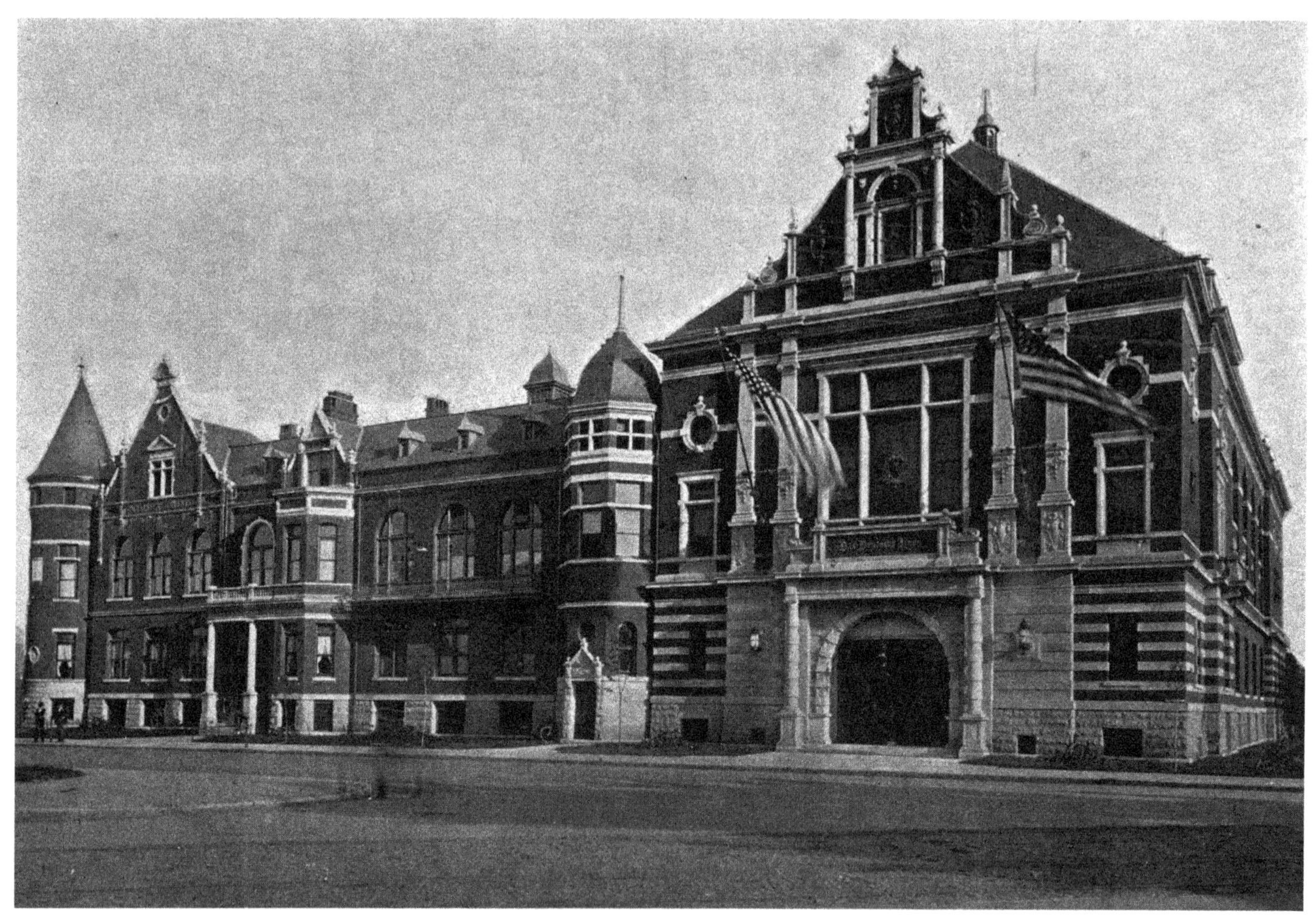

In addition to being a splendid example of Romanesque and Renaissance architecture, Das Deutsche Haus—or the German House—was the center of German cultural and athletic activity in the late nineteenth century. Designed by architect Bernard Vonnegut and located in Indianapolis, it was renamed the Athenaeum when World War I sparked anti-German sentiment.

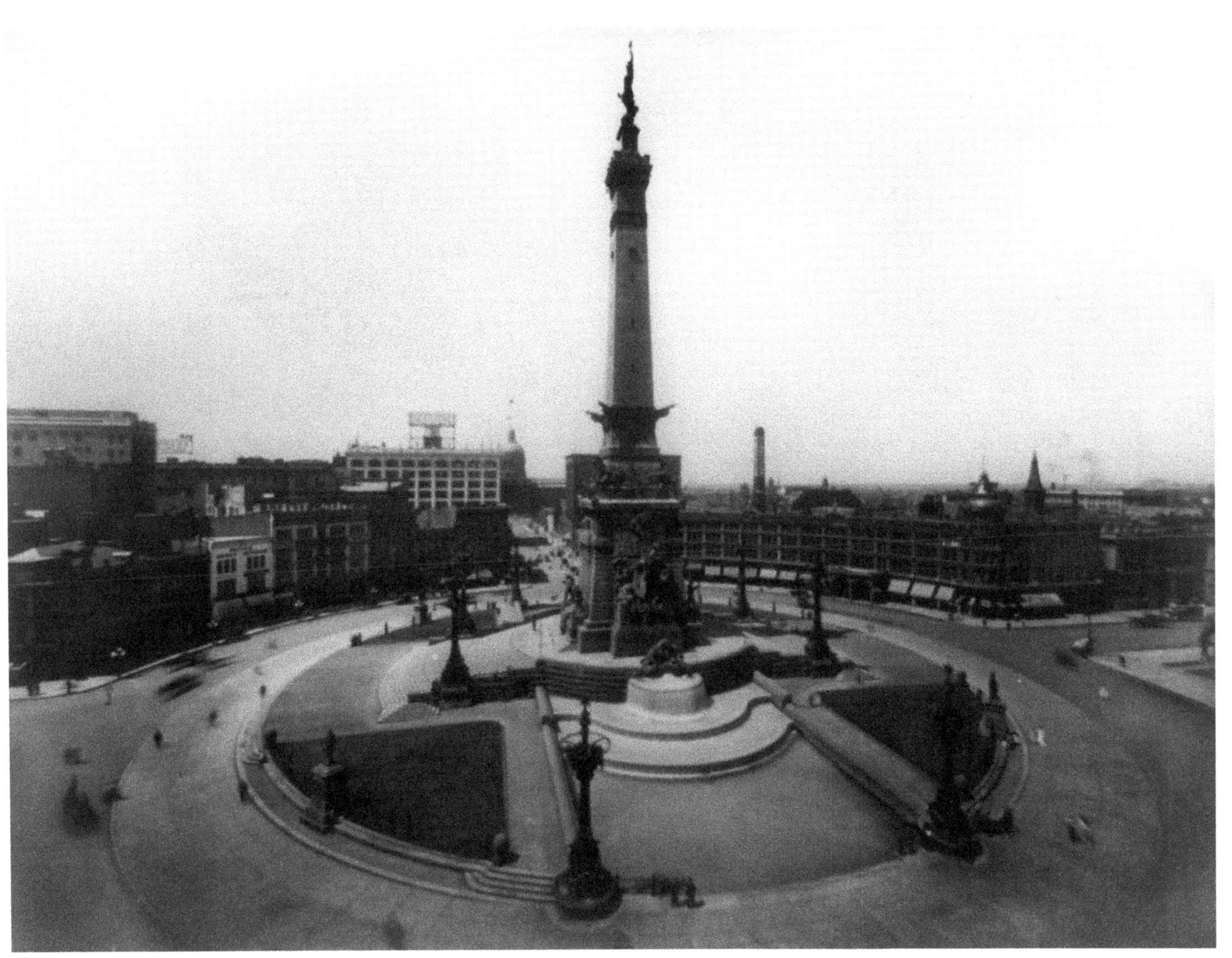

This early morning photograph of the Soldiers' and Sailors' Monument in Indianapolis shows the symmetry of its design with streets leading into the circle like the spokes of a wheel. Constructed of limestone quarried at Stinesville, the 284-foot-tall monument was dedicated in 1902 as a memorial to the soldiers and sailors of the Civil War.

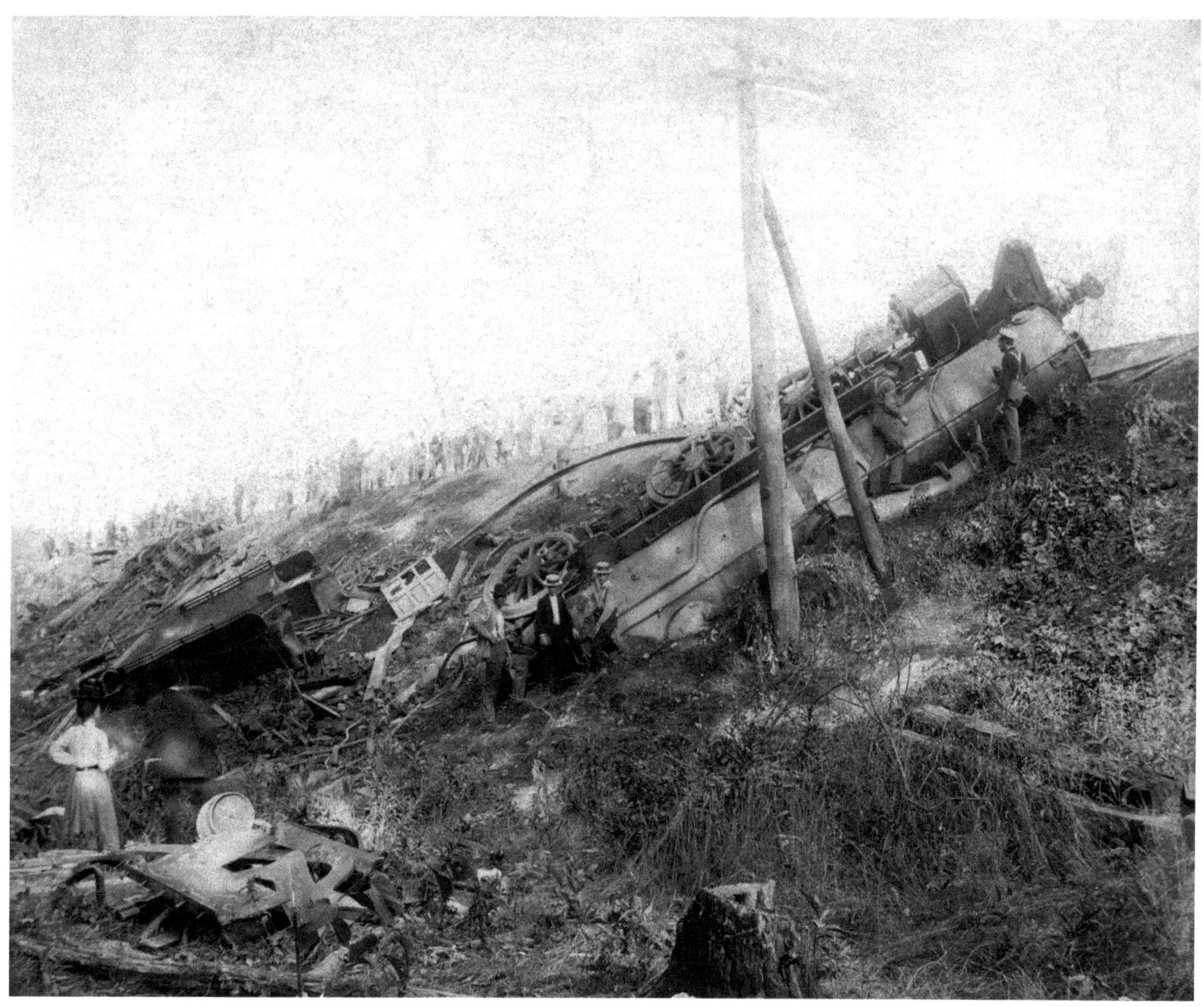

More than 25 railroad accidents resulted in fatalities in Indiana in the first decade of the twentieth century. These wrecks were scenes of carnage and twisted metal, a spectacle of overturned locomotives and crushed passenger cars that always drew the curious. This crash of a Wabash Railroad locomotive in Cass County in 1901 had its share, including the three men at center posing for a photograph before the engine.

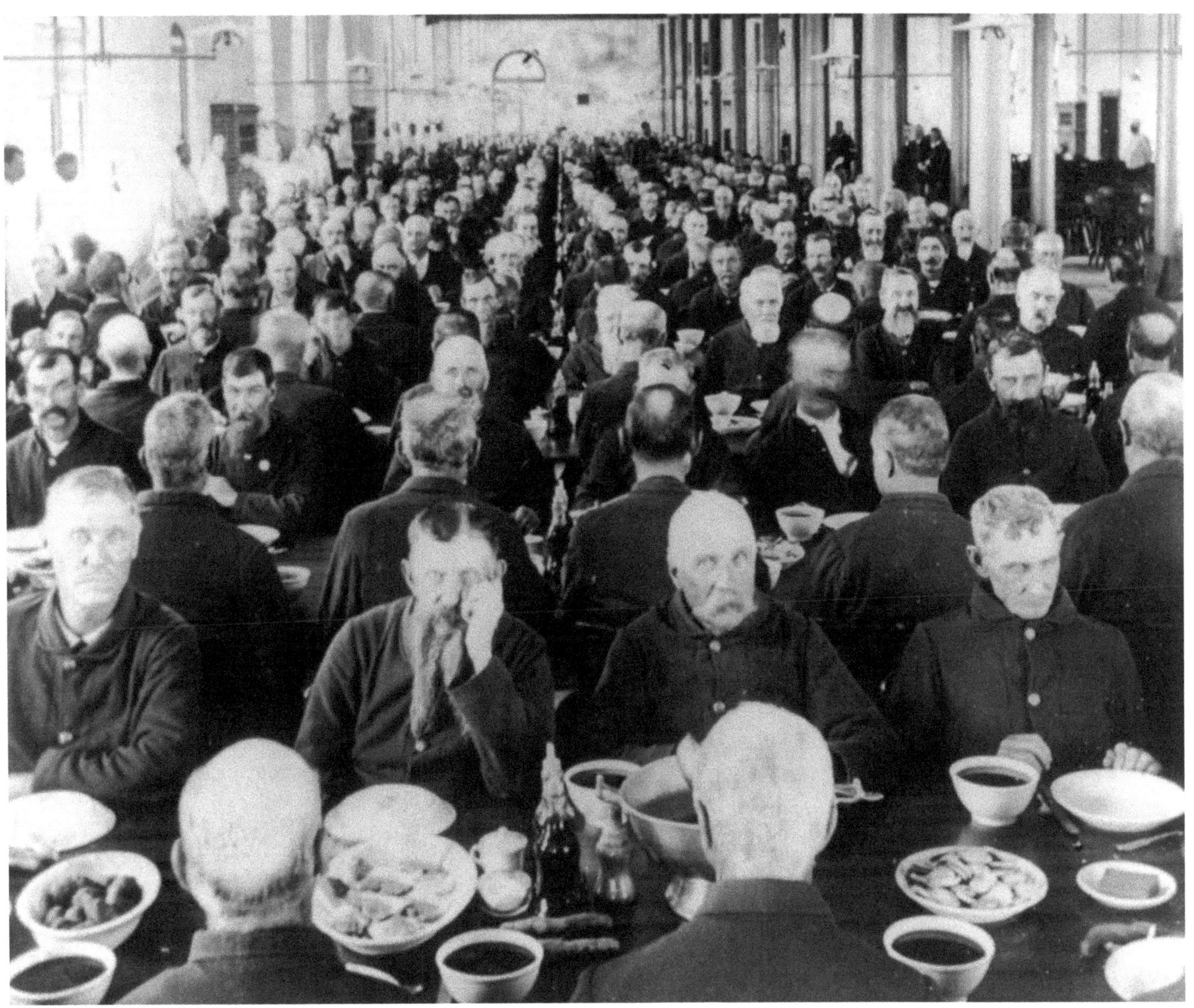

The faces in the dining room of the National Military Home of Indiana in 1898 are a stark commentary on the impact of the Civil War. The facility opened in Marion with 586 disabled and impoverished veterans in 1890 and grew to be a city within itself with 14 barracks and other buildings serving more than 2,000 men.

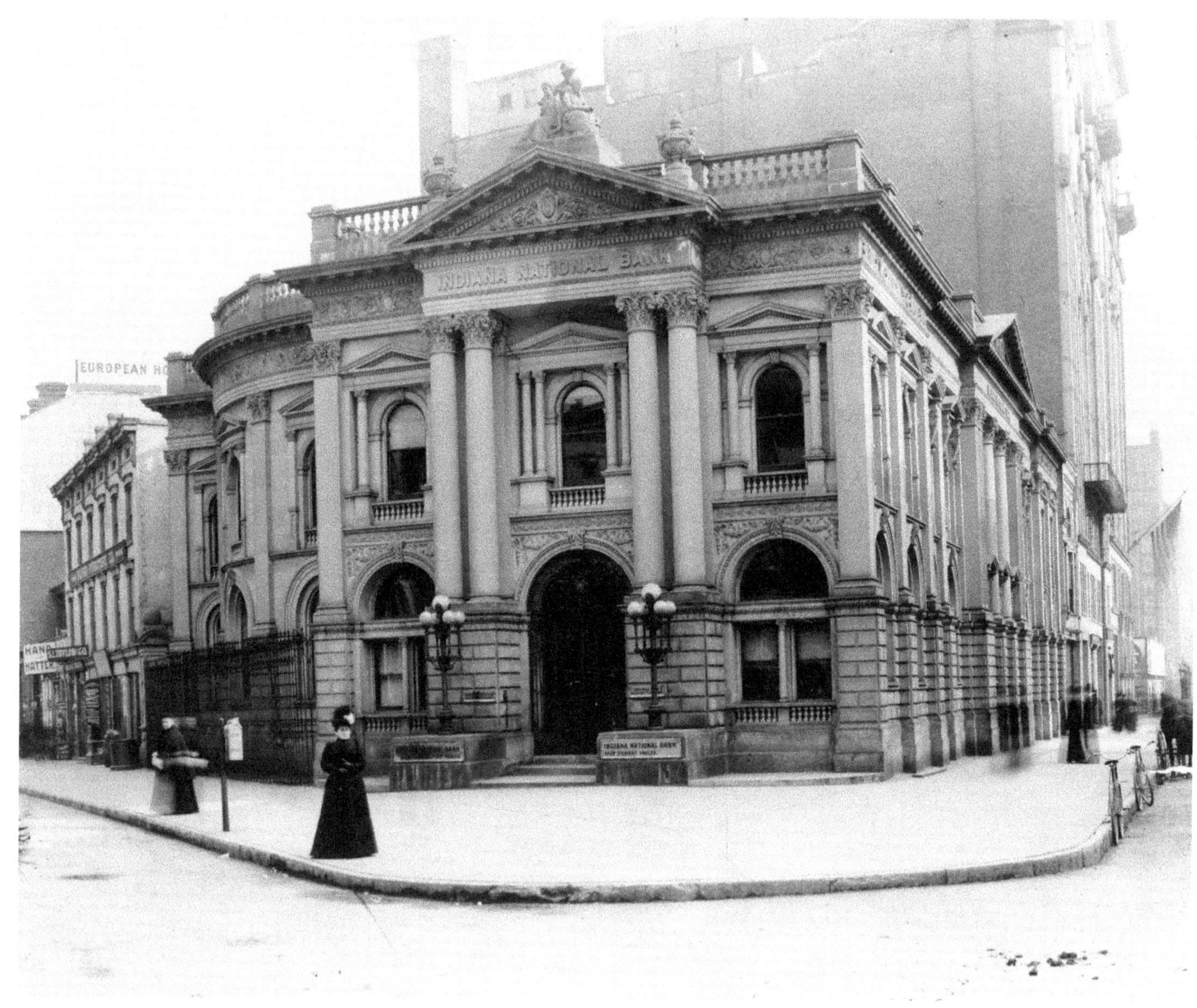

The Indiana National Bank was one of the oldest financial institutions in the capital city, with roots dating to 1857. It became a national bank after the Civil War and survived even when its building burned on September 18, 1895. Its home when this photograph was taken in 1898 was at Indianapolis' busy Virginia Avenue and Pennsylvania Street.

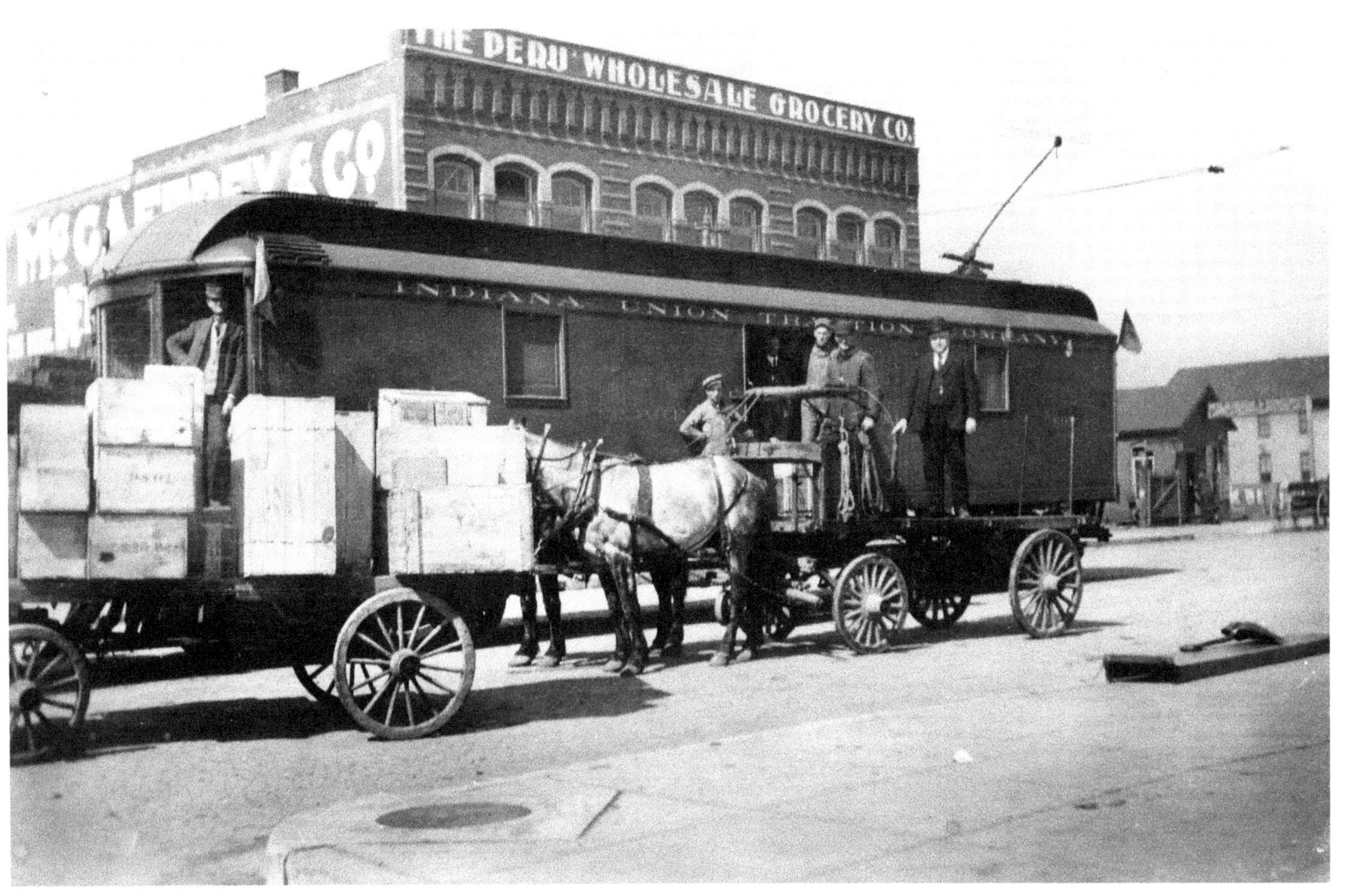

The 1890s saw the rise of interurbans, providing convenient rail travel for Hoosiers and rapid shipment of goods and materials by cars like this Indiana Union Traction Company freighter on North Broadway in Peru. Interurban shipments were at first unloaded at depots. When the economic potential of delivery to homes and businesses was recognized, traction companies began offering the service and profited from it.

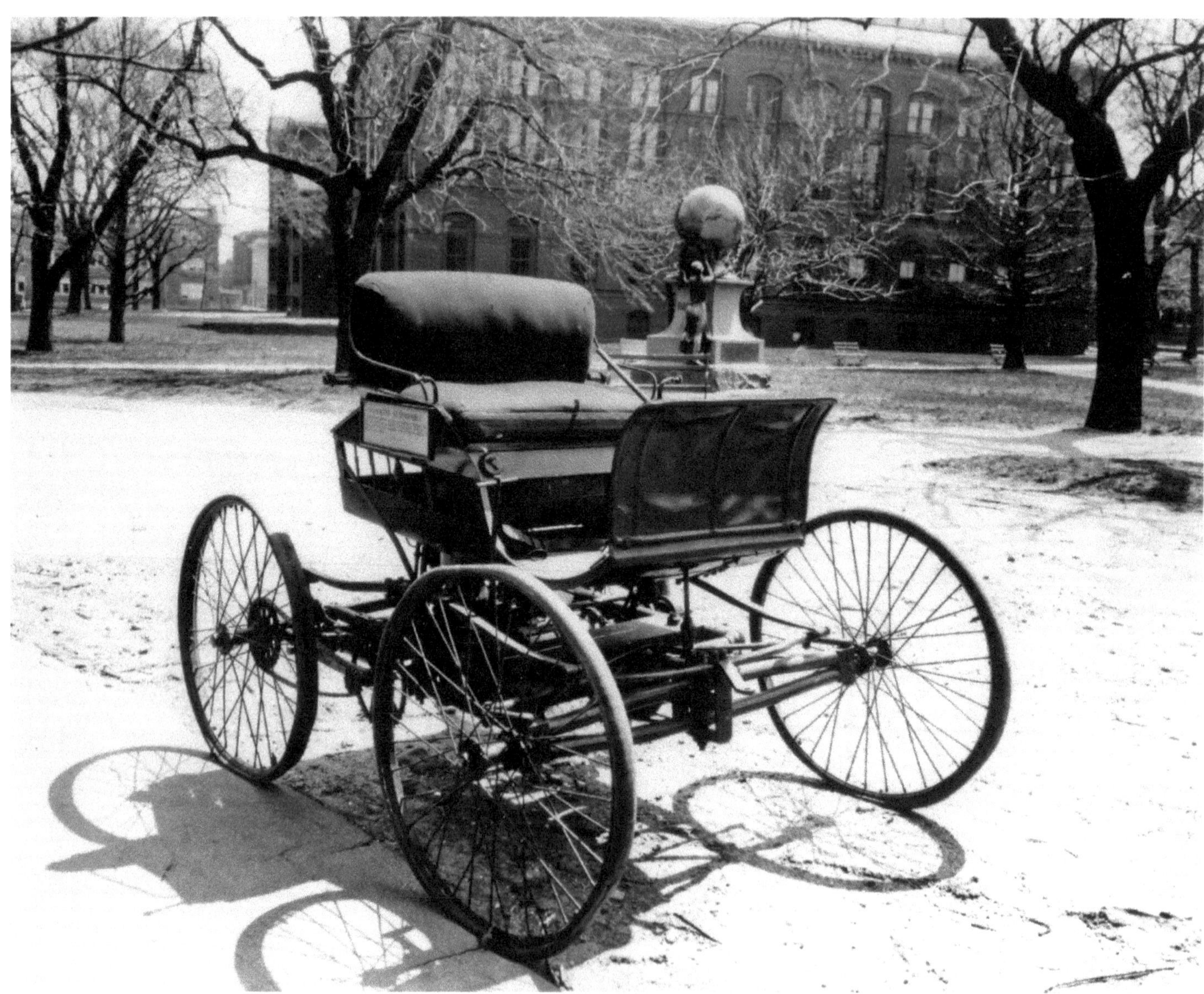

Elwood P. Haynes is credited with building one of the first gasoline-powered automobiles in the United States and later becoming one of the first mass manufacturers of cars in the nation. Haynes successfully tested the automobile he called "Pioneer" before a large crowd in Kokomo on July 4, 1894. He was joined by Elmer and Edgar Apperson in 1896, and soon they were producing autos at a then unheard-of rate of a car every two or three weeks. By 1900 their Haynes-Apperson Automobile Company was producing 100 cars a year.

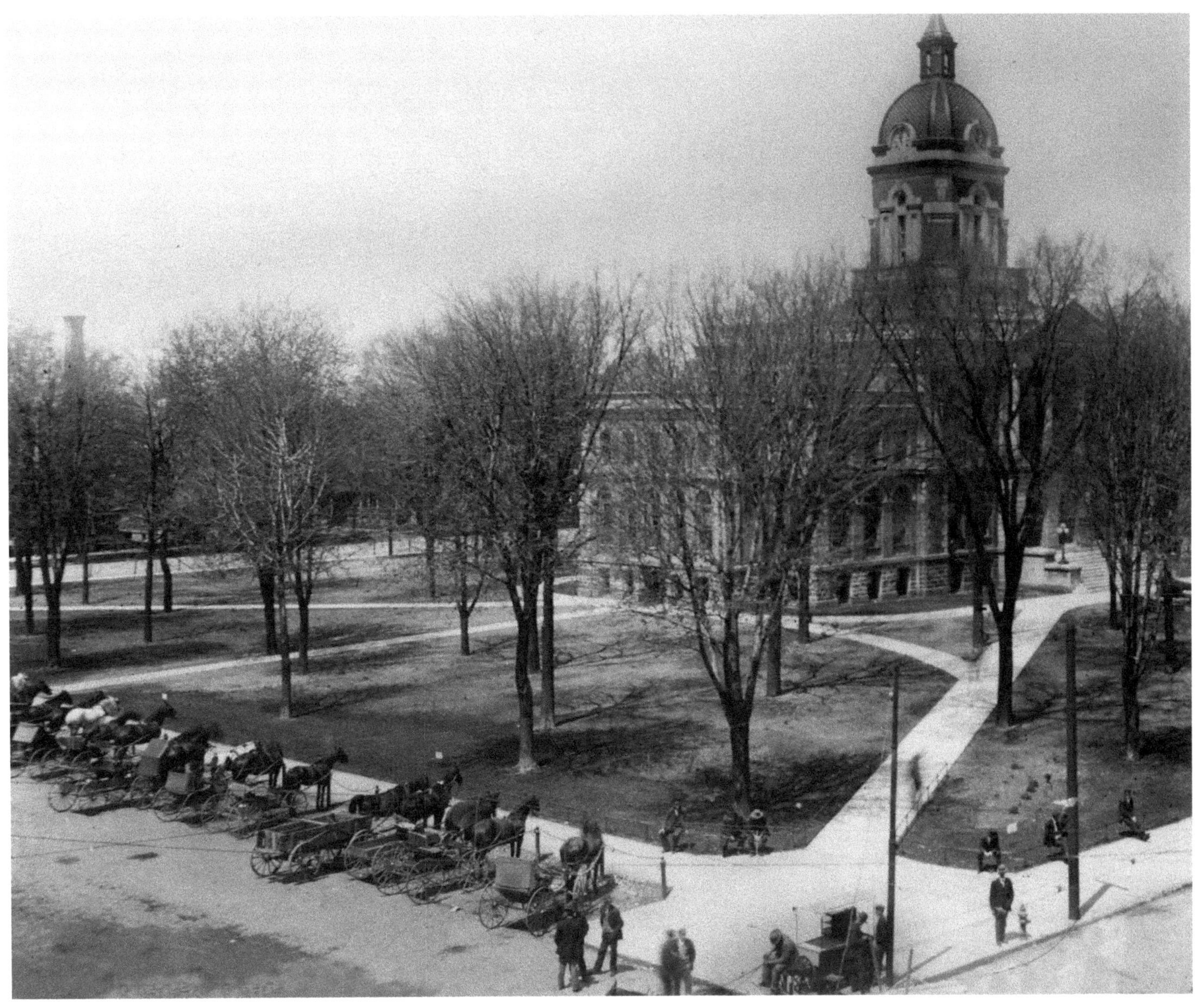

The Elkhart County Courthouse was a magnificent structure built three years after the end of the Civil War. Thirty years later, this rooftop view of the building and town square demonstrates how it dominated the vistas in Goshen.

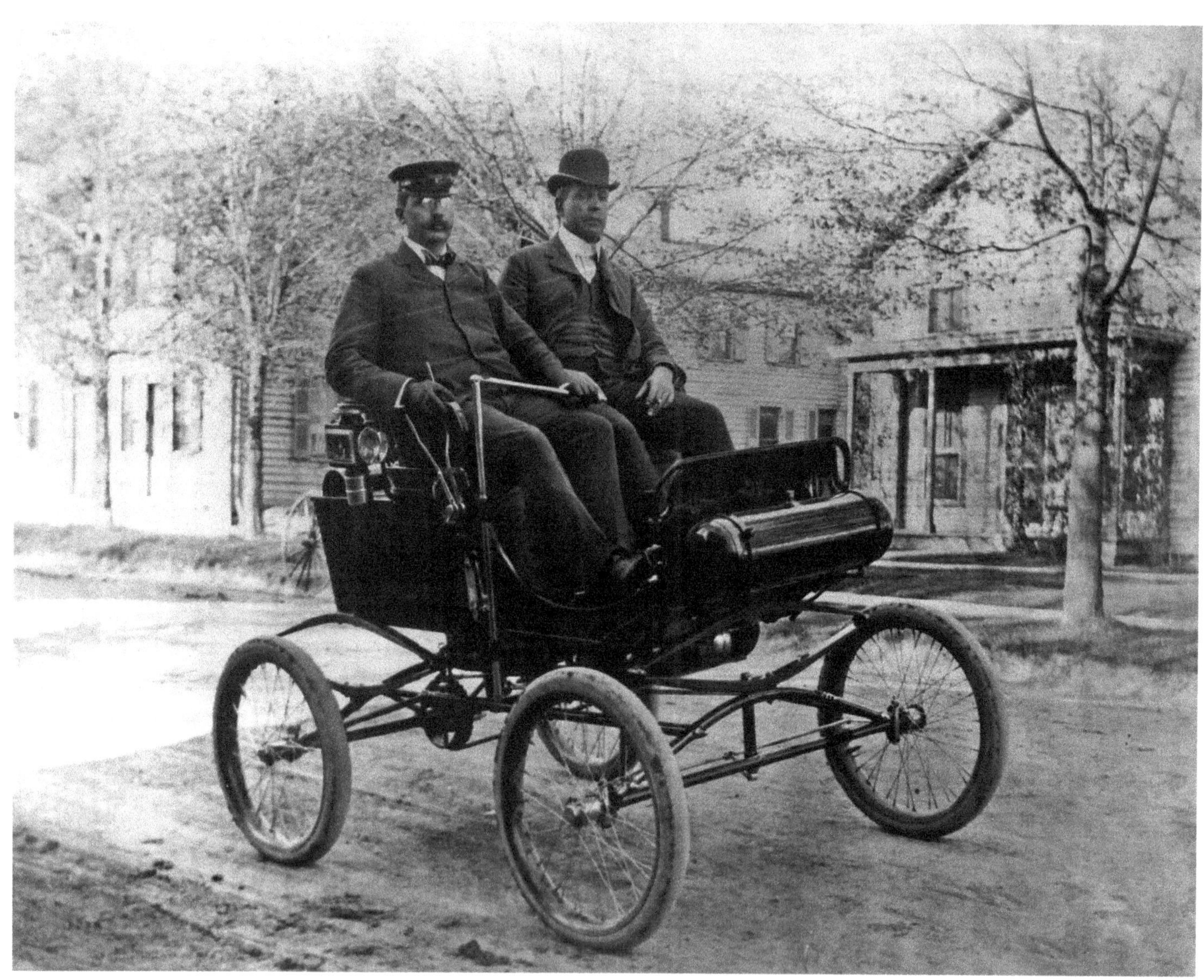

In the early days of automobile design, steam power was harnessed by some inventors as a competitive option. W. H. McIntyre, left, who would become an innovator in the early automotive industry, pauses with friend Harry C. Henry, as they test a Milwaukee Steamer along Main Street in Auburn around 1900. At its height, McIntyre's company operated five automotive plants in Auburn.

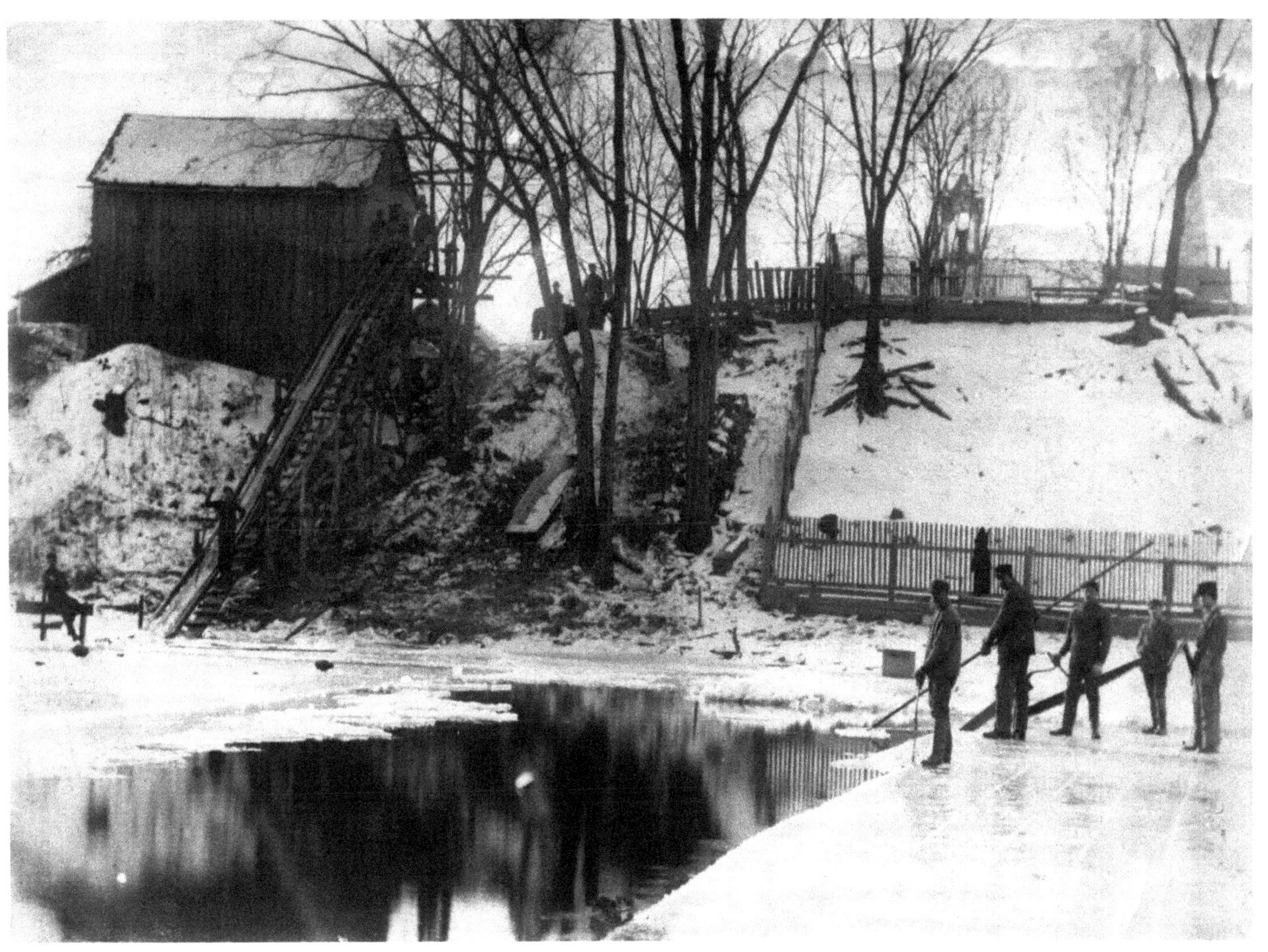

Some of the winter work engaged in by Americans a century ago was aimed at warm weather relief. This group of men and boys are shown cutting ice from the St. Joseph River in Spencerville, to be pulled uphill to the ice house at upper left for use in summer. The ice was scored and then cut and moved about using the hand saws and poles visible in the image. The photograph was taken around 1900.

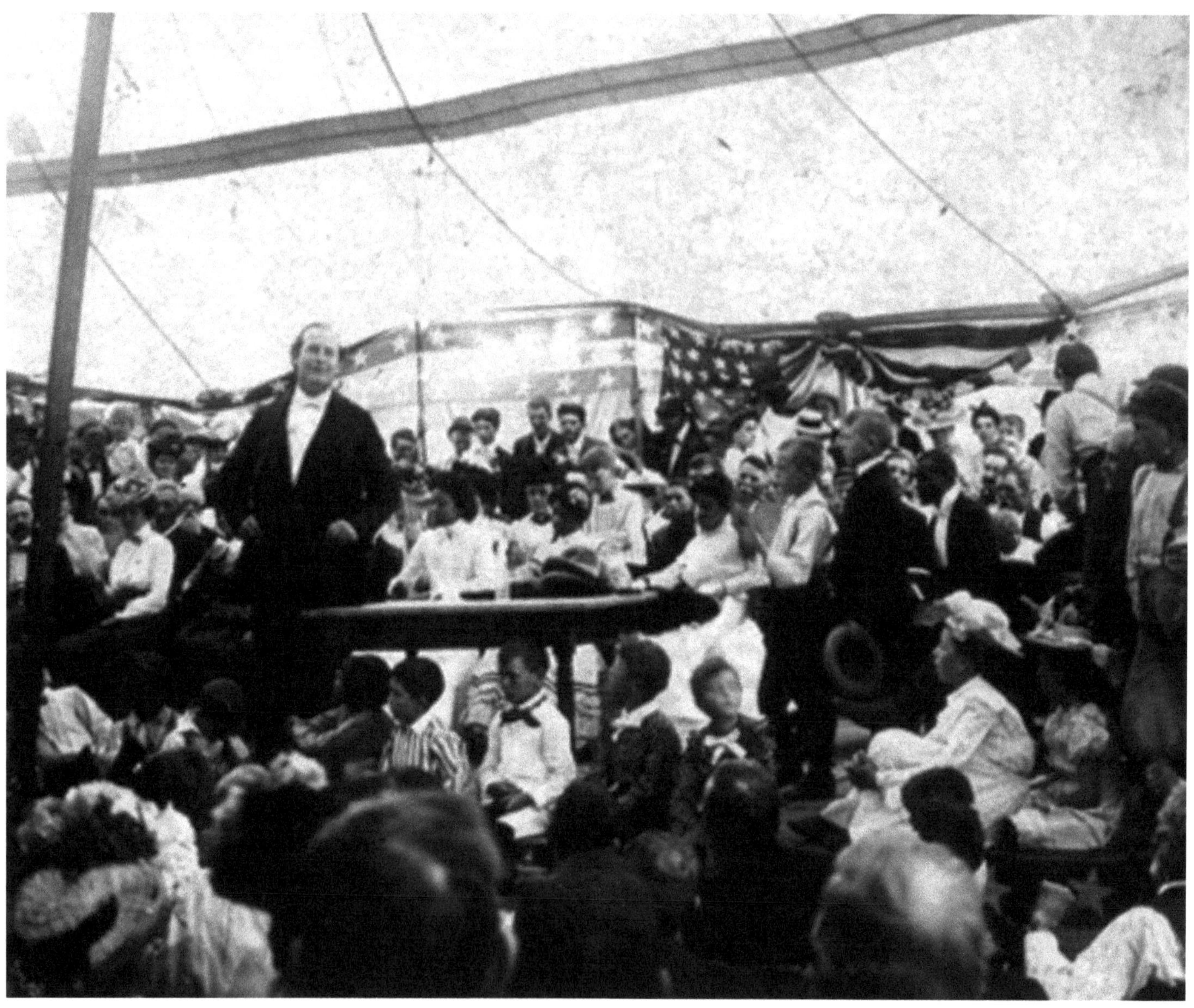

Even though twice defeated for the presidency of the United States in 1896 and 1900, William Jennings Bryan remained one of the most popular orators in the nation as demonstrated in this image from an address to thousands at a Chautauqua in Madison on July 6, 1901. Bryan would make a third unsuccessful run for the presidency in 1908.

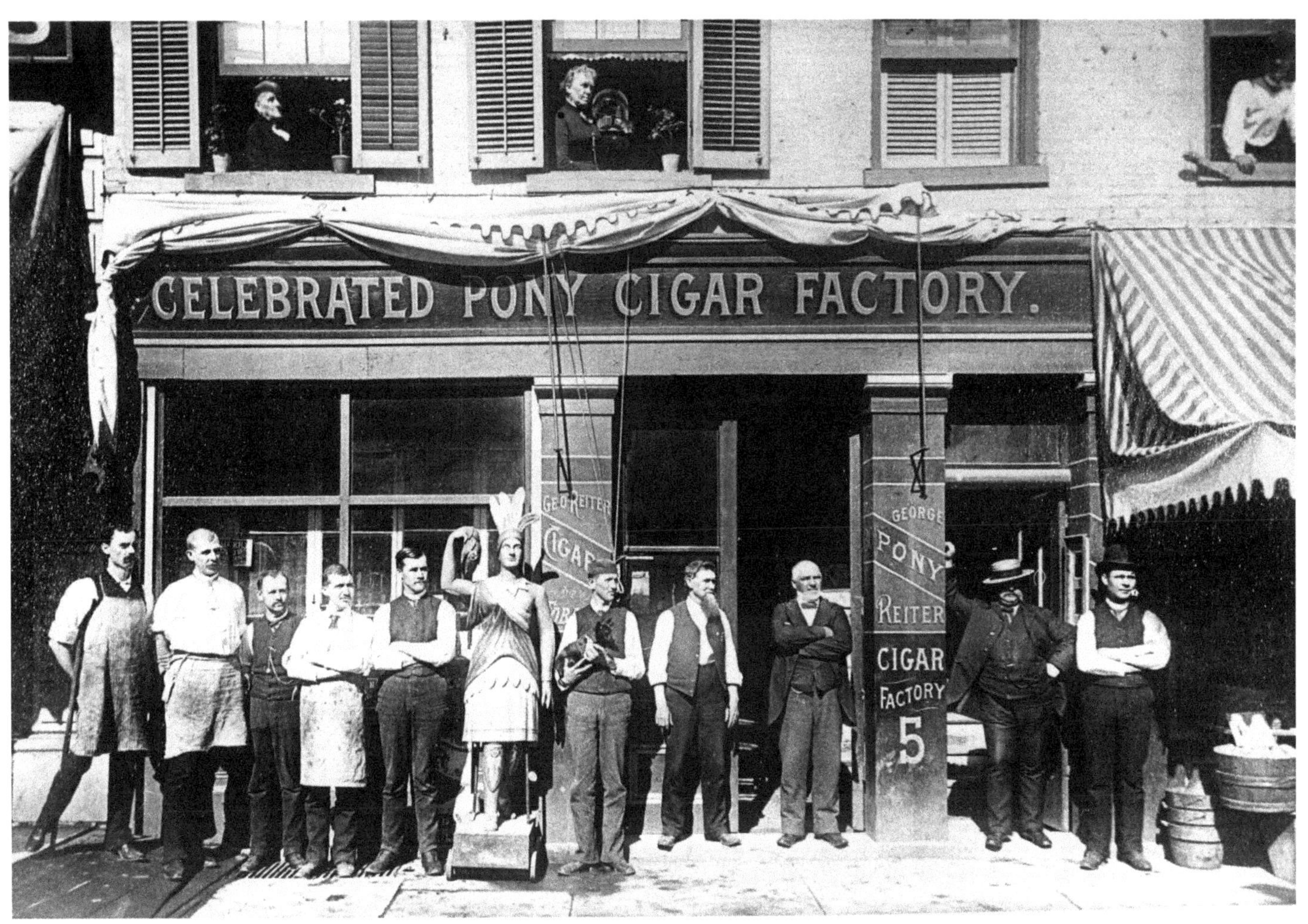

Nearly 350,000 different brands of cigars were made in America in 1900, and almost every large community in Indiana included a cigar maker of its own. The Pony Cigar Company in Fort Wayne was among the favored brands in northeastern Indiana—in part perhaps for its life-size cigar store Indian. Equally ubiquitous but today seldom noted was the fanciful signage on every building front in America, hand-lettered by skilled craftsmen without recourse to computers, electronic printing devices, or much of anything but paint, brushes, chalk, and a yardstick, and the satisfaction derived from well-executed brush strokes.

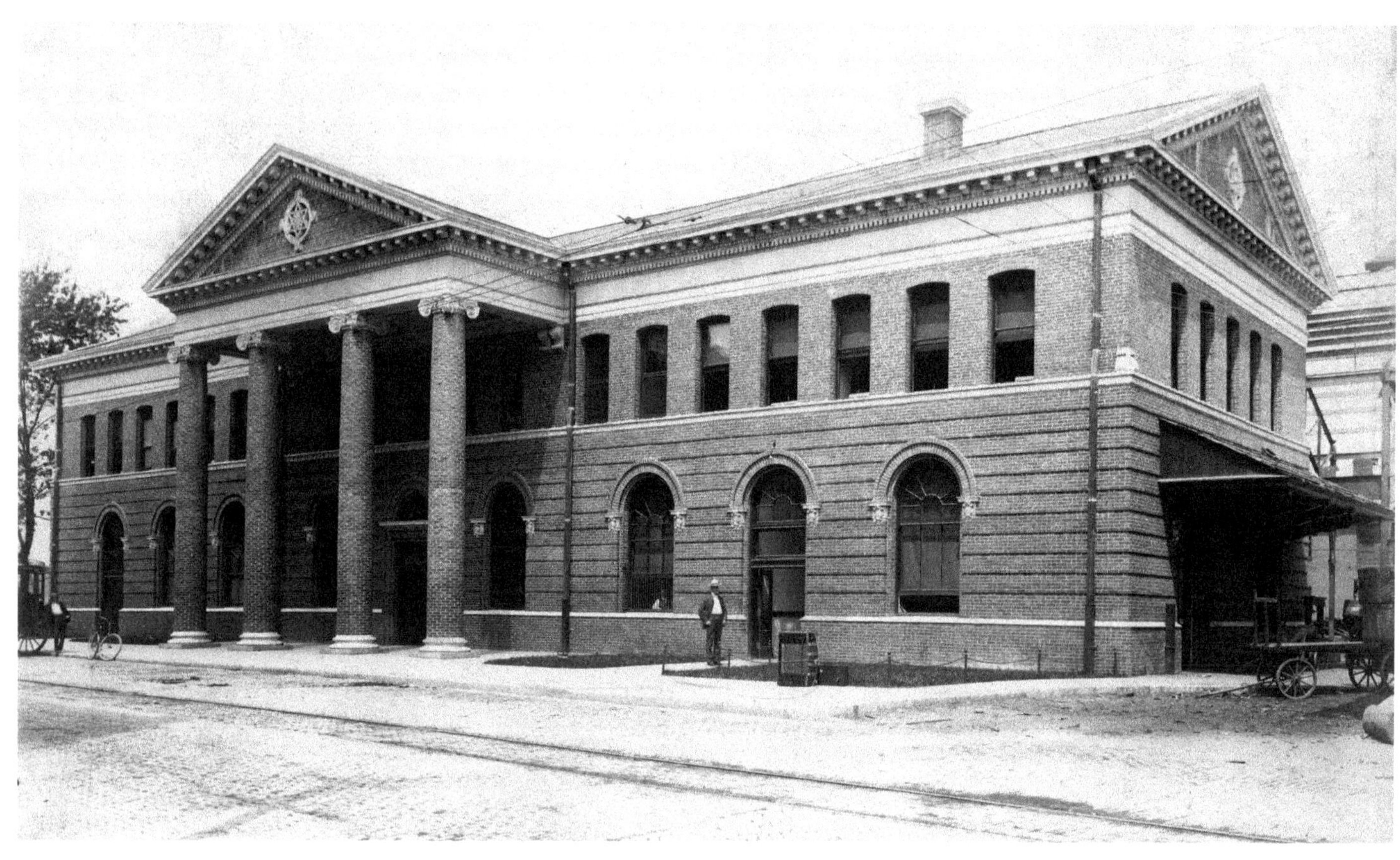

The Union Depot in Richmond completed in 1902 could boast two very distinctive architectural features. First, the columns in front were made of brick. Second, the depot had an enclosure over its tracks that could accommodate nine trains at a time regardless of the weather. The station was later known as the Pennsylvania Railroad depot and remains standing, in large measure through the efforts of local historic preservation groups.

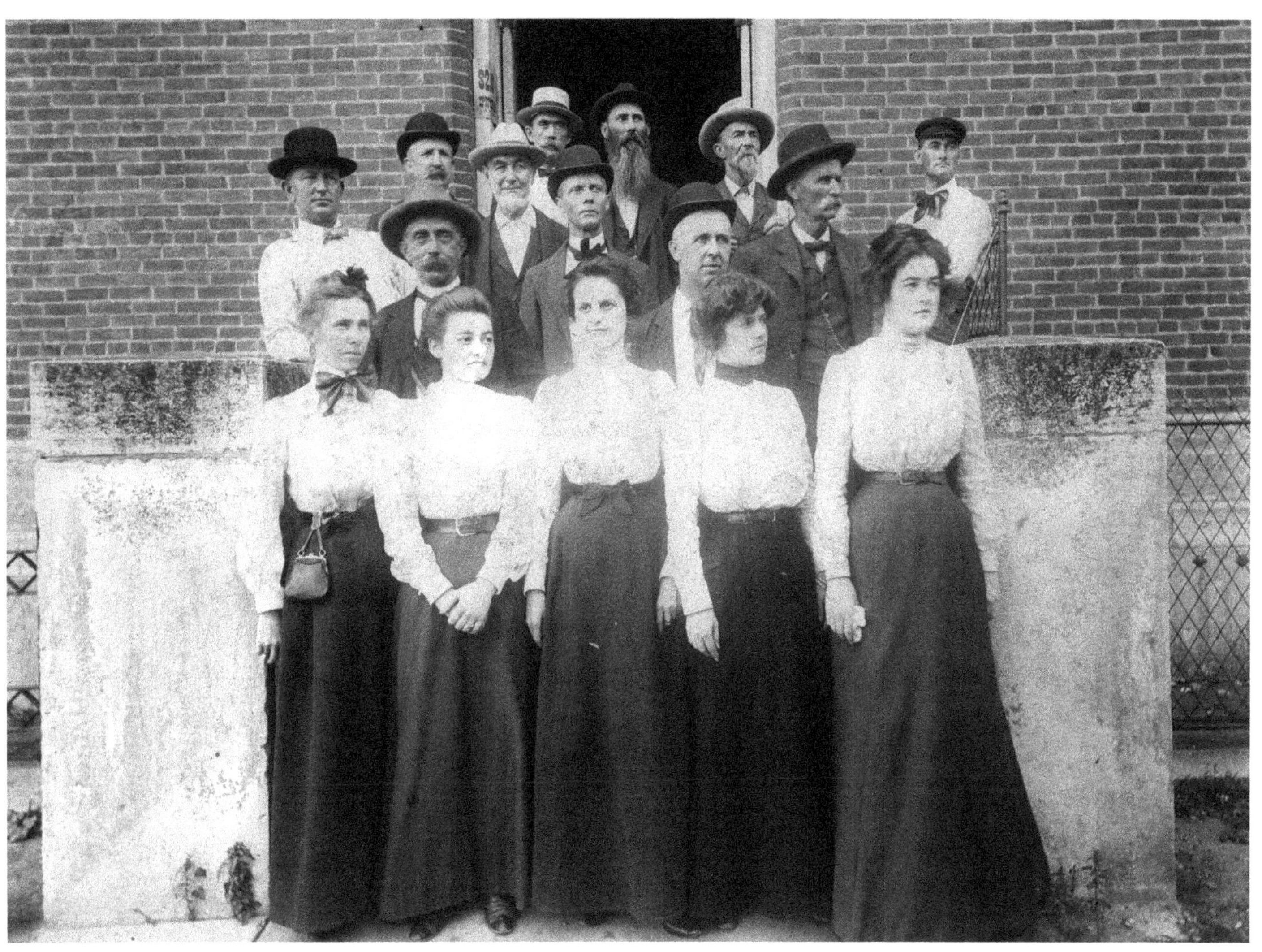

Miami County officials and assistants pose for a photograph on the steps of the second county courthouse around 1901. Fashion in the new century included a trend toward lighter colors, exemplified here in the blouses worn by these women.

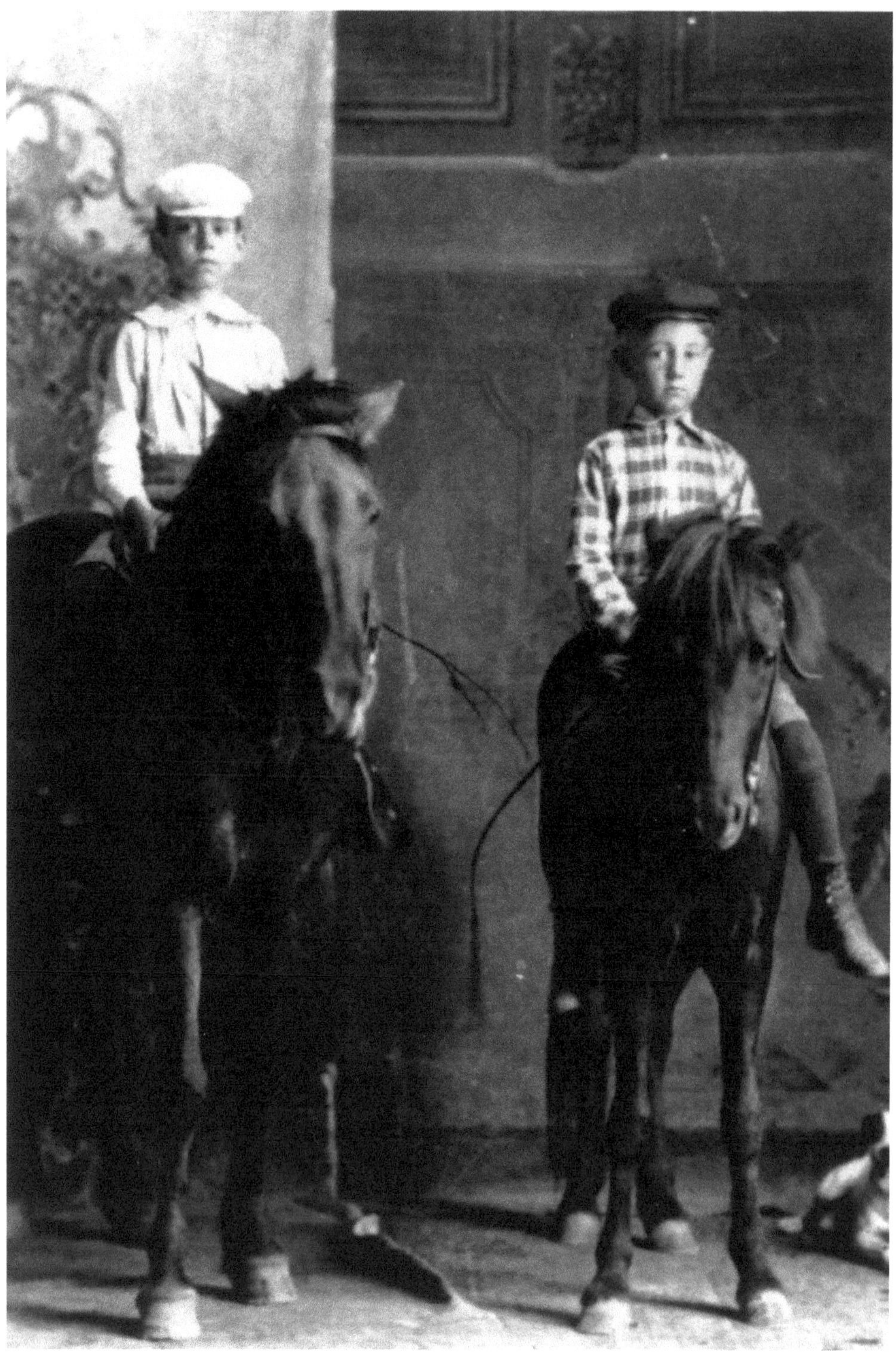

The young lad on the horse at left would become one of the greatest lyricists and composers in U.S. history, Cole Porter. Born and raised in Peru, Porter is 11 years old in this 1902 photograph showing him and his cousin, Louis Cole. Cole Porter's ultimate success on Broadway was preceded by years spent in Europe as a member of the Lost Generation and enlistment in the French Foreign Legion. Ironically, Porter suffered compound fractures in his legs when he fell from a horse in October 1937, requiring many surgeries and changing his life dramatically.

Gabriel Godfroy (Wapanakekapwah, or White Blossoms) poses with his son, George Durand Godfroy, in Butler Township, Miami County, around 1903. The once-great landholder of the Miami tribe wears the Francis Slocum blanket, named for the woman who lived most of her life with the Miami after being captured as a five-year-old by the Delawares.

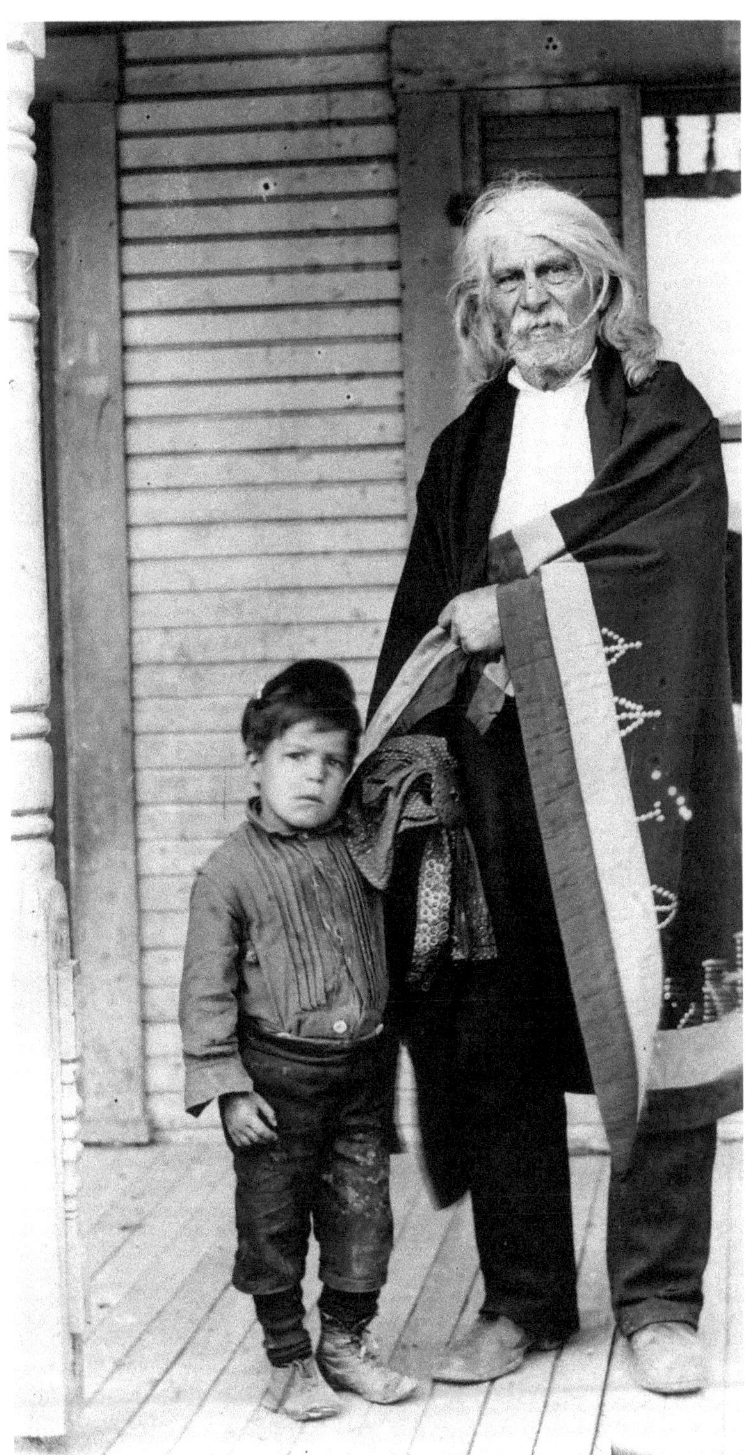

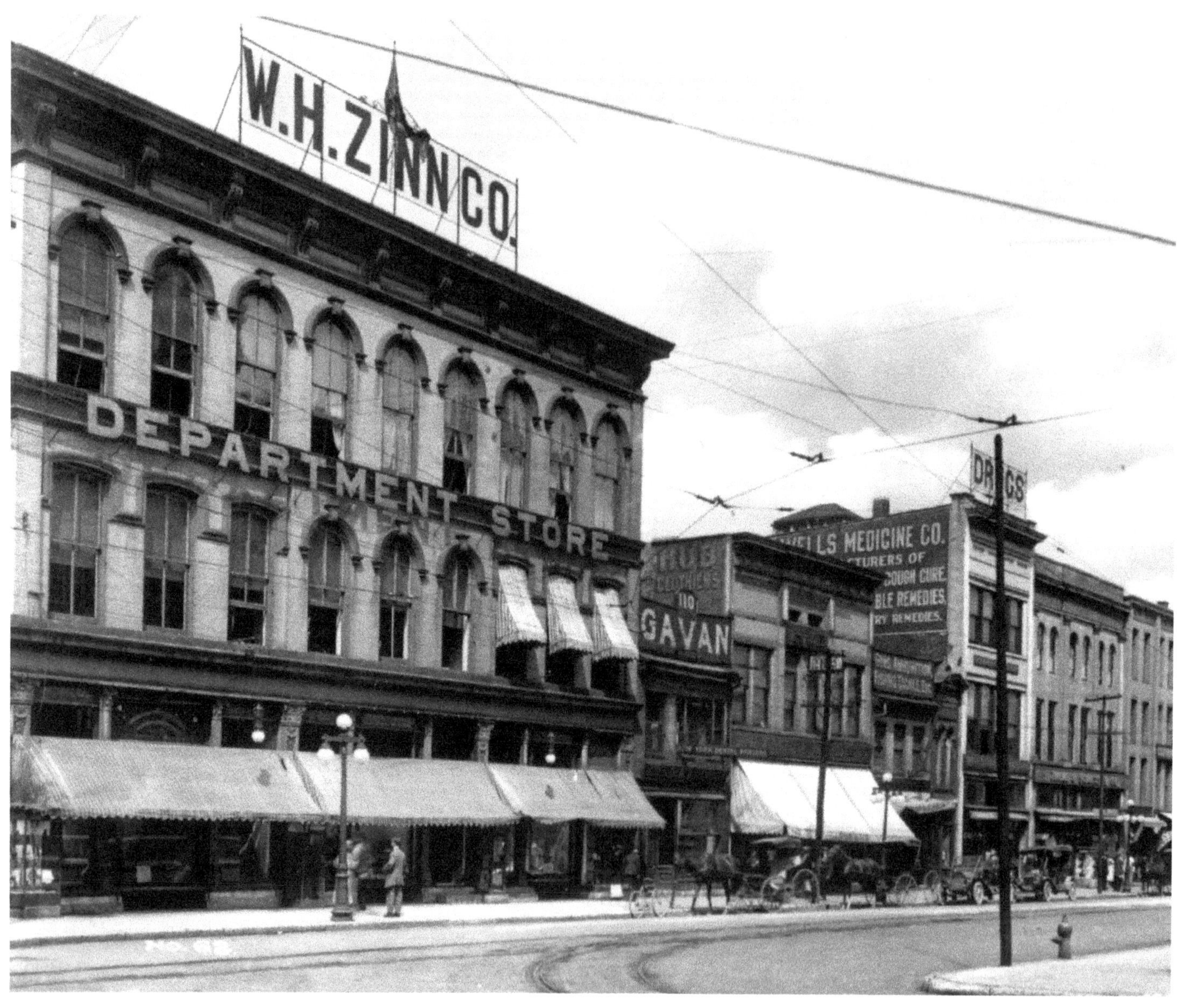

Given its name in 1825 when the Marquis de Lafayette was touring the United States, Lafayette became the county seat for Tippecanoe County in 1826. In 1959, the United States Post Office issued an air mail stamp commemorating an experimental air mail flight which had departed the city a century earlier—by balloon.

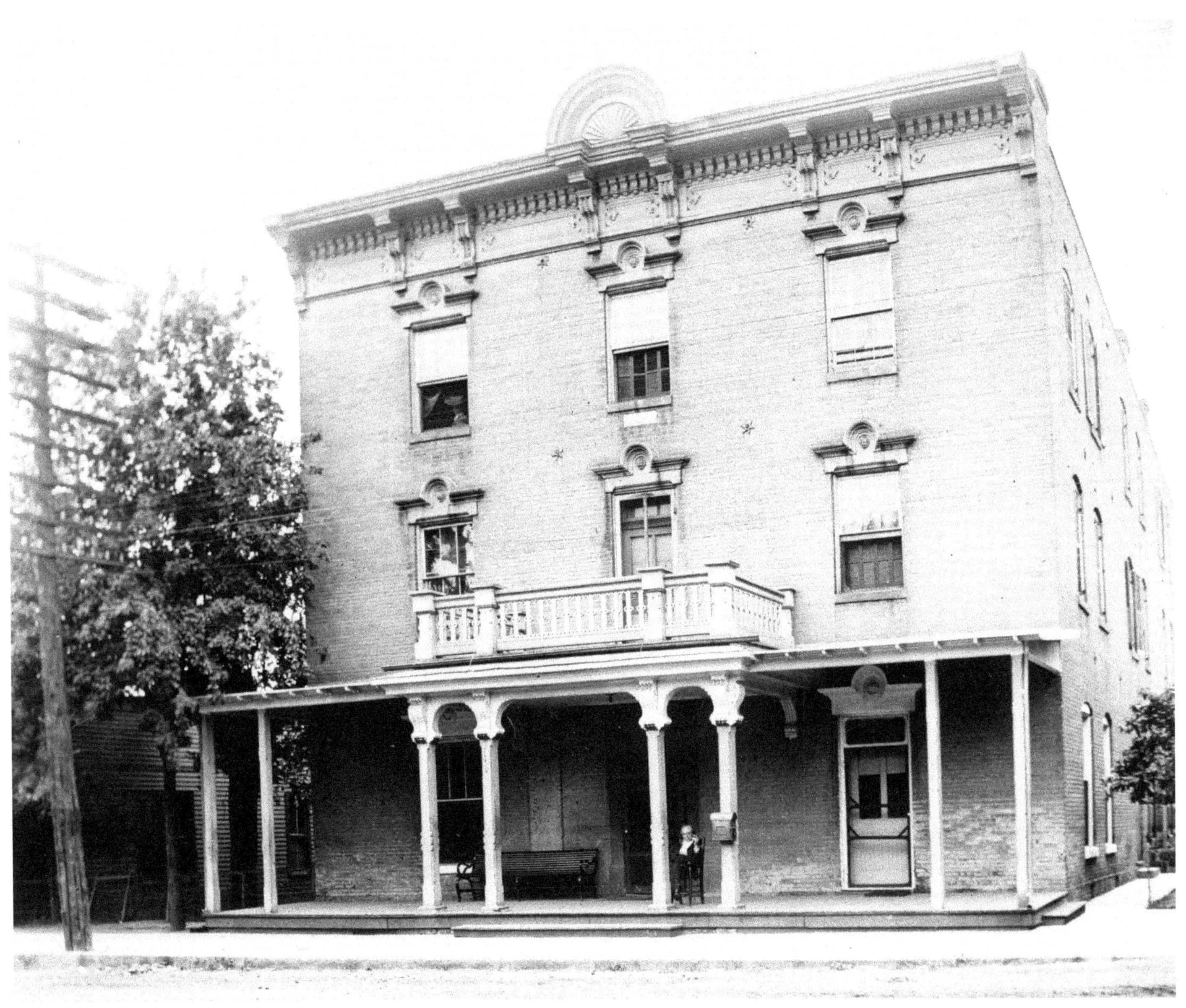

The Rappite Tavern on Church Street in New Harmony was built as a dormitory in 1823 for the utopian communities of George Rapp and Robert Owen. Three years later it was converted into a tavern.

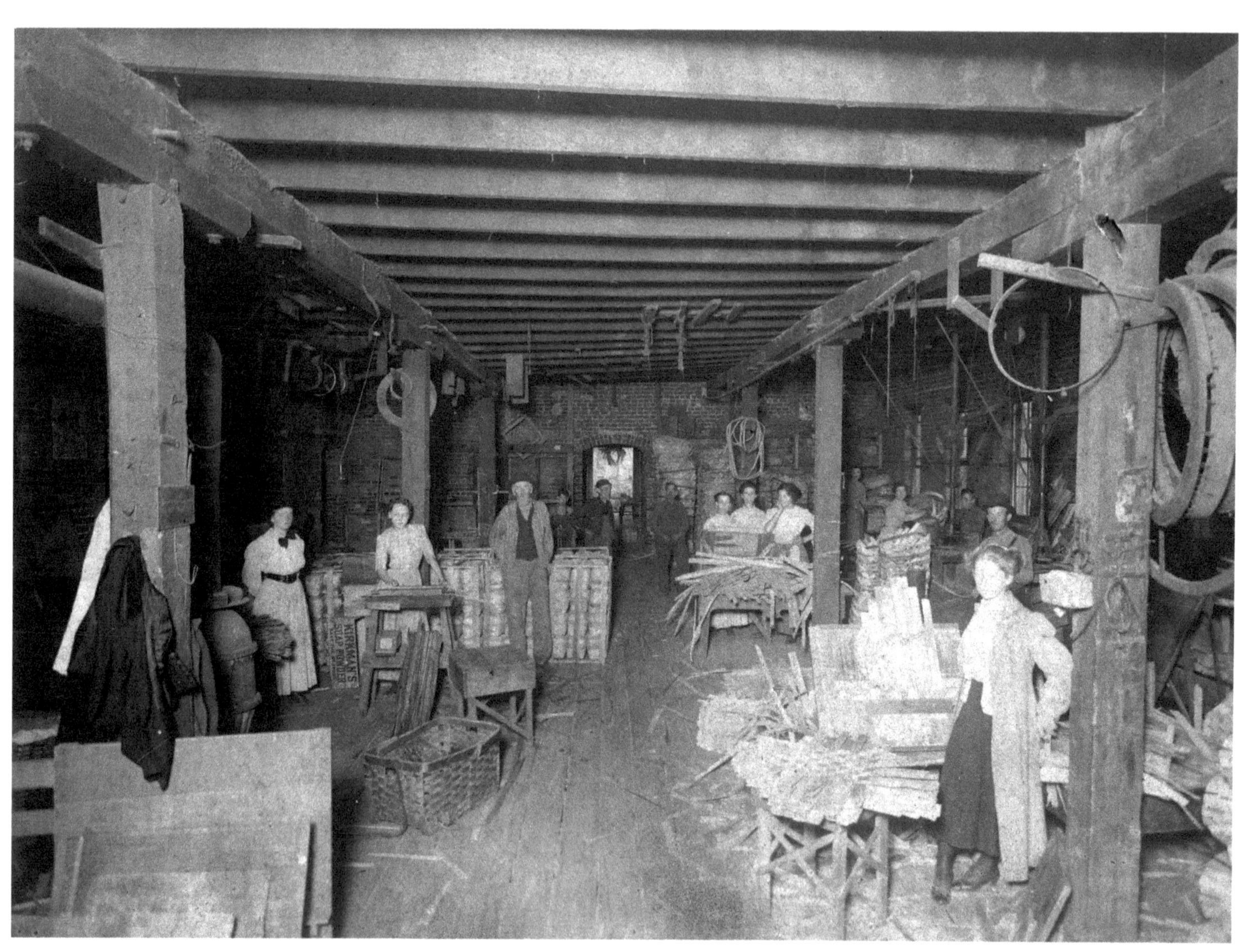

Dark and dingy working conditions are very evident at this basket factory in Peru. More than a dozen individuals have interrupted their work to pose for the photographer.

Gilbert and Sullivan's *The Mikado* swept the nation in song and fashion at the turn of the century. Like thousands of other little girls, five-year-old Anna Brandon of Auburn, at left, and her friends dress up to play "the three little maids" of the comic opera in 1904.

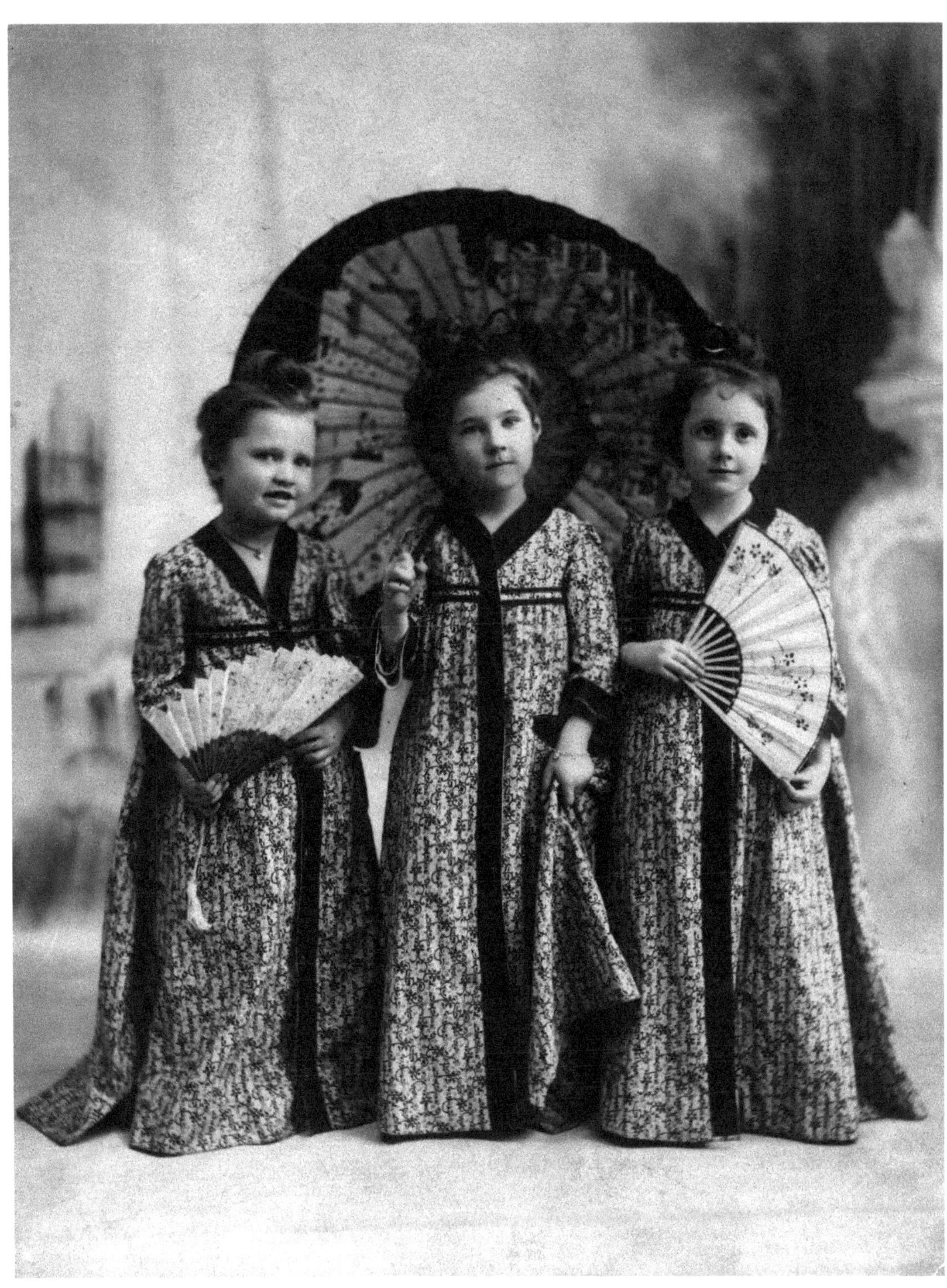

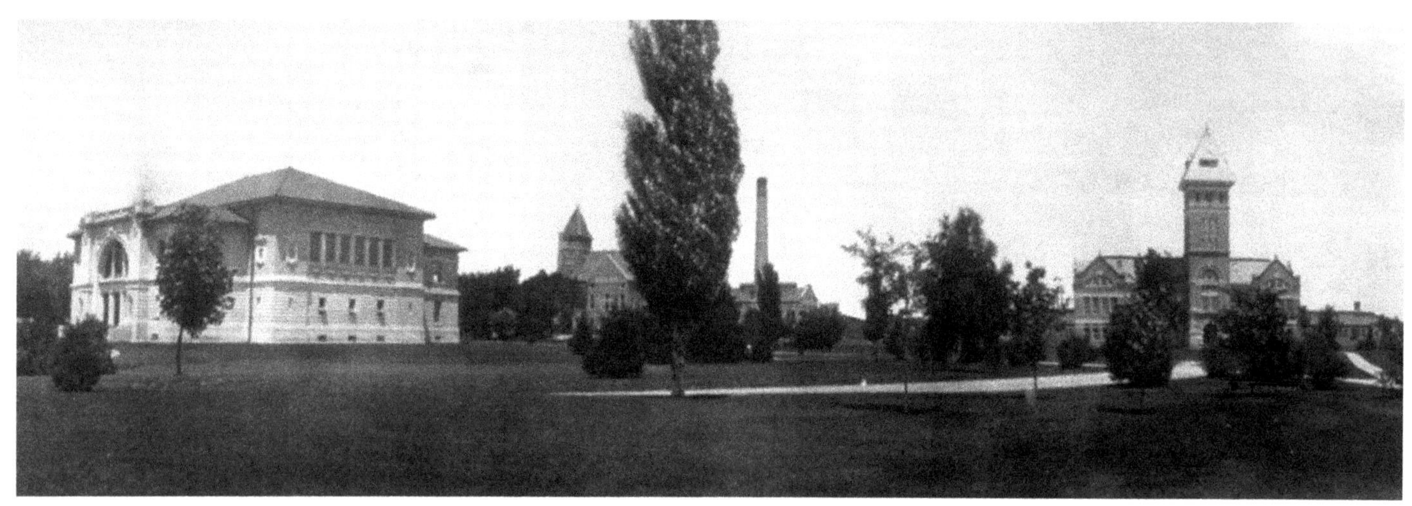

This panorama of the Purdue University campus as it appeared in 1904 speaks to the vision of the grand institution of higher learning it has become. The 140-foot-tall tower of Heavilon Hall, rebuilt in 1895 after an explosion and fire, is visible at right.

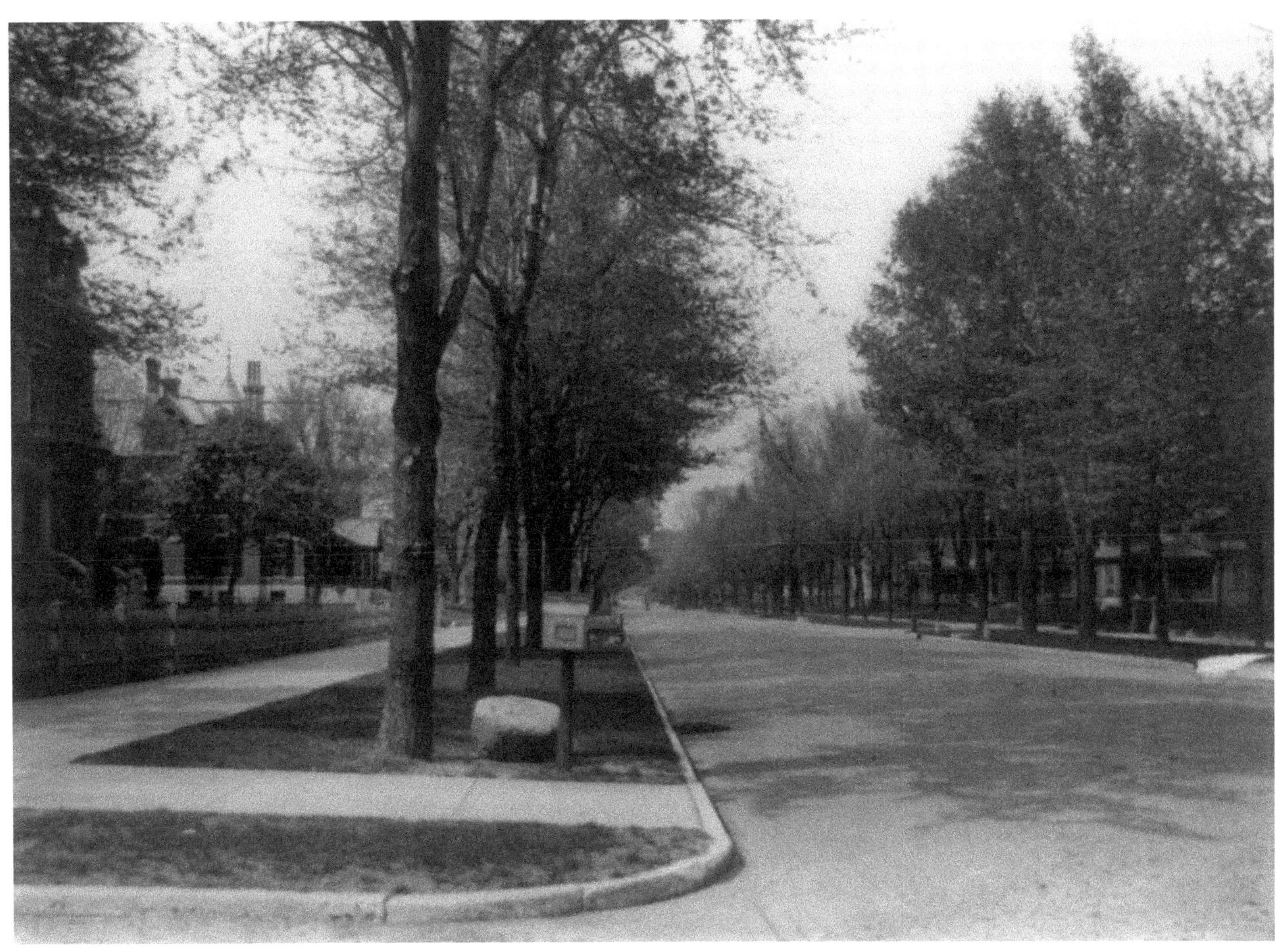

One of the goals for Indianapolis at the turn of the century was to create pleasant, tree-lined streets, exemplified in this photograph of North Delaware Street. Guides to Indianapolis at the time touted it as preferring to be "a city of comfortable homes" rather than one of mansions signifying great wealth.

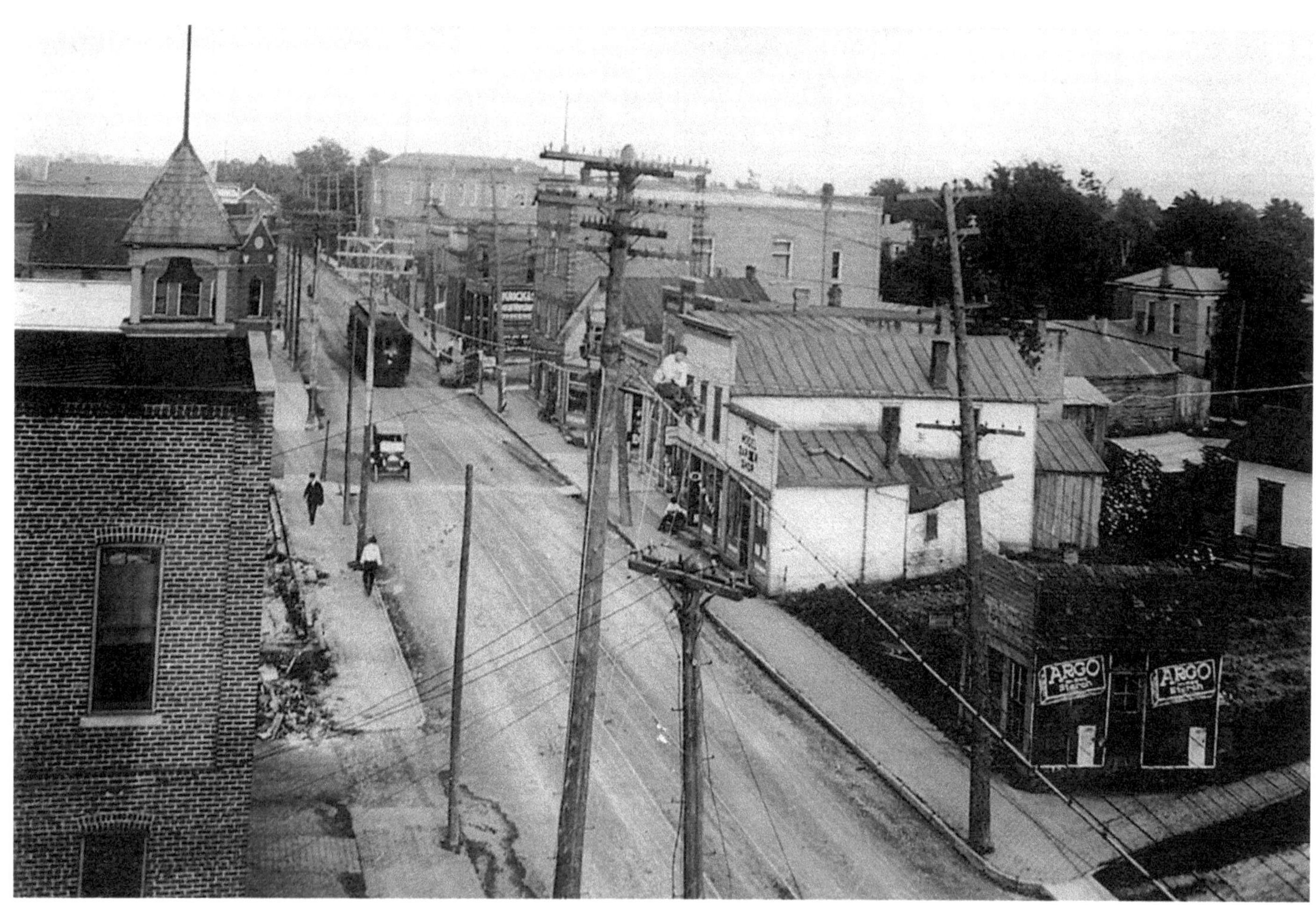

A lonesome-looking automobile, a few pedestrians, and a trolley wend their way along South Street in Monroeville in what seems to be an ordinary day in the early twentieth century. Life evidently was just too quiet for the fellow eyeing the photographer—from the top of the tall telephone pole in the foreground.

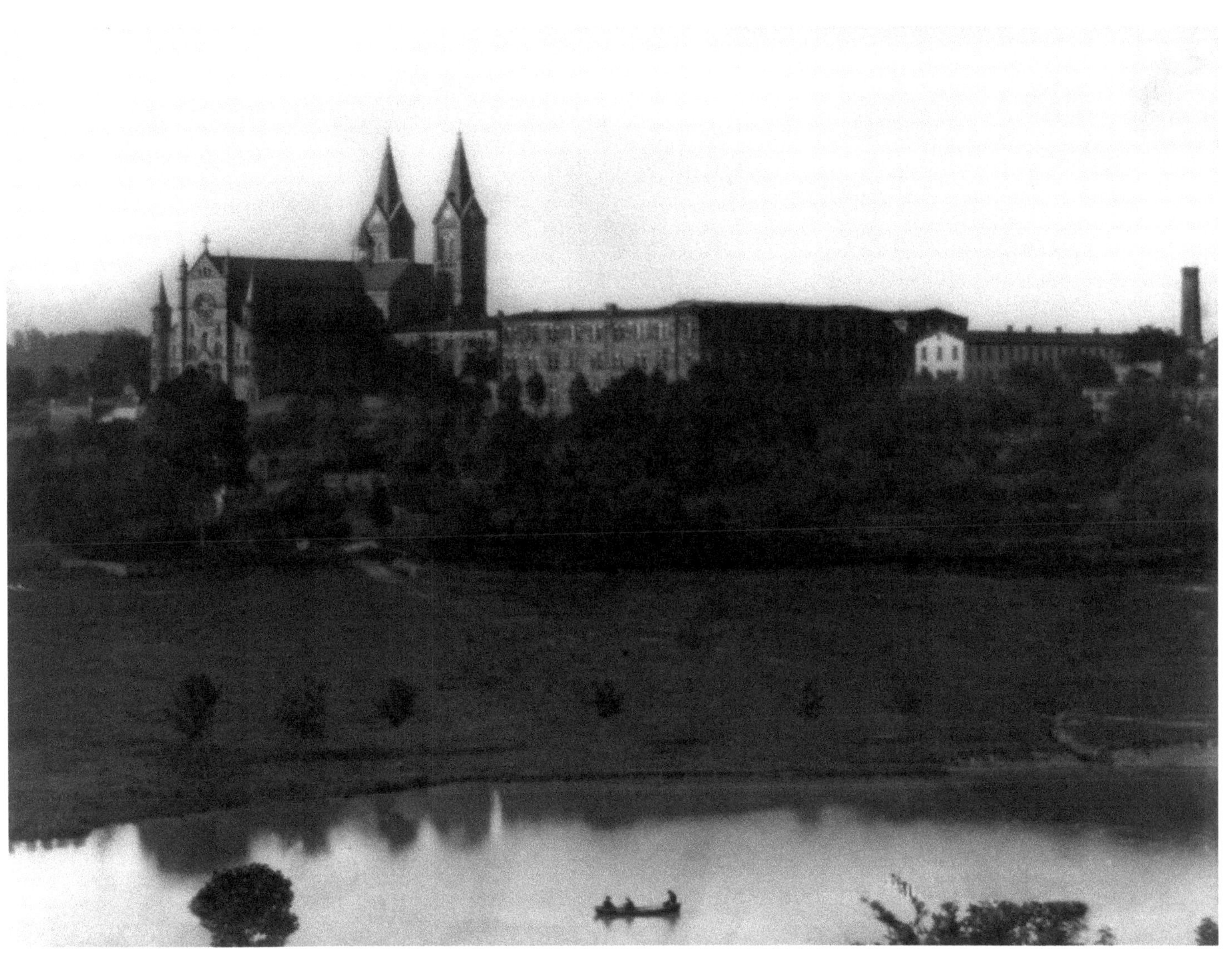

The sylvan scene at St. Meinrad Abbey and college from the early 1900s gives no hint of the 1887 fire that destroyed the monastery and two-thirds of the 10,000 volumes in its library. Named for a Swiss Benedictine monk martyred in 861, St. Meinrad is one of a handful of archabbeys in the world.

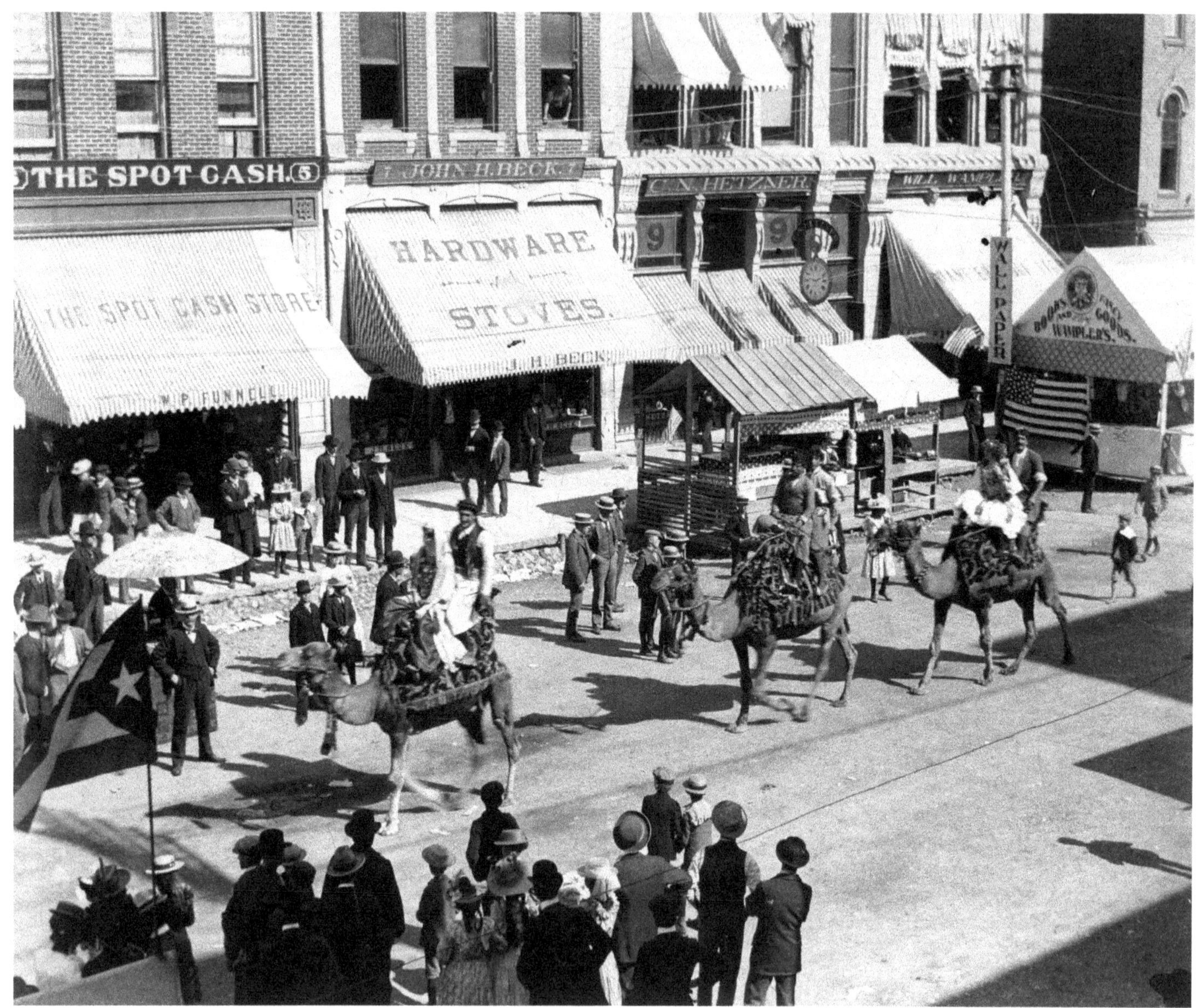

Every community loves a parade, but in Peru—known as Circus City for the many troupes that have wintered there—the "homecoming parade" along Broadway is a special event. This line of camels seems to be receiving critical attention from the spectators while fascinating the young boys trailing behind these "ships of the desert."

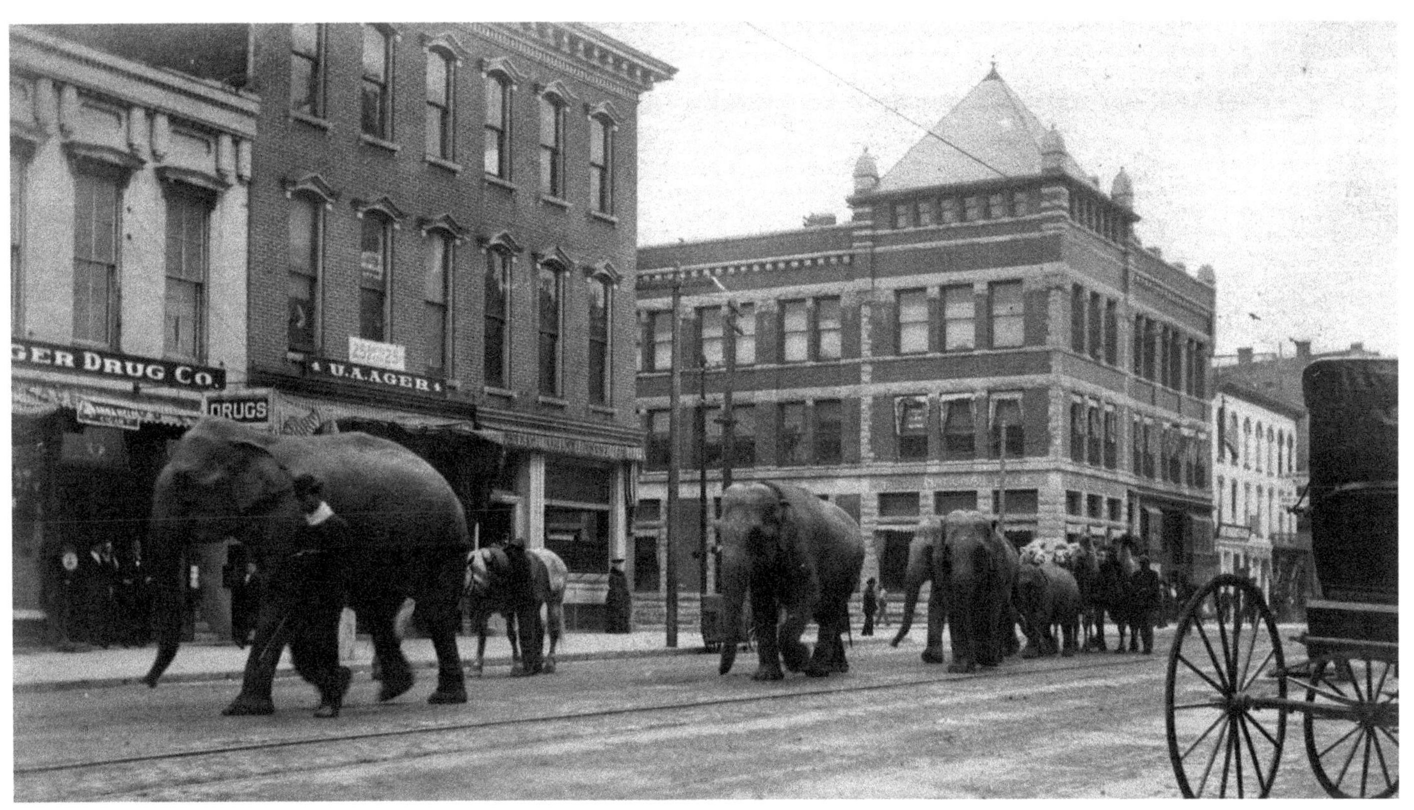

The elephant parade was the highlight of any circus arriving in town in the early twentieth century, especially in Peru where the animals, acrobats, clowns, and trainers had wintered since the 1880s. The lead elephant in this parade seems eager to reach its destination, reflecting the writing on the original image: "Home, Sweet Home."

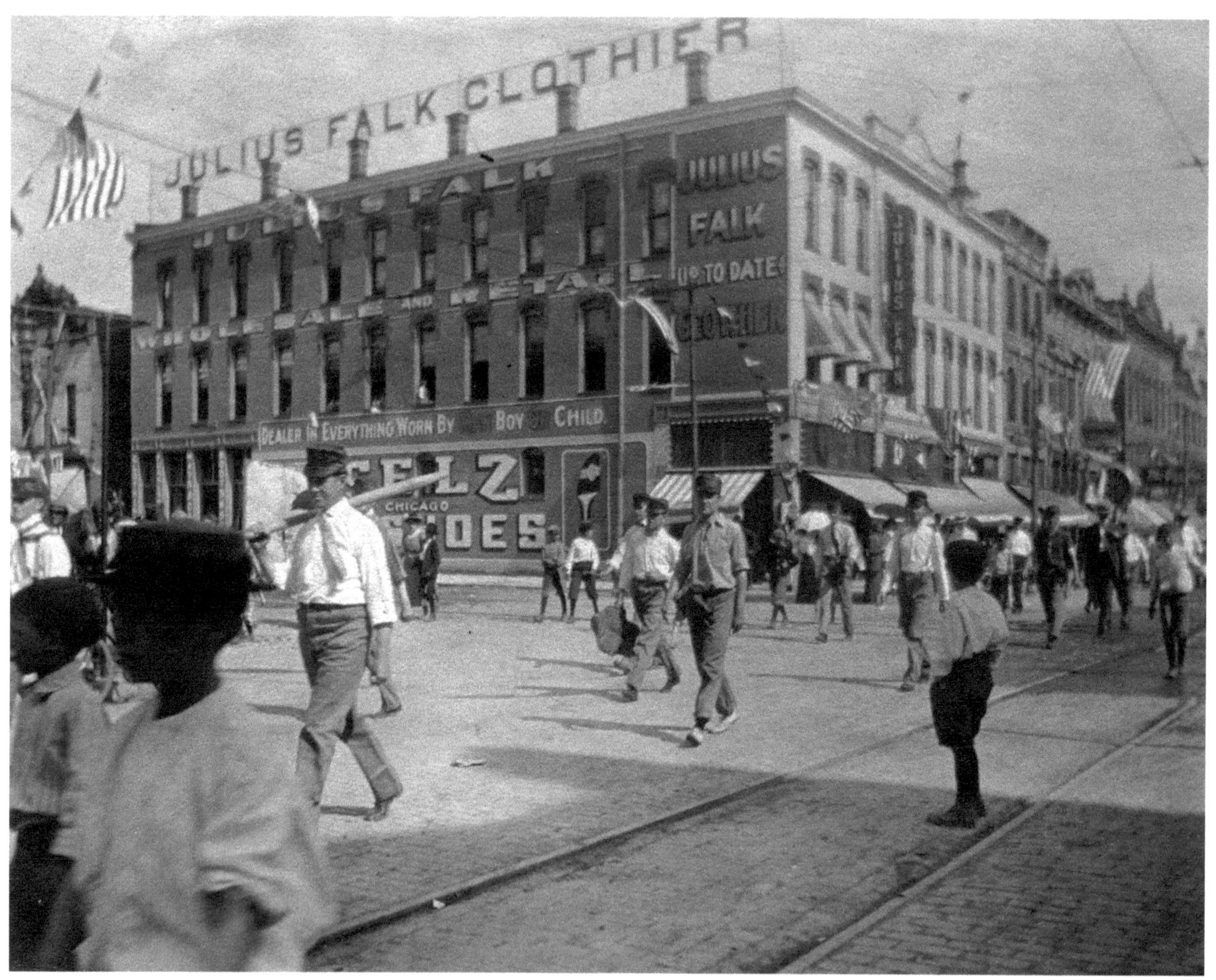

It's Homecoming Day in Peru in 1905 and, in keeping with tradition, the two teams in the baseball game between the Lawyers and Doctors parade to the ballpark. A handwritten note on the original photograph reports that this was the game in which Ross Lockridge, Sr., broke his leg. Lockridge, who was a catcher on the Indiana University baseball team in the late 1890s, was the father of Ross Lockridge, Jr., author of the acclaimed novel *Raintree County.*

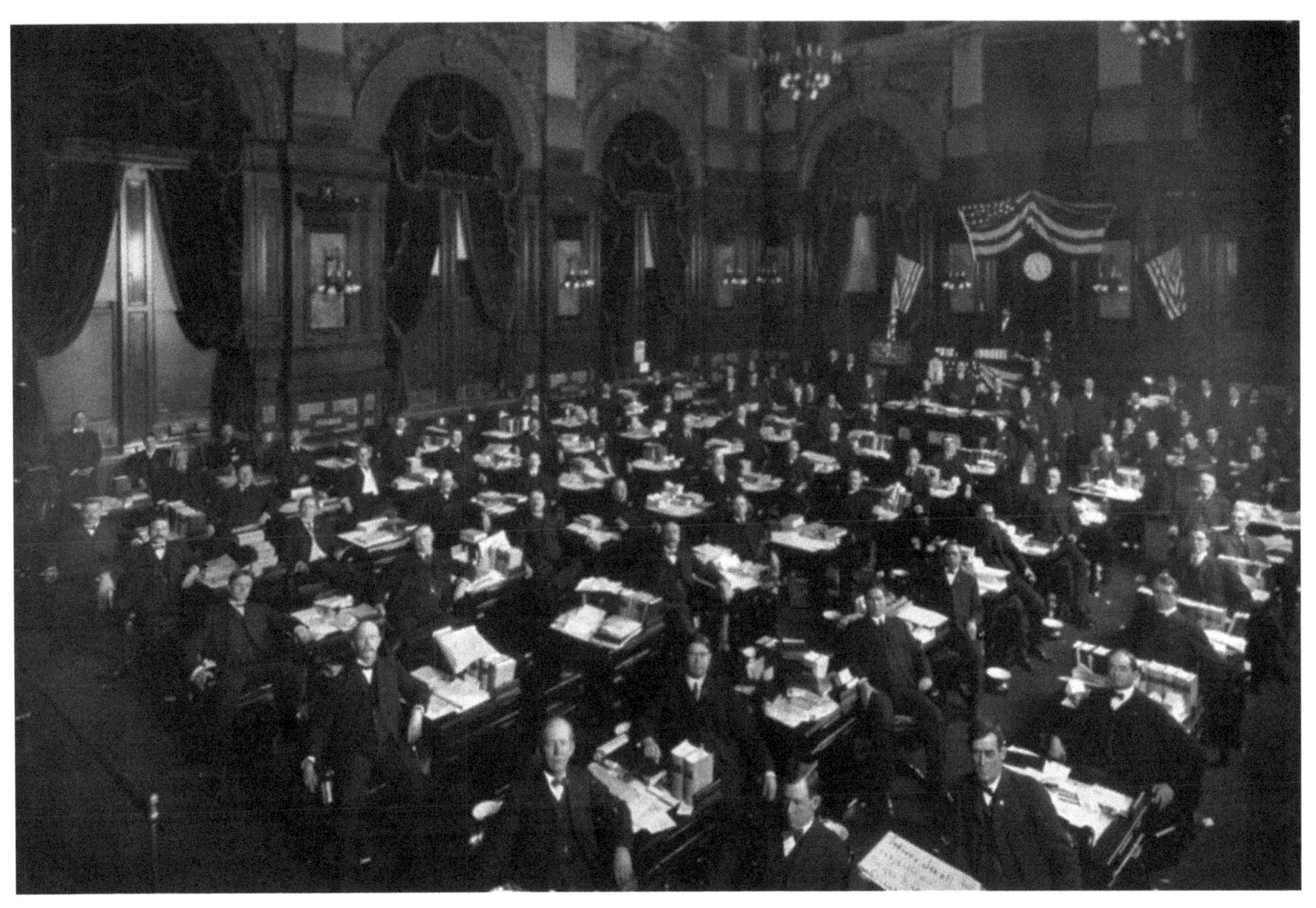

It was a rare day that unanimity could be found in the Indiana Senate in 1905, but one photographer apparently convinced lawmakers to pause from their politicking long enough to pose for the camera.

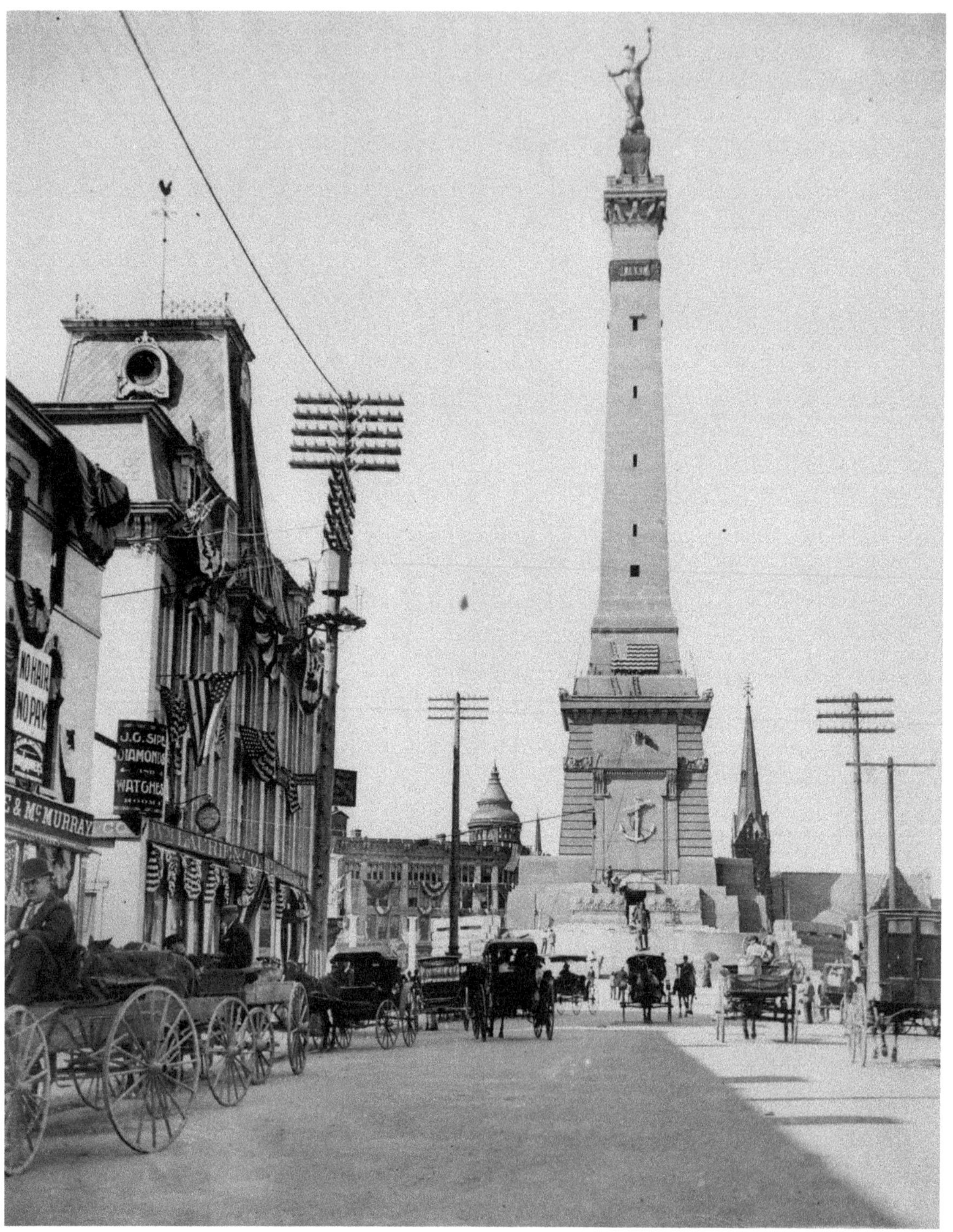

This view of the Soldiers' and Sailors' Monument in Indianapolis provides some idea of its immense scale and why it was called the "grandest of all memorials" to the Indiana men who died in the Civil War. The monument was designed by Bruno Schmidt and built at a cost of $500,000. This image was recorded amid flags and bunting festooning the businesses at left, suggesting a Fourth of July celebration.

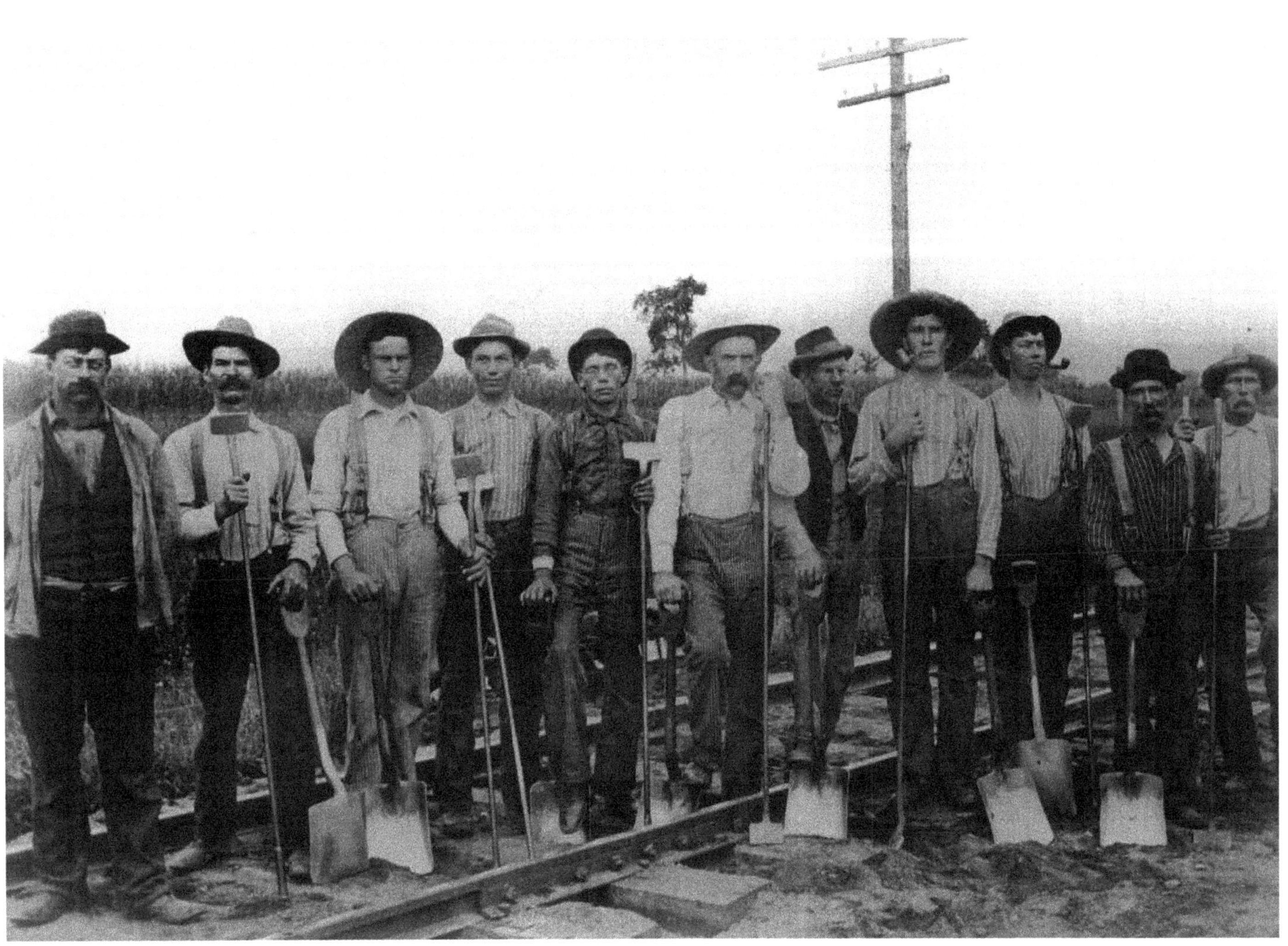

Looking scrubbed and clean-shaven before another day of working on the railroad in 1905, these gandy dancers on the New York Central near Butler pose for a group portrait holding the tools of the trade. Year-round, daily maintenance was essential to keeping the rail lines in service, and most of the work was done by hand by local crews like this one.

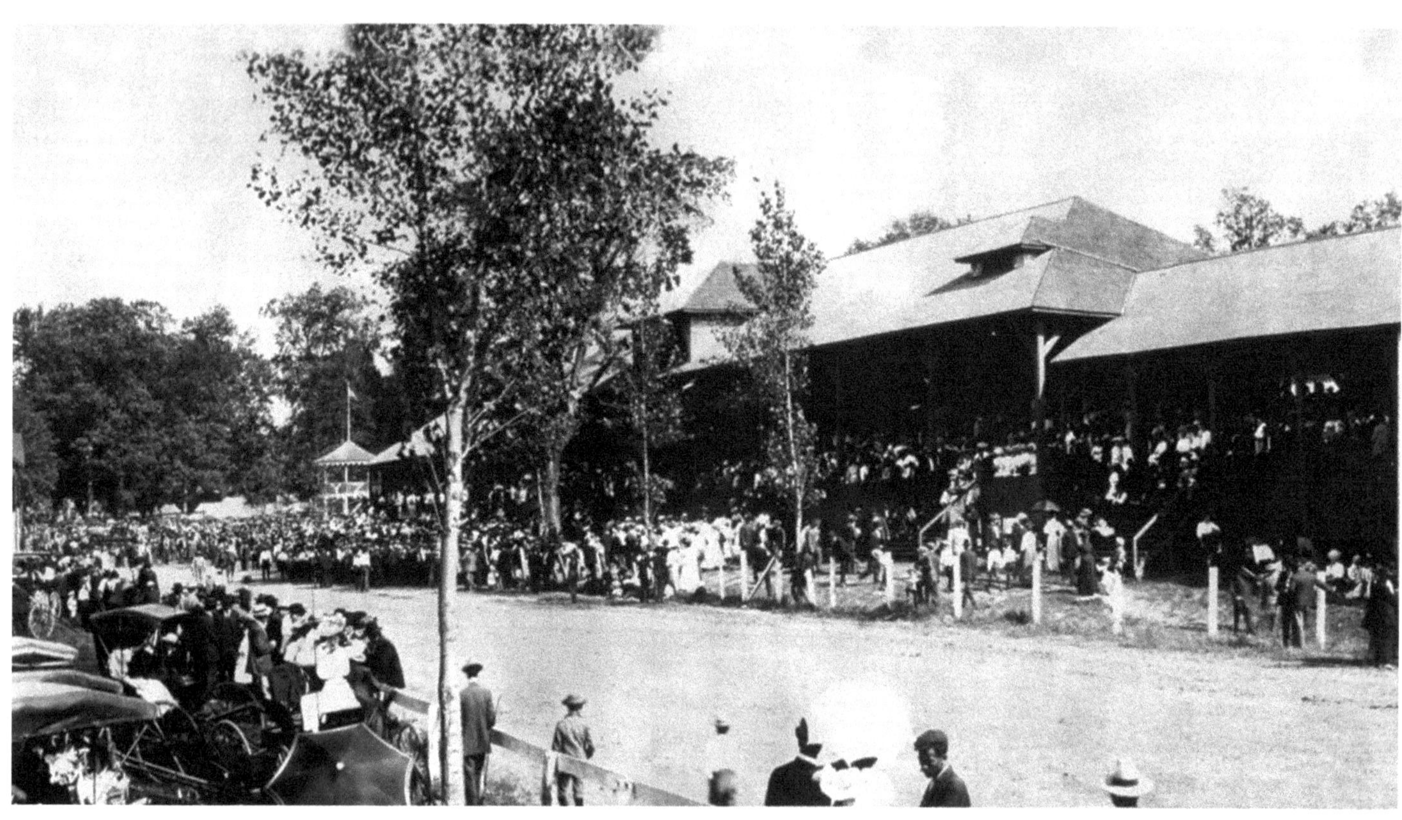

It was said that 20,000 people attended the annual county fair at Princeton grounds on September 5, 1907. This number was more than two-thirds of the population of Gibson County, for which Princeton was the county seat.

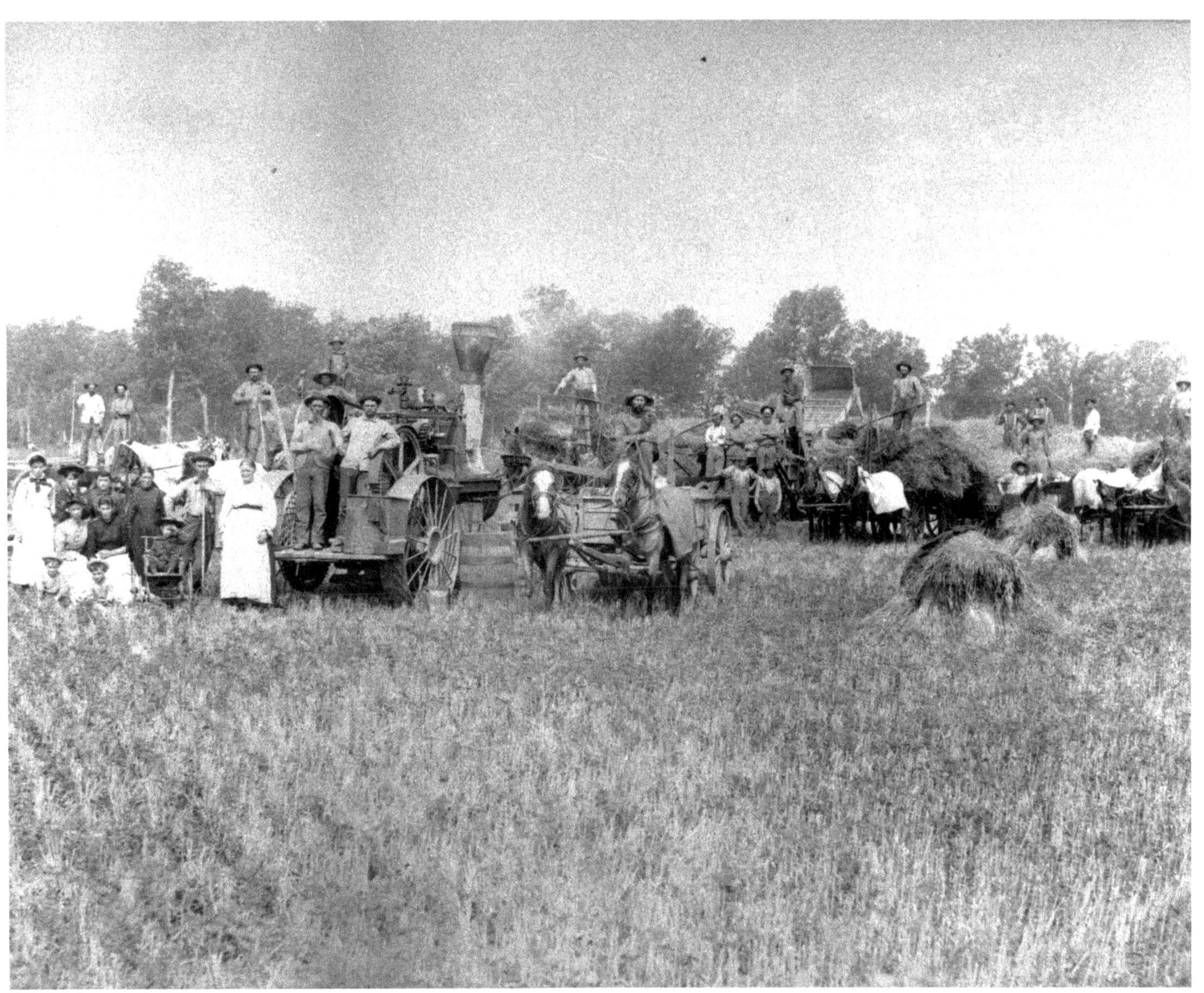

Harvesting was a community affair. Families and neighbors gathered to bring in the harvest when a threshing machine visited, such as here at Mill Creek in La Porte County. Labors were generally divided but the goal was shared: while the men worked the fields, the women prepared meals for the large number of ravenous laborers looking forward to their next hour of rest.

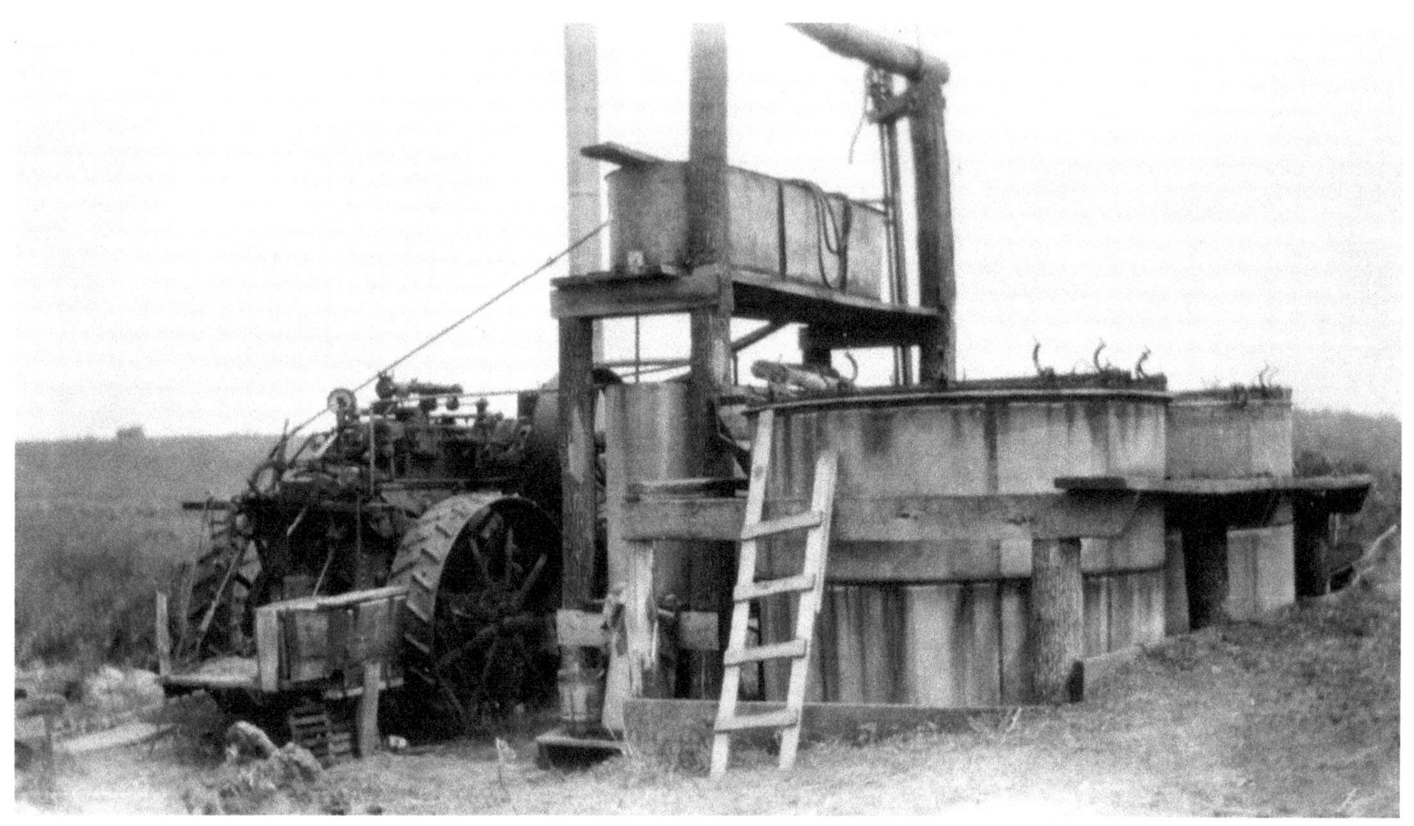

The manufacturers of chewing gum probably would not have been so successful without the invention of this farm device. Found in western DeKalb County, this is a mint still used to extract and distill the oils from spearmint and peppermint leaves. Mint flourishes yet today in the fields of northern Indiana.

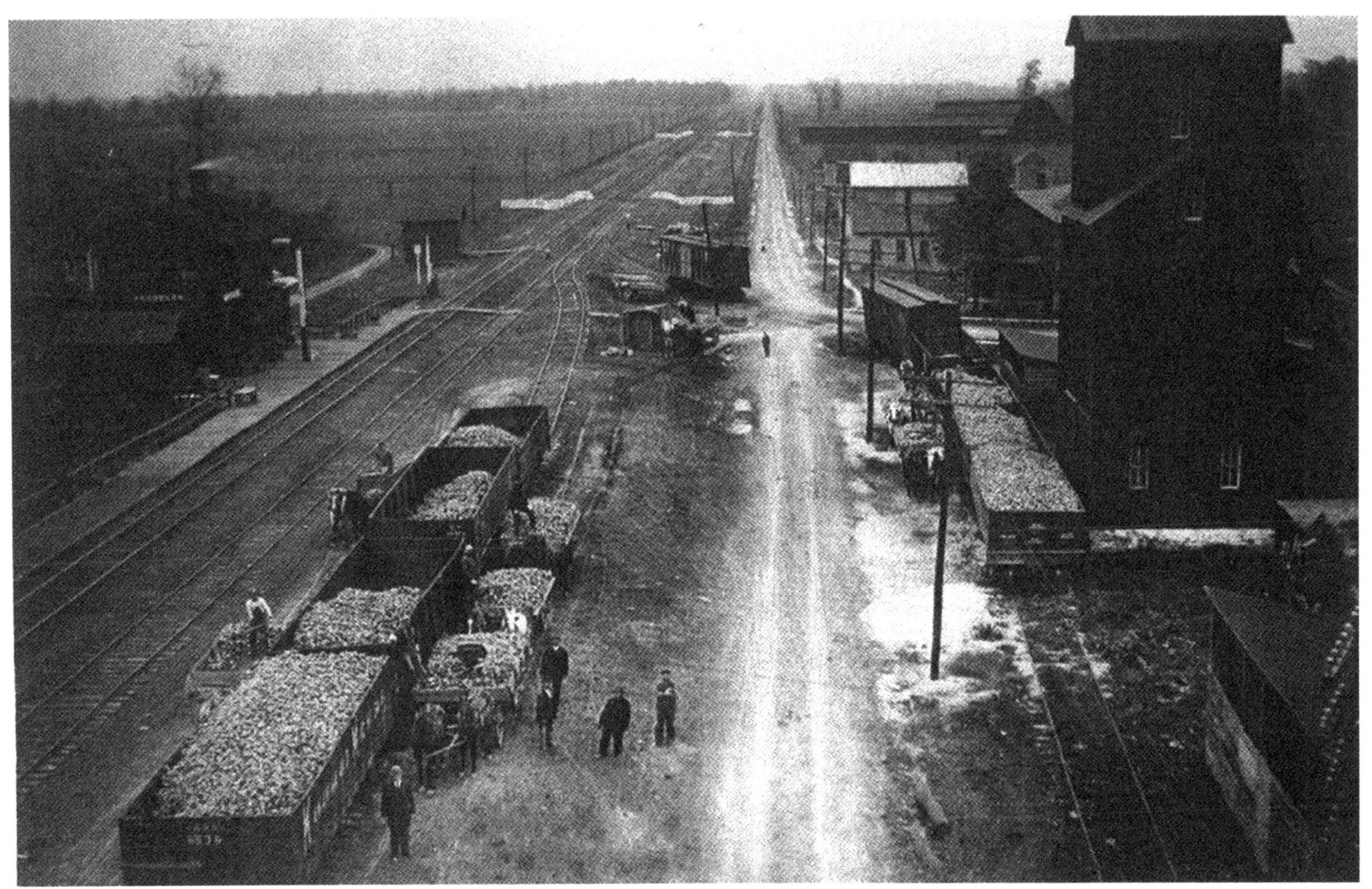

Sugar beets were once a prominent root crop in parts of Indiana. The harvest of one crop is visible here in horse-drawn wagons and hopper cars along a Wabash Railroad siding in Woodburn. Sweet products also flowed from sugar maple trees abundant in the state. Maple syrup was produced on farms in areas where wintertime temperatures and a springtime thaw caused maple trees to flow with sap.

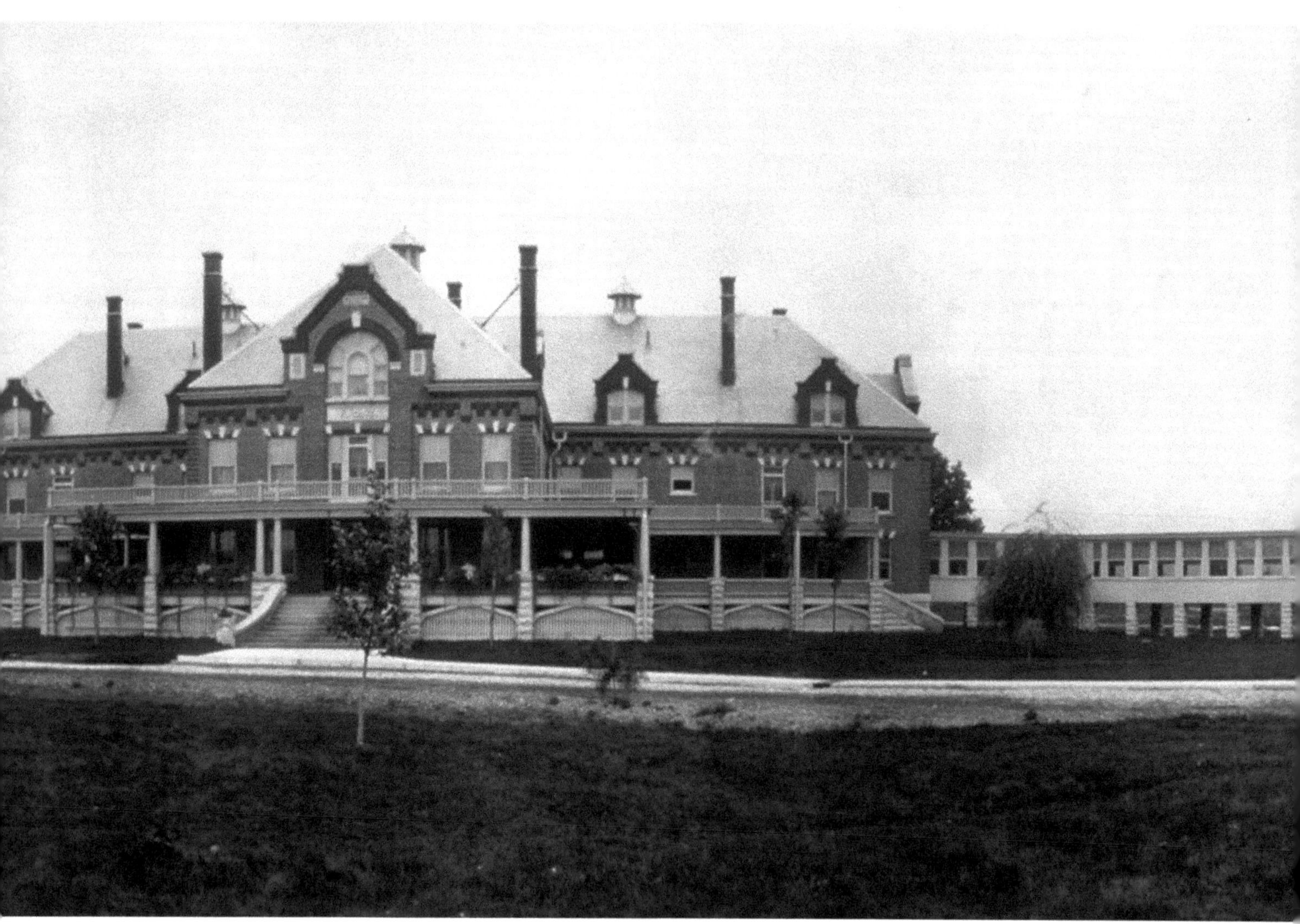

The Odd Fellows Home in Greensburg (seen here circa 1906) reflects the sizable role the fraternal order played across the state and the nation. Throughout Indiana, members of the Odd Fellows visited the sick, relieved the distressed, buried the dead, and educated orphans.

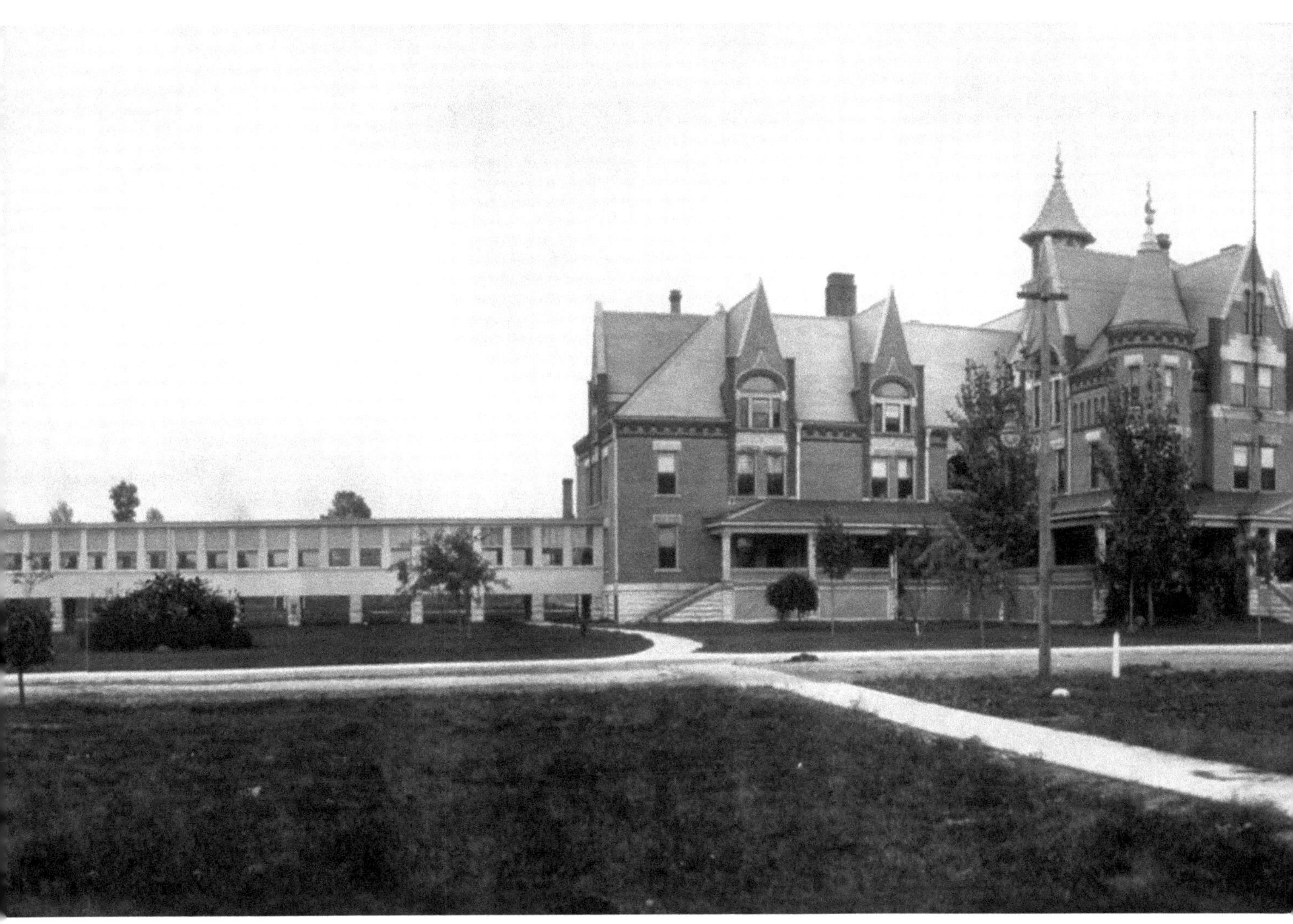

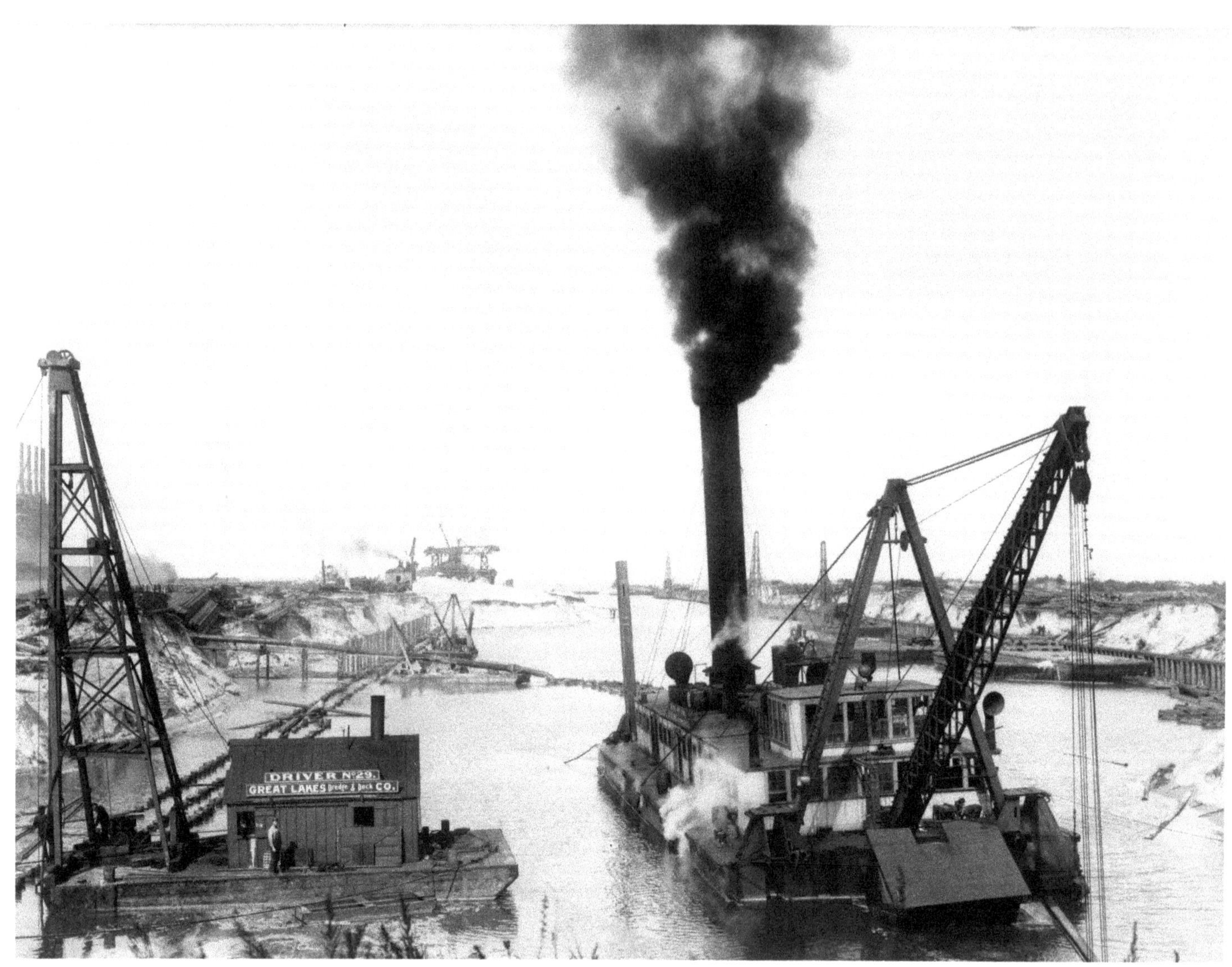

U.S. Steel began building its great steel-making plants in 1906 in the barren lands of northwestern Indiana now known as Gary. Success came in part as a result of the foresight to build a harbor with a slip and a turning basin for ore carriers plying the Great Lakes. The turning basin permitted a steady stream of ore to enter the mills.

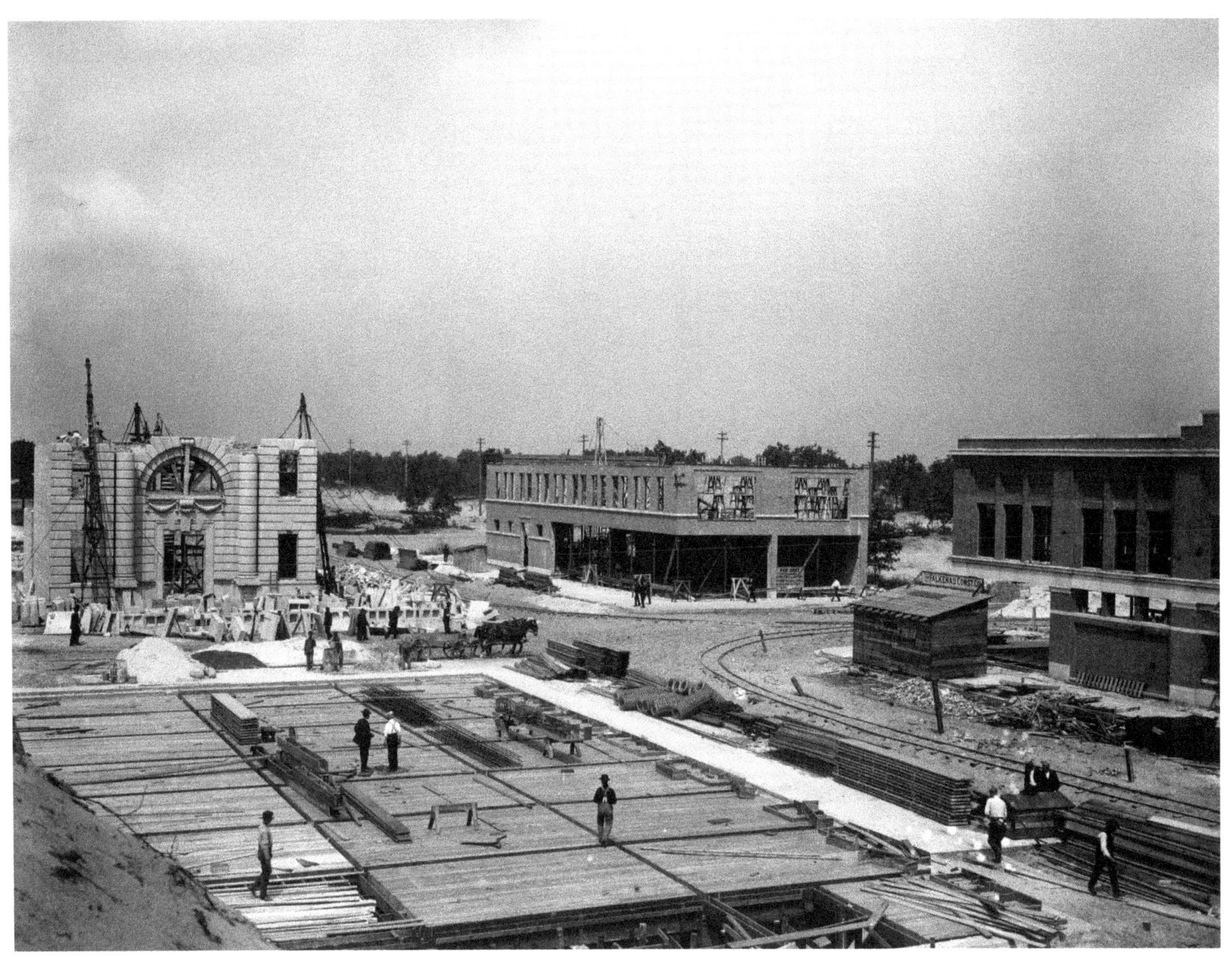

What was once considered wasteland became a modern city in 1907 as U.S. Steel built the city of Gary along with its mammoth mills. Banks, stores, roads, and rail tracks were part of what was called a modern miracle.

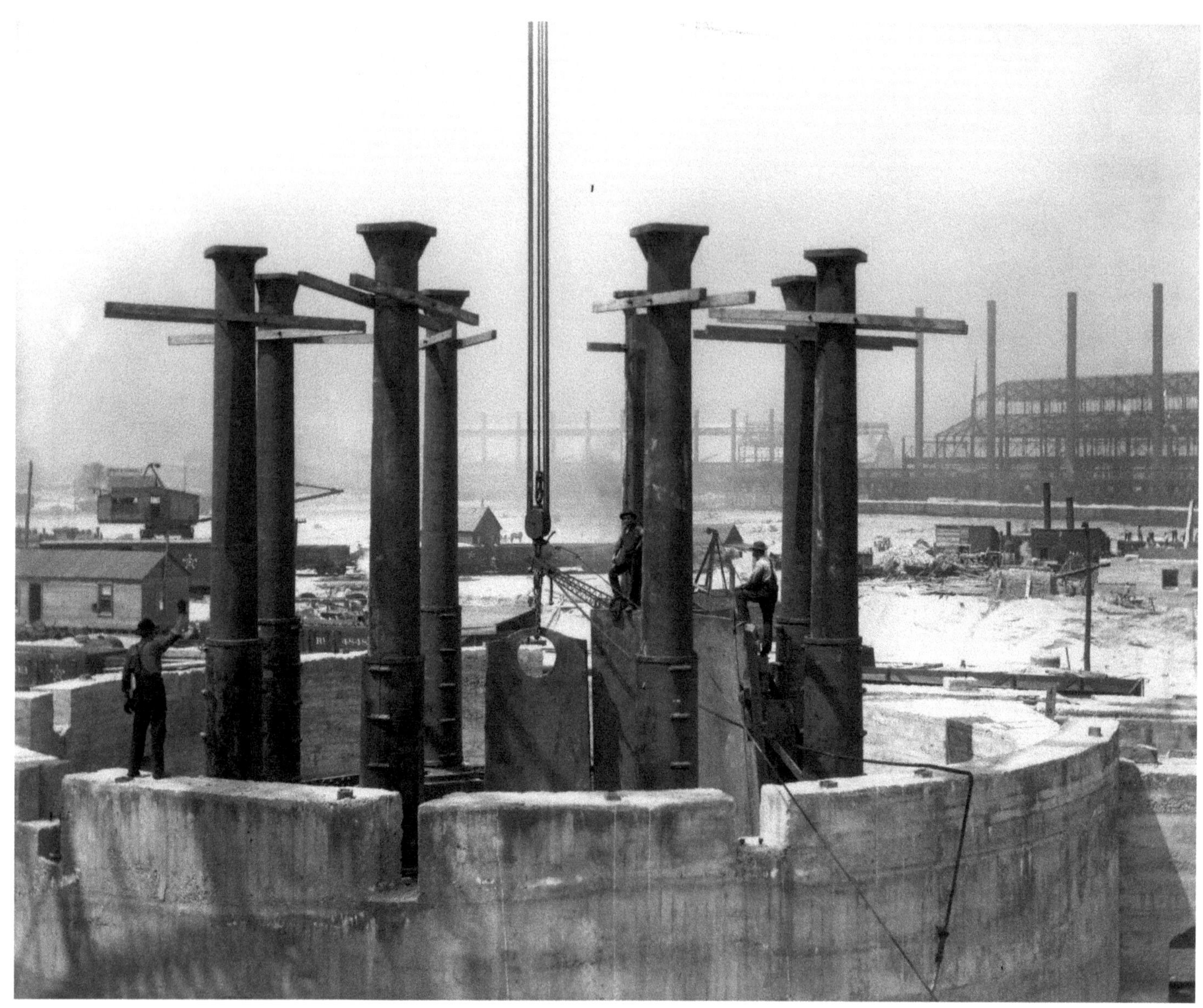

The size of the steel mills being built in Gary in May 1908 was evident in the construction of Furnace No. 6. The city was named for Judge Elbert H. Gary, president of U.S. Steel, whose vision attracted other industrialists to the region.

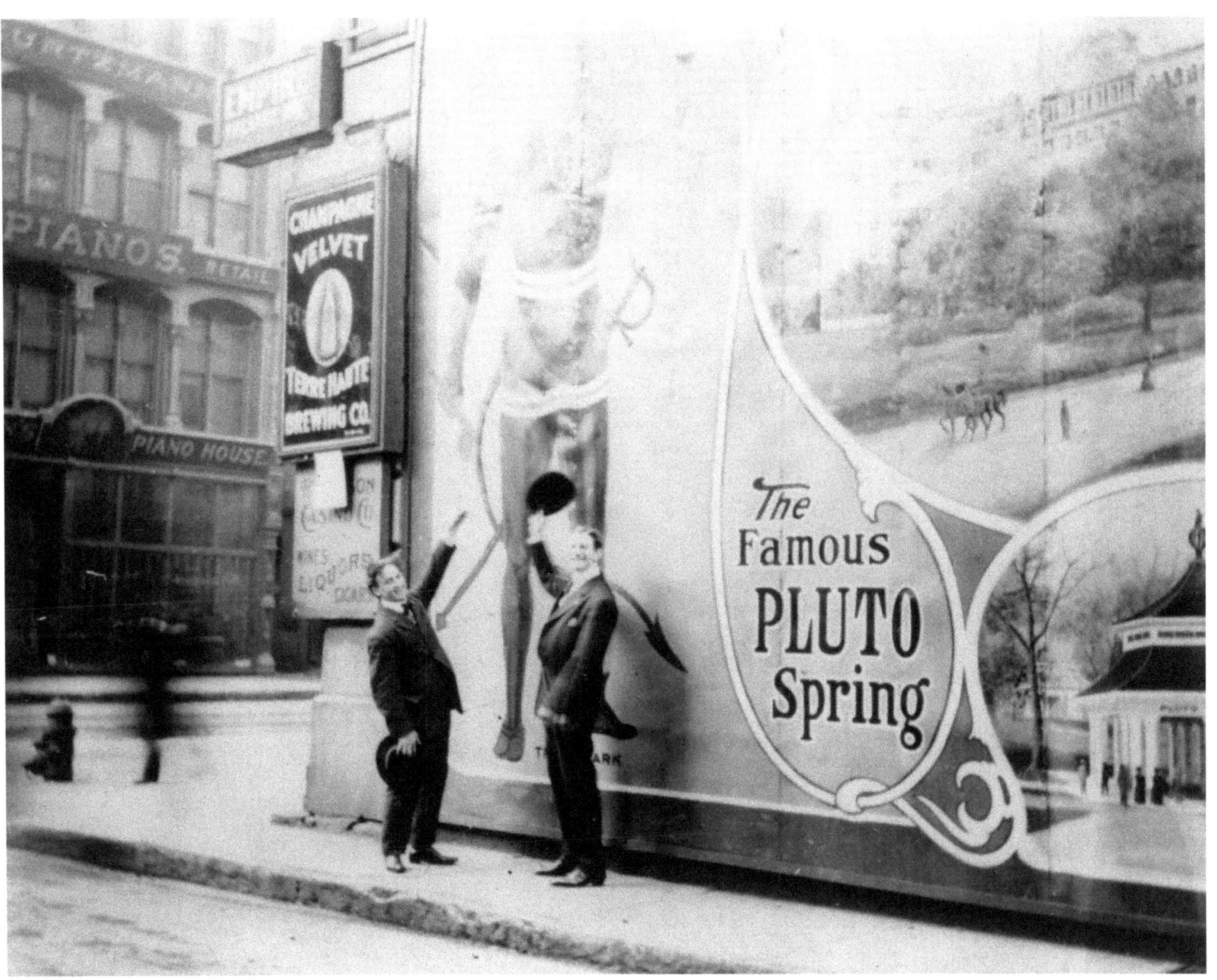

Renowned for his ability to escape from chains while underwater, Harry Houdini brought his act to Indianapolis from December 29, 1907, to January 4, 1908. At far left, Houdini poses here with a companion, amused at an ad for his act "pinned" between advertisements for the Terre Haute Brewing Company and for the healthful Pluto Spring waters from French Lick.

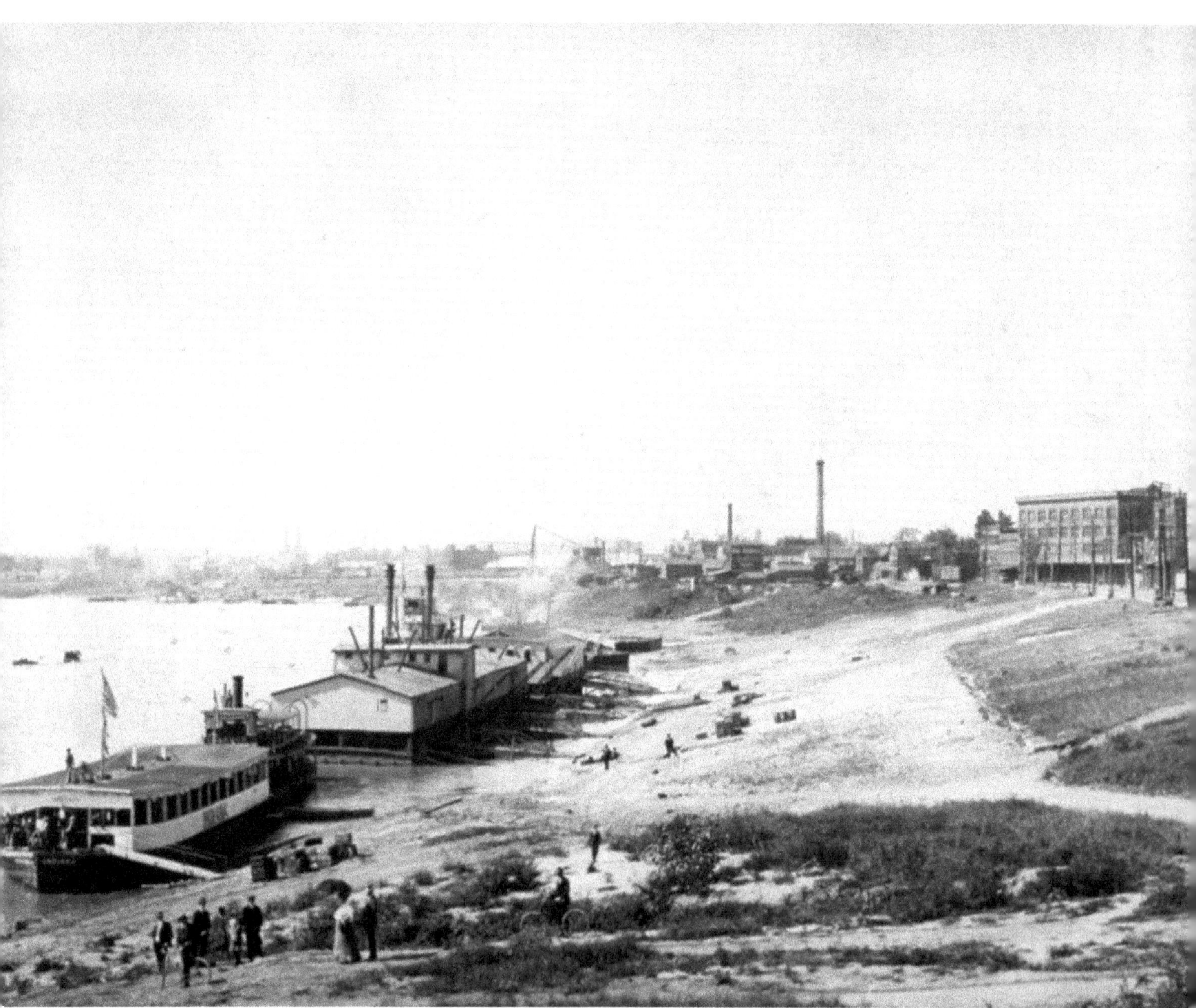

Evansville was a busy commercial center and the state's second-most populous city when this photograph was taken along the Ohio River waterfront in September 1907. The city remained smaller than Indianapolis, which was home to three times as many residents.

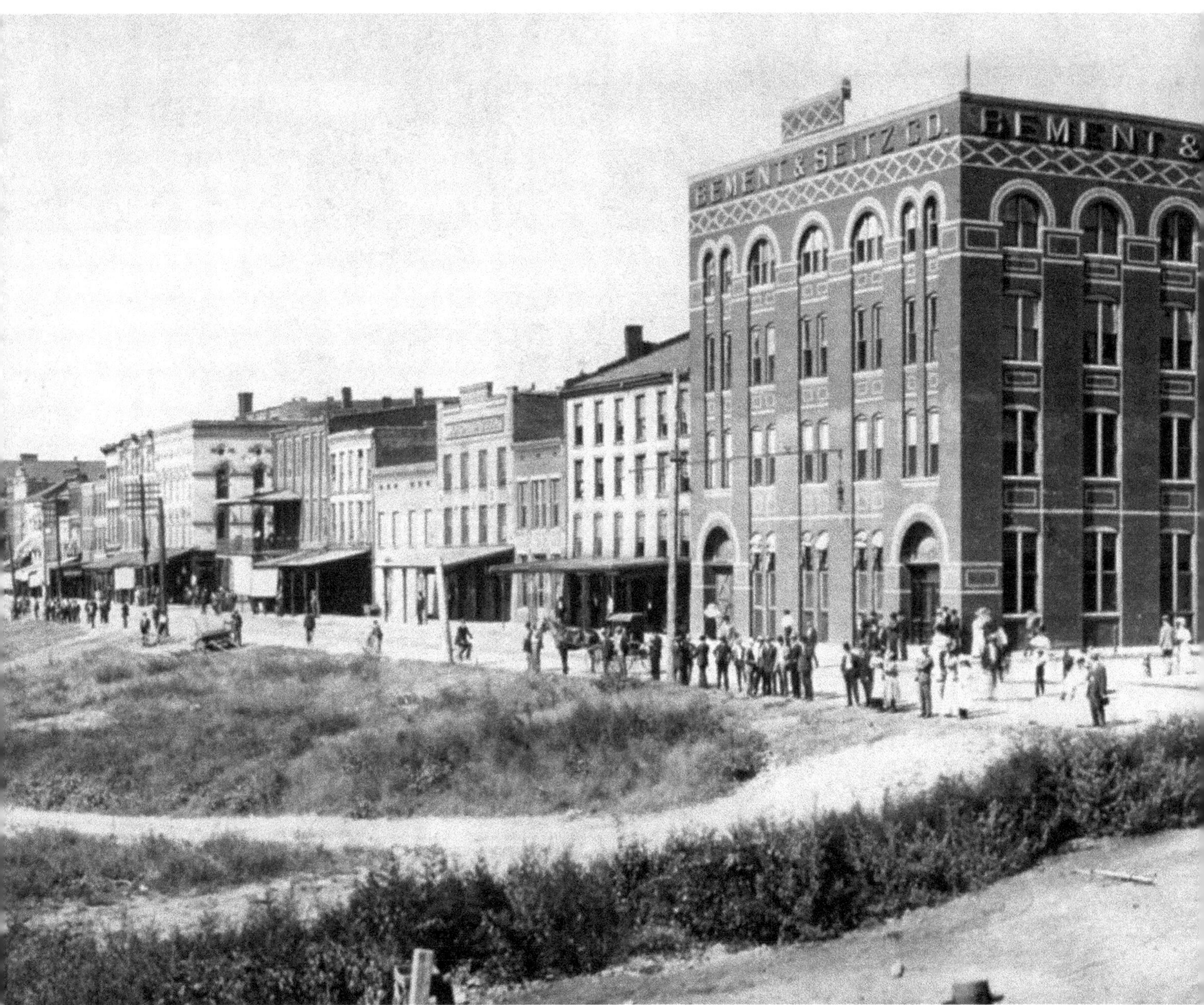
BEMENT & SEITZ CO.
BEMENT &

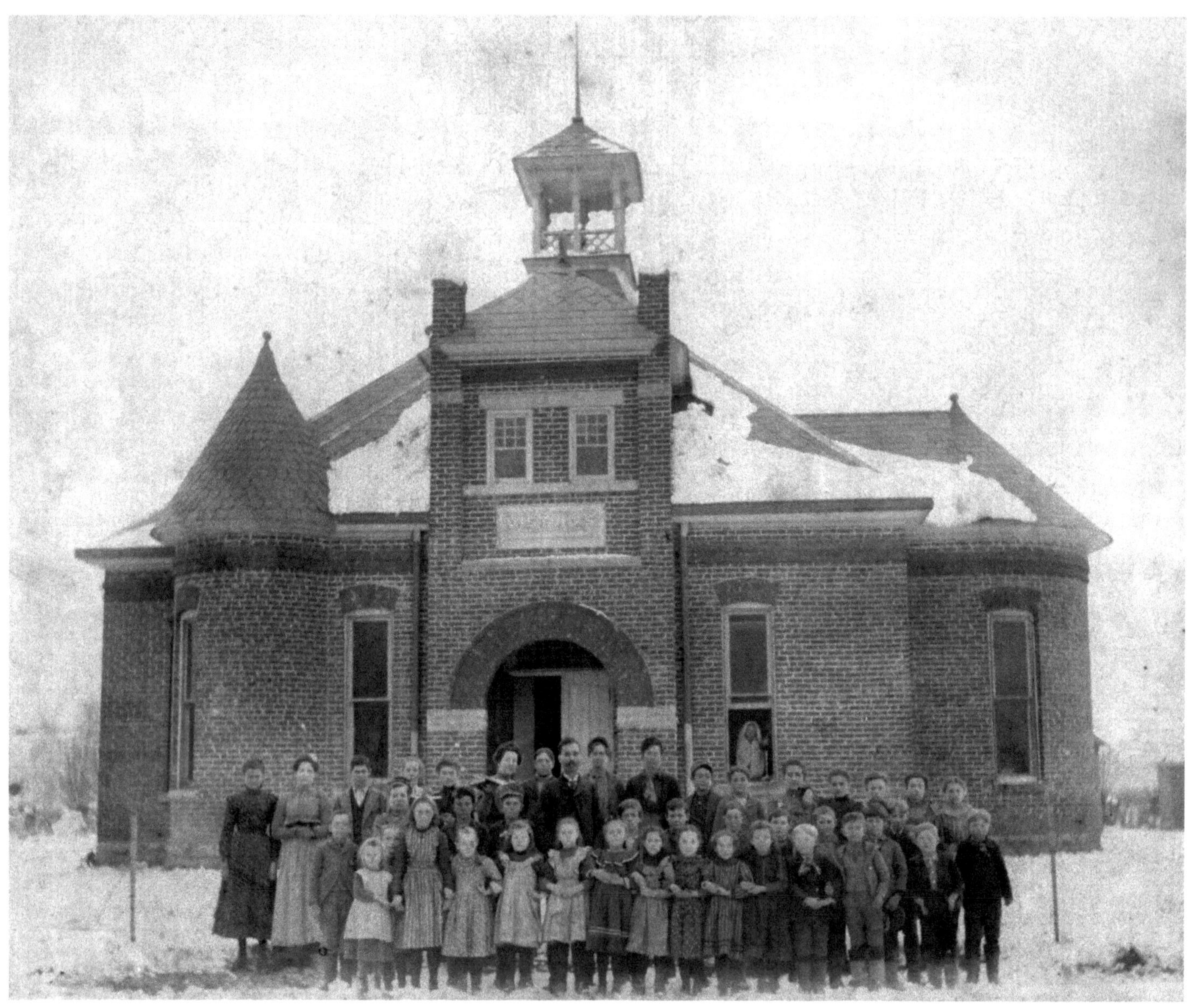

Not all schools were the same in Indiana in the early 1900s. One architect who built schoolhouses in central Indiana and north-central Illinois was evidently fond of turrets, castlelike rounded walls, and cupolas. This photograph of children without coats arm-in-arm in the snow shows Evans School in Tipton.

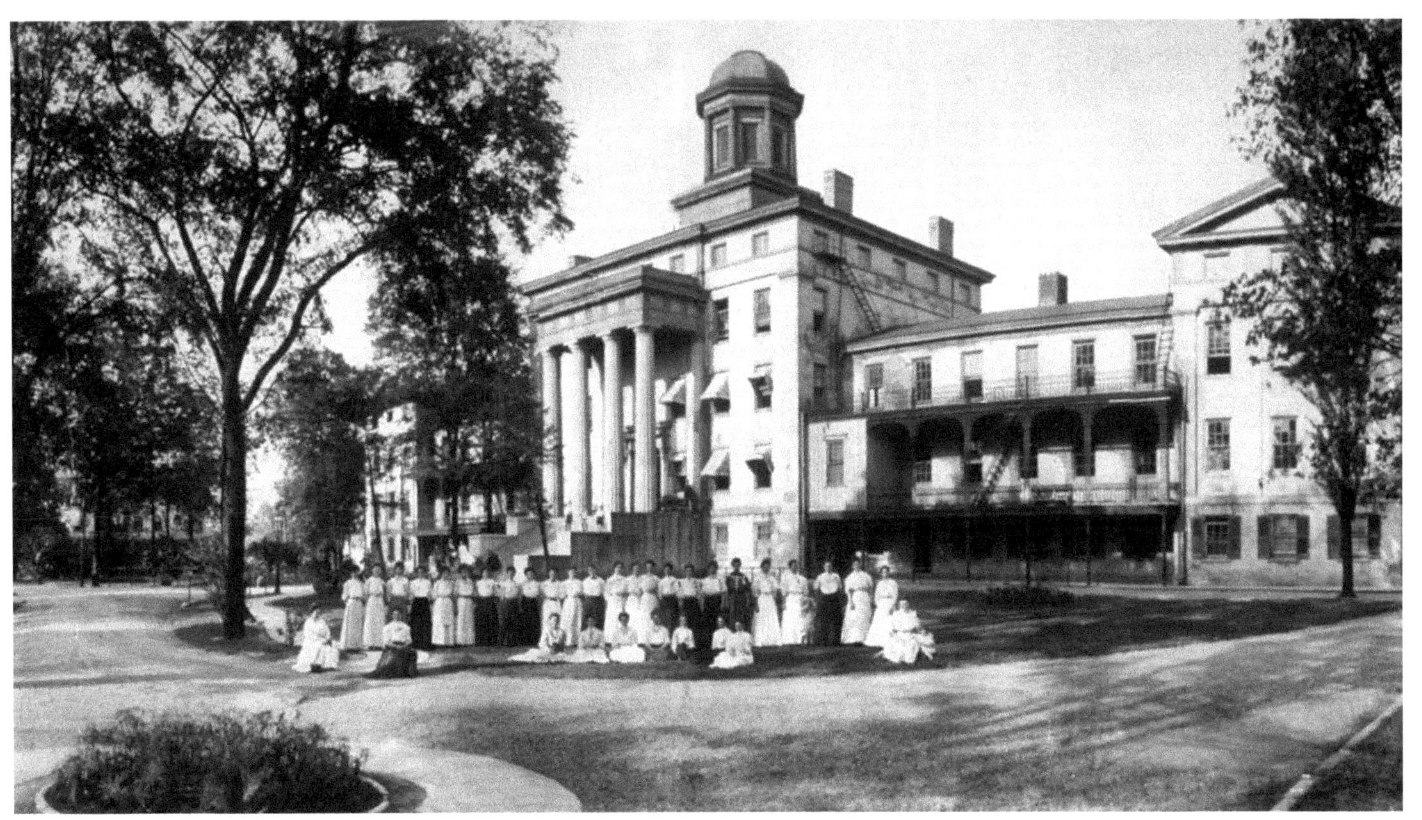

A group of alumnae gather on the lawn of the Indiana State School for the Deaf at Indianapolis on June 6, 1908, one week after the grounds were named Willard Park. William Willard founded the school in 1843, and the institute remained at this location until 1911.

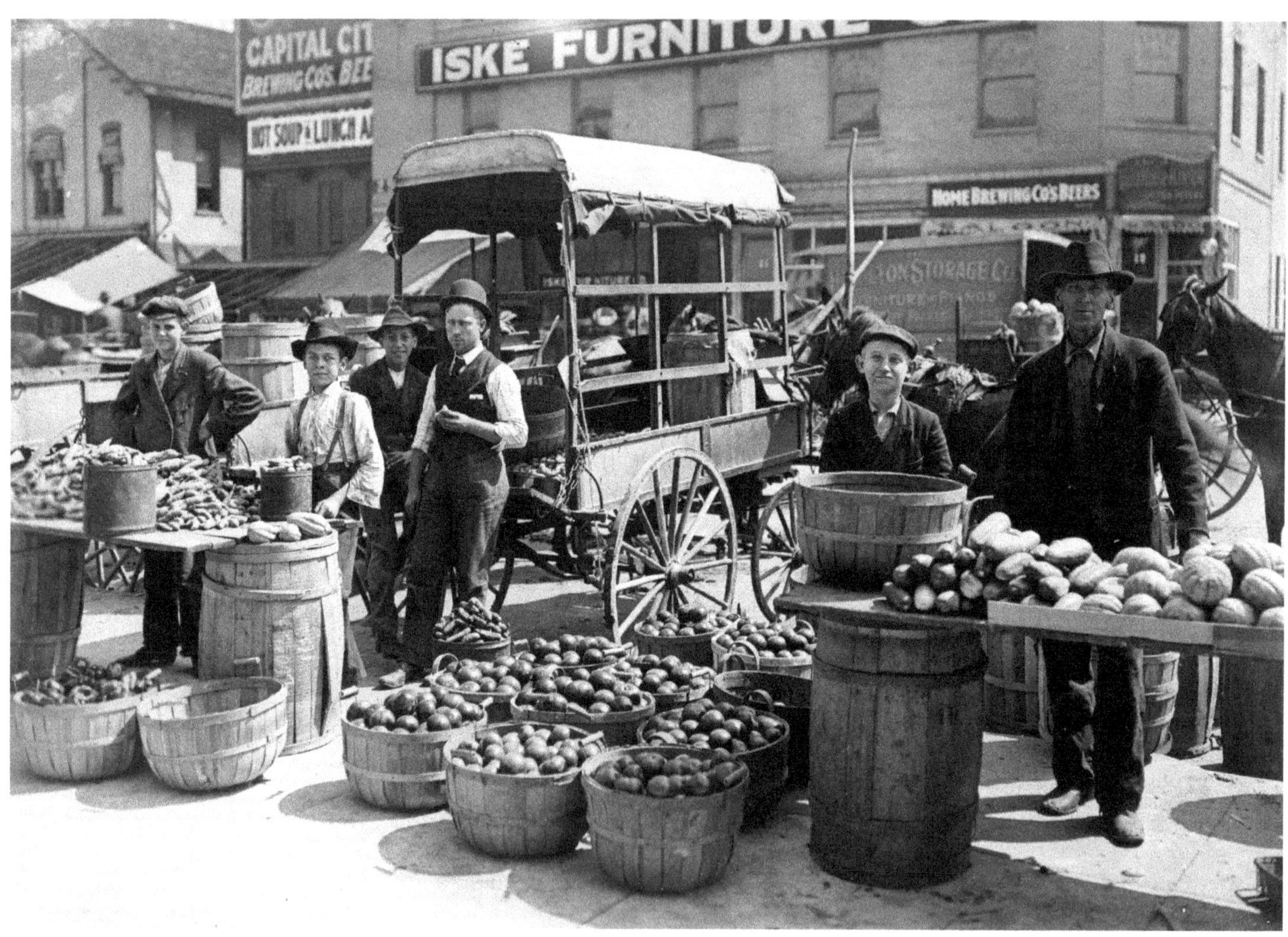

In 1908, vendors of fresh farm produce at an Indianapolis market display their crops for the camera. For sale to friends and neighbors are potatoes, muskmelons, cucumbers, peppers, and other homegrown vegetables. And for home canning, Ball fruit jars were readily available, manufactured in the company factory at Muncie.

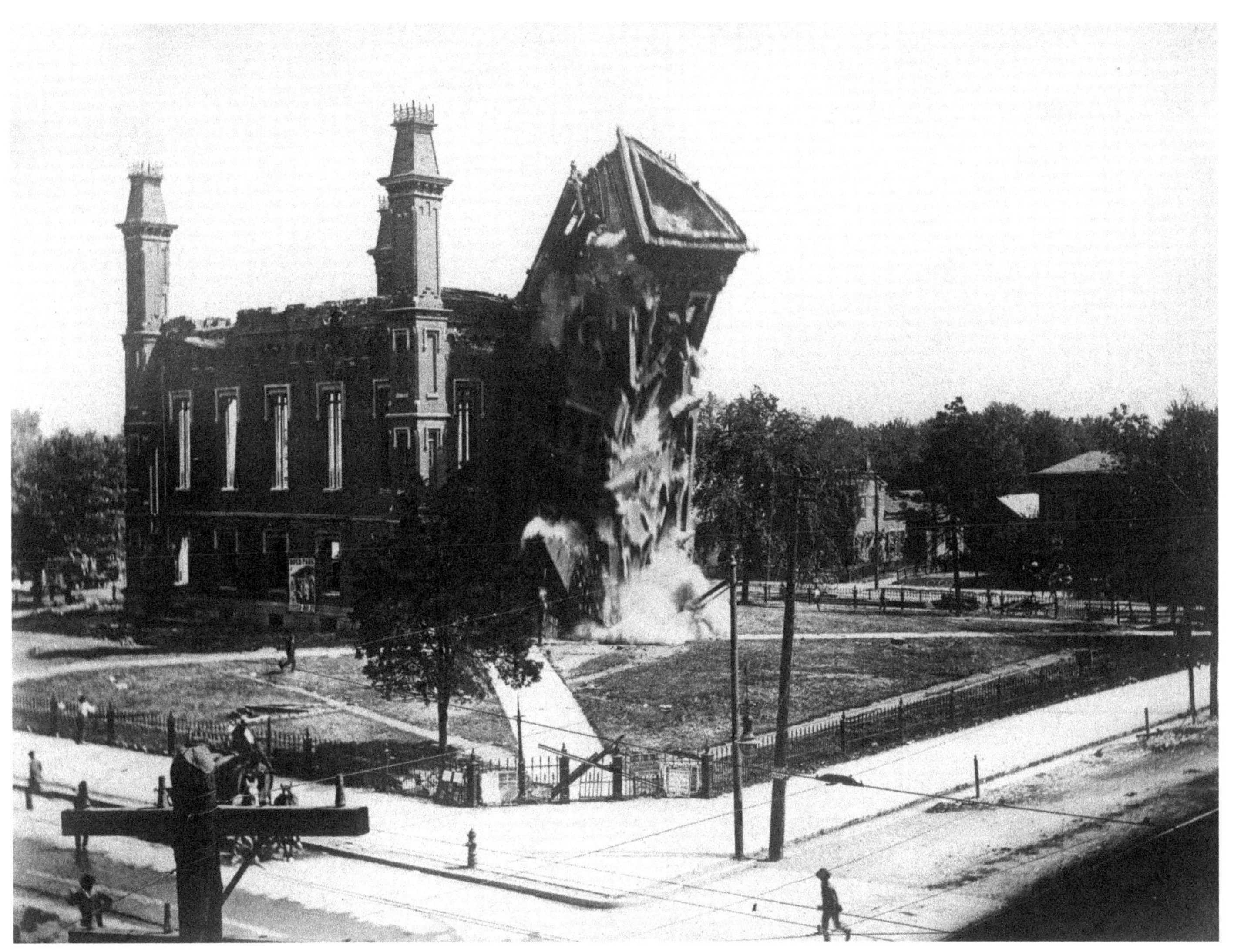

Workmen went scurrying for safety when the second Miami County Courthouse in Peru was demolished in early 1908. Dynamite had been placed at the base of the building and the explosion proved greater than expected.

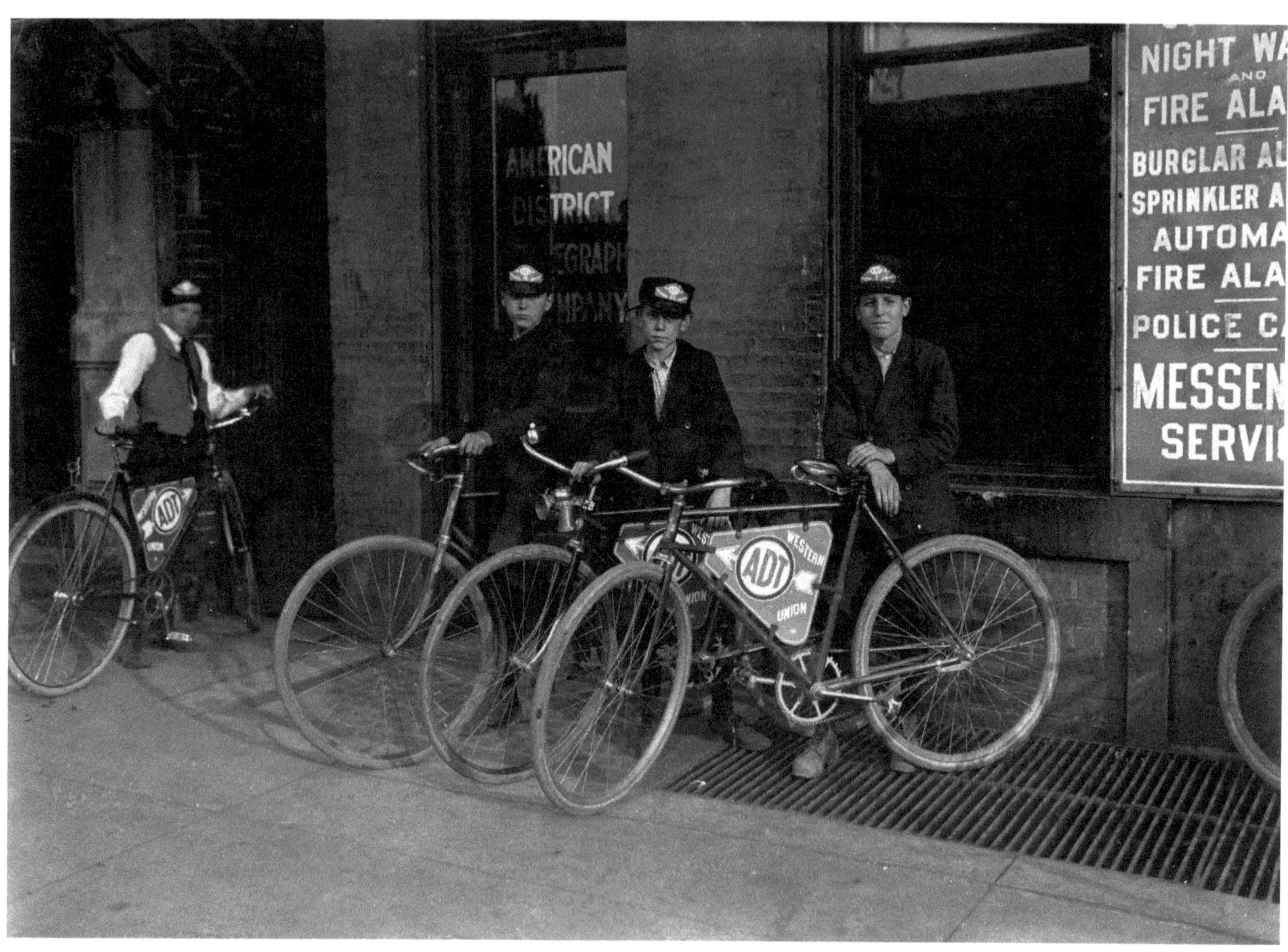

Working for the National Child Labor Committee with his simple box camera, Lewis Hine brought to public attention questionable child labor practices in mines, fields, factories, and cities. In 1908, he took more than 800 photographs of underage children in the workforce. Hine's travels brought him to the Midwest, where he captured these Indianapolis messenger boys in August. The boys worked from noon to 10:30 P.M., delivering notes, as one youngster said.

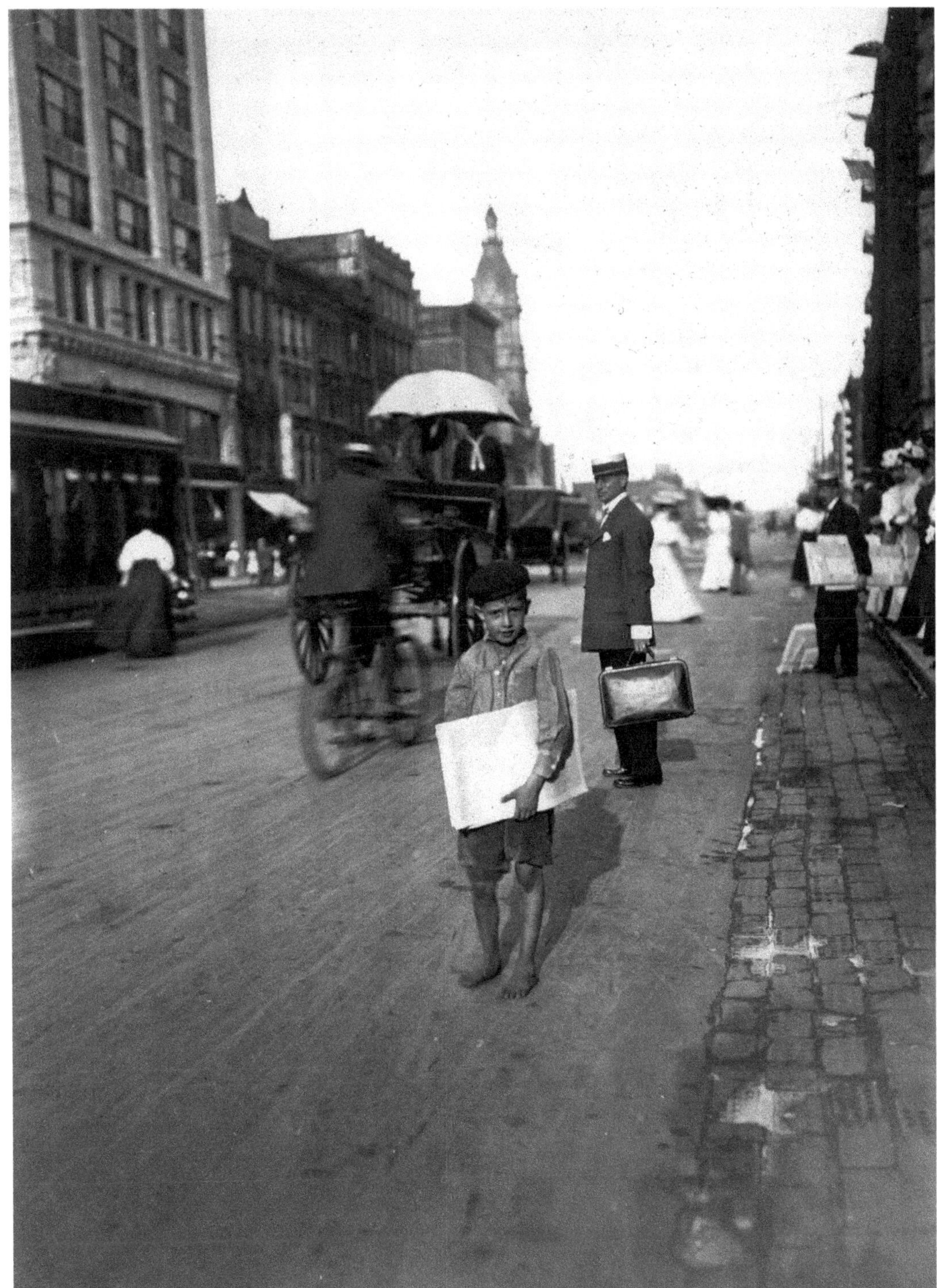

Newspaper boys were to become a leading subject of Hine's photography as he crisscrossed the nation to show the conditions under which underage children worked. Hine photographed this barefoot Indianapolis newsie in August 1908.

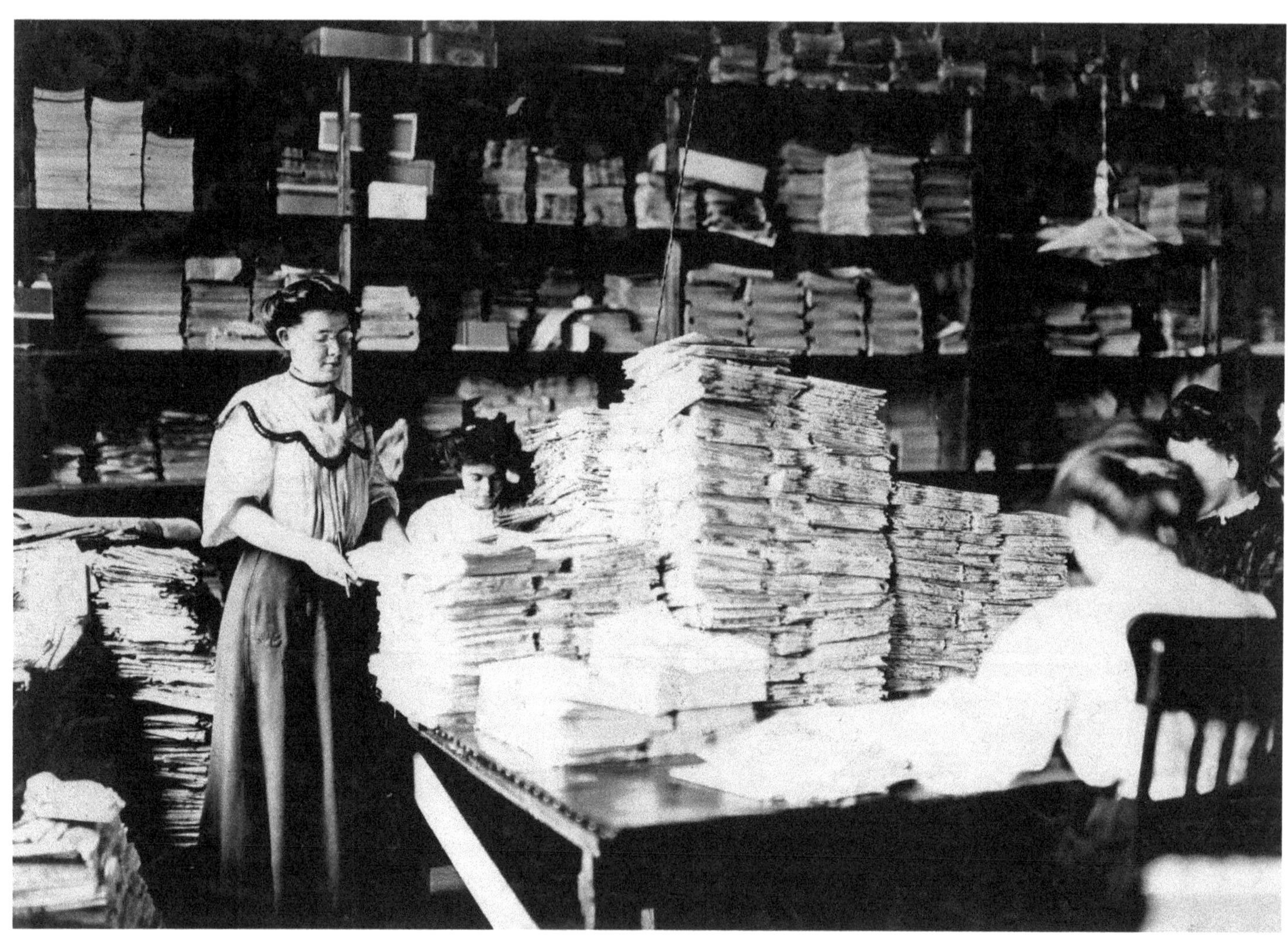

Not all of Lewis Hine's investigative work uncovered abuse. The images taken at Frank S. Betz Company, an optical instruments firm in Hammond, in October 1908 showed "very few young boys or girls" laboring under questionable circumstances.

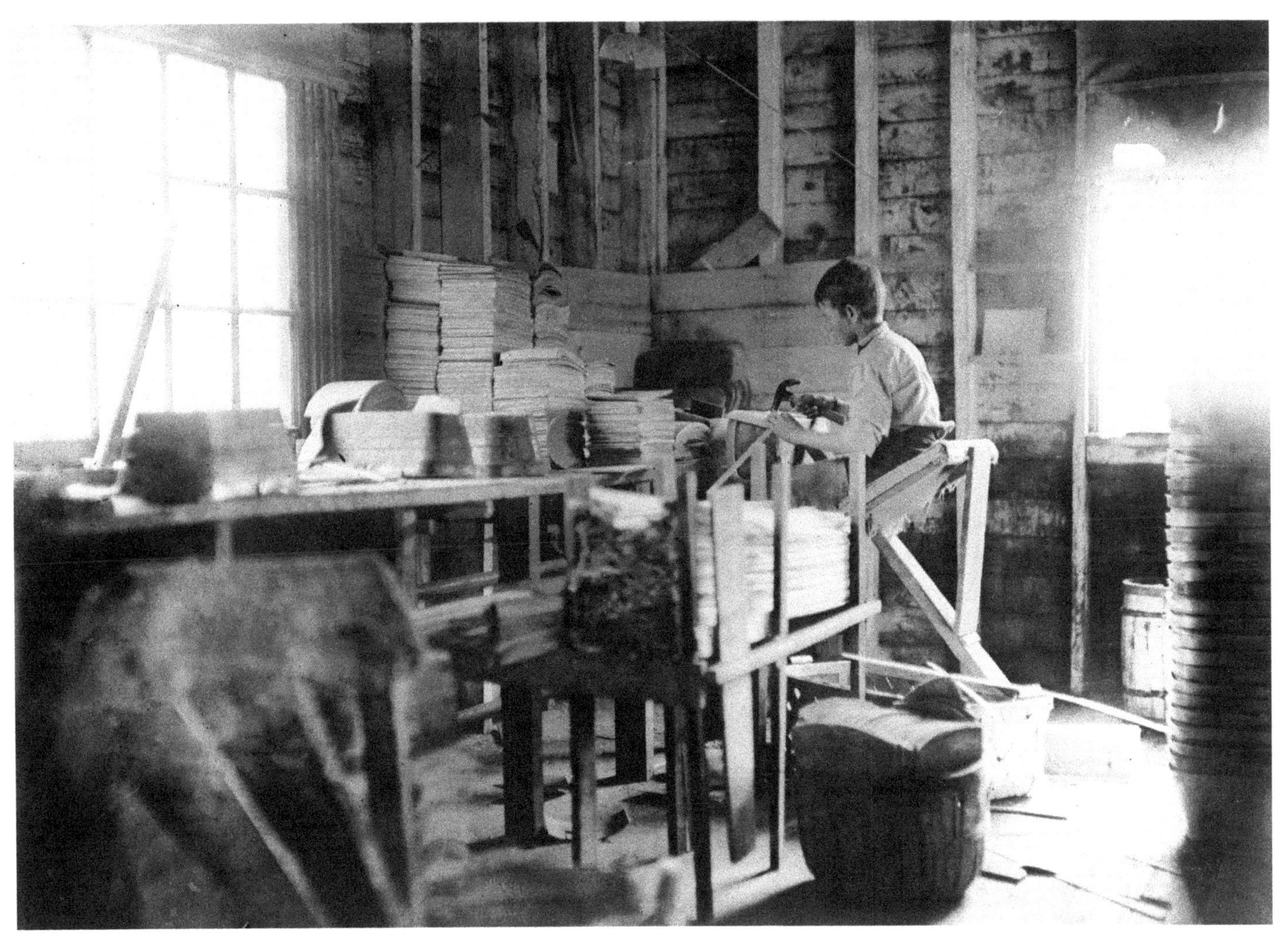

This boy is engaged at making melon baskets in an Evansville factory in late 1908.

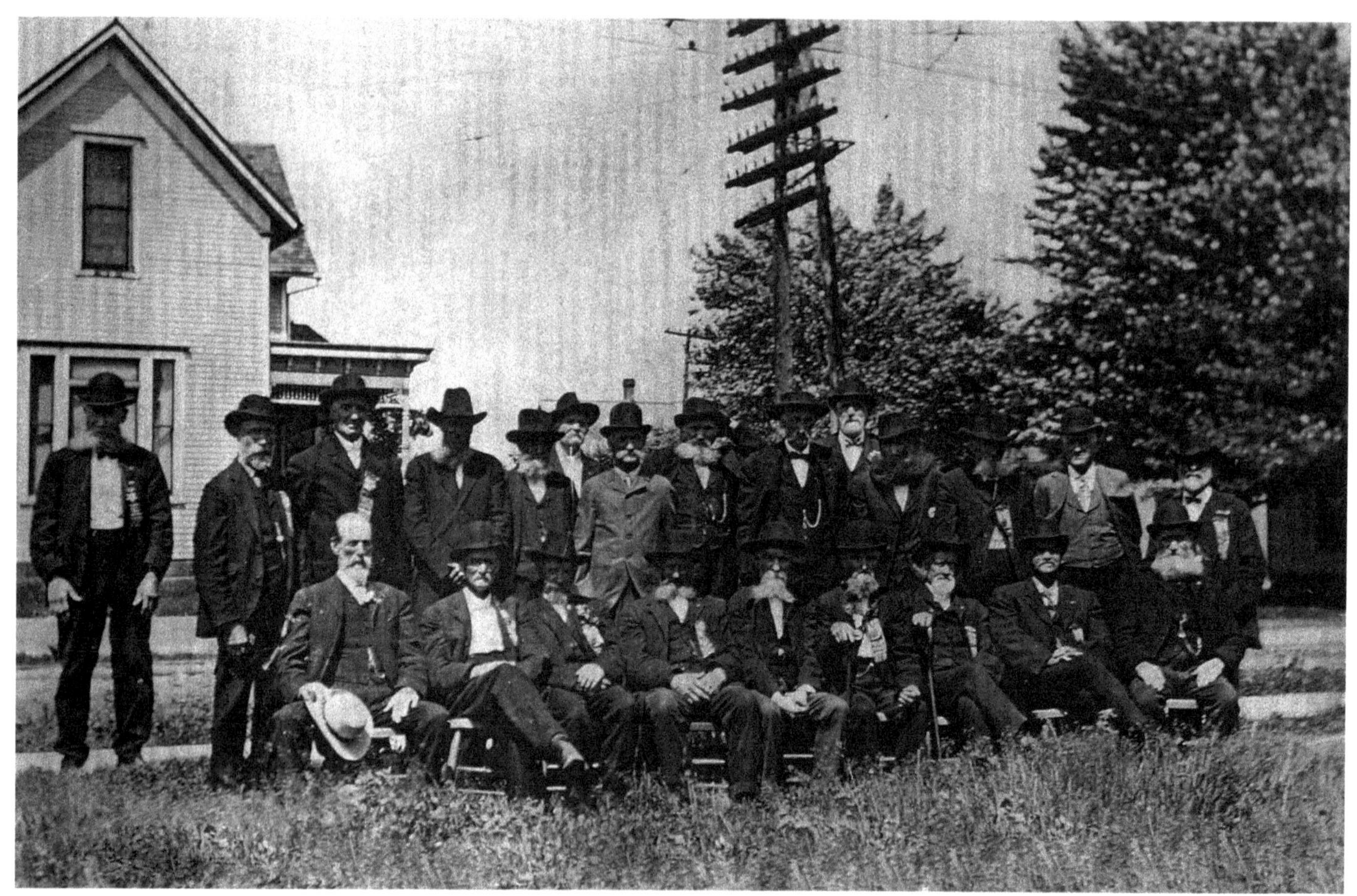

Forty-three years after Appomattox, area Union veterans of the Grand Army of the Republic gather for their annual get-together in Monroeville on May 30, 1908. Of the 210,000 Hoosiers who fought to preserve the Union, 24,416 lost their lives and more than 50,000 suffered injuries. Confederate forces entered the state in three offensives during the war—at Newburgh; from Leavenworth to Paoli; and from Mauckport to Corydon and towns farther north, including Salem, most of which was burned to the ground.

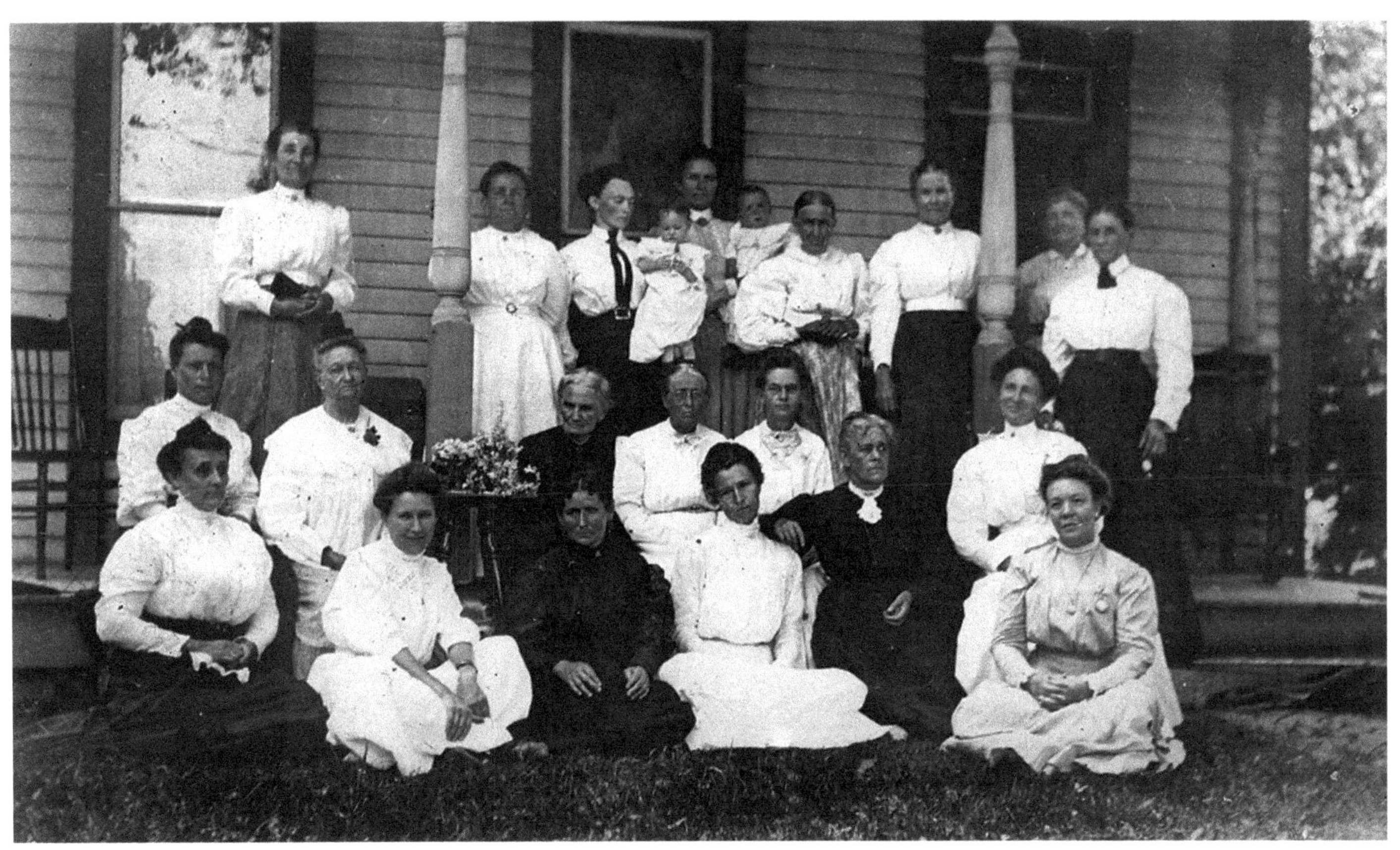

Veterans of the Grand Army of the Republic are featured in many photographs in Indiana collections, fewer of which portray the Ladies of the GAR. This one depicts old and young (with several infants) assembled for a meeting in August 1909 in Monroeville. The Ladies of the GAR continue to serve as ambassadors for patriotism, loyalty to the union, community service, historic preservation, and honoring the memory of our collective past.

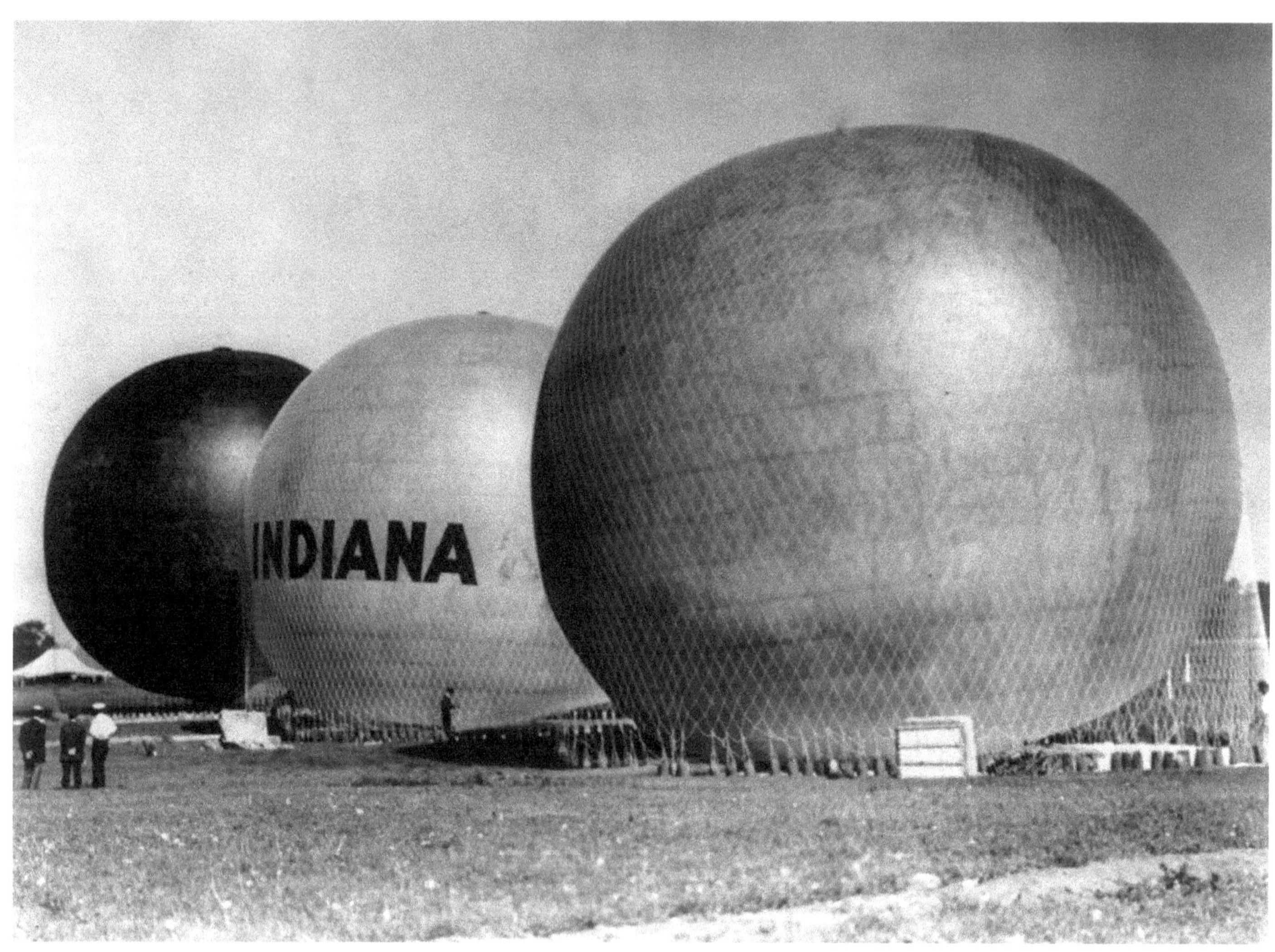

Balloon racing was, excuse the pun, big business in 1909. Thousands of spectators crowded into the Indianapolis Motor Speedway to see the "1st National Balloon Race" here on June 5, where the *Chicago, Indiana,* and *Hoosier* entries are set for what was described as an exciting launch. The race was the work of Carl Fisher, who developed the speedway where the first Indianapolis 500 would be held a year later. Fisher piloted the *Indiana* with the help of aeronaut George Bumbaugh.

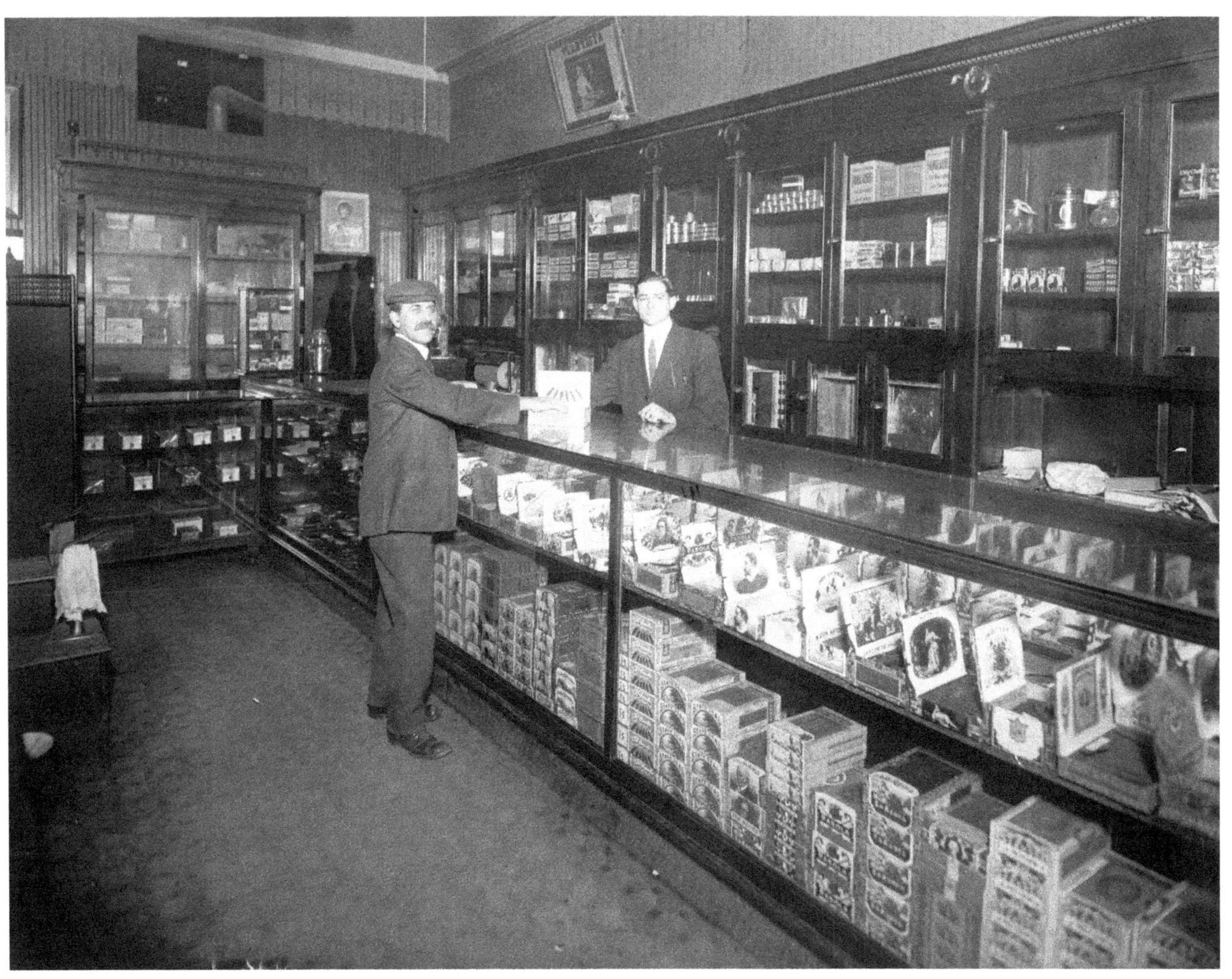

The profusion of brands is overwhelming in Blue's Cigar Store, a manufacturer and retailer in Peru. There were 6.7 billion cigars produced in the United States in 1909, or about 75 cigars per capita for the year.

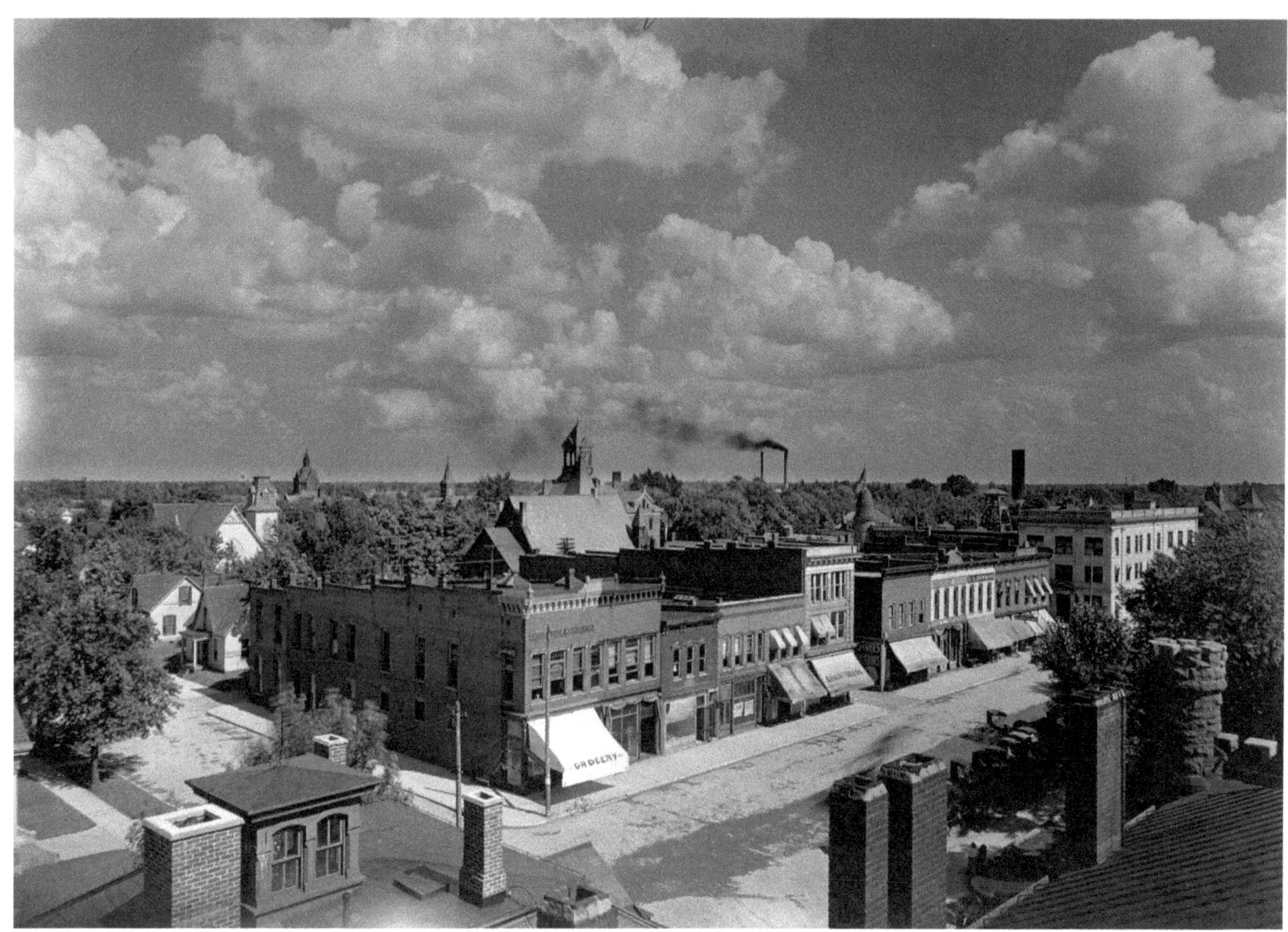

On a summer morning in 1909, E. S. Harvey captured this bird's-eye view of the east side of courthouse square in his hometown of Lebanon. The Heflin Building is the square structure at far-right and remains standing today. The cylindrical dome just to the left of the Heflin is part of the tower on Lebanon's third courthouse, built from bricks made on a local farm in 1856. It was razed shortly after this photograph was taken, to make way for construction of the courthouse standing there today.

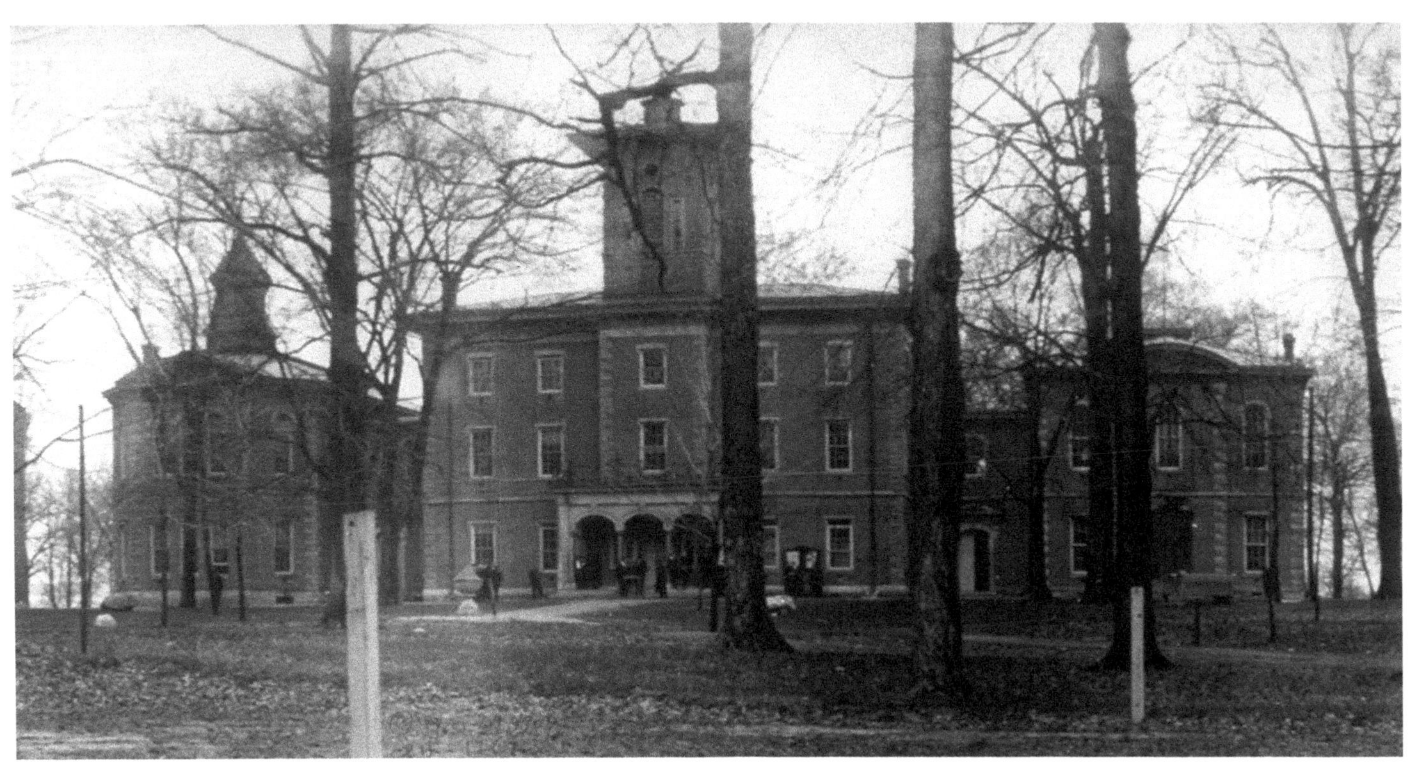

Wabash College was already in its 75th year of operation when C. F. Bowden photographed the campus in Crawfordsville in 1909. Caleb Mills, who taught the first class in Forest Hall, later became known as the father of the Indiana public school system. Wabash continues today as a four-year liberal arts college in Crawfordsville.

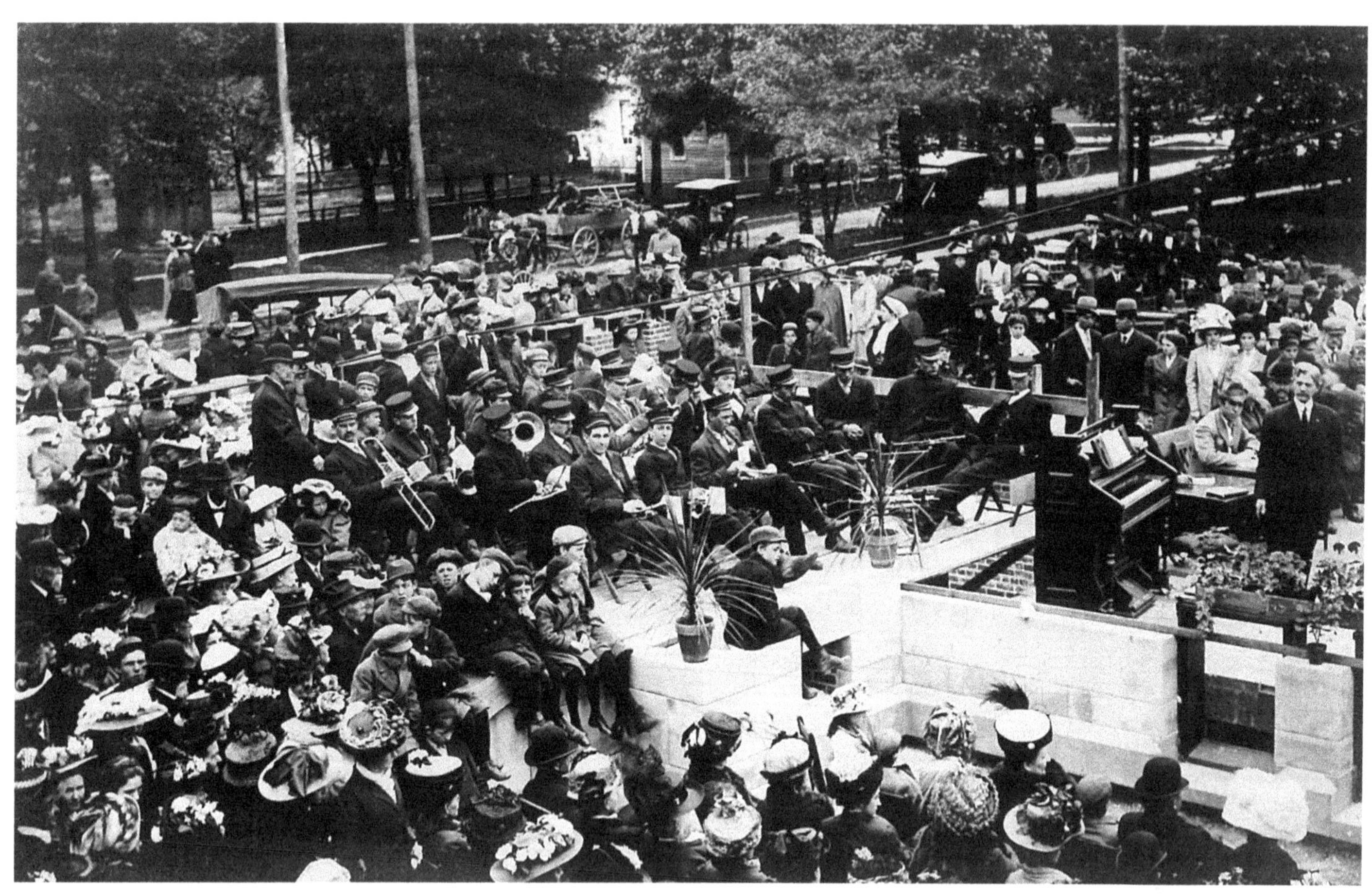

Governor Thomas R. Marshall, at lower-right, looks around before making his remarks at the cornerstone-laying ceremony for the Eckhart Public Library in Auburn on May 13, 1910. Attendance at the ceremony included a gaggle of reporters visible behind the governor, a troupe of tired-looking musicians, and a bevy of women attired in fashionable millinery.

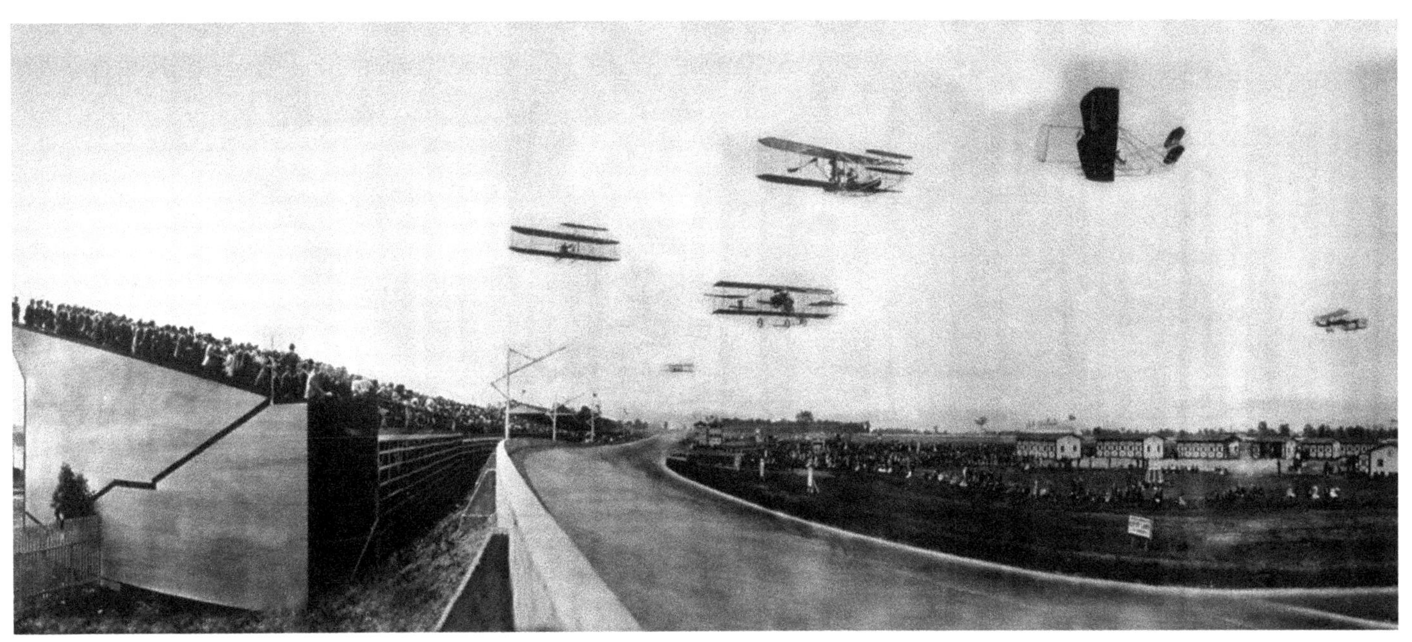

The Indianapolis Motor Speedway was the scene of the First National Aviation Meet in June 1910. In addition to pursuit races and flight demonstrations, a world record was set by Walter Brookins, who flew his plane to an altitude of 4,000 feet. The meet featured a company of aviators employed by the Wright Brothers, whose Wright Flyer designs can be delineated in at least three of the planes in flight.

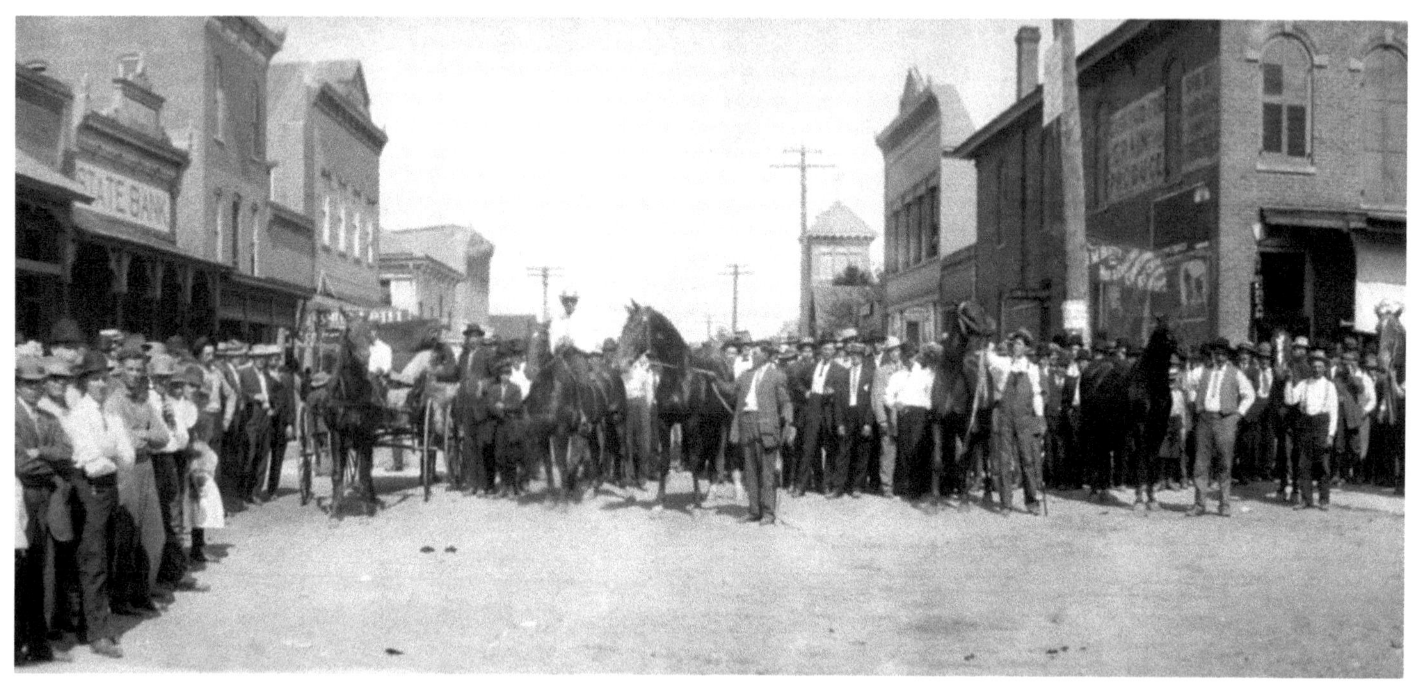

The advent of cameras with wide-angle capabilities made for the best cityscapes of many Indiana communities in the early part of the century. This wide-angle bit of Hoosier humor depicts a "Horse Show and Moter Cycle Meet" in Mulberry in June 1910. The motorcycles all seem to have been horse-powered.

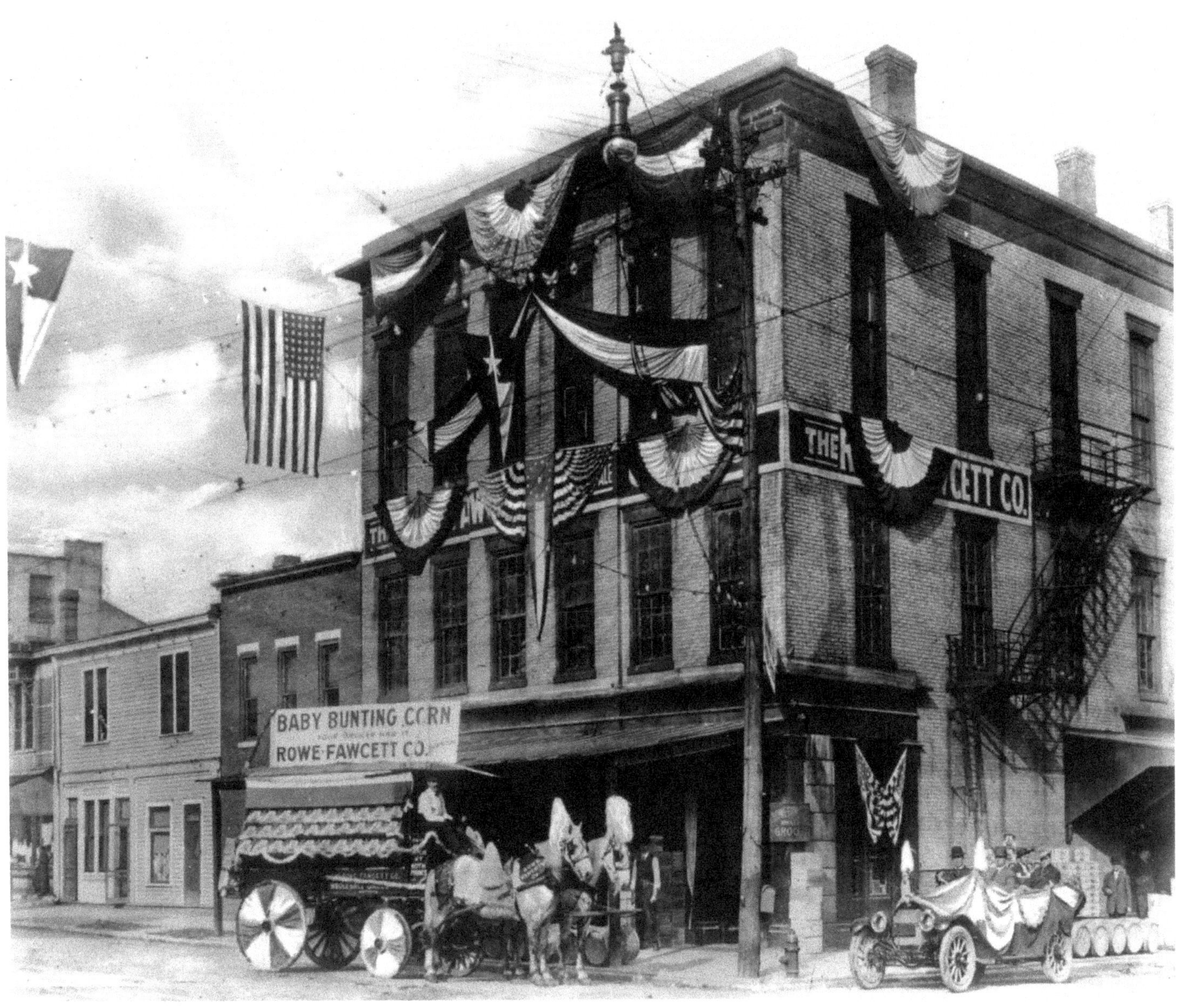

New Albany's Rowe Fawcett Company wholesale grocery and delivery vehicles are draped with bunting in 1913 to celebrate the town's centennial. Platted by the Scribner brothers, who named it for the capital of their home state of New York, New Albany had grown to more than 20,000 residents when this photograph was taken.

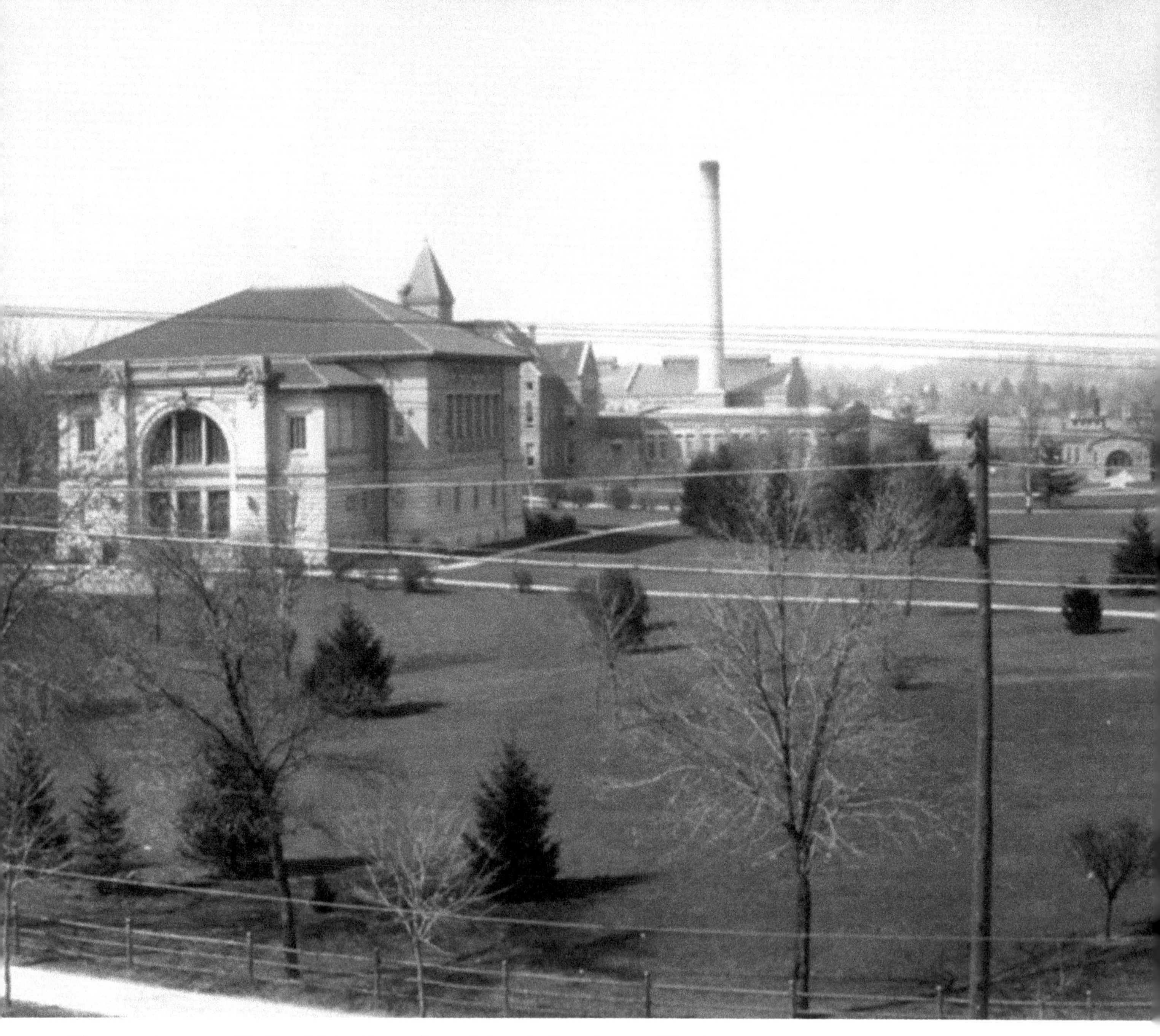

The second campus of Indiana University was located about half a mile east of the Bloomington town square. This photograph shows the grow[illegible] campus in what was known as Dunn's Woods around 1910. The Student Building and its tower, at right, are prominent in the image.

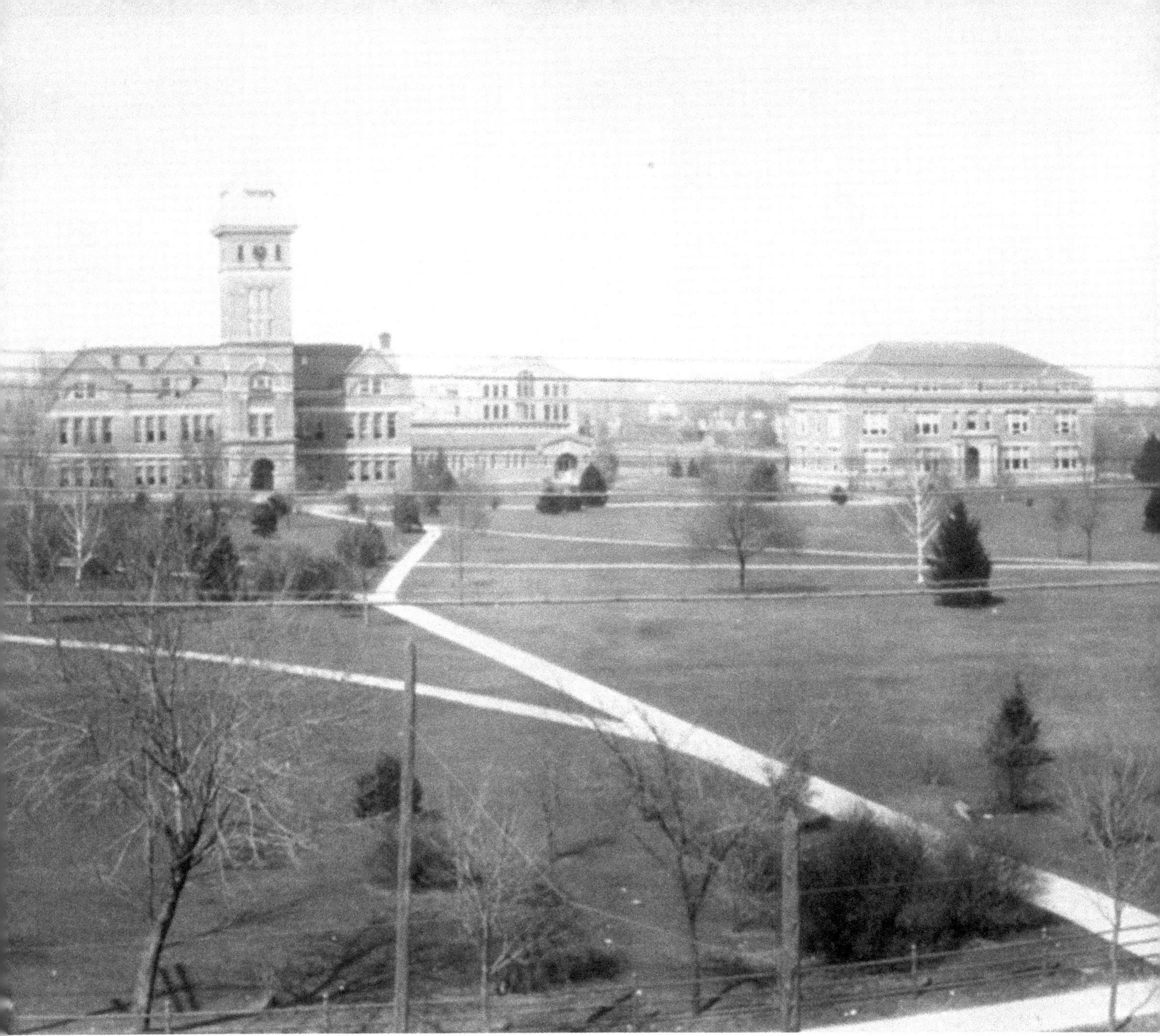

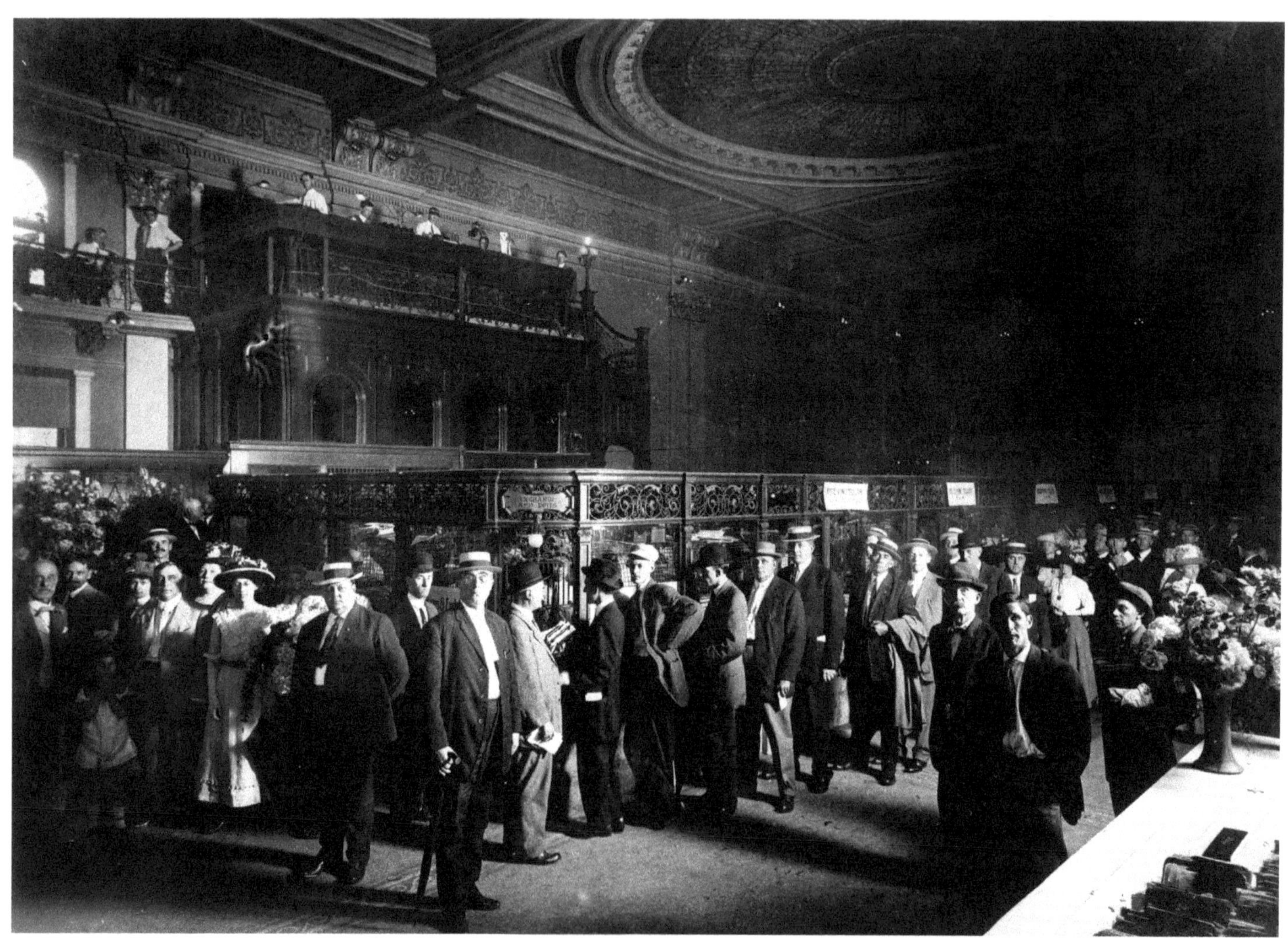

The celebration of the merger of the Indiana National Bank and the Capital National Bank in July 1912 filled the INB lobby with well-wishers up to its balcony. The bank's combined assets were $20 million, reason enough for any financial institution that had survived the Panic of 1907 to cheer.

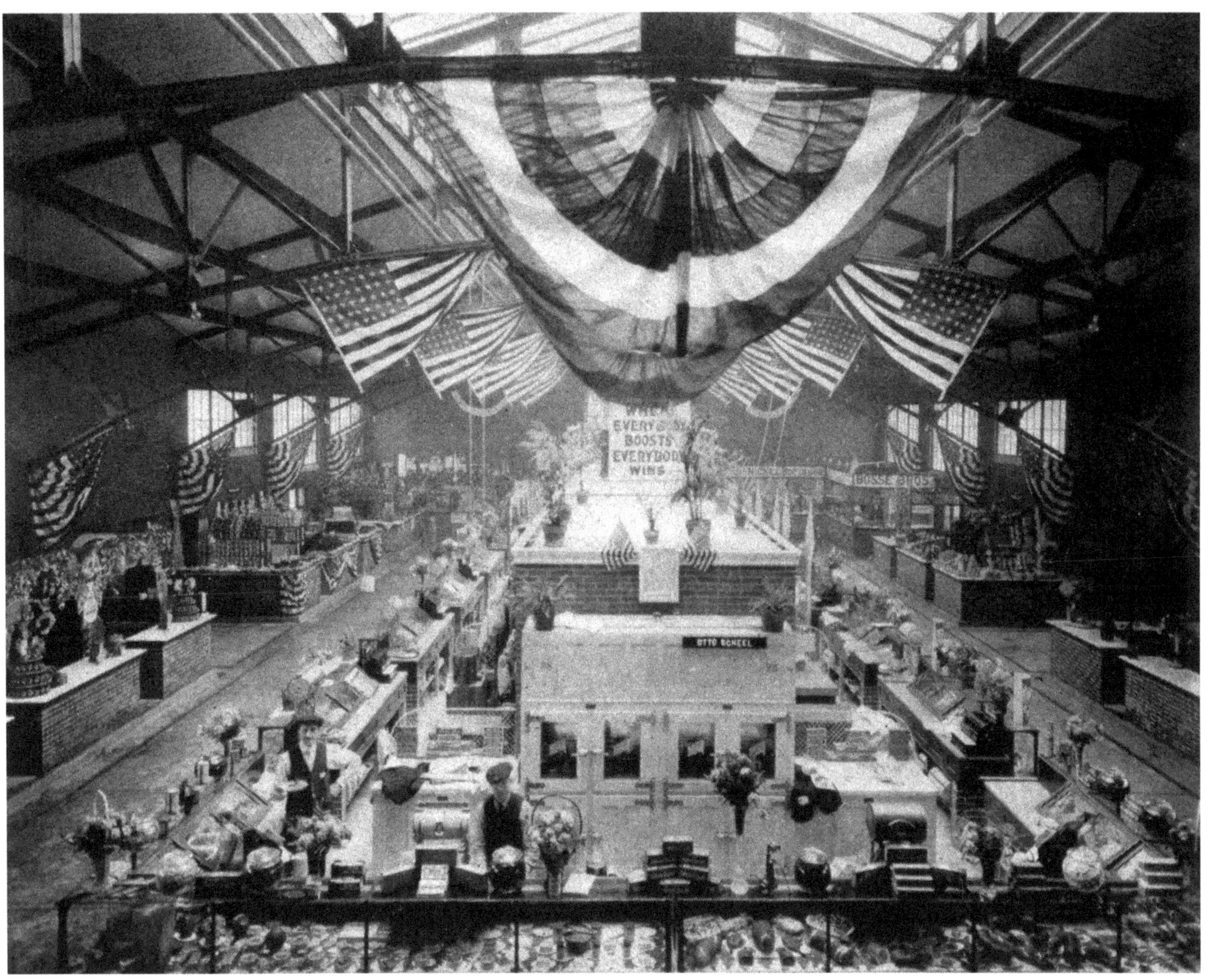

The Municipal Market for the city of Evansville could boast a handsome Prairie School design with its brick-and-mortar exterior, but it was its massive, well-organized interior that was the real attraction. The sign beneath the bunting, "When Everybody Boosts, Everybody Wins," suggests a cooperative among the merchants.

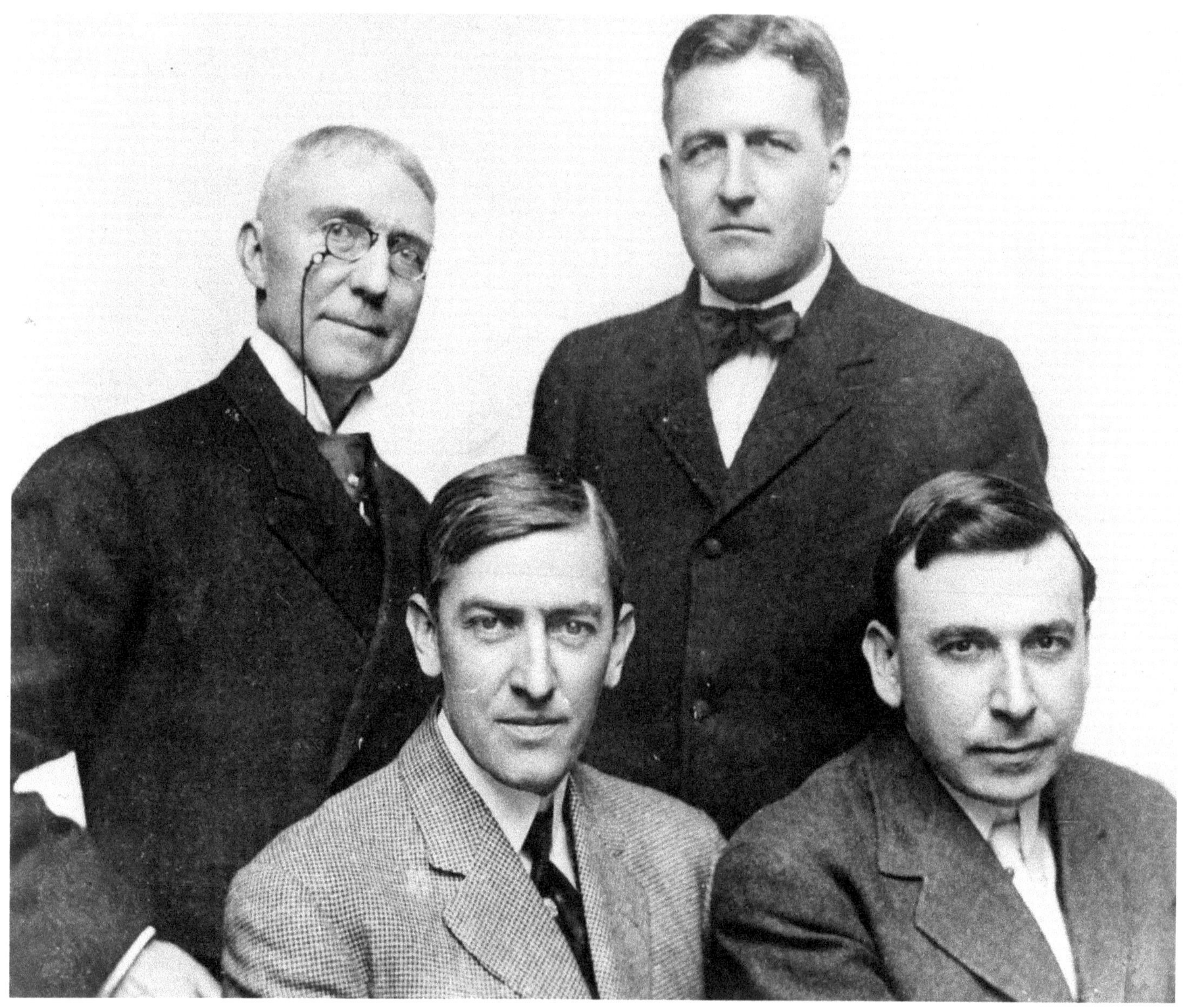

What some call the "golden age" of Indiana literature is found in this publicity photo. Clockwise from top-left are poet James Whitcomb Riley from Greenfield, novelist Meredith Nicholson from Crawfordsville, novelist Booth Tarkington from Indianapolis, and playwright George Ade from Kentland. Born between 1849 and 1869, all four conveyed a sense of "Hoosierdom."

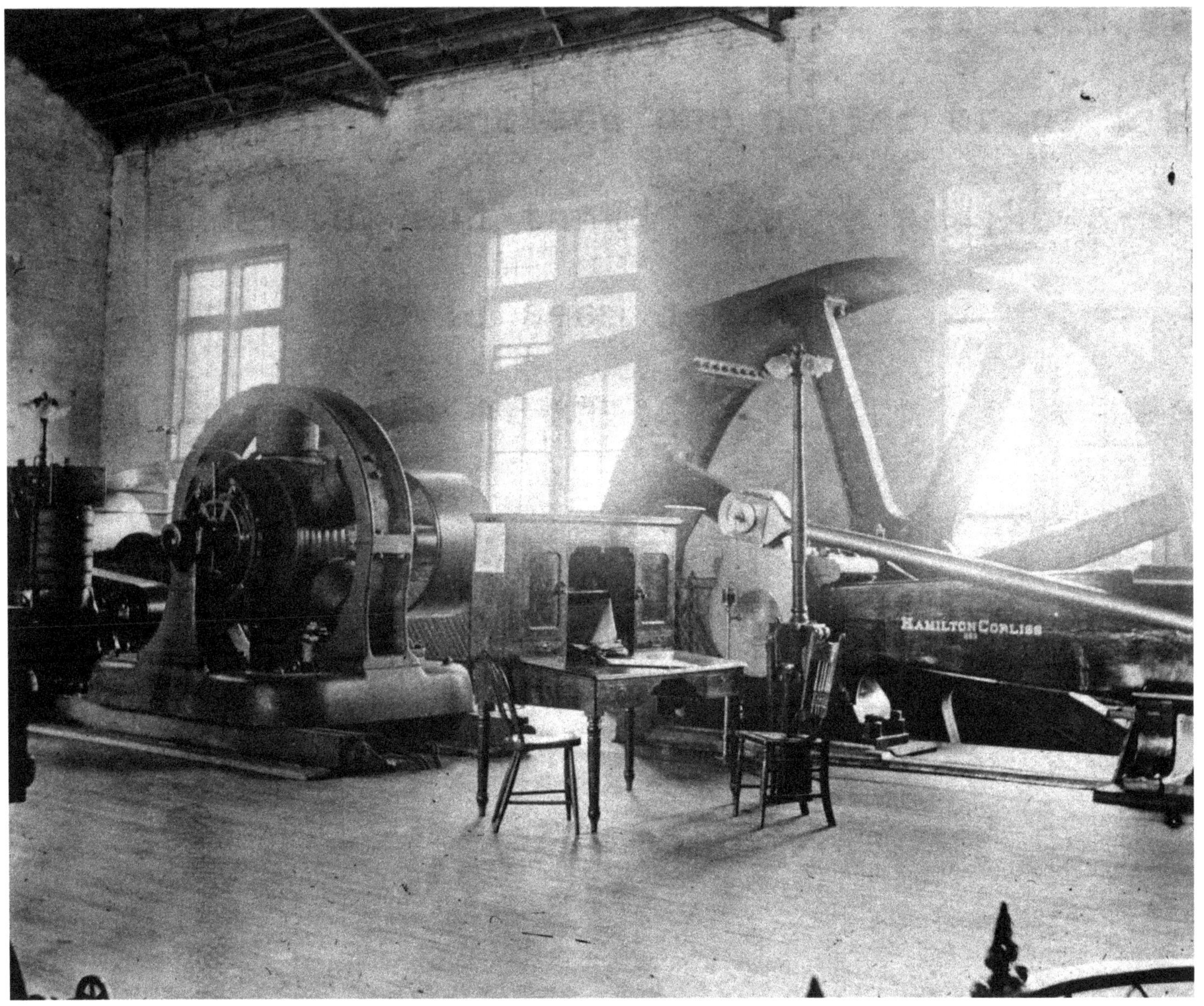

In 1888, Lafayette became one of the first cities in the United States to convert its street railways from horse power to electric traction. This photograph of the powerhouse on South Street shows the Westinghouse generator and Hamilton-Corliss engine.

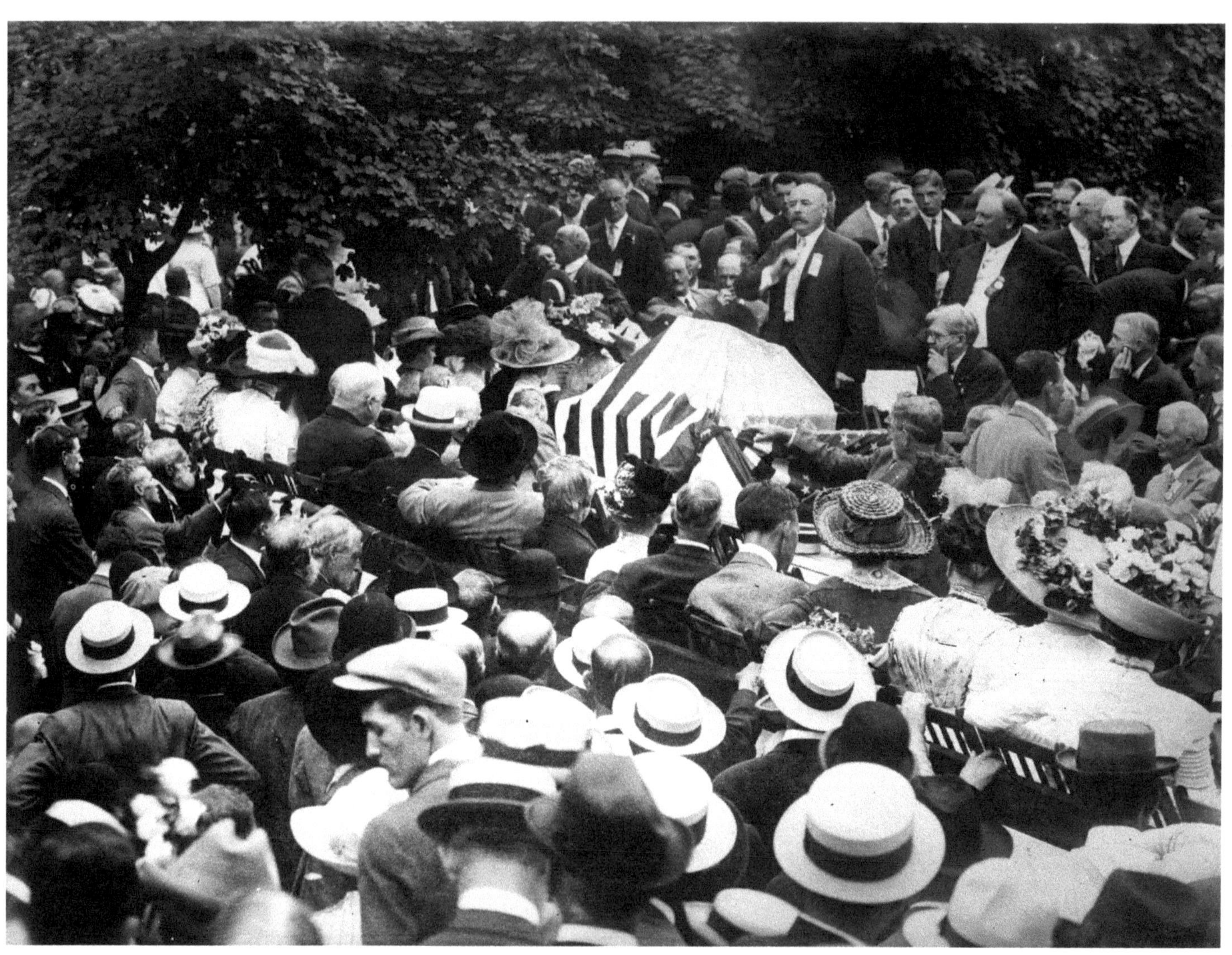

Judge Alton B. Parker addresses a political rally in Indianapolis in 1912 to formally announce the selection of Indiana governor Thomas R. Marshall as the Democratic Party's candidate for vice-president. Parker had been the party's unsuccessful presidential candidate in 1904.

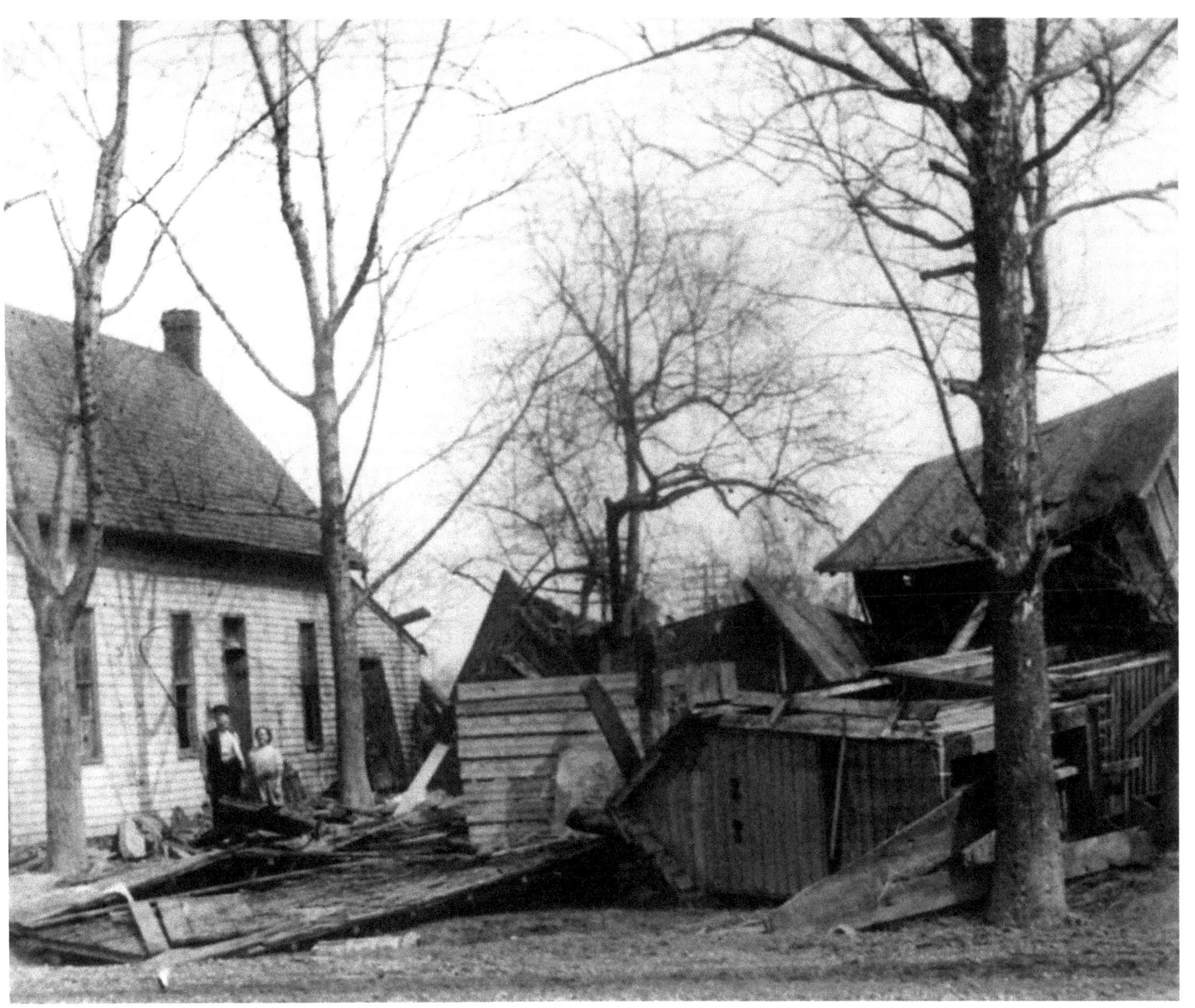

Much of the Midwest was devastated by the Great Flood of 1913. After a winter-long ice pack on rivers and streams began to thaw, a violent string of thunderstorms unleashed torrents of water on communities throughout Indiana and other states. This scene in Logansport typifies the destruction.

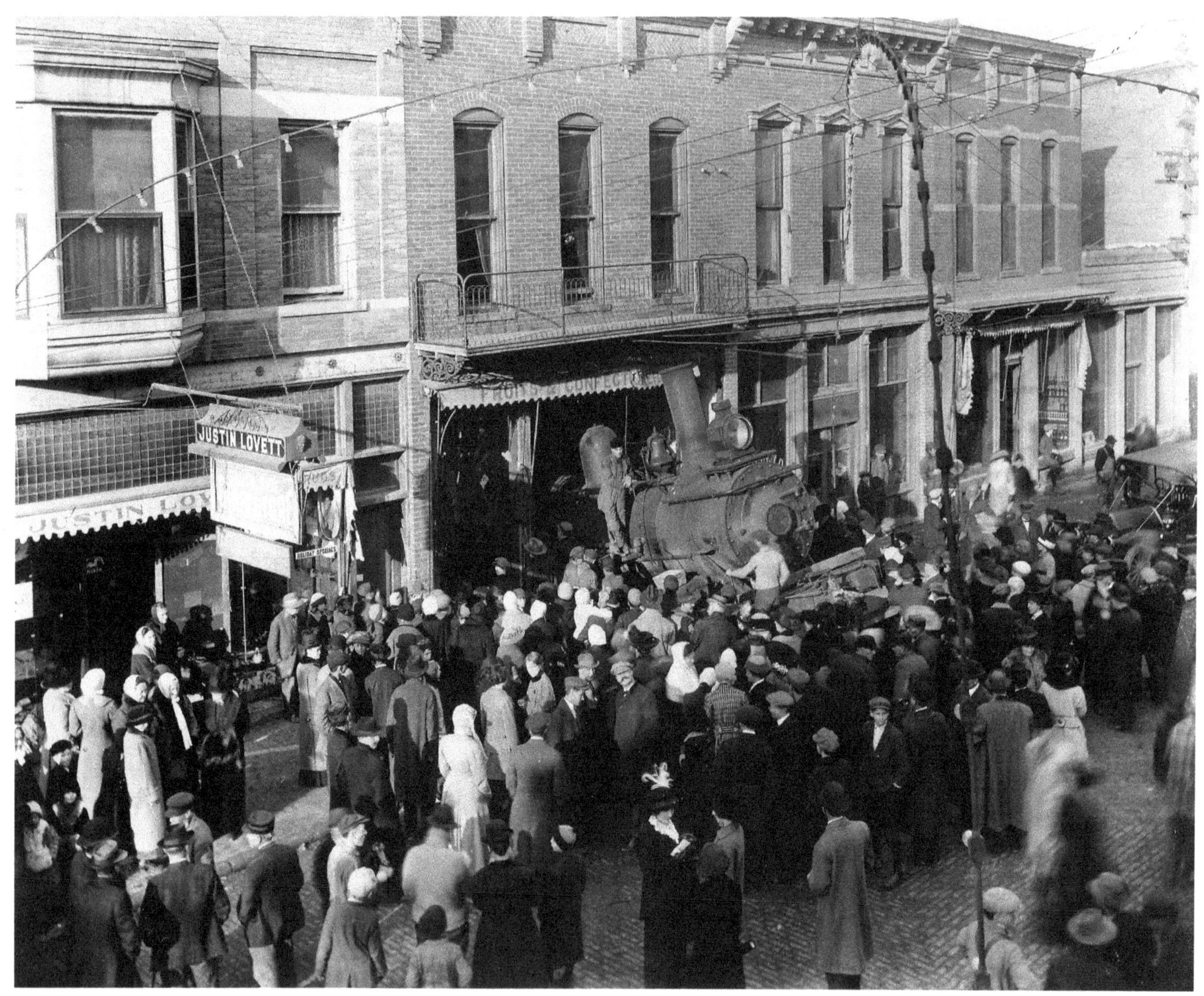

Most train wrecks had tragic consequences, but the element of humor helped alleviate the trouble of a few. The engineer of this Chicago, Bluffton & Cincinnati Railroad locomotive in Huntington apparently failed to set the brake in 1913, causing the engine to roll backward on the tracks, down the street, and into a fruit and confectionery store.

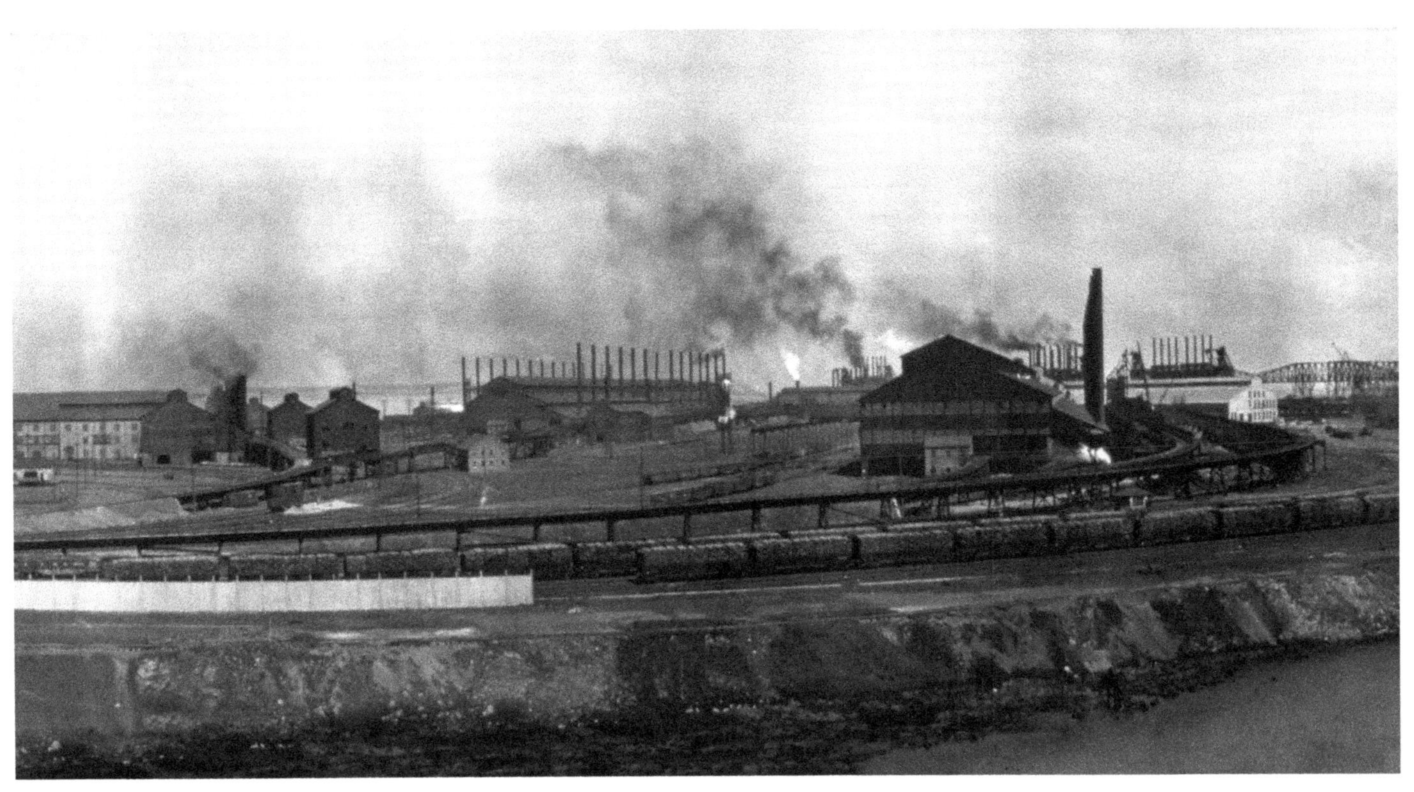

By summer 1912, the once-barren land along Lake Michigan was quickly becoming "Steel City." The impact of the industry and its awe-inspiring structures can be appreciated in the fact that Gary does not appear as a city in the 1900 census, but would have more than 100,000 citizens by 1930.

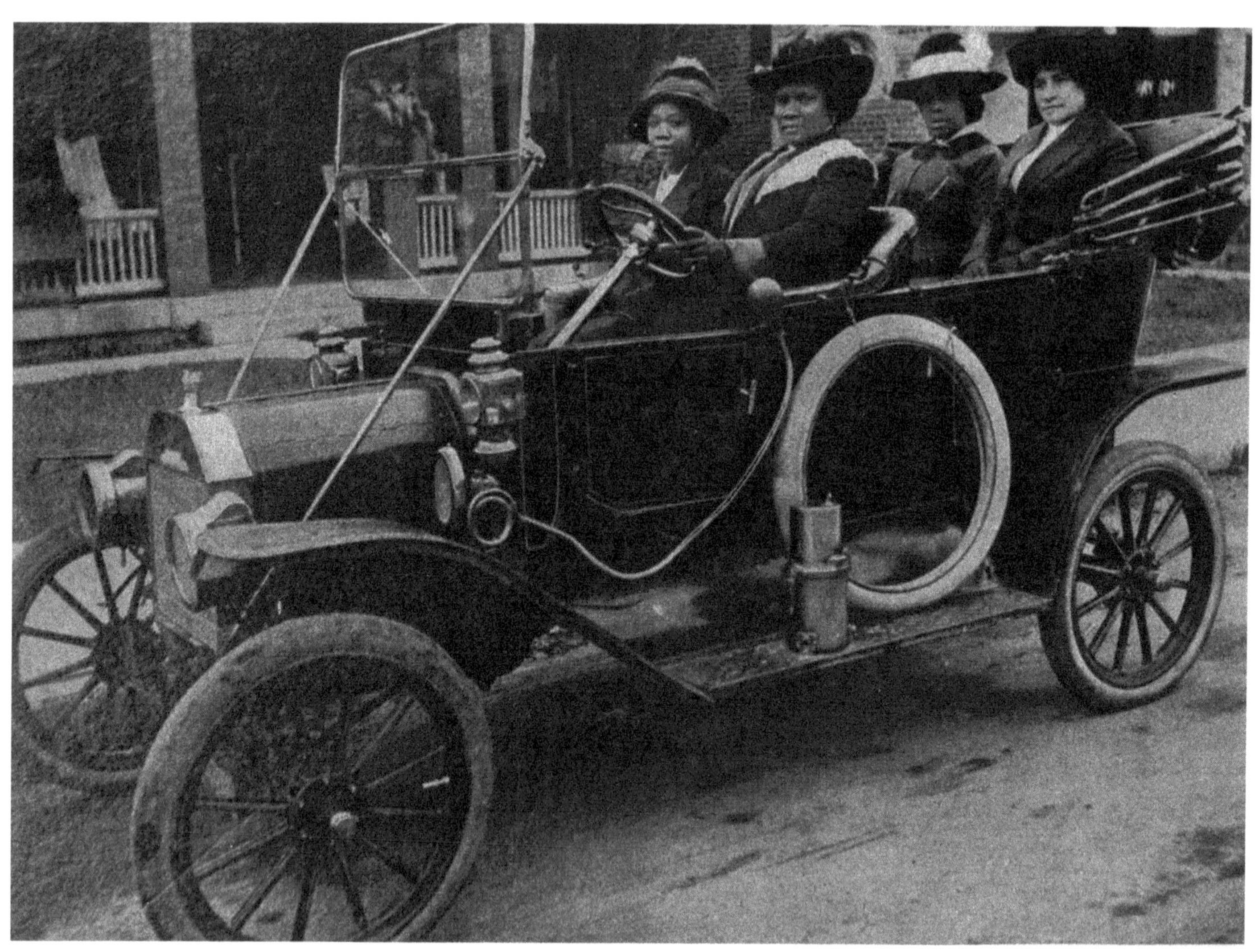

The driver of this handsome Model-T Ford was Madam C. J. Walker, who revolutionized the hair-care product market for African-American women. Here she poses outside her home in Indianapolis in 1912 with her niece, Anjetta Breelove, and two employees, Lucy Flint and Alice Kelly.

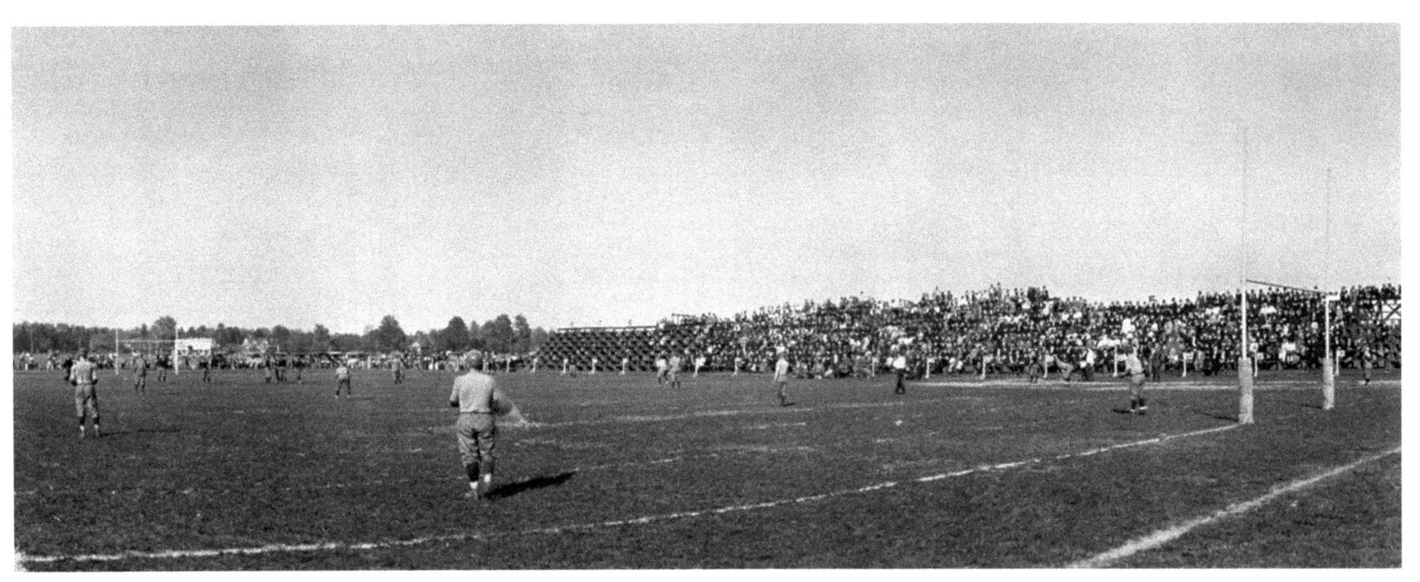

Stuart Field in West Lafayette was packed for the Purdue-Wabash game on October 24, 1913, which Purdue won, 26–0. Legend has it that Purdue's trouncing of Wabash in 1891 resulted in Purdue's nickname "Boilermakers," awarded them by a sportswriter from Crawfordsville, the home of Wabash College.

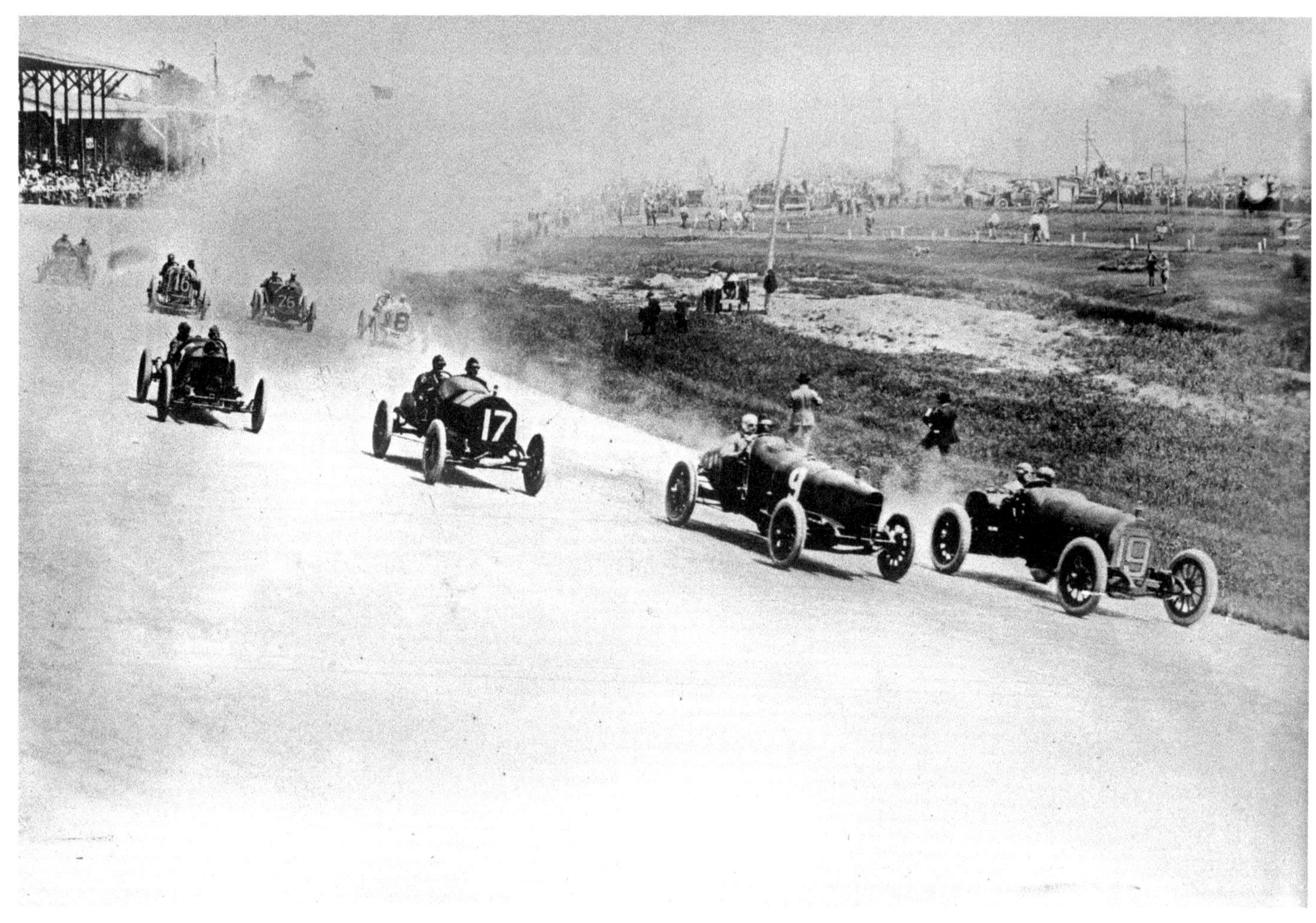

Caleb Bragg (19) takes the lead over Albert Guyot (9) and Bill Liesaw (17) at the first turn in the 1913 Indianapolis 500. Jules Goux (16), whose car can be seen in the dust at upper-left, won the race with an average speed of 75.93 miles per hour. The race was the third Indy 500 held.

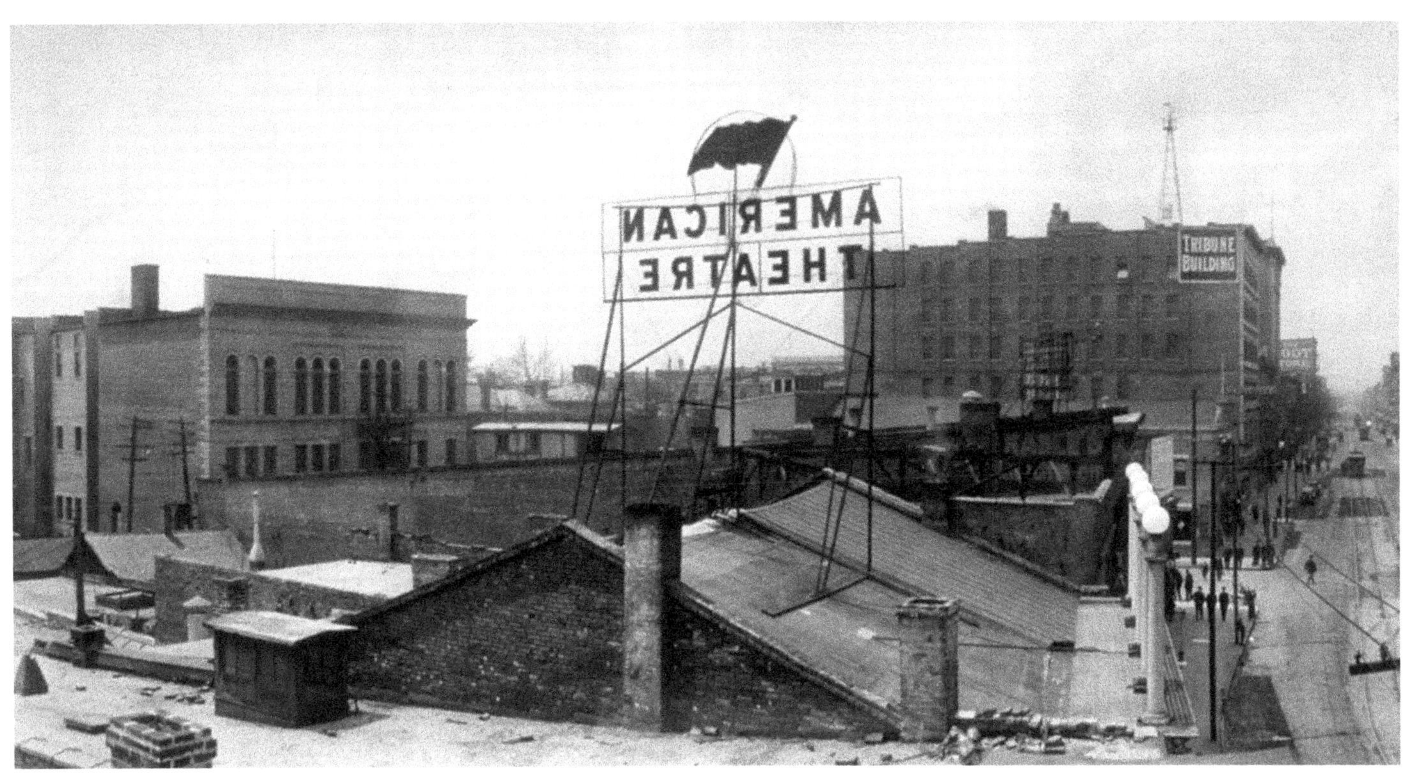

Early in the century, Terre Haute aspired to be the "Pittsburgh of the West" through its myriad industries, including mining, milling, and transportation. In any prosperous city, one measure of success is the arts, and the American Theatre's sign flies high above Ninth and Main streets in this image from 1913. Hoosiers from Terre Haute famous in literature and the arts include Claude Thornhill, Paul Dresser, Max Ehrmann, and Theodore Dreiser.

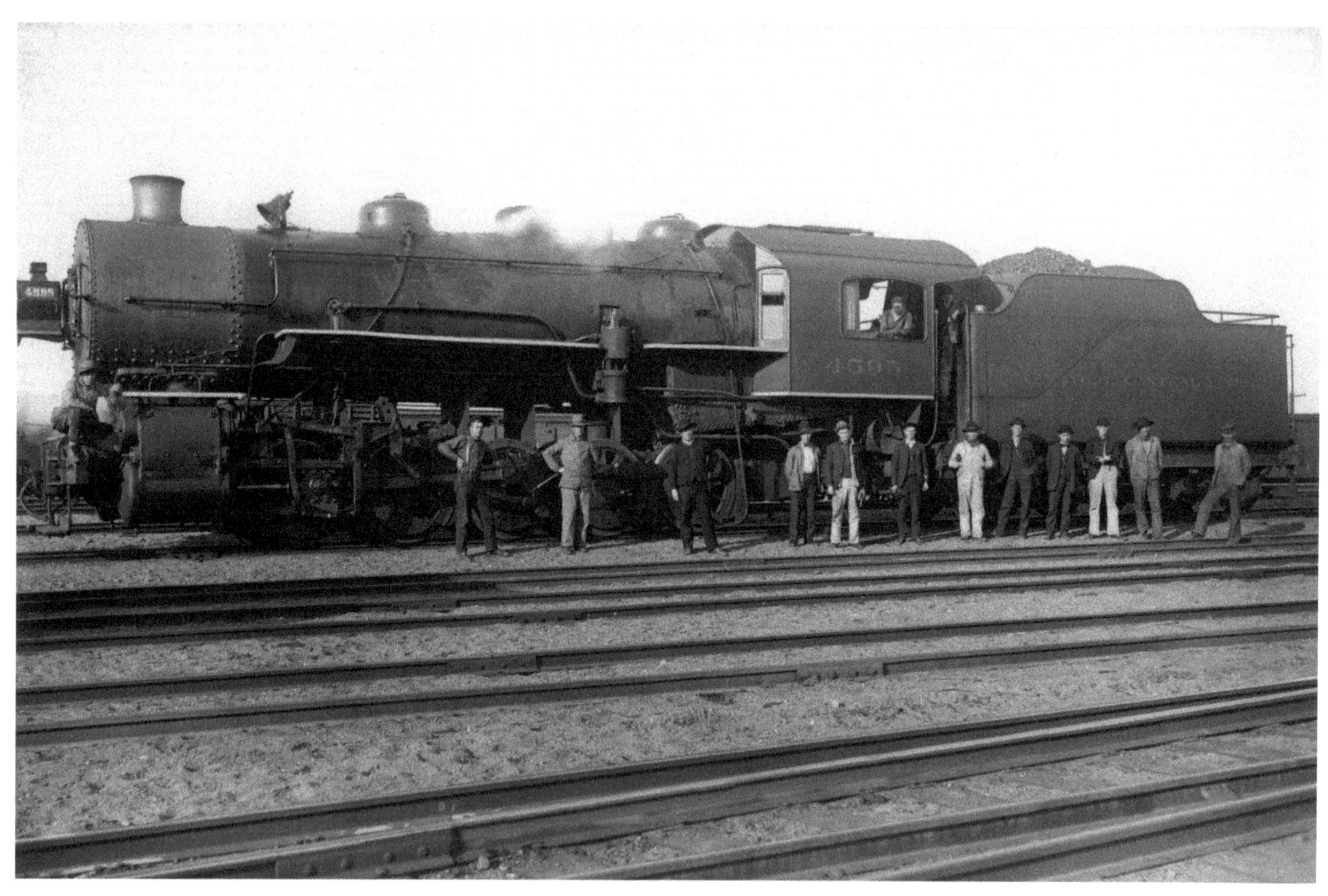

This massive locomotive was known as a hump pusher, one that shuttles lines of freight cars onto different tracks in a rail yard to form a train. Lake Shore & Michigan Southern Railway trainmen pose with the engine for a group shot in the Elkhart rail yard.

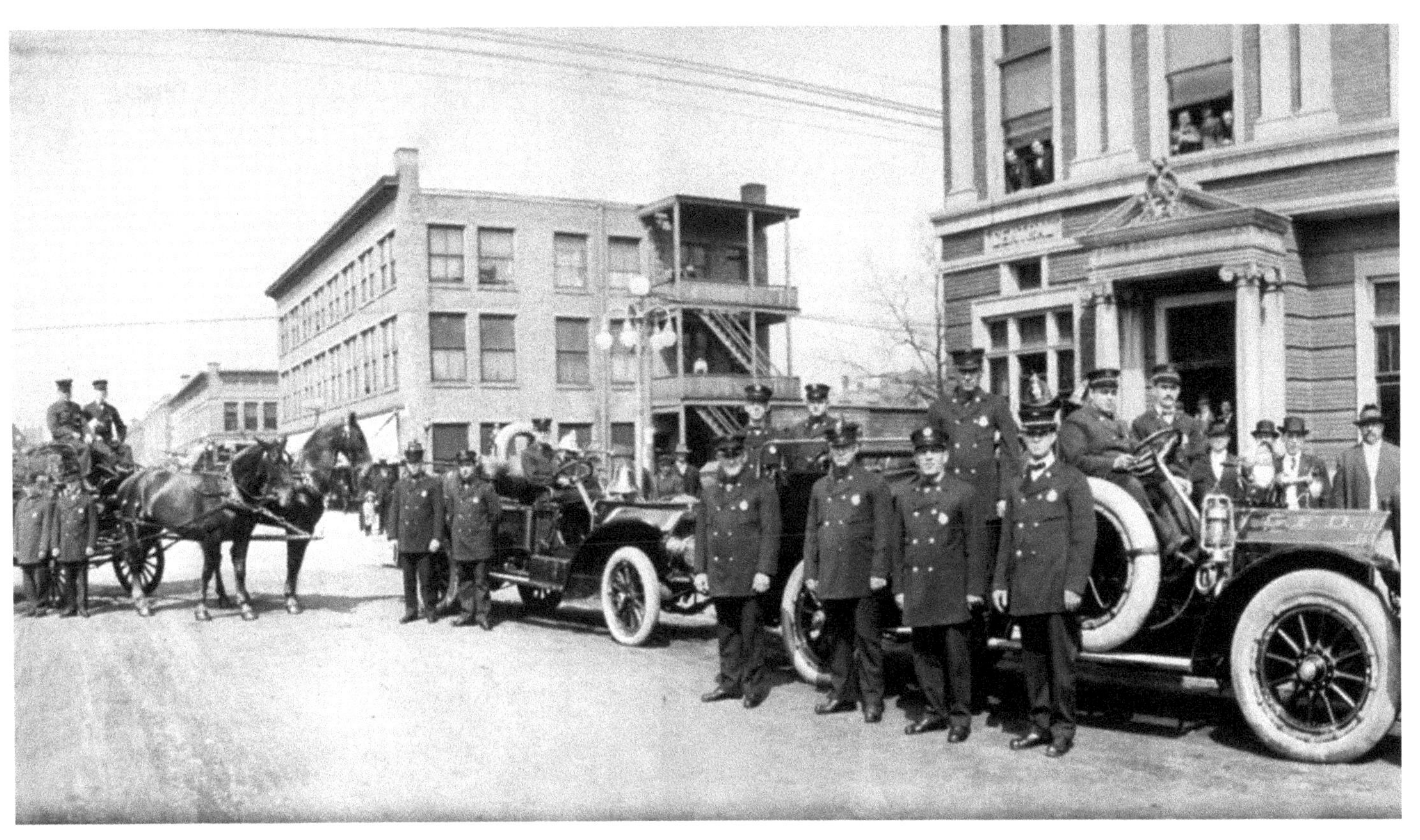

The pride of Gary's fire department turned out in full dress and full force in 1914 as the northwestern city grew by gigantic strides. The transition to mechanized equipment was under way but incomplete in many cities across the state and nation, as the horse-drawn wagon at far-left reveals.

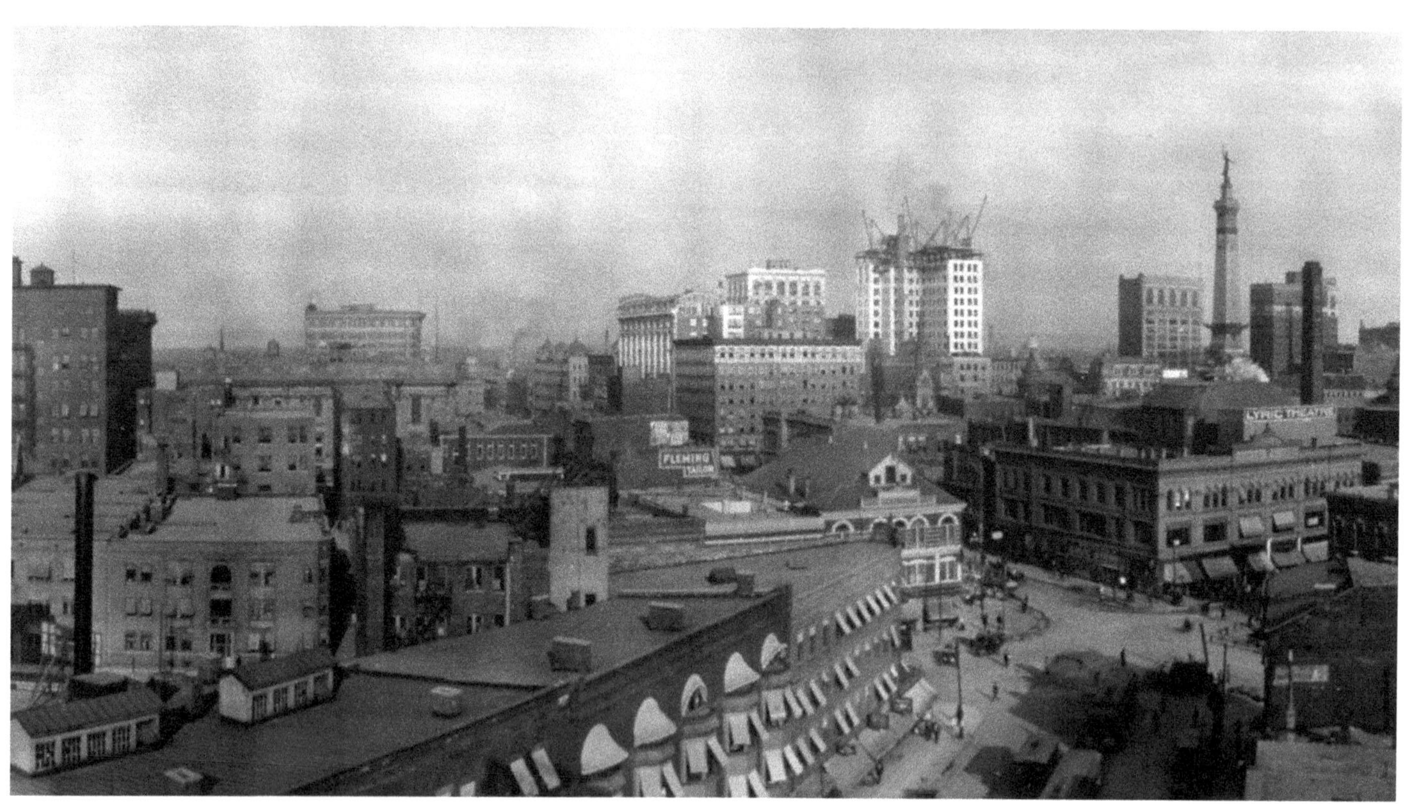

The skyline of Indianapolis sweeps across the horizon in 1914, reflecting the time when Indianapolis was not only the seventh-largest city in the Midwest, but could also make the claim that more than one-quarter of the nation's population lived within 300 miles of the city.

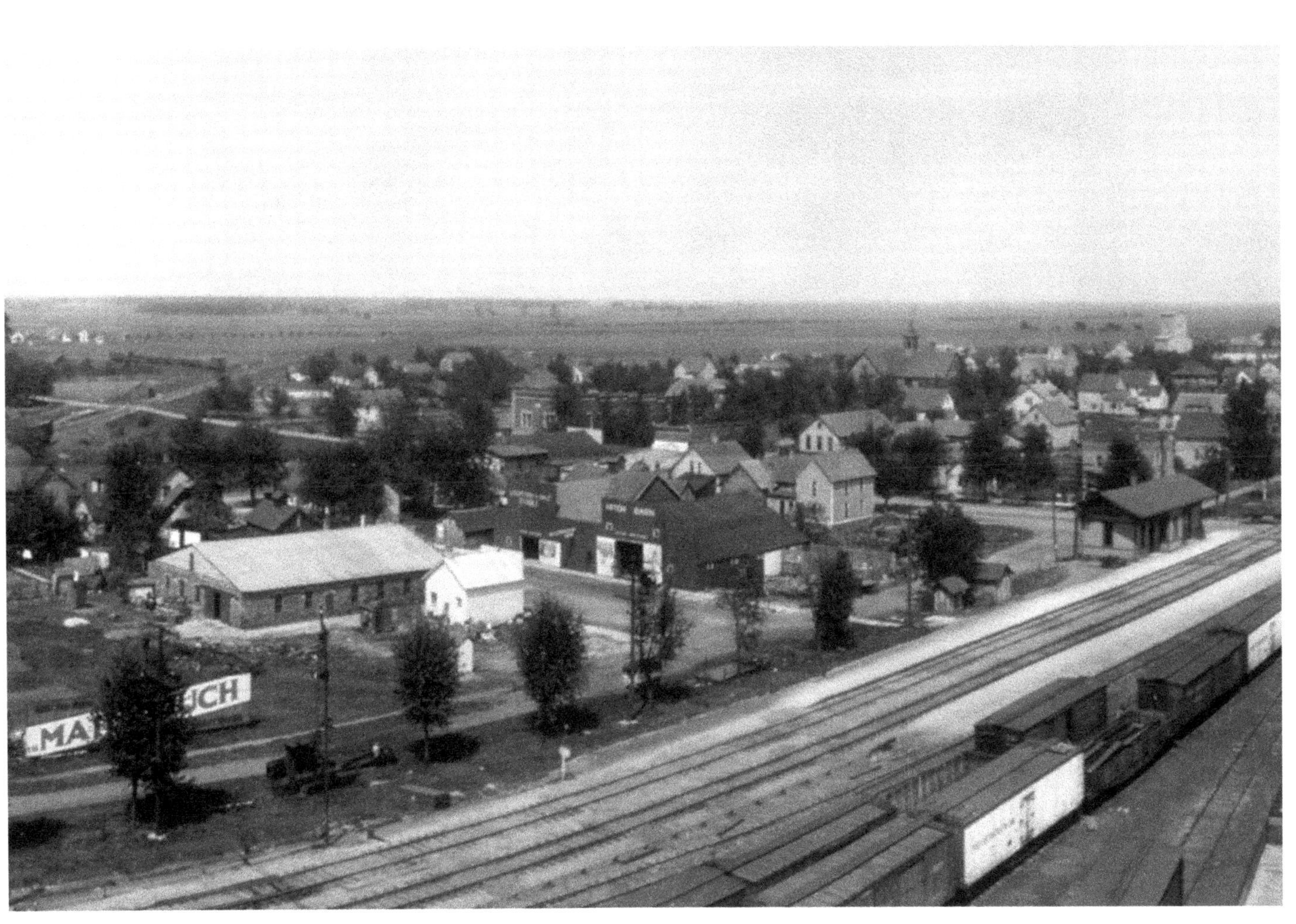

This 1915 view of the town of La Crosse was probably taken from a water tower or grain elevator alongside the railroad. The view faces southward across the La Porte County community, revealing farmland on the great level plain of the northwest Indiana horizon.

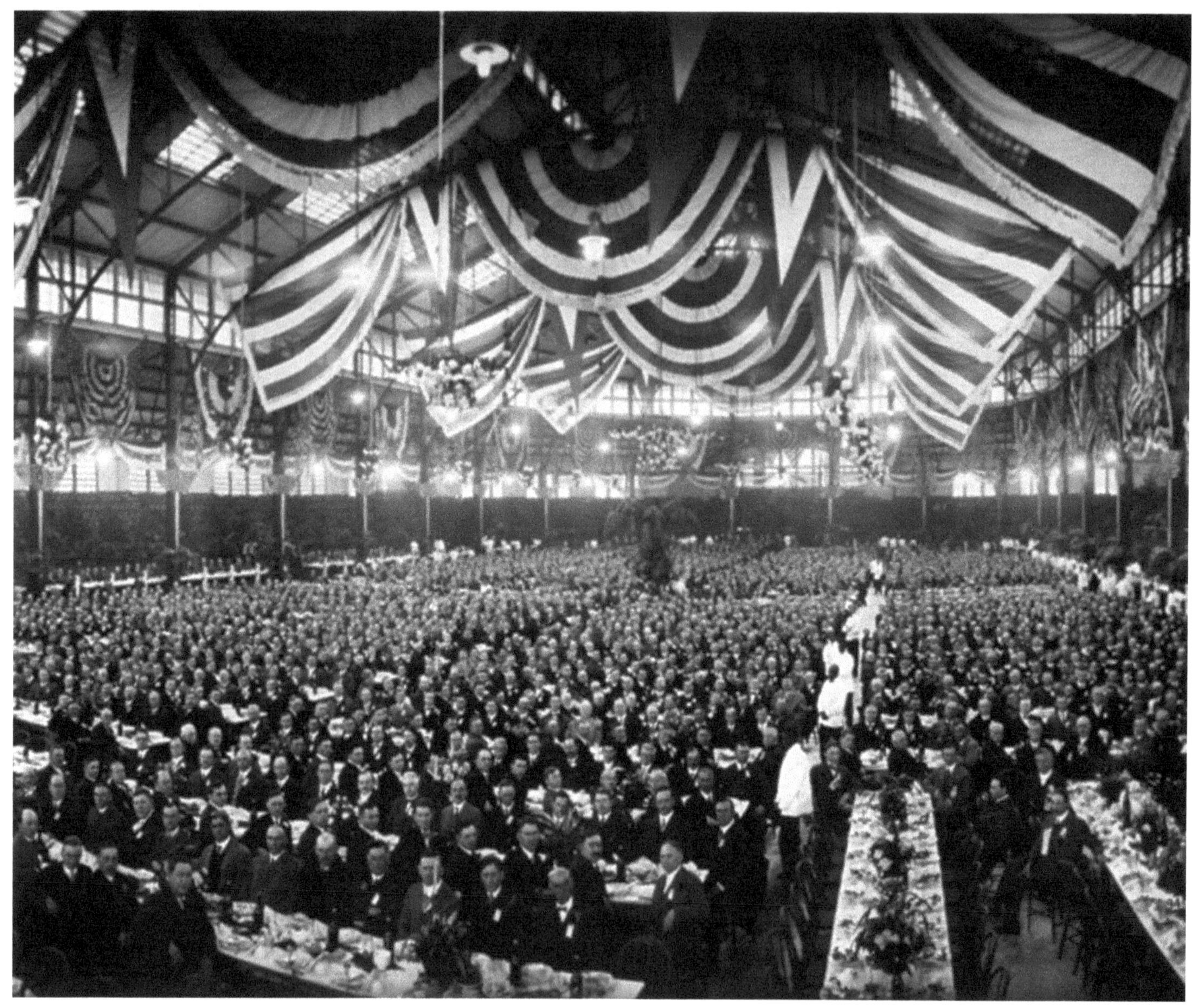

More than 4,000 Masons attended the banquet to celebrate the golden jubilee of the institution of the Scottish Rite in the Valley of Indianapolis at the city auditorium in May 1915.

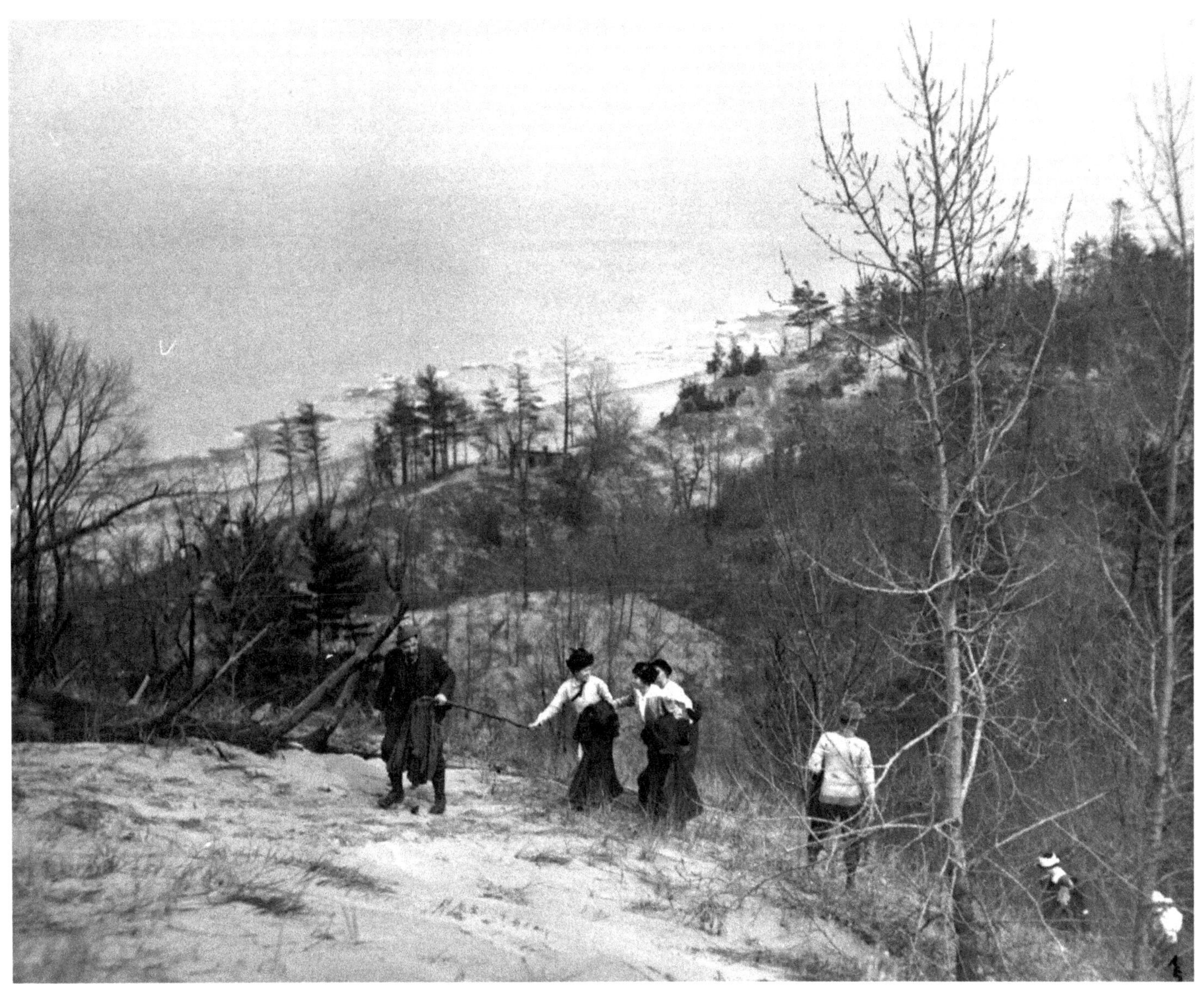

Chicago's Prairie Club championed saving the Indiana dunes—that thin strip of shore, wetlands, and woods along Lake Michigan in the northwestern corner of Indiana. Early conservationists and visitors explored the variety of habitats found at the dunes, among them this group climbing Mount Tom in 1915, eight years before the state set aside 2,200 acres for a park.

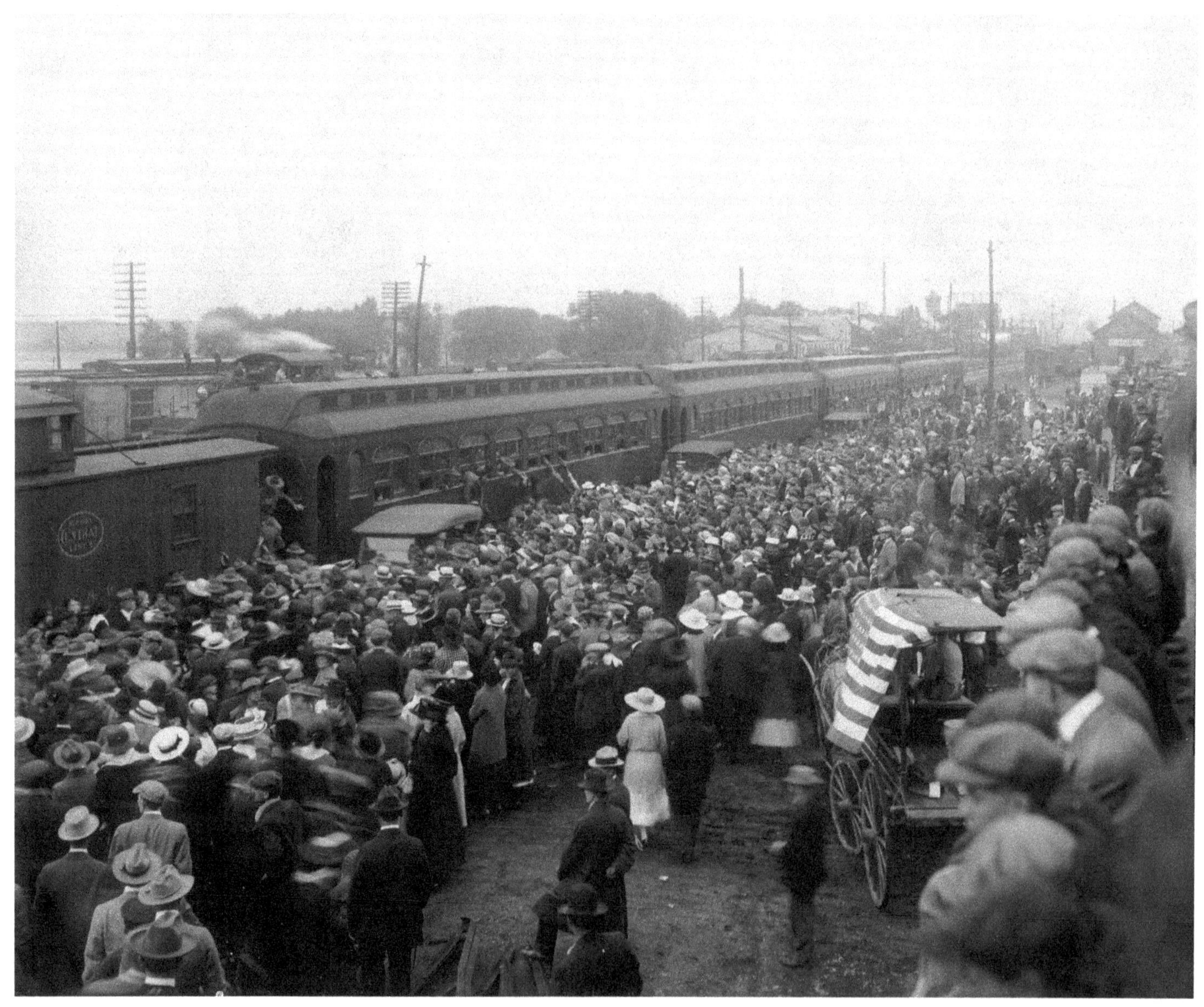

Spirits were high in La Porte in 1916 as the nation geared up to fight Pancho Villa and his bandits along the border with Mexico. A large crowd gathers at the La Porte depot to cheer the soldiers of Company B of the Indiana Guard as they embark for training.

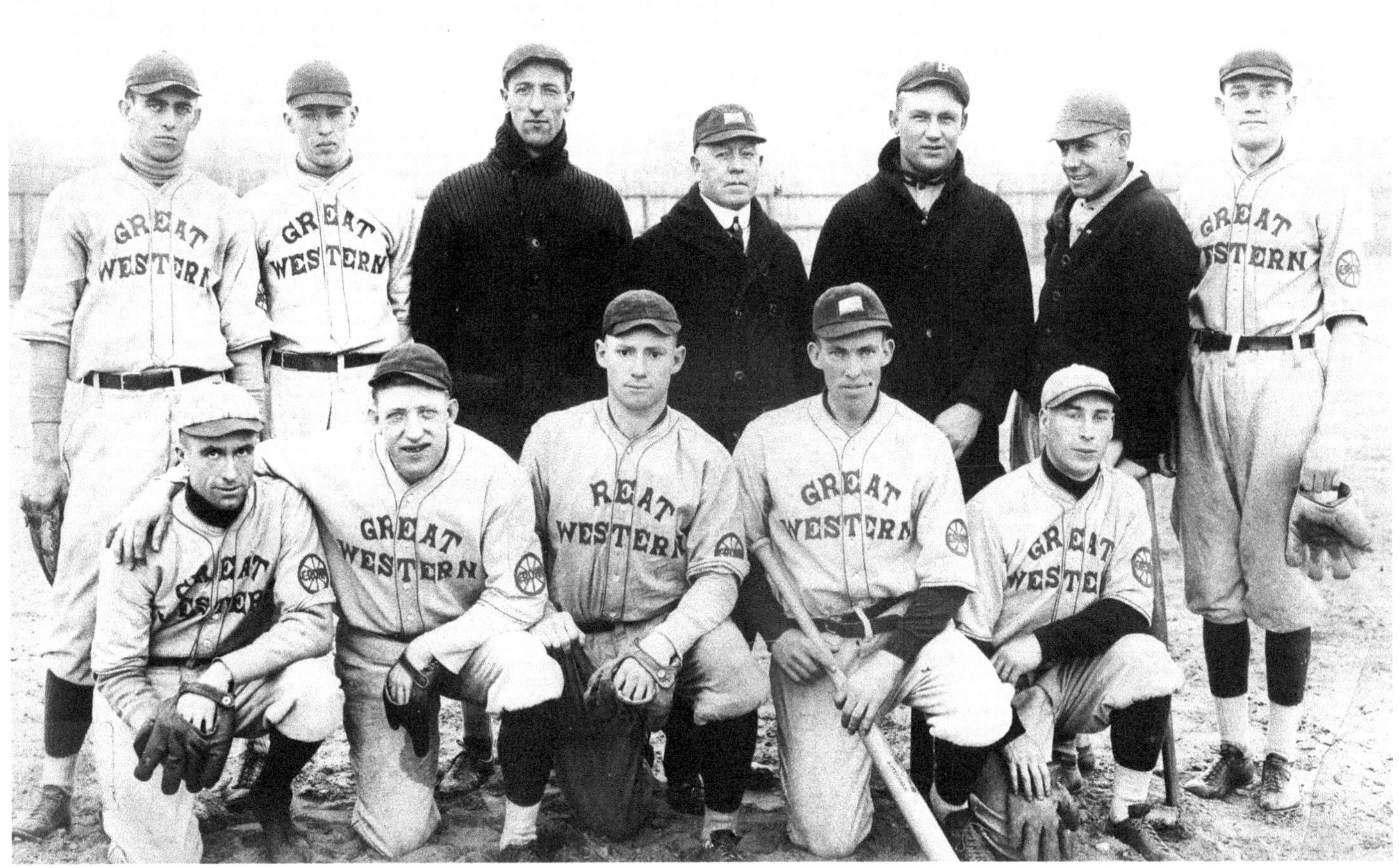

Like almost every town in America, La Porte had a semi-pro baseball team. The 1916 Great Western Bicycle factory team, however, was unusual. The second player from the left in the back row is Babe Adams, hero of the Pittsburgh Pirates' 1909 World Series championship. Born in Tipton, Adams had been released by the Pirates because of a sore shoulder but would return to the Major Leagues team in 1918.

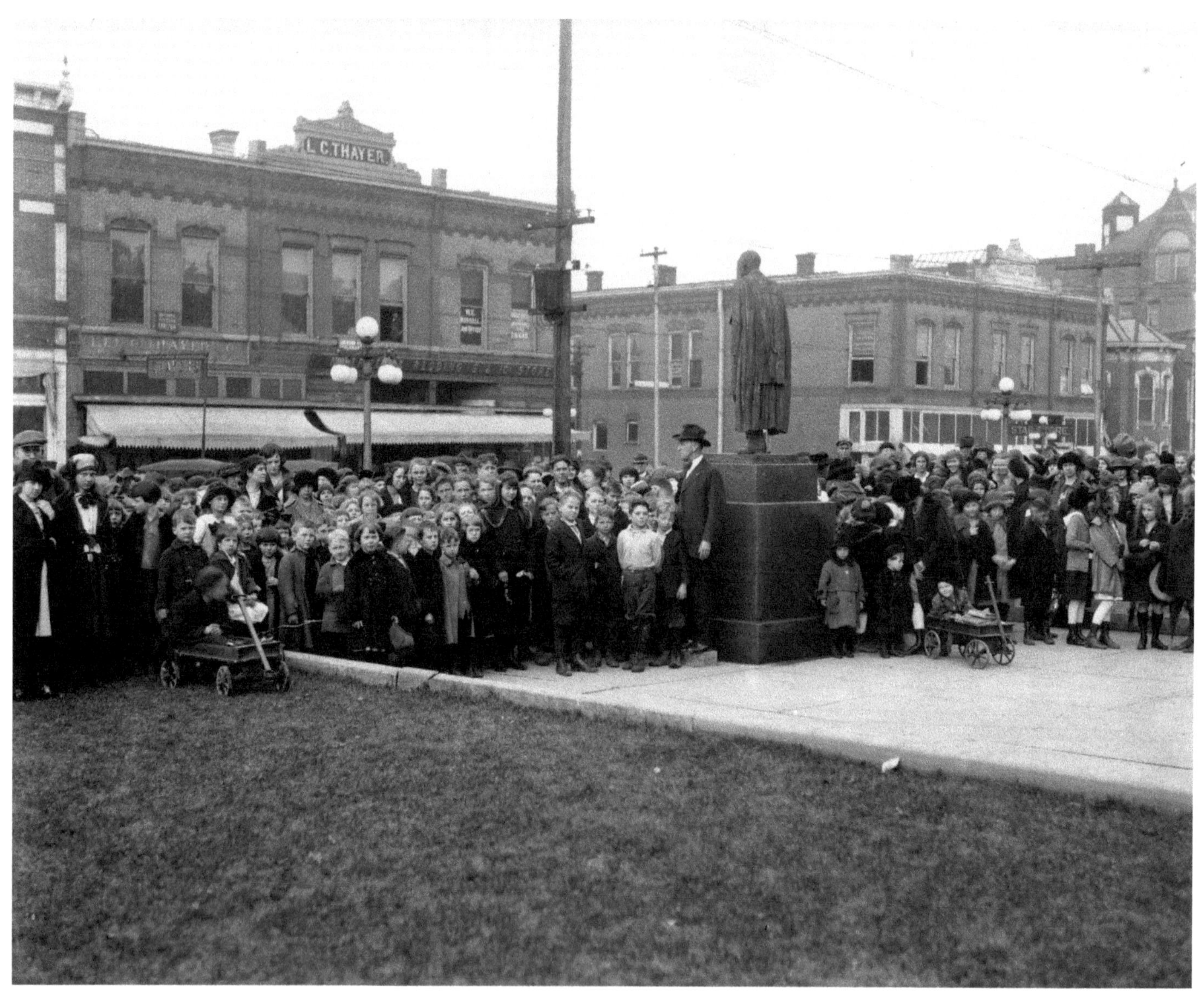

Schoolchildren gather around for the unveiling of a statue of James Whitcomb Riley, sometimes called the Children's Poet, in his hometown of Greenfield in 1918. Donations from schoolchildren across the United States helped finance the statue erected on the courthouse lawn. Another gift in the poet's memory came from 40,000 Hoosiers who financed Riley Hospital for Children in Indianapolis.

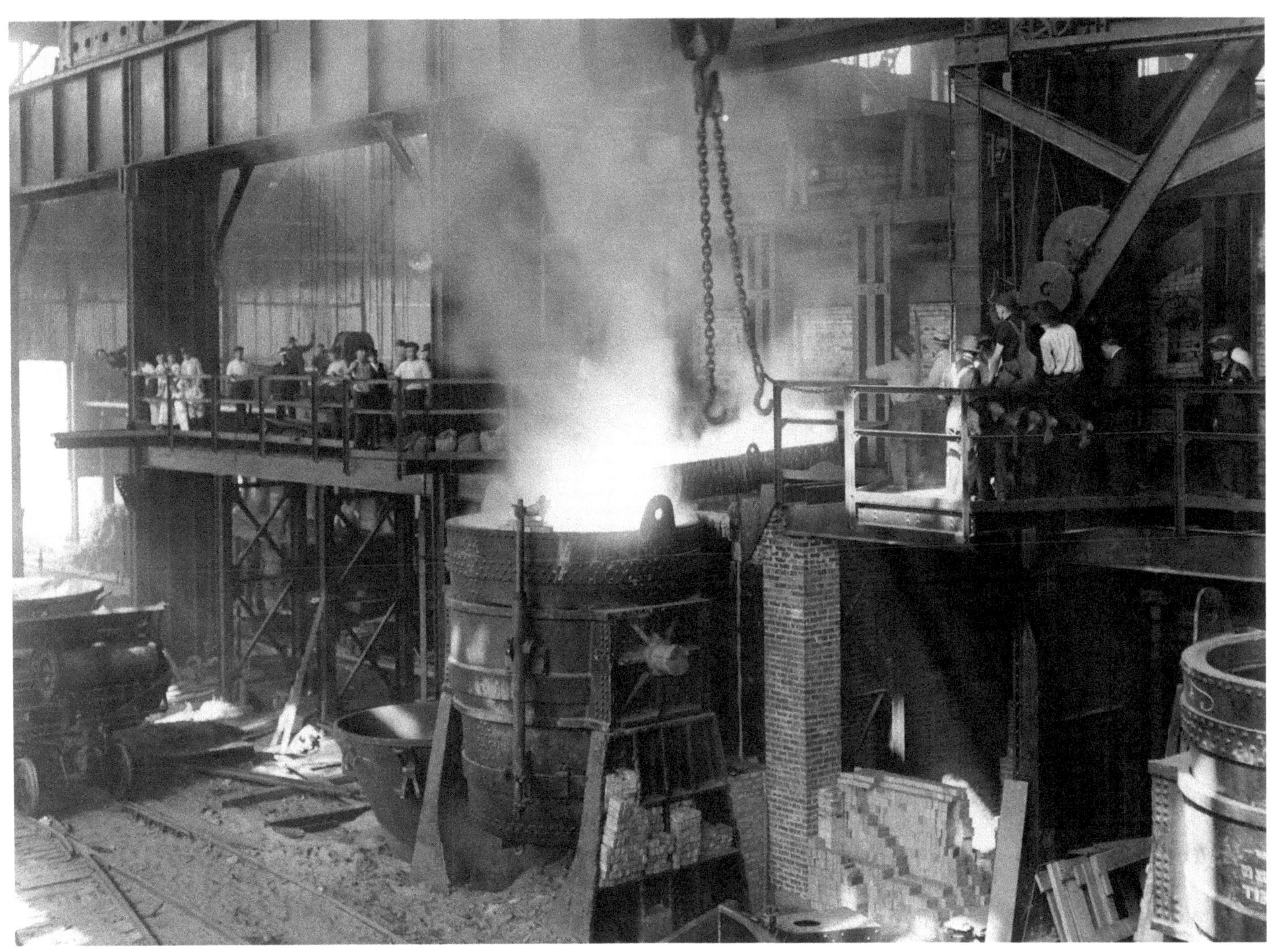

This remarkable photograph shows the "christening" of an open hearth furnace at the U.S. Steel plant in Gary. The camera was able to capture the figures of the workers as the first metal came forth on the morning of August 23, 1916.

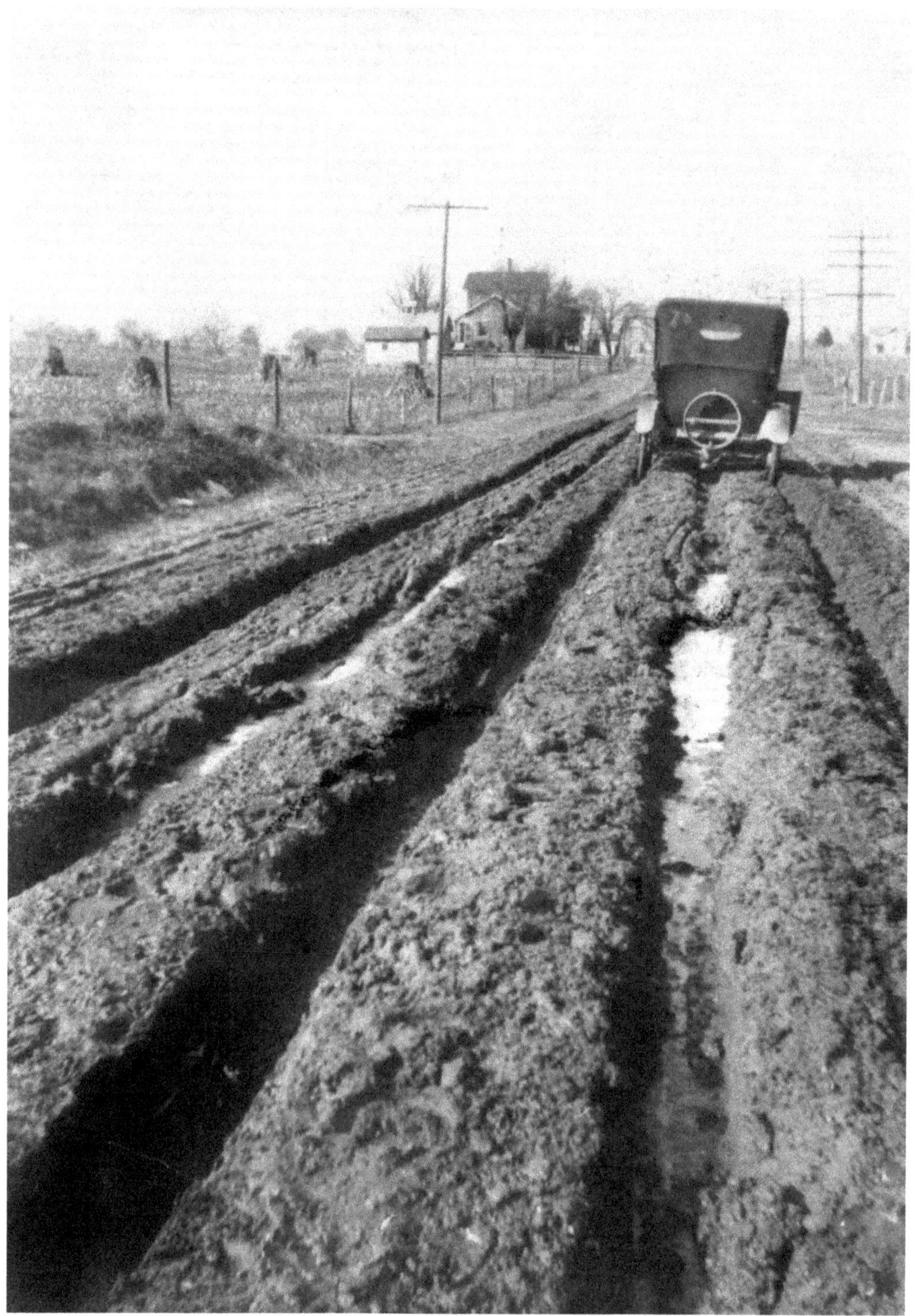

Before there were paved roads, one sure way to bury a car was to try navigating wagon wheel ruts along the seemingly bottomless glacial soils found in much of the state. With enough rainfall, country roads became sloughs rife with automobiles axle-deep and deeper and drivers ripe for conversion—back to horses if one was handy.

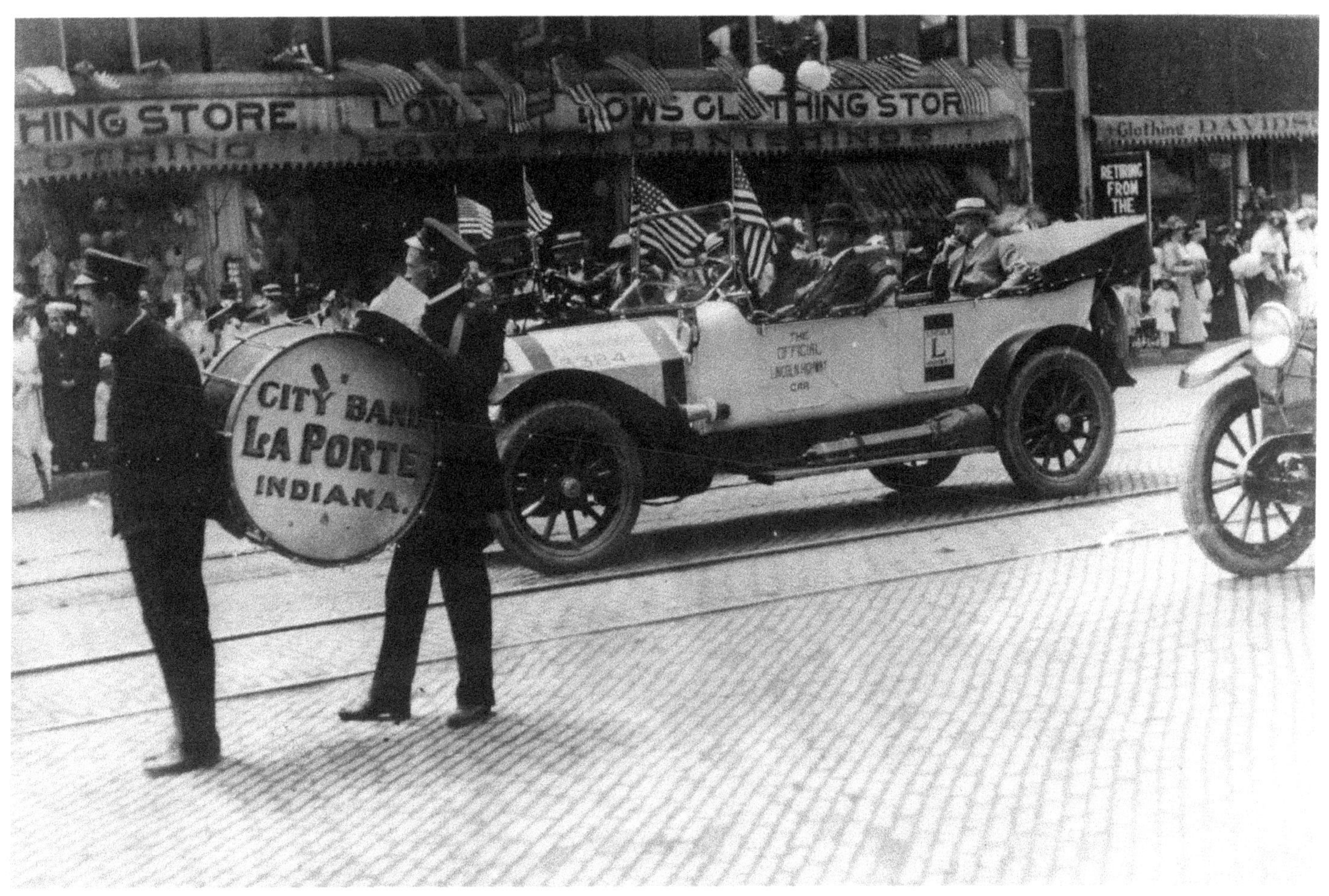

The Lincoln Highway was the dream of legendary Greensburg native Carl Fisher and others who recognized what a paved transcontinental road could mean for the country. The Indiana portion of the highway was dedicated in the summer of 1915, with parades and rallies along the way. Fisher also championed the Dixie Highway to Florida, where he successfully promoted the development of Miami Beach. In this image, he is seated in the official Lincoln Highway automobile in the La Porte parade.

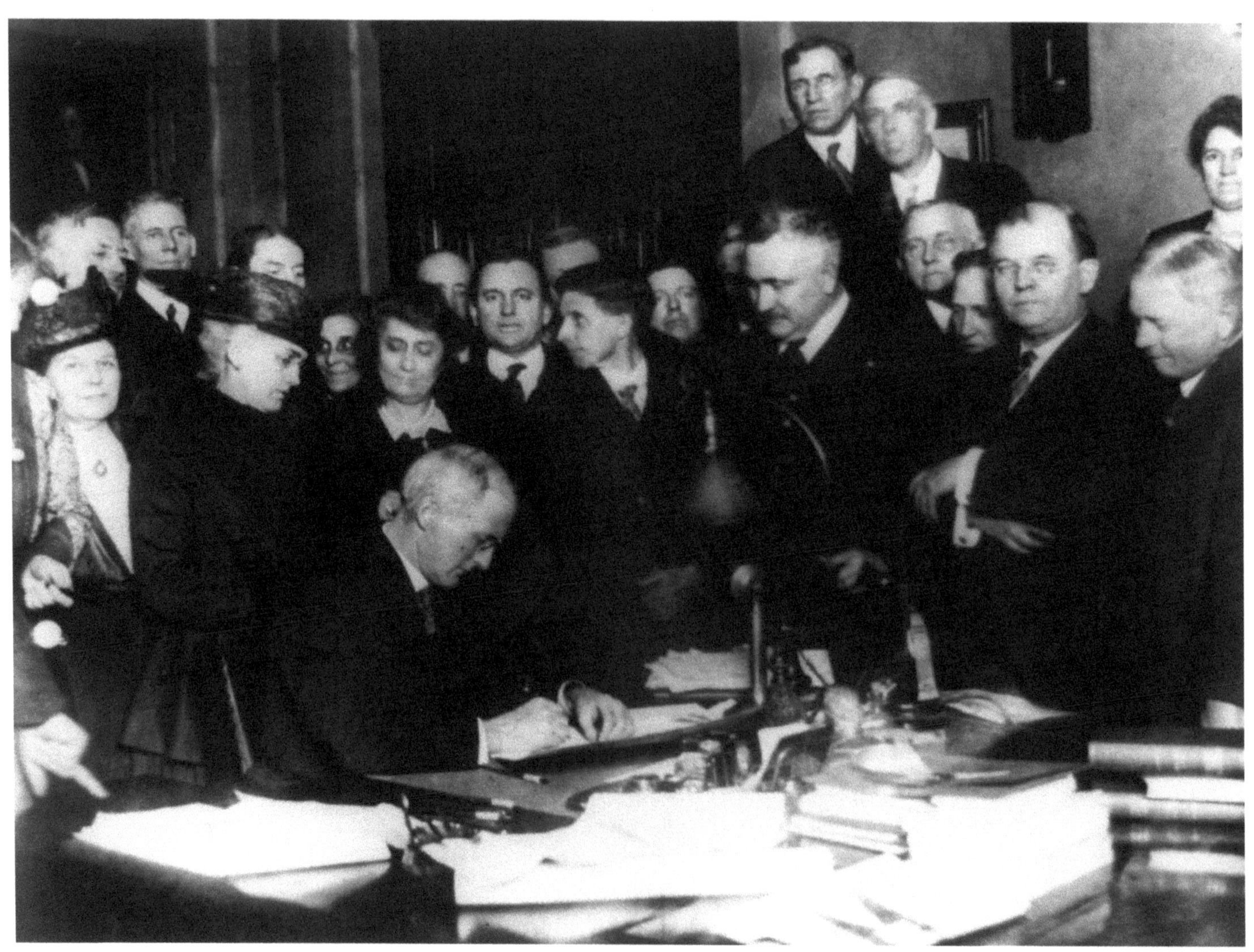

Governor James P. Goodrich signs the bill prohibiting the manufacture, sale, and distribution of alcoholic beverages in the state as a group of supporters looks on. Statewide prohibition became law on April 2, 1918, two years before national prohibition.

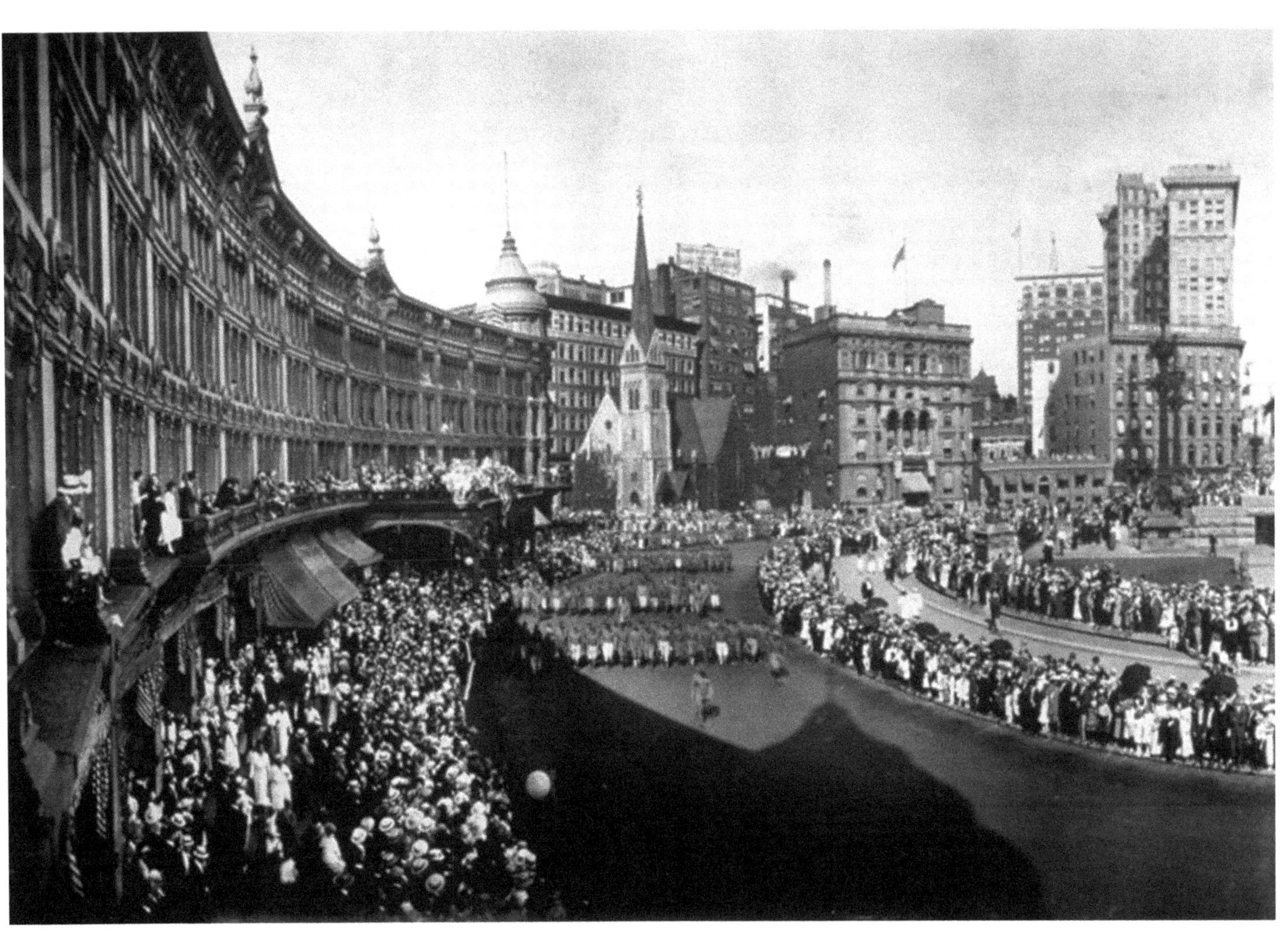

Charles F. Bretzman's 1918 panorama of the soldiers' farewell parade around Monument Circle in Indianapolis reveals the passion and patriotism sparked by U.S. entry into World War I in 1917. The role of the United States in the war, which brought the conflict to a successful conclusion for the Allies on November 11, 1918, would prove paramount.

Spectators watch warily as one of the walls of the Scott Building crumbles onto the street of downtown La Porte. The structure was being demolished to make way for construction of a building to house the First National Bank.

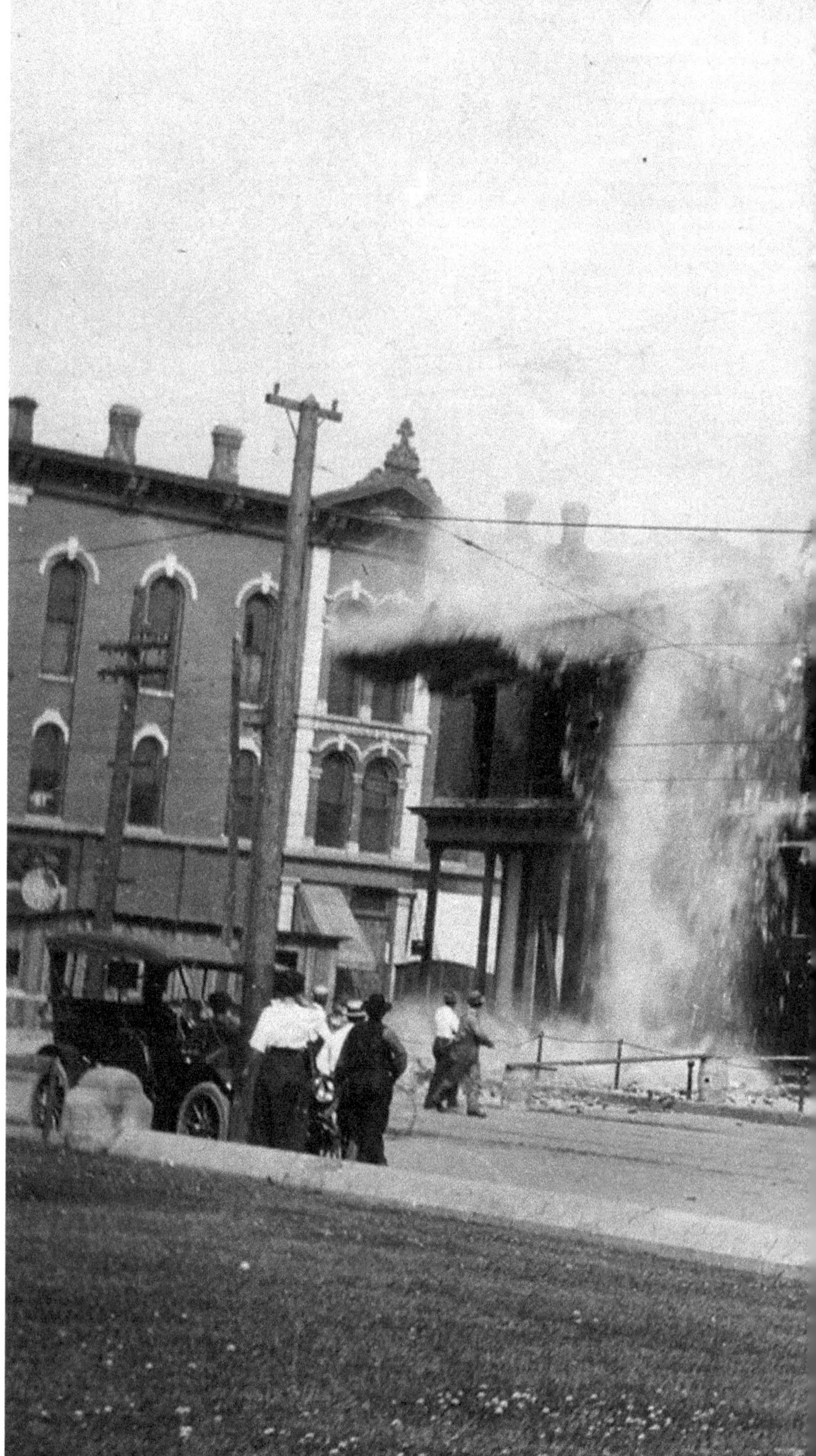

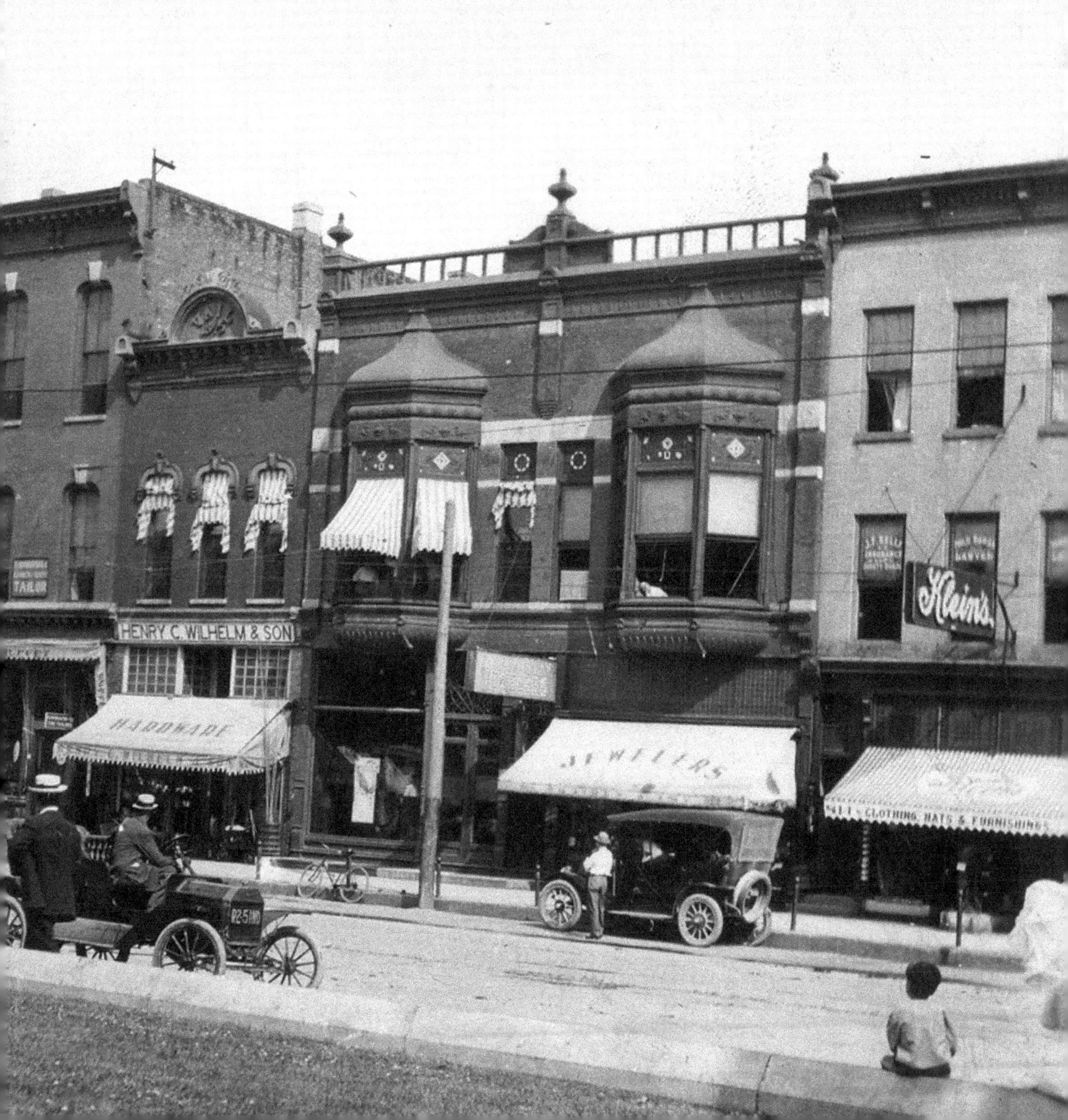
HENRY C. WILHELM & SON
HARDWARE
JEWELERS
Klein's
CLOTHING, HATS & FURNISHINGS

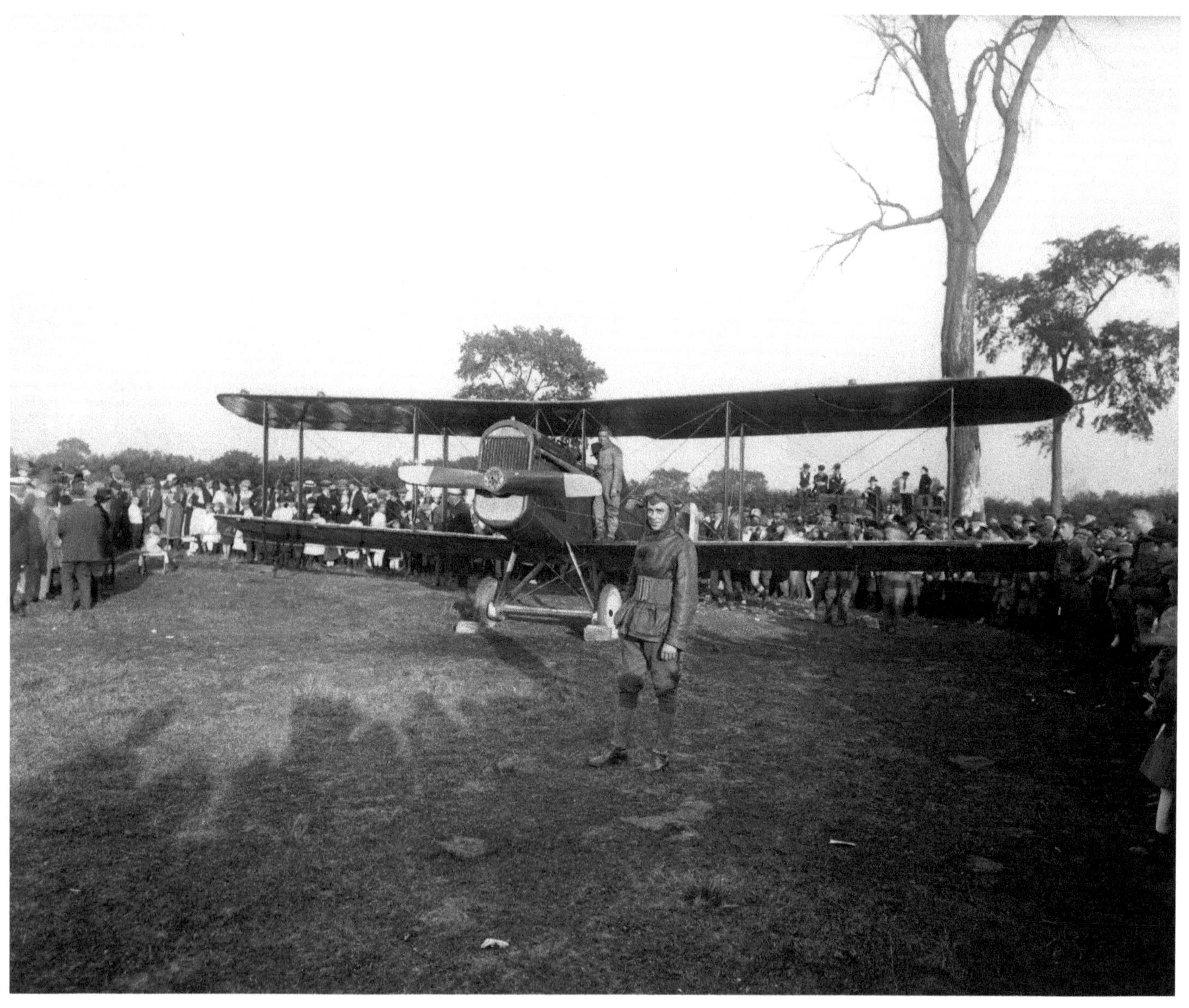

Not only was Art Smith a pioneer aviator, he was also a natural showman. Wherever the young flier from Fort Wayne traveled to do his "death loops" or nighttime phosphorescent "skywriting," he attracted great crowds. Smith would die in an airplane crash in 1926, the fate of more than one barnstorming daredevil of the era.

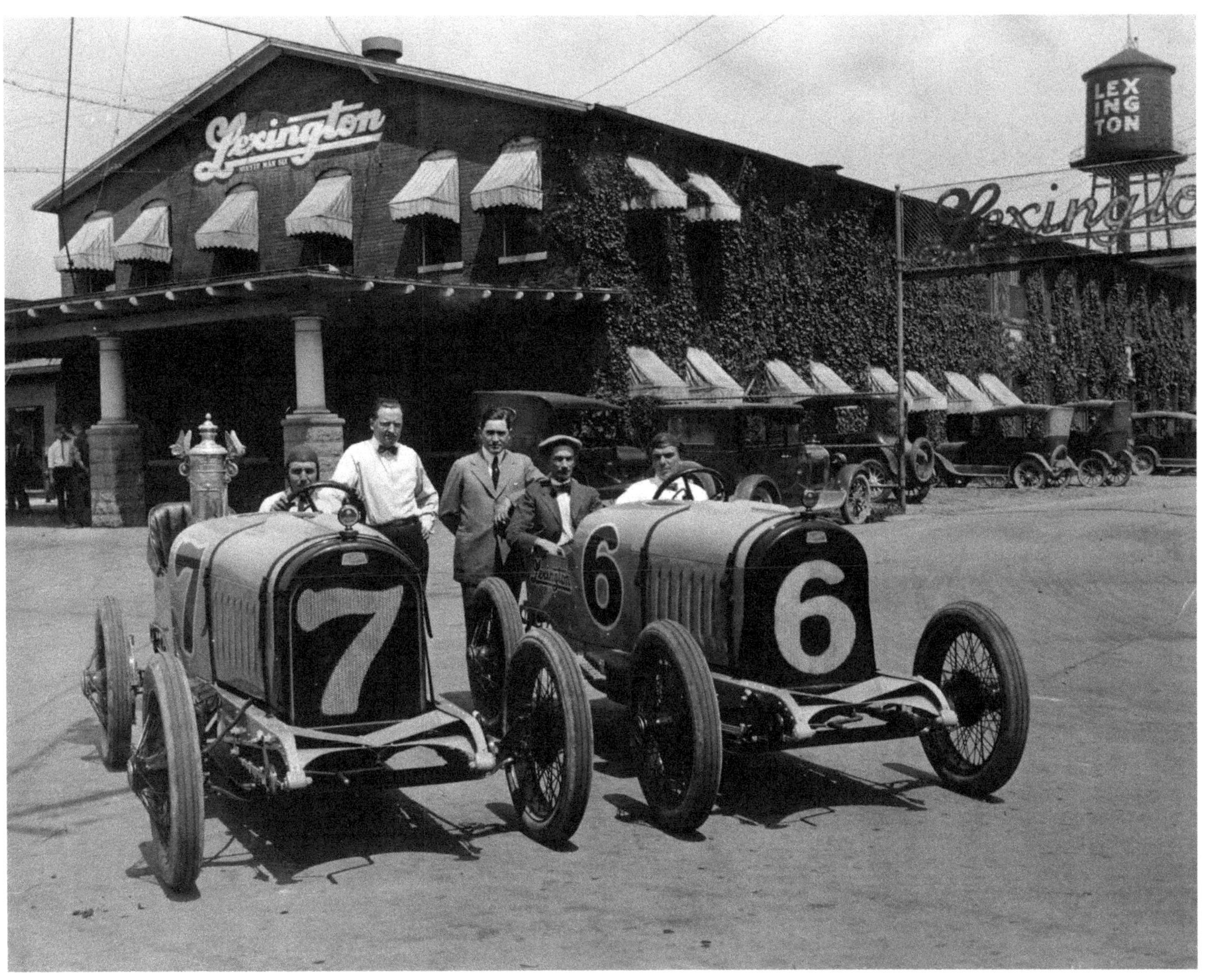

The Lexington Motor Company in Connersville proudly displays its winning entries in the 1920 Pikes Peak International Hill Climb. Otto Loesche won the race in car No. 7 with a finish time of 22 minutes, 25 seconds. Albert Cline in car No. 6 took second, 5.4 seconds behind the winner.

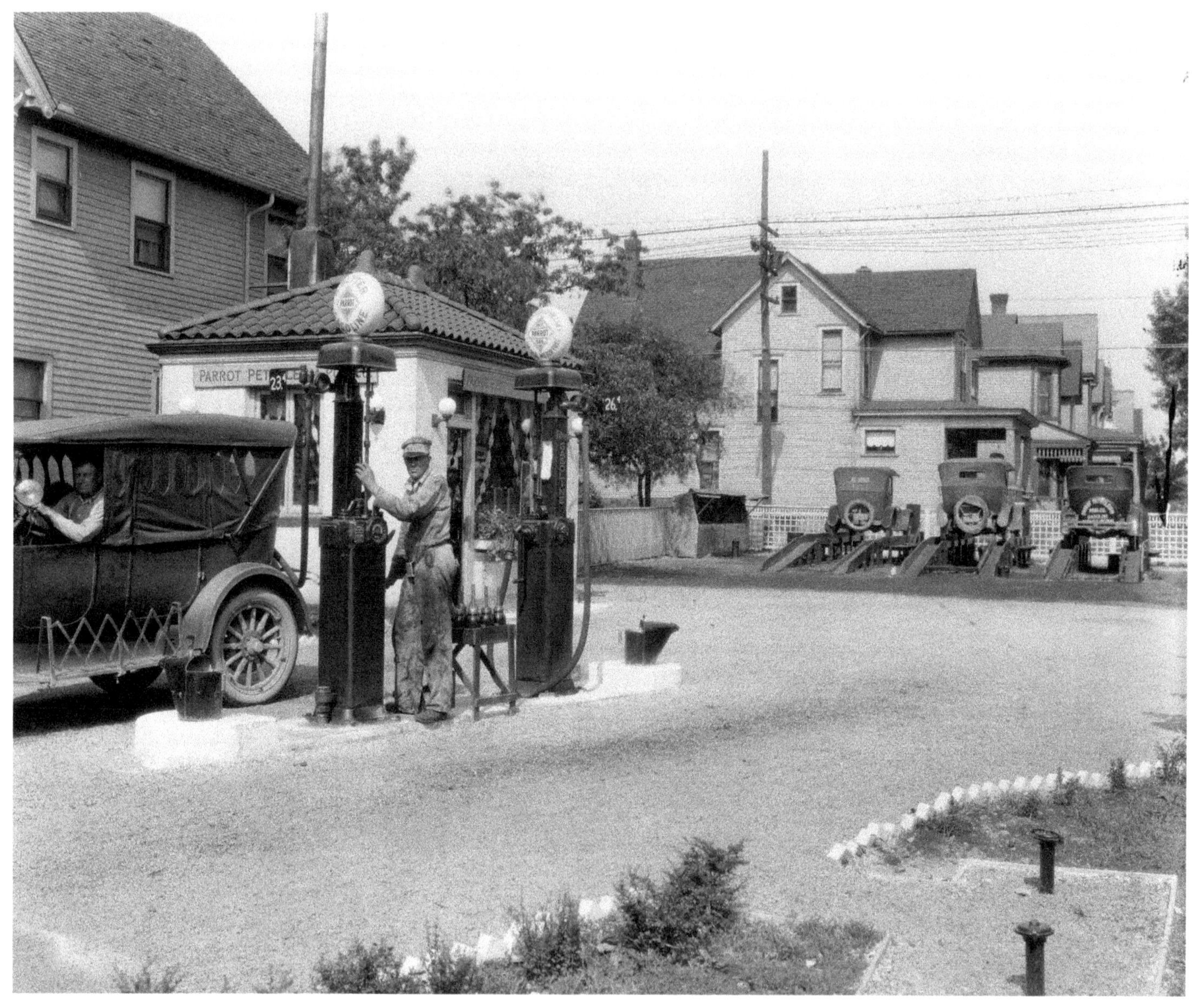

Although Parrot Petroleum in Fort Wayne sported modern gasoline pumps, its ability to make repairs may have depended on the weather, as the three automobiles at right indicate. It would be a few years before larger stations were designed with one or more service pits, so that an oil change or work beneath a car could be accomplished indoors. Early filling stations often featured whimsical architecture, frequently including terra cotta roofing.

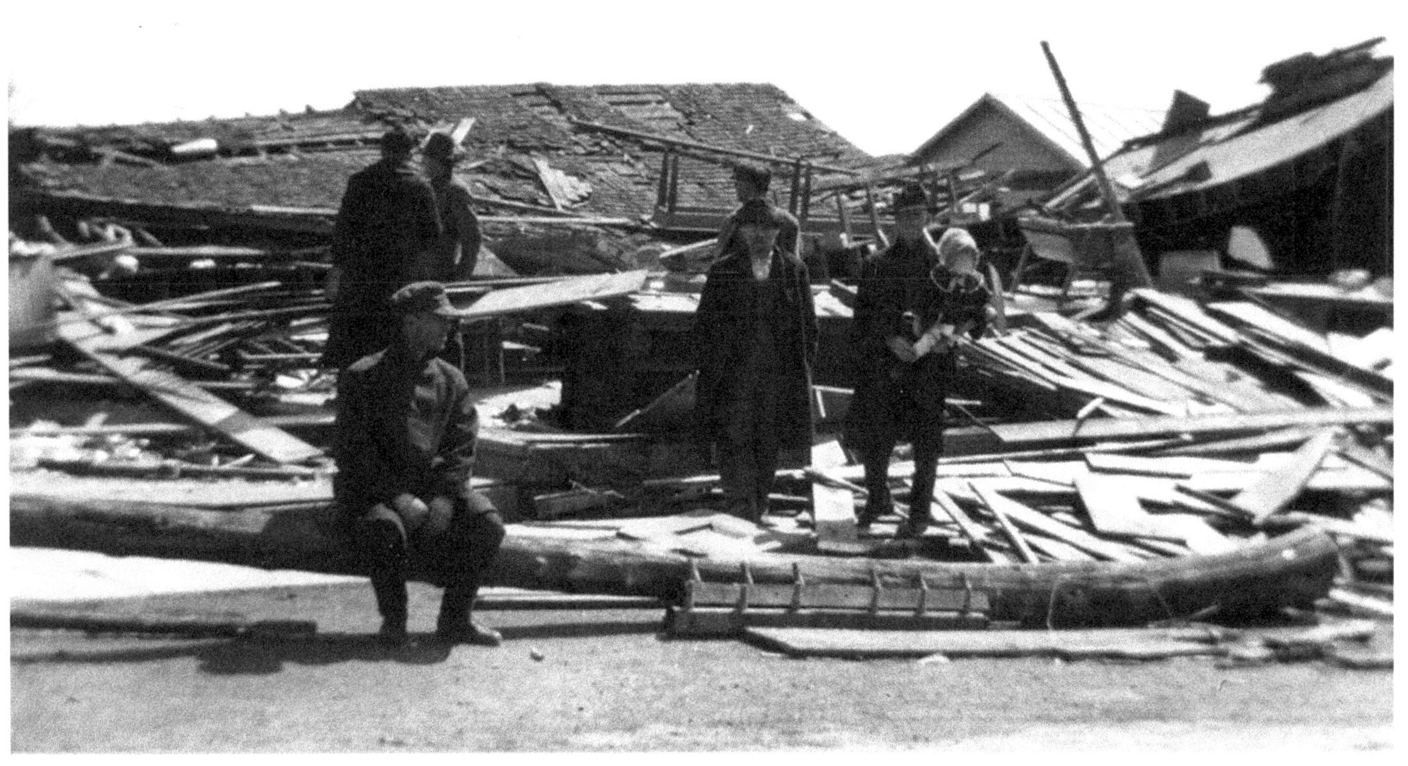

A tornado swept through Townley in northeastern Indiana on March 28, 1920, causing widespread destruction. Townspeople survey the destruction in front of what had been the school building for the community's children.

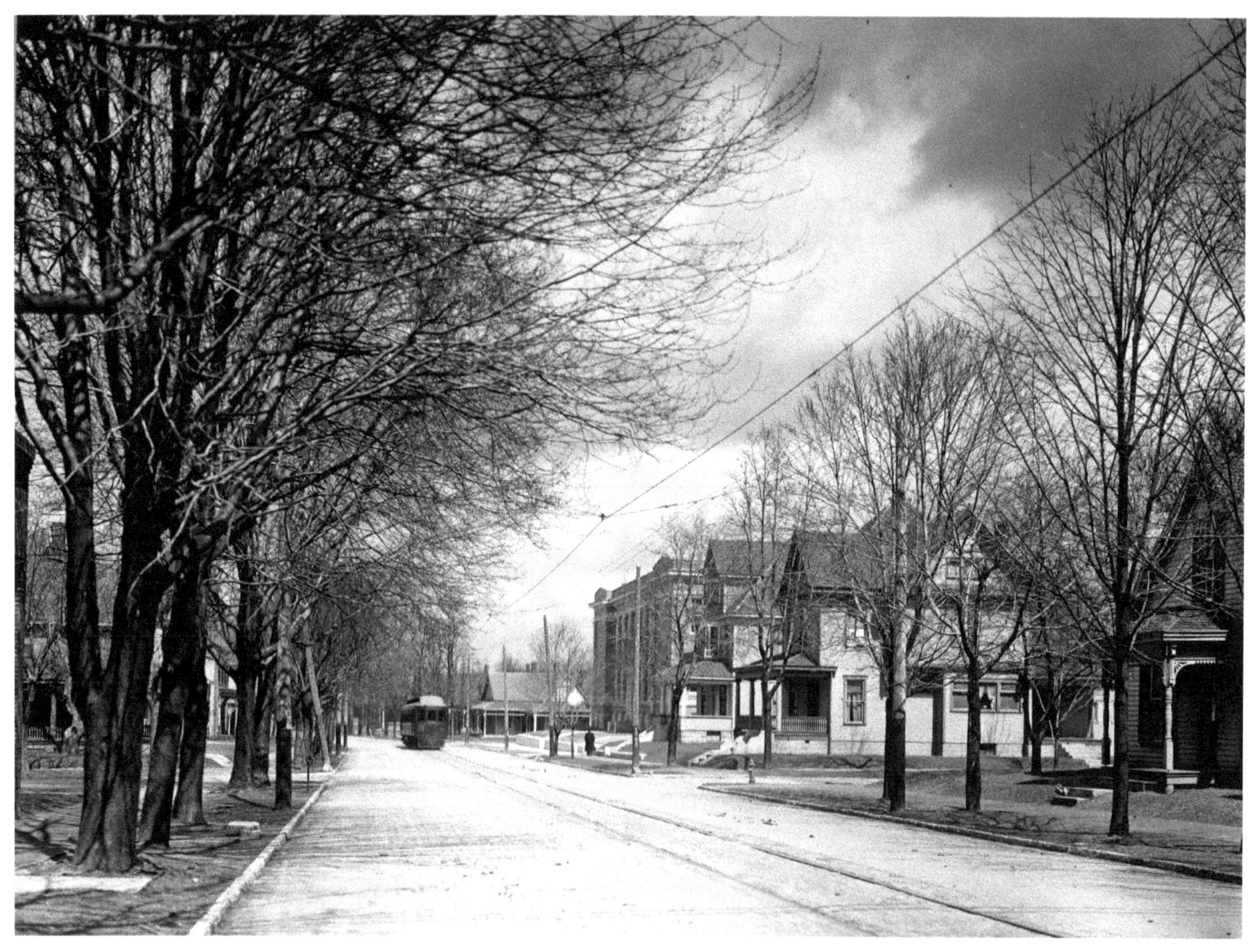

A wintry sky highlights the tranquil scene of an interurban plying its way along one of Lebanon's tree-lined residential streets around 1920.

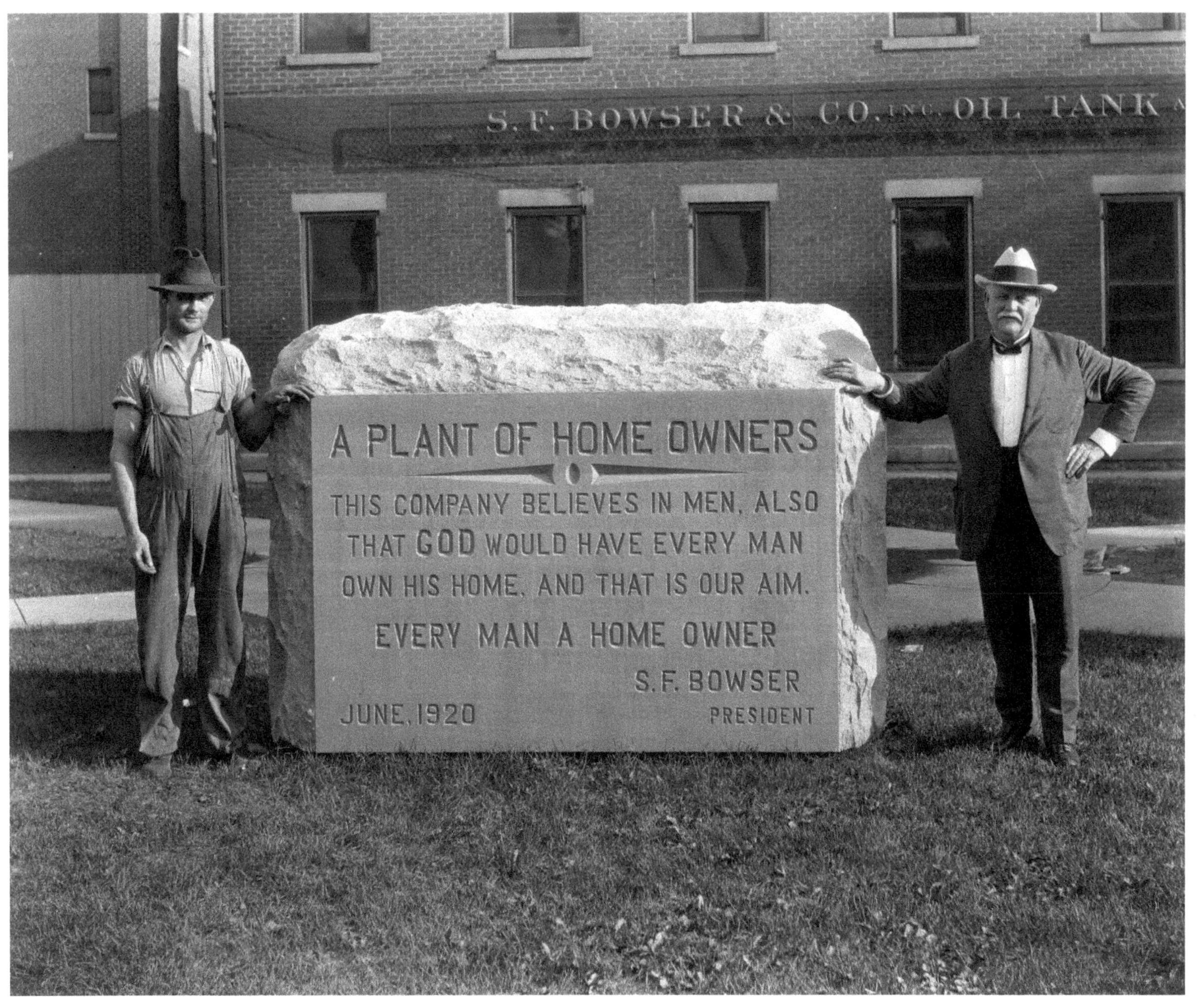

Sylvanus F. Bowser, at right, made his fortune in Fort Wayne during the Gilded Age with the invention of the self-measuring oil pump, the forerunner of the gasoline pump. He also had regard for Americans trading their services for a paycheck, opening a bank to help them afford their own homes, as this stone monument in front of Bowser Pump Works attests in 1920.

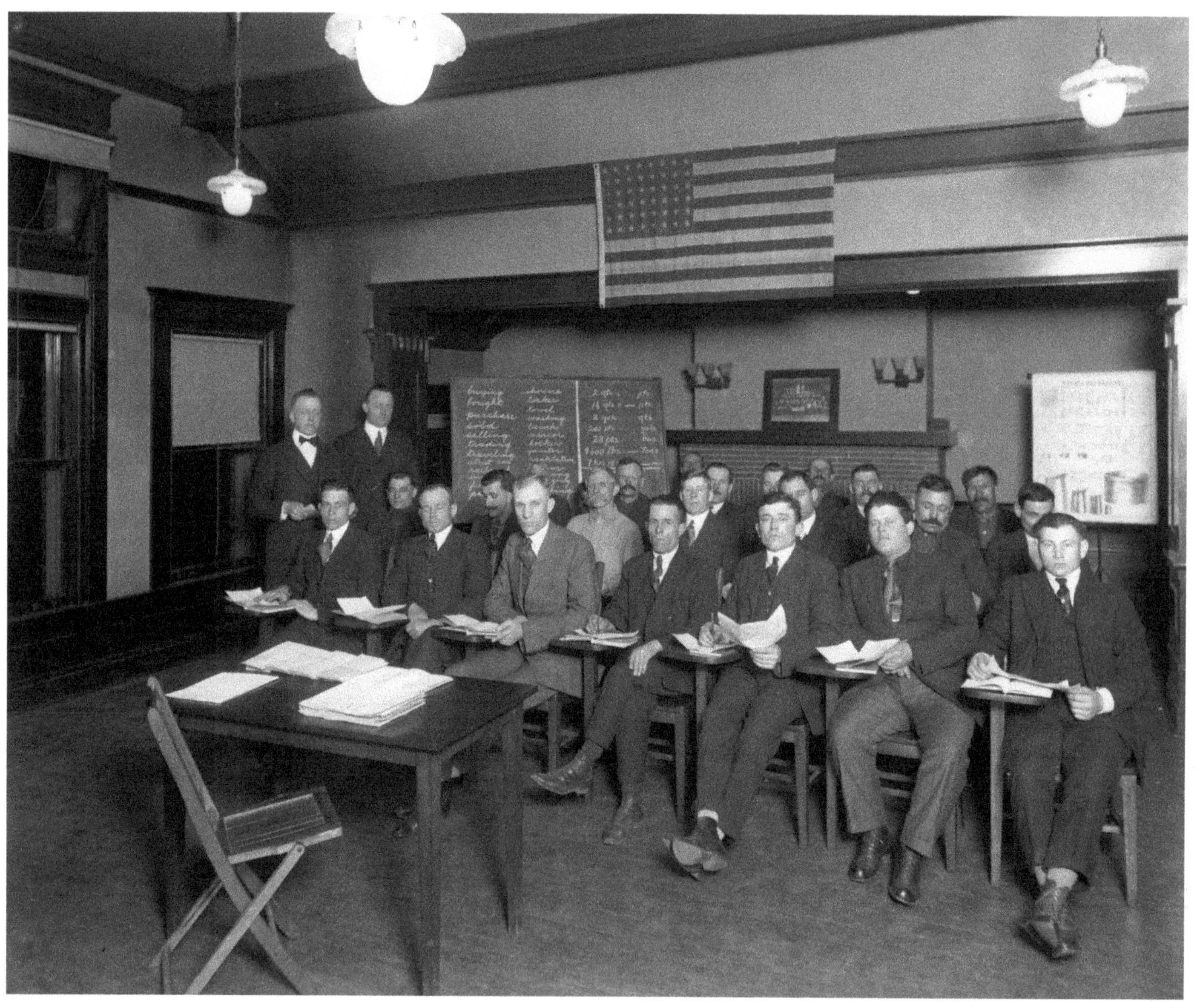

The steel industry in Gary attracted thousands of immigrants from eastern and southern Europe. By 1920, Gary had tripled its population to more than 50,000 residents, and by 1921, Americanization classes were mandatory for immigrants working at the steel mills.

Good Times, Bad Times, and War

(1921–1945)

The opening for *A Tale of Two Cities* is as apropos for this period as it was when Charles Dickens wrote it in 1859: There was wisdom and foolishness, belief and incredulity, hope and despair, the worst and the best. The end of the War to End All Wars brought high hopes, dampened somewhat by Prohibition. There was tremendous growth on Wall Street, on Main Street, in the cities and towns, all devastated by the onset of the Great Depression. There was the comfort of America First and protectionism, torpedoed by Germany, Italy, and Japan in World War II. "It was the season of Light, it was the season of Darkness, it was the spring of hope, it was the winter of despair," as Dickens wrote.

Indiana's golden age of literature was ending as the new era was beginning. James Whitcomb Riley's buoyant verse was succeeded by Theodore Dreiser's novels, noted for what was then considered dire realism in literature. Much of Indiana's artistic repertoire shifted to the likes of Cole Porter, whose most productive period was the 1930s. Other actors, composers, and entertainers native to the state gained national recognition, including Hoagy Carmichael, Carole Lombard, Red Skelton, James Dean, and Irene Dunne.

The numbers of people leaving the farms for work in the cities was on the upswing. The 1930 census showed that for the first time there were five cities in Indiana with populations of more than 100,000 residents. There were also successful innovations in industry. Miles Medical Company in Elkhart, for example, released a new bubbly pain reliever called Alka-Seltzer in 1931.

Perhaps the most difficult place to be was on the farm. Great changes in agriculture were taking place, but little of the impact reached small farmers. During the depression, about one in nine American farms had electricity, with slightly fewer rural areas in Indiana having access to it.

With the onset of World War II, Indiana changed again. Leading cities like Evansville, Fort Wayne, Gary, and Indianapolis became centers for military production. Evansville, for example, produced naval landing craft and P-47 fighter planes around the clock during the war. There were 250,000 Americans from Indiana who served in the military, more than 10,000 of whom died in service to the nation.

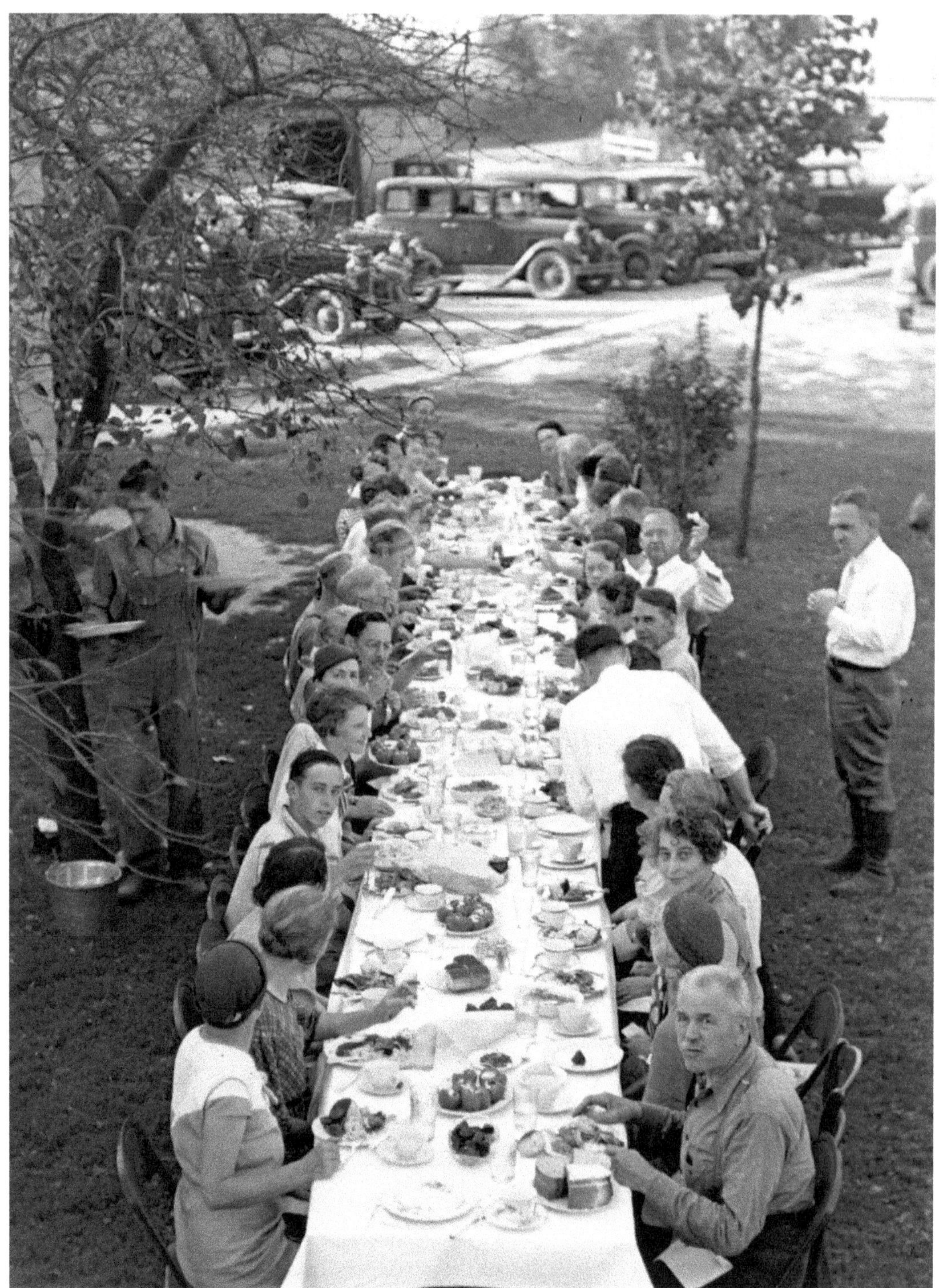

An invigorating day of exploring the Indiana dunes ends with a stylish picnic for the Prairie Club. Founded in 1908, the group began as a way for Chicagoans to escape the city. For more than a century it has sponsored hikes and joined in conservation efforts in Cook County, Illinois, and the Indiana Dunes State Park and National Lakeshore.

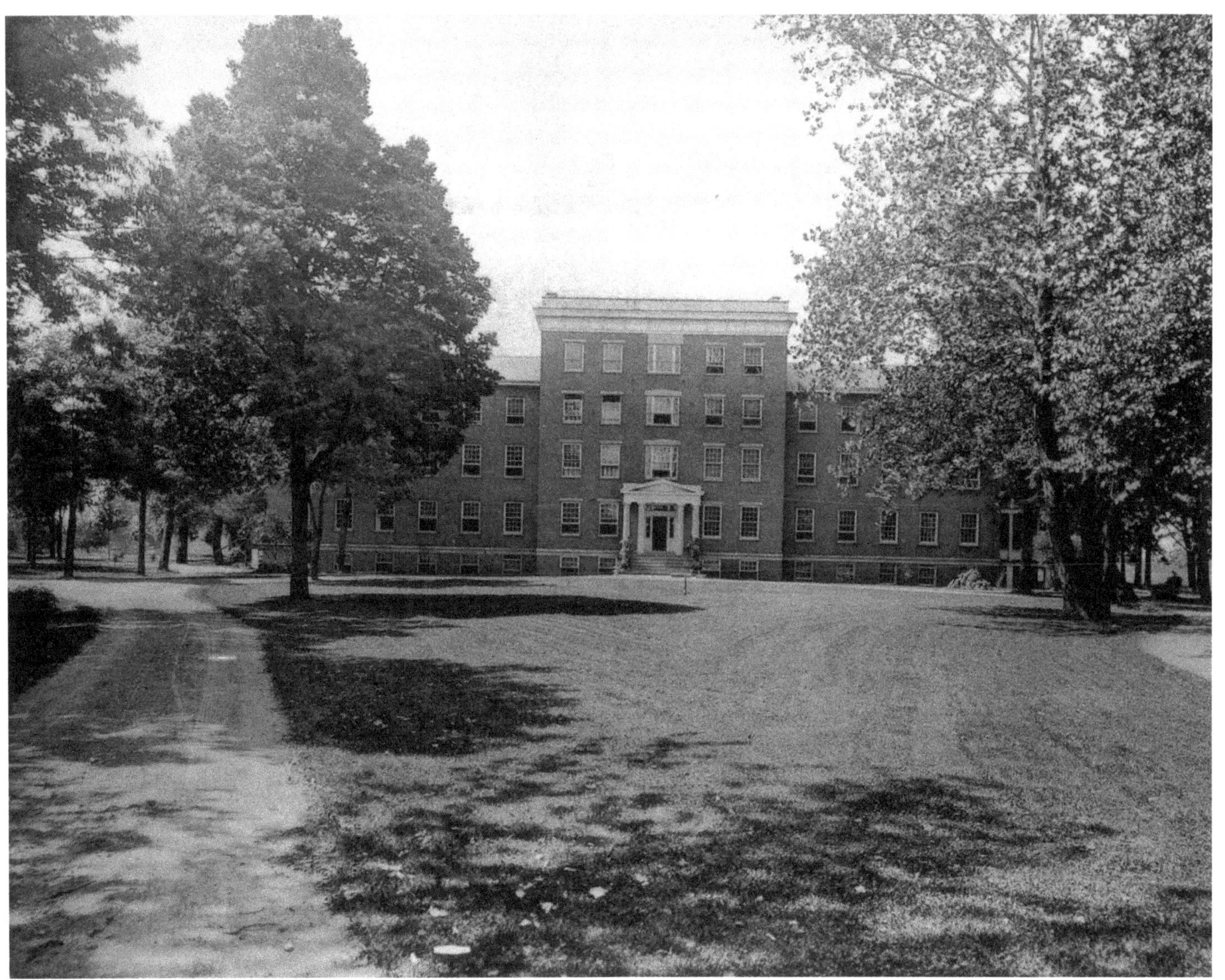

It took 16 years for Earlham Hall to be completed in 1855 at the Friends' boarding school, which became known as Earlham College in Richmond. It served as a dormitory until the 1950s when it was torn down and succeeded by a new Earlham Hall whose exterior appearance looked almost identical to the original.

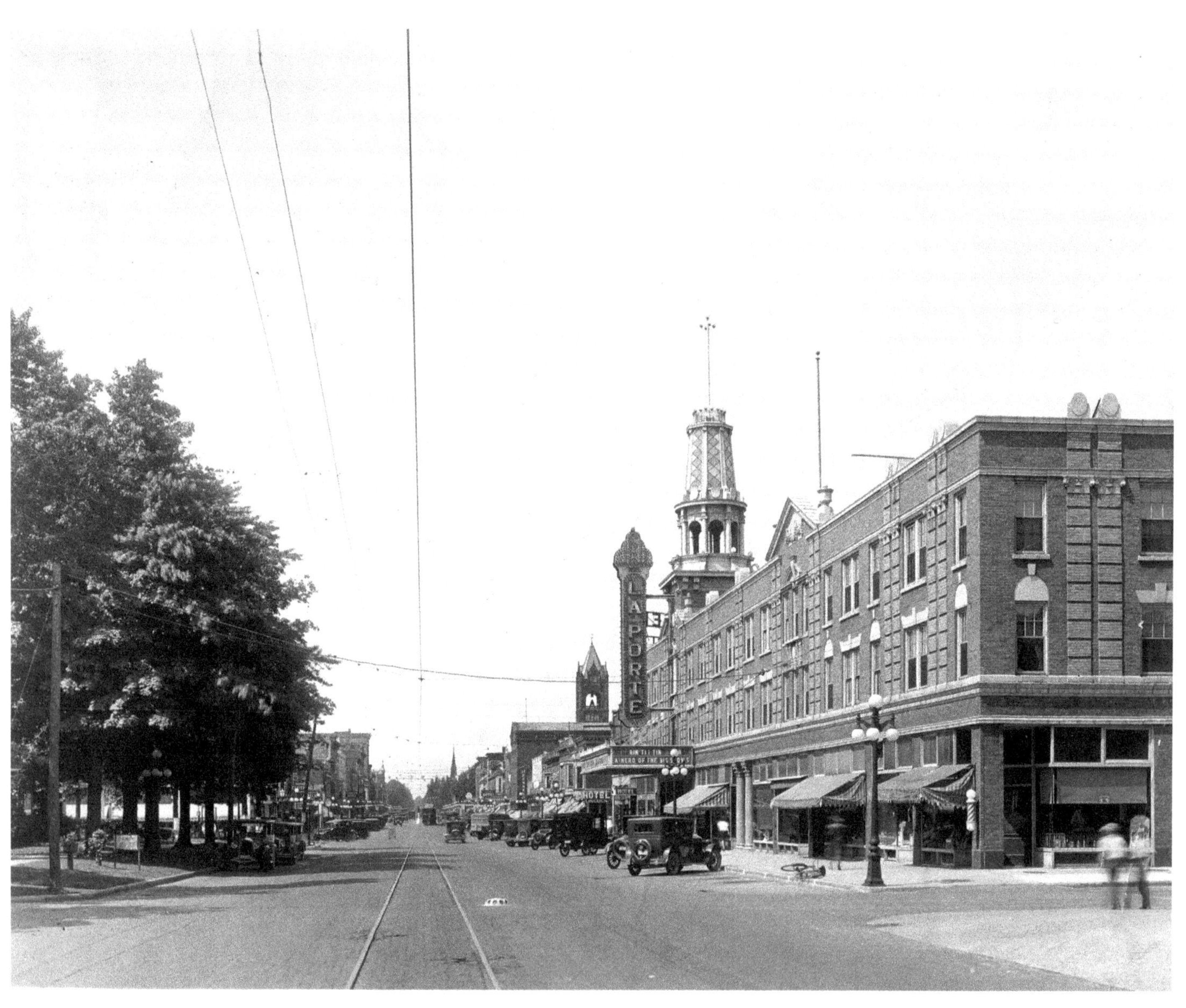

The La Porte Theatre ushered in a new era for the city when it opened in 1920. In addition to the 1,300-seat theater, the building included apartments, the Lincoln Hotel, offices, and commercial spaces.

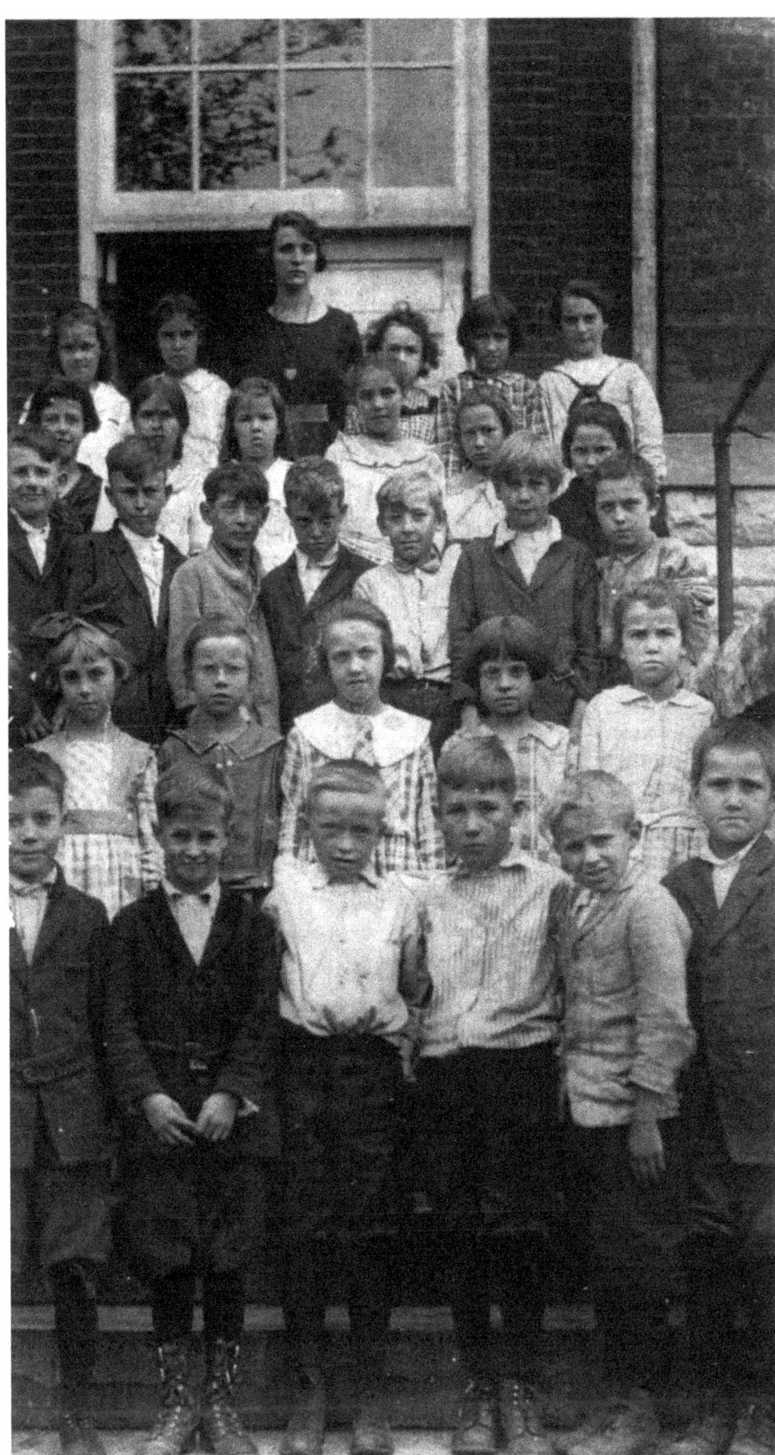

This teacher and her young scholars pose for a class portrait in Brazil, Indiana, in the 1920s. Not every child of the Wabash Valley would be remembered as a model student. Jimmy Hoffa and John Dillinger both came of age in the region before pursuing their separate rendezvous with infamy. And for derring-do not afoul of the law, there were other talents. Eyewitness accounts of John's affable cousin Ken Dillinger describe his fearless exploits meant to amuse friends: a climb to the top of a telephone pole, topped at the tip by standing on his head. At home in the heights, Ken would become a skilled crop-dusting pilot in service to American farms.

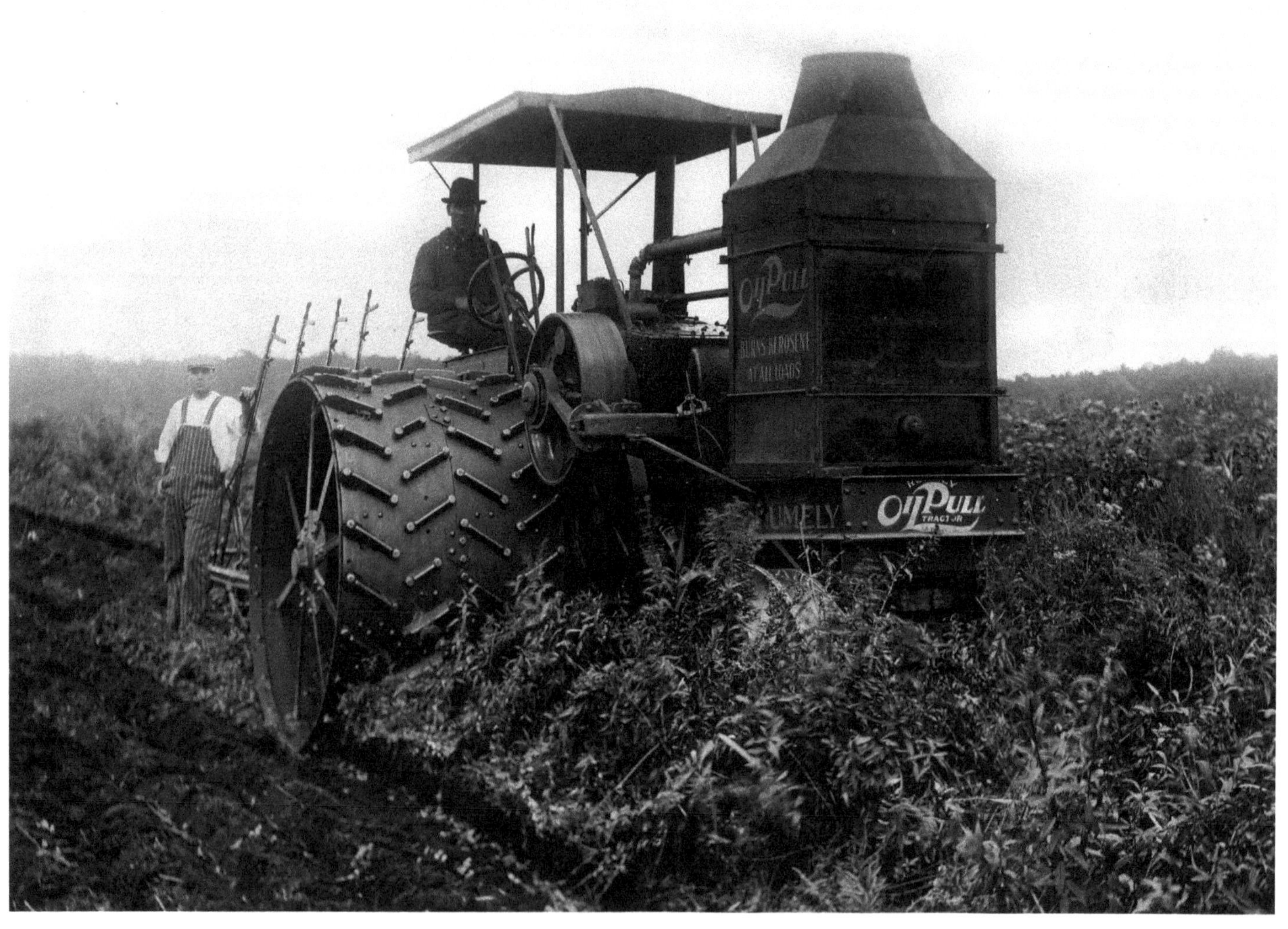

The Rumely Oil Pull was a tractor credited with opening the Grand Kankakee Marsh to farming. The tractor, shown here pulling a gang plow through the fertile soil of the marshland, is recognizable for its characteristic cooling tower, which relied on oil, not water. The early models were powered by kerosene, with a special carburetor that used water to control the combustion. Started by Meinrad and Jacob Rumely, the success of the Rumely Company contributed significantly to La Porte's development, where Rumely tractors and equipment were manufactured.

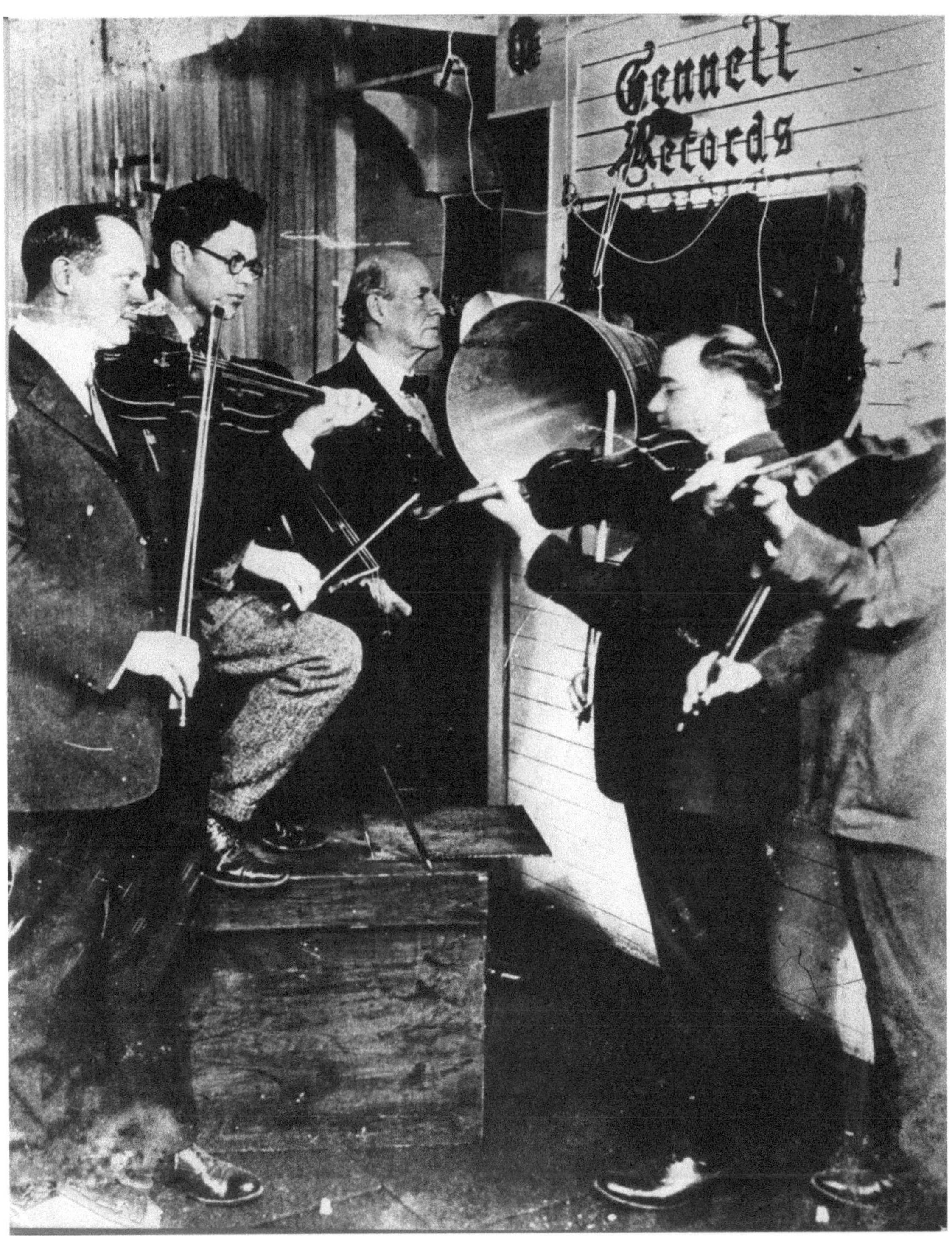

It was at Gennett Records in Richmond that William Jennings Bryan preserved a historical piece of oratory in June 1921. Bryan is shown speaking into one horn while four musicians play into another to make a recording of his "Cross of Gold" speech that won him fame and the 1896 Democratic presidential nomination. Gennett Records was renowned as "the birthplace of recorded jazz."

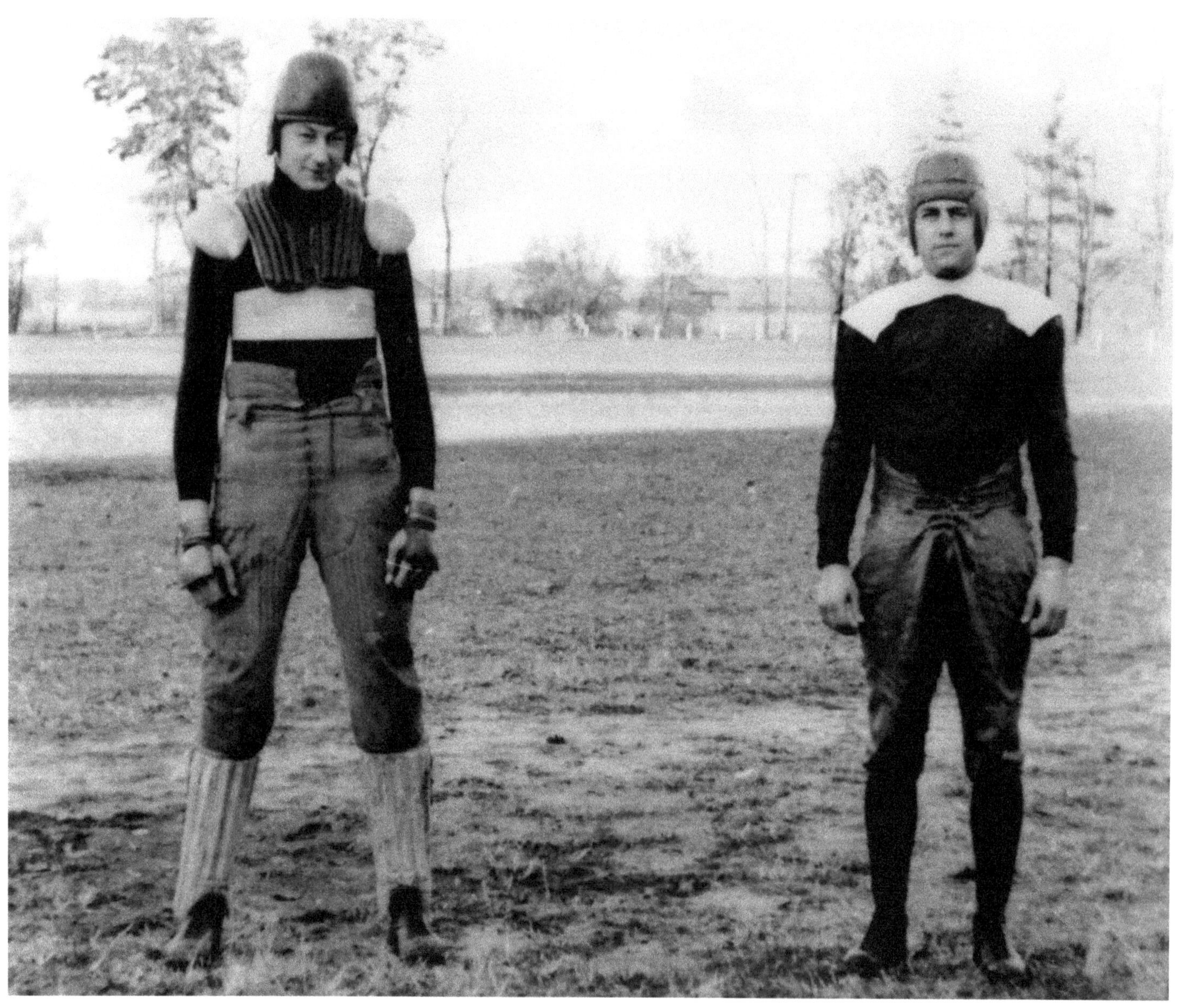

Years of injuries on the gridiron led to calls for protective uniforms for football players. The changes are evident in this photograph of one Notre Dame player wearing gear from the 1880s while another displays the more padded uniform of the 1920s. Notre Dame University is located in South Bend.

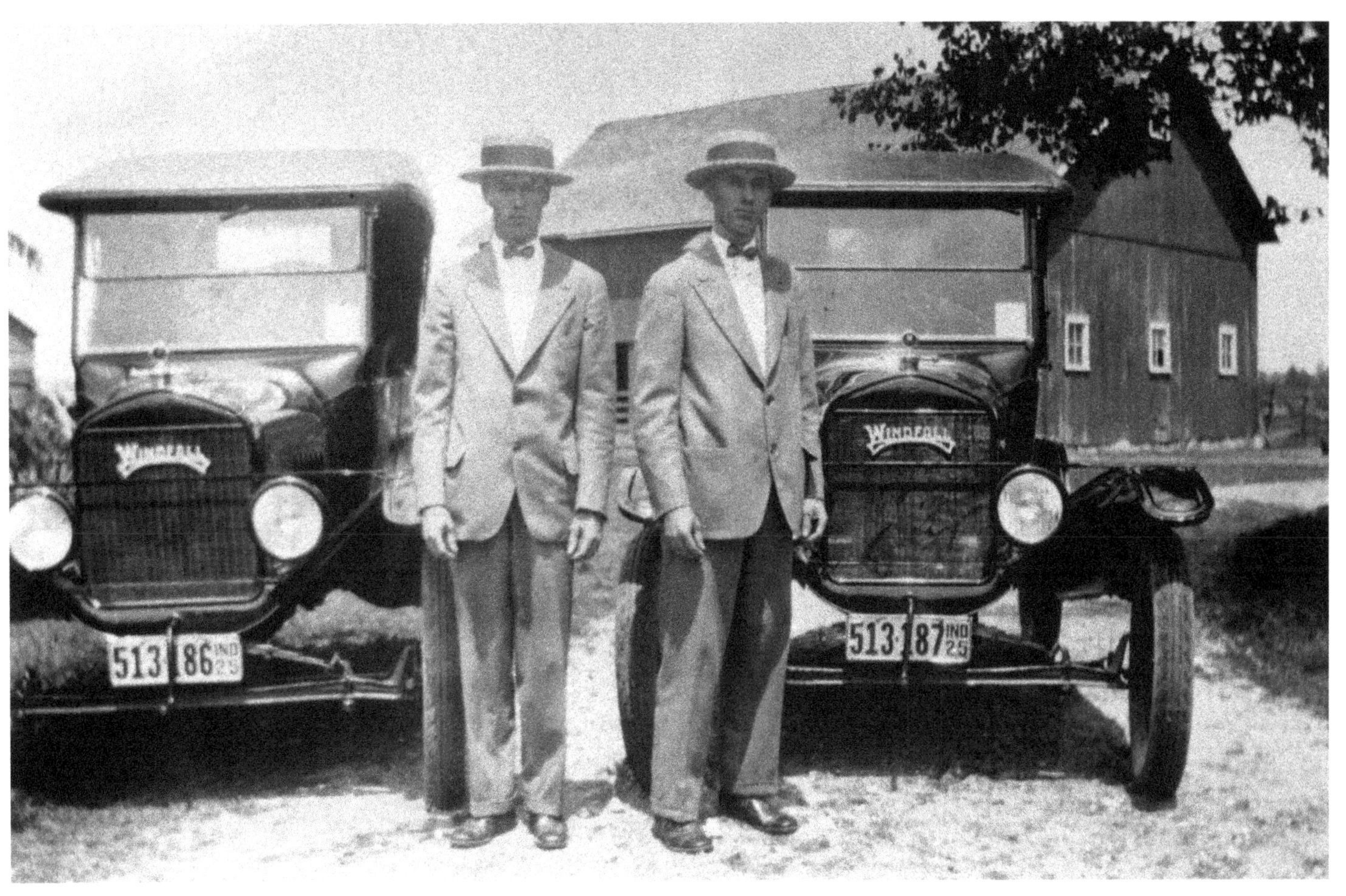

If you lived in the Wildcat Township town of Windfall in the 1920s, wore clothes like your twin brother's, and had a sequentially numbered license plate, what kind of car would you drive?

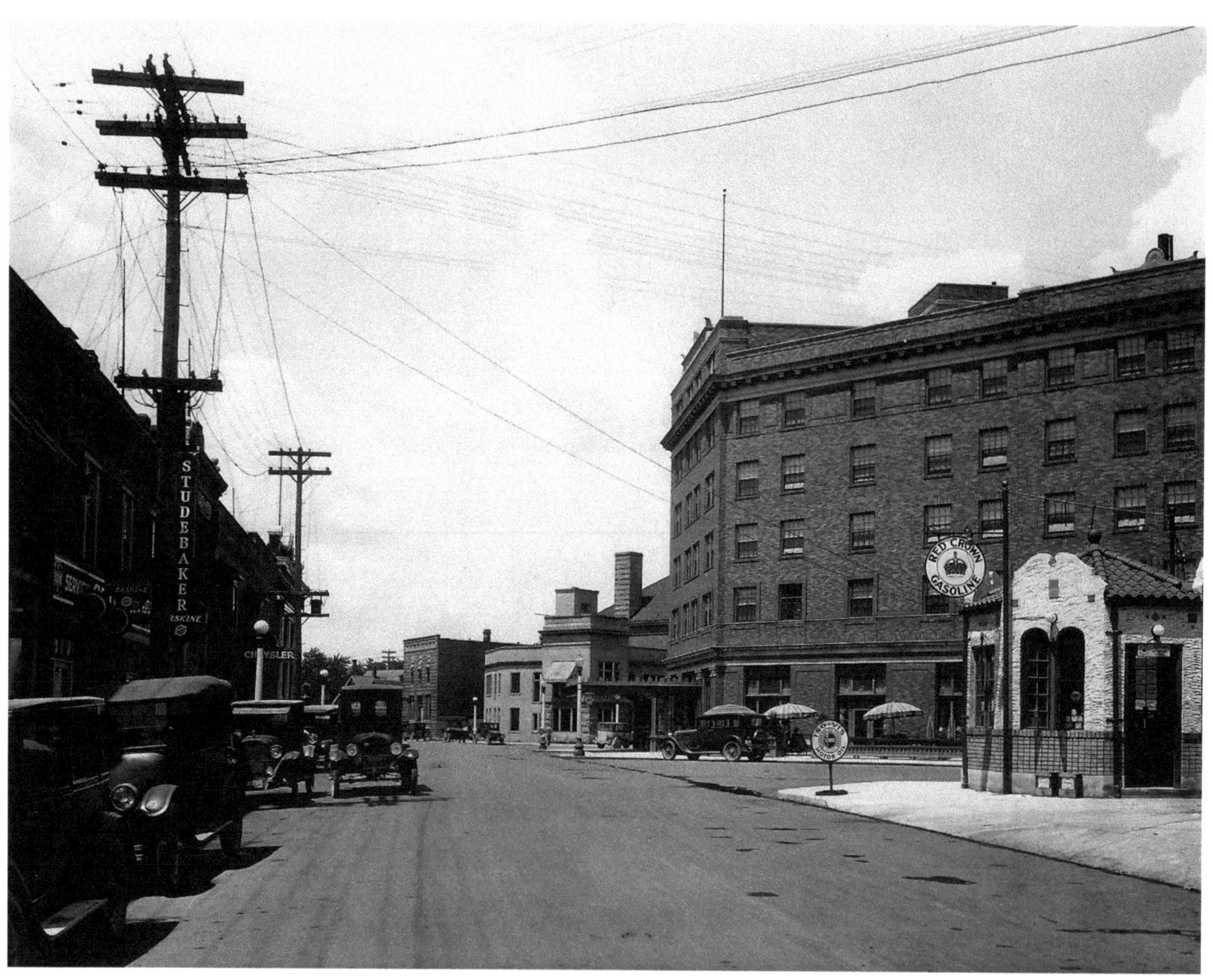

The LaFontaine Hotel, on the right, was considered "the finest hotel of its size in the United States" when it opened in Huntington in October 1925. It contained 120 rooms, a grand lobby with Moorish-style arched ceilings, electric elevators, reading rooms, a tea room, a soda fountain, a barbershop, and an "inditing room" where one could write a speech or letter or dictate it to a stenographer. The LaFontaine proudly boasted of an Egyptian-design swimming pool with purified water, reportedly the largest among hotels in the United States. And there was more: a recreation area in the hotel held eight alleys for bowling.

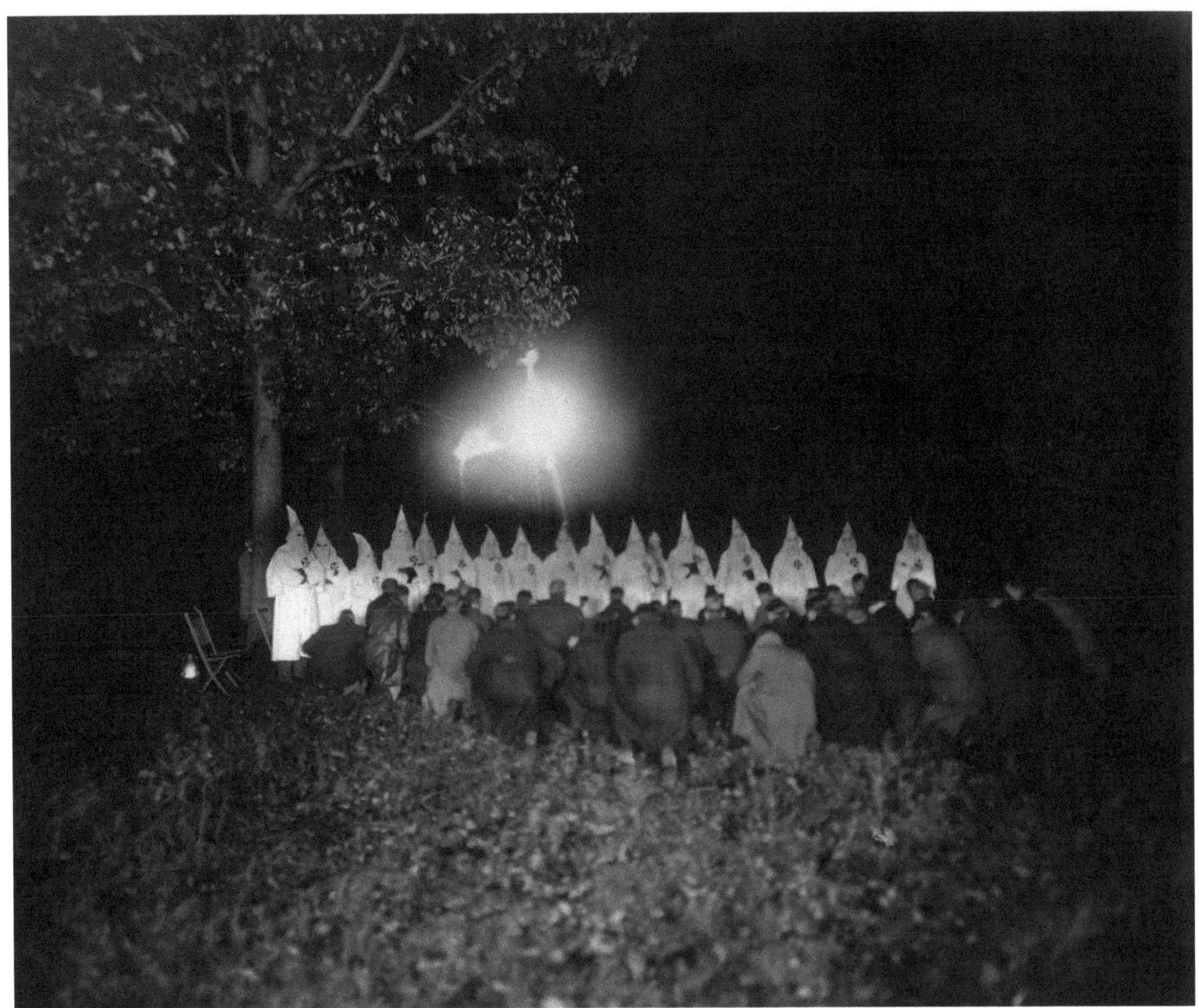

The Ku Klux Klan emerged in the South following the Civil War as a vigilante organization aimed at settling war-related grievances. A second incarnation of the group was organized in 1915, primarily in northern and southern states experiencing migration to the cities by blacks and other minorities in search of work. The Klan was especially strong in parts of Indiana, reaching its greatest strength in Tipton at this rally when more than 100 members were inducted in a very public ceremony in the center of town. By 1925, with the murder conviction of the Klan's state leader, the white supremacist organization was falling into rapid decline.

Following Spread: Travel in Peru would never be the same after installation of the first traffic signal in August 1925.

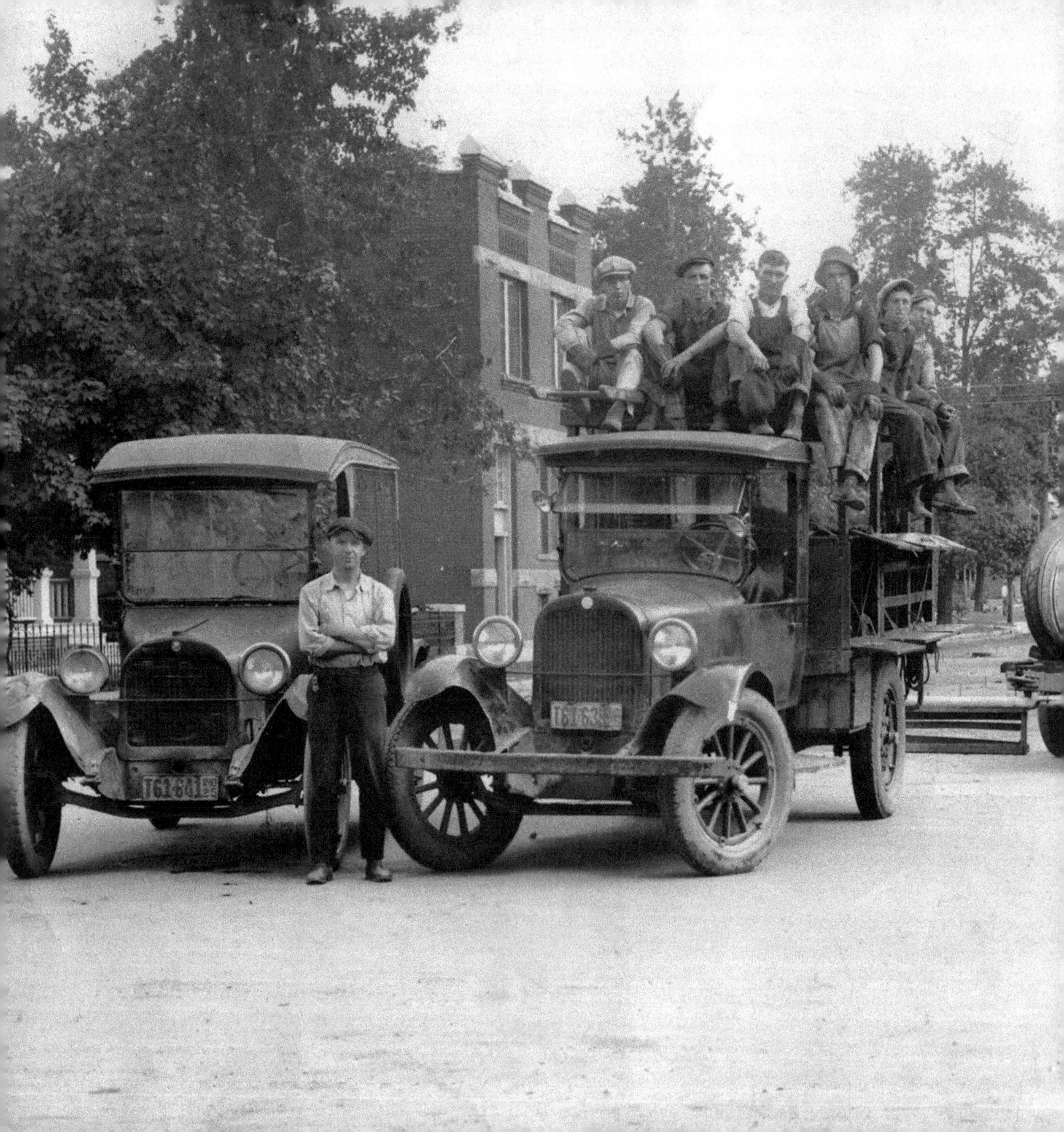

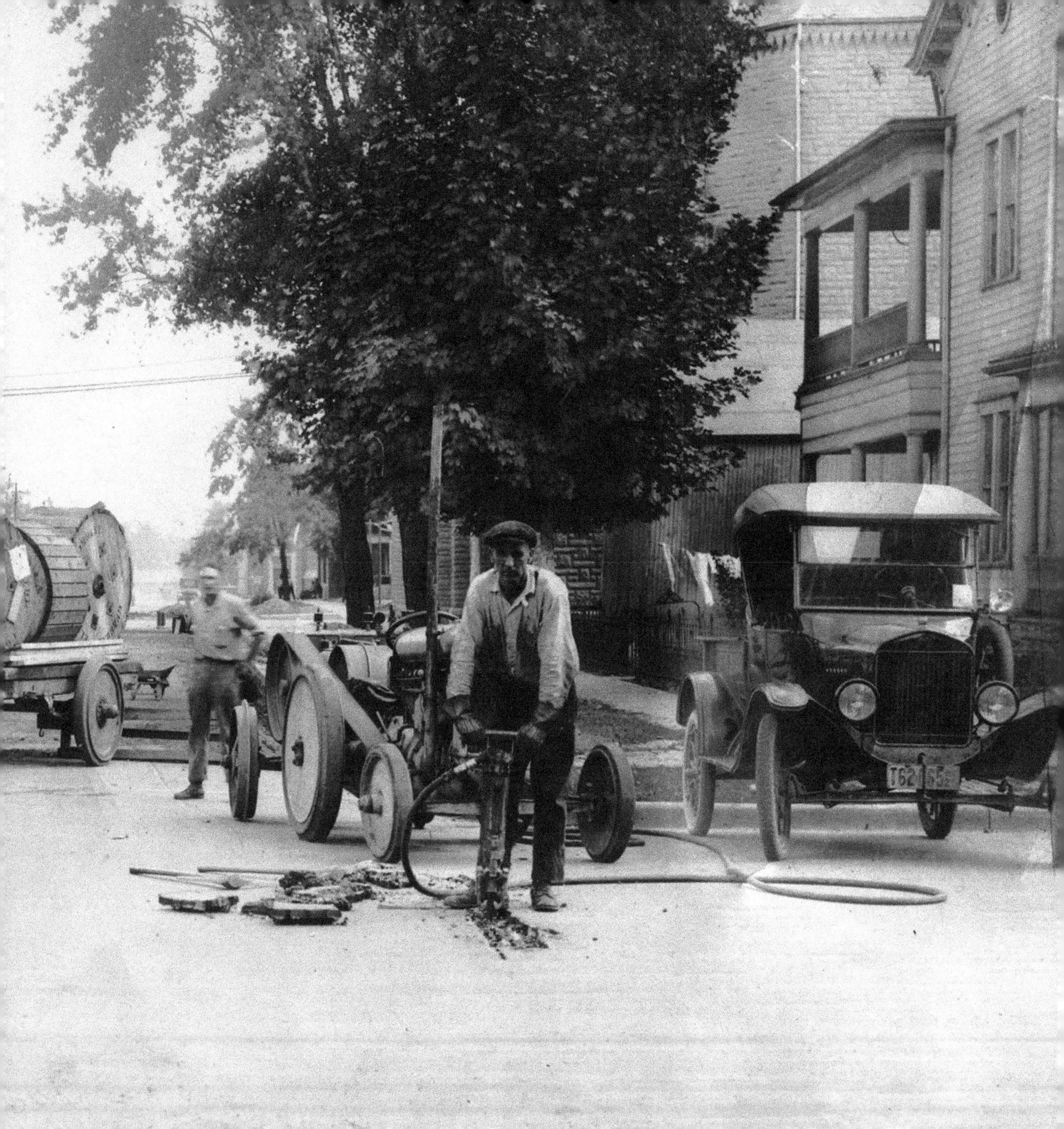

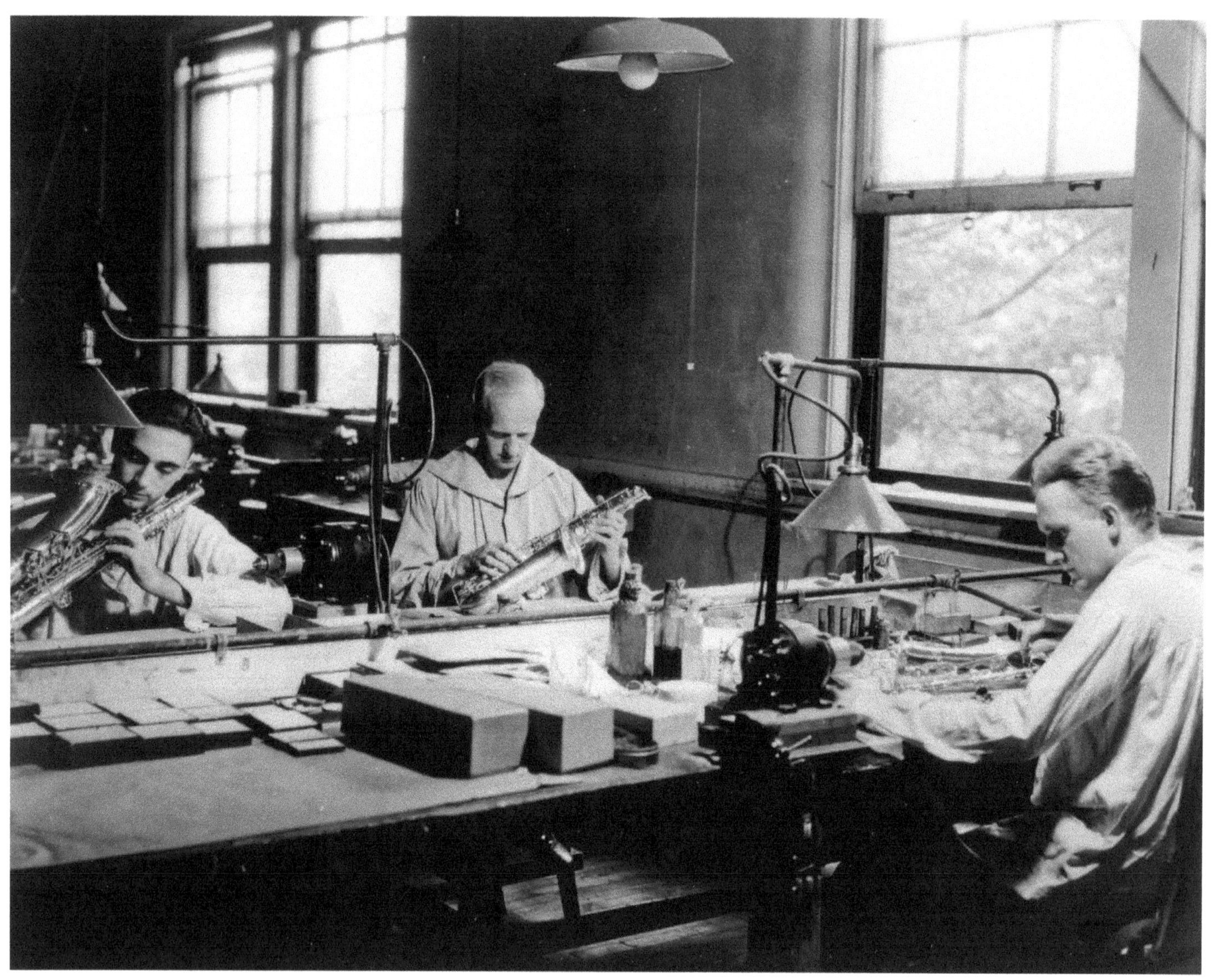

In the 1920s, Elkhart was renowned for its manufacture of musical instruments. In this image, workers are carefully mounting keys on saxophones in the H. & A. Selmer plant. Other manufacturers of note were the C. G. Conn Company, the Buescher Music Company, and the Elkhart Musical Instrument Company.

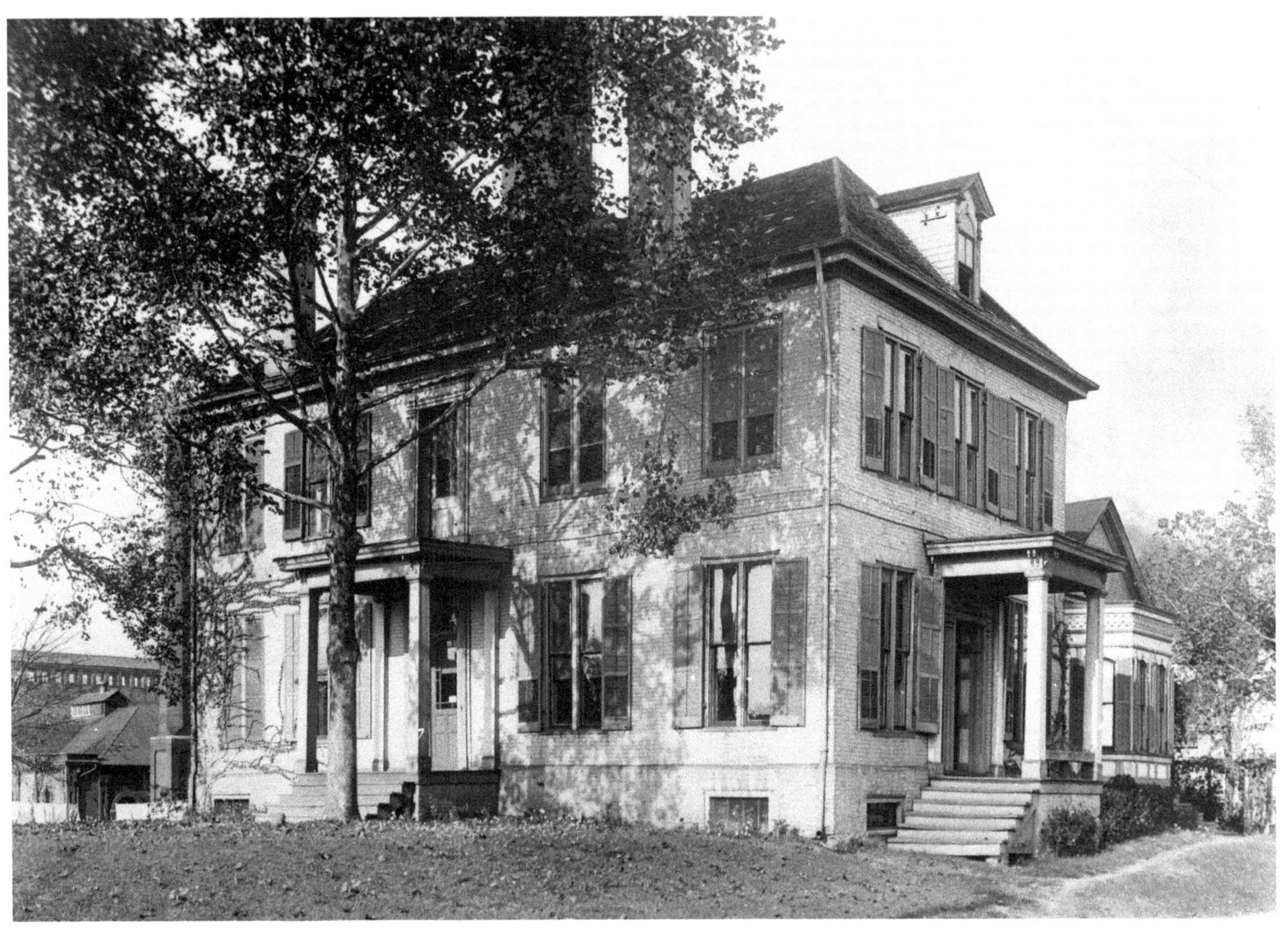

Known as Grouseland, this is the home in which William Henry Harrison lived from 1804 to 1812 when he was territorial governor. The house at Park and Scott streets in Vincennes was one of the first brick structures in the territory. Harrison went on to become a congressman and senator from Ohio, ambassador, and ultimately the nation's 9th president.

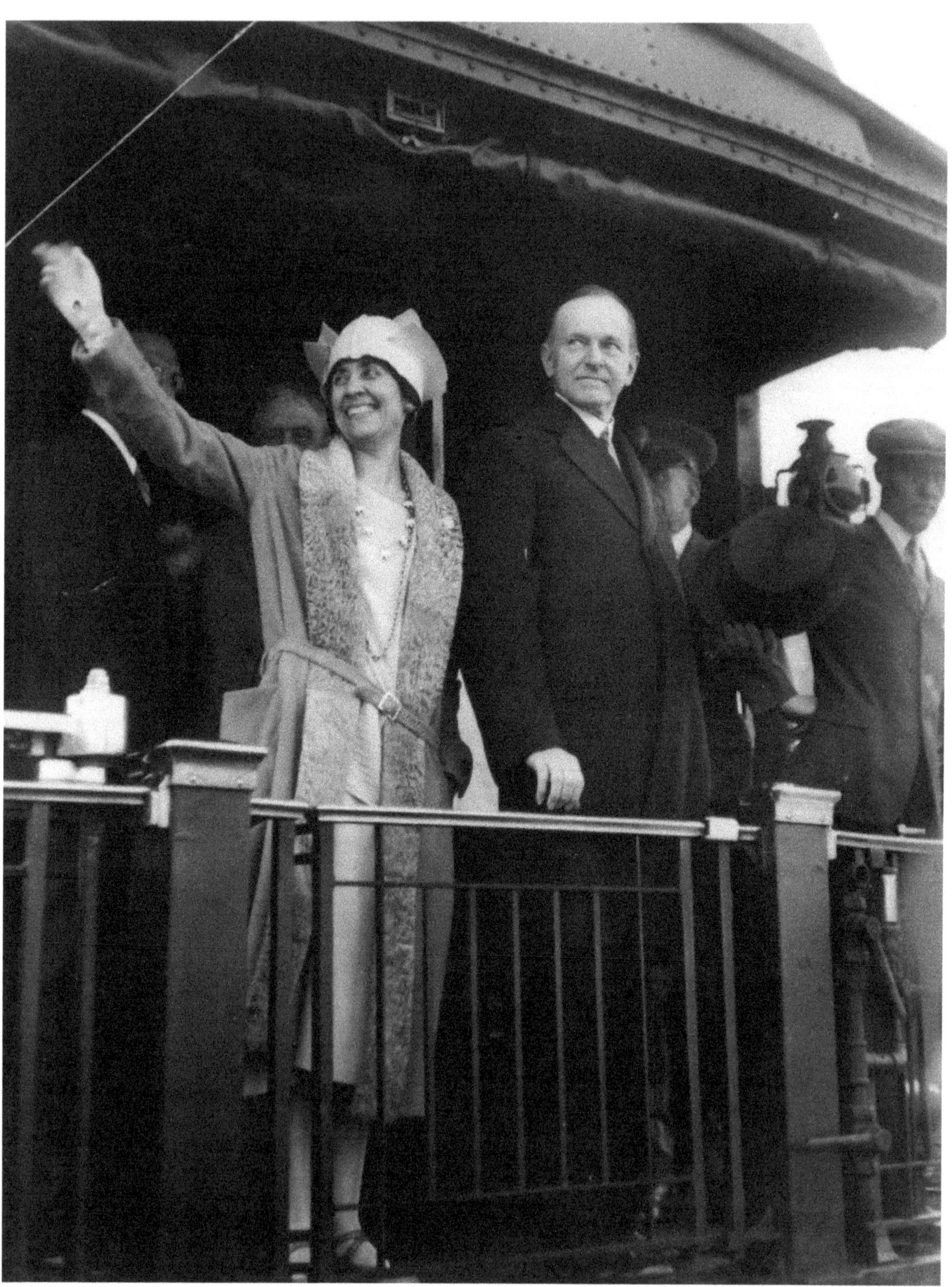

President Calvin Coolidge, accompanied by his wife, Grace, visited Hammond in mid-June 1927 to dedicate Wicker Memorial Park, honoring the township's war dead. An estimated 200,000 people attended the ceremonies.

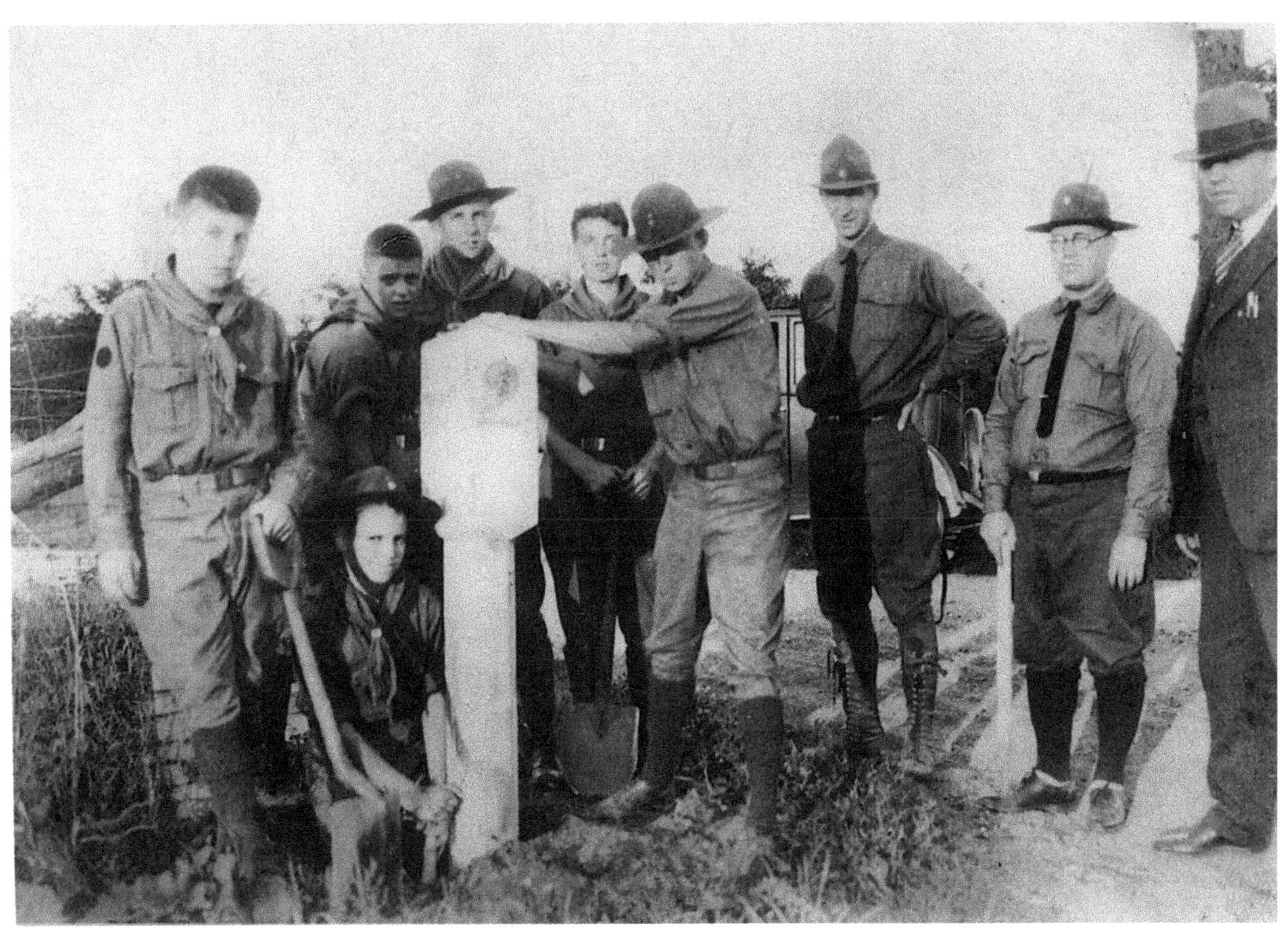

The Lincoln Highway was a source of commerce and community pride along its route through Indiana. This Monroeville Boy Scout troop is shown placing three distinctive Lincoln Highway markers between the Ohio State Line and Zulu, in Allen County, in 1929.

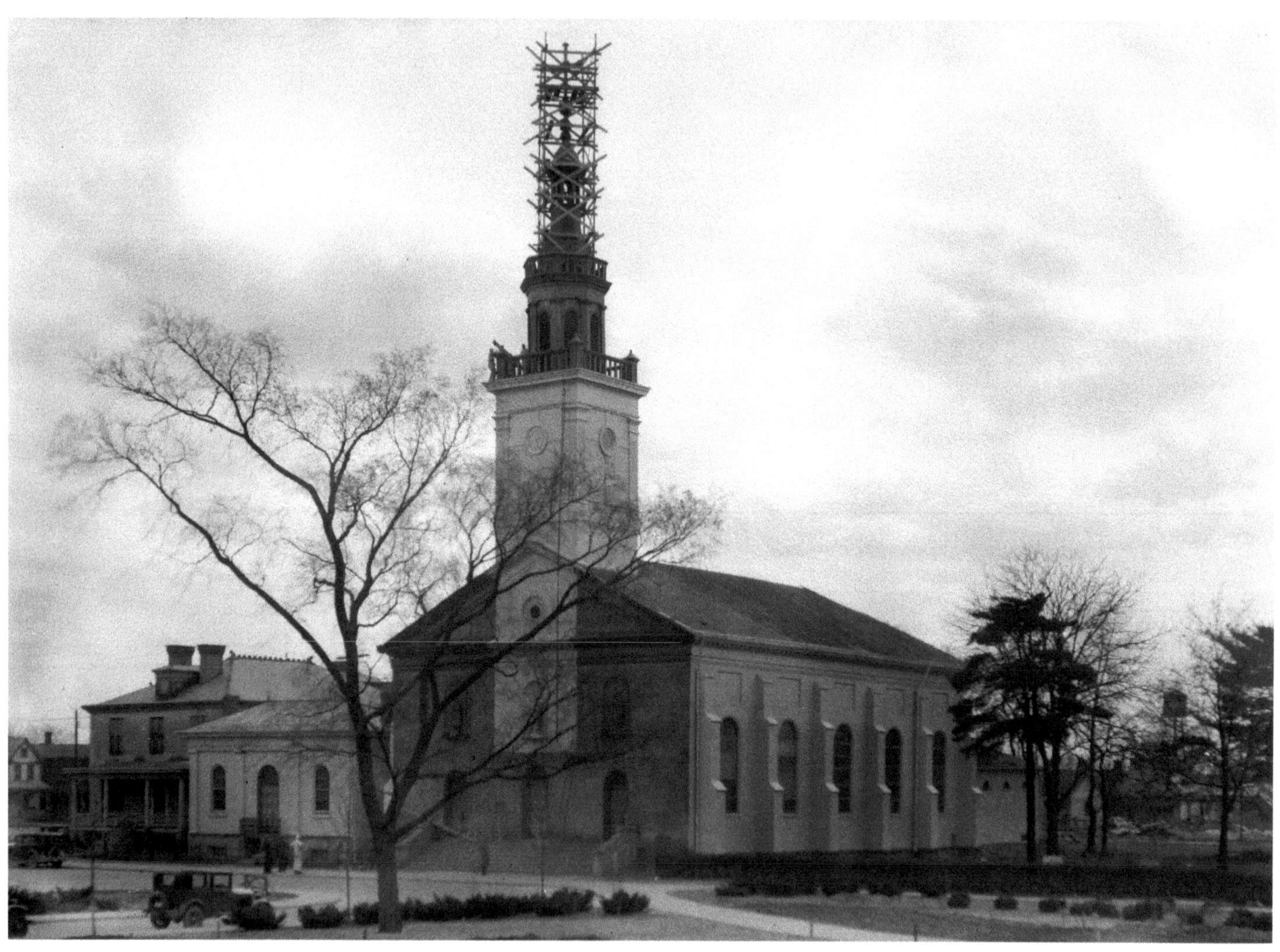

The oldest church in the state of Indiana, St. Francis Xavier Cathedral in Vincennes is shown undergoing repairs to its steeple. Built in 1826, the Old Cathedral, as it is known, actually stands on the site of three earlier churches. The first held worship in a log structure built in 1732. Today the state is headquarters or home base for many church bodies, including the Free Methodist Church; the Wesleyan Church; the Christian Church; the Church of God, Anderson; the Friends United Meeting of the Religious Society of Friends; the Church of the United Brethren in Christ; and the Missionary Church. The Mennonites and Amish and other groups also have a strong presence.

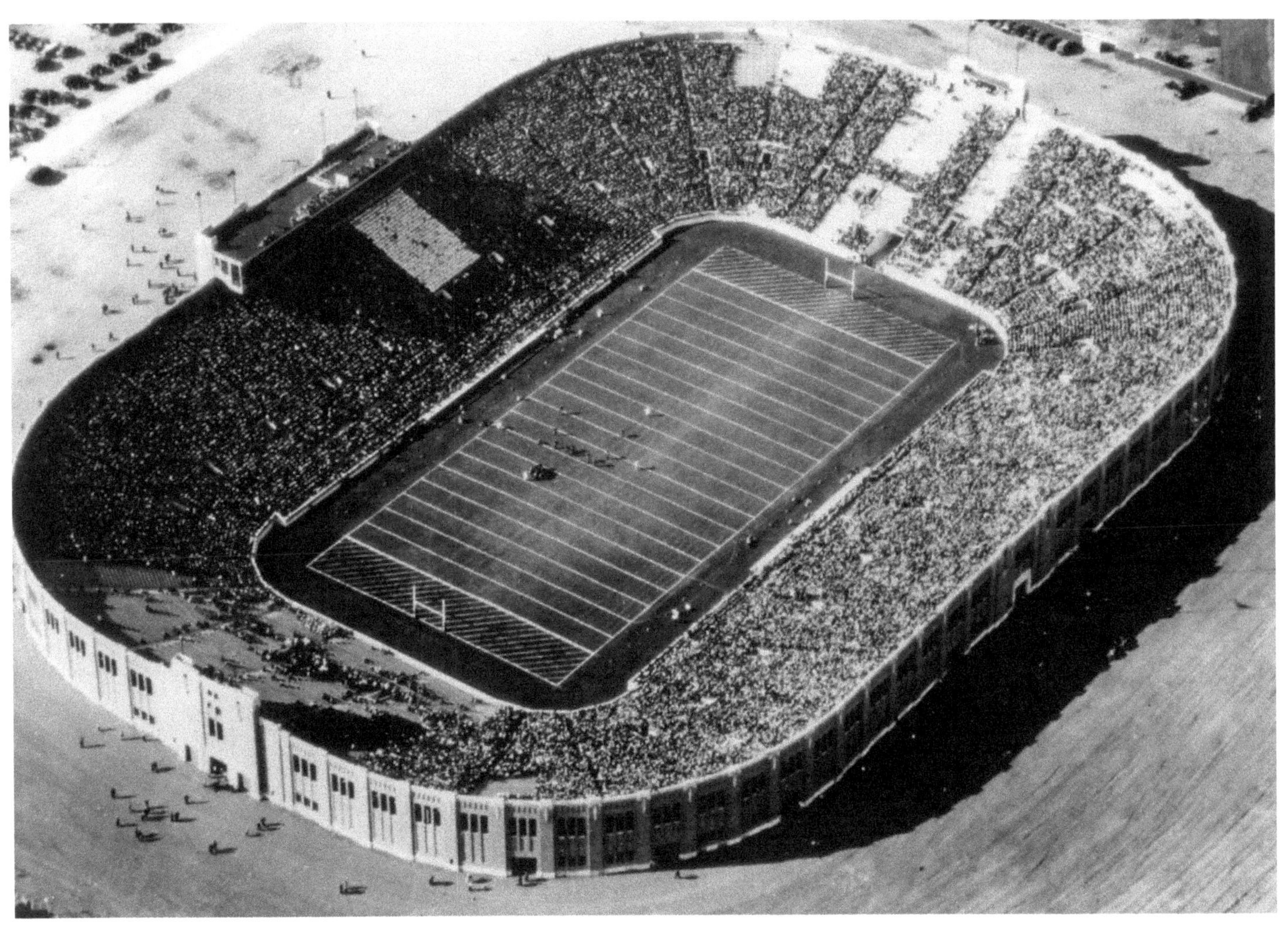

This aerial view shows the capacity crowd for the dedication game of the new Notre Dame Stadium on October 13, 1930. The Irish beat the Navy, 26–2, for Coach Knute Rockne in the game broadcast nationally on radio. It was also the first game at which the students sang an alma mater, "Notre Dame, Our Mother," at the end of play, a tradition that continues.

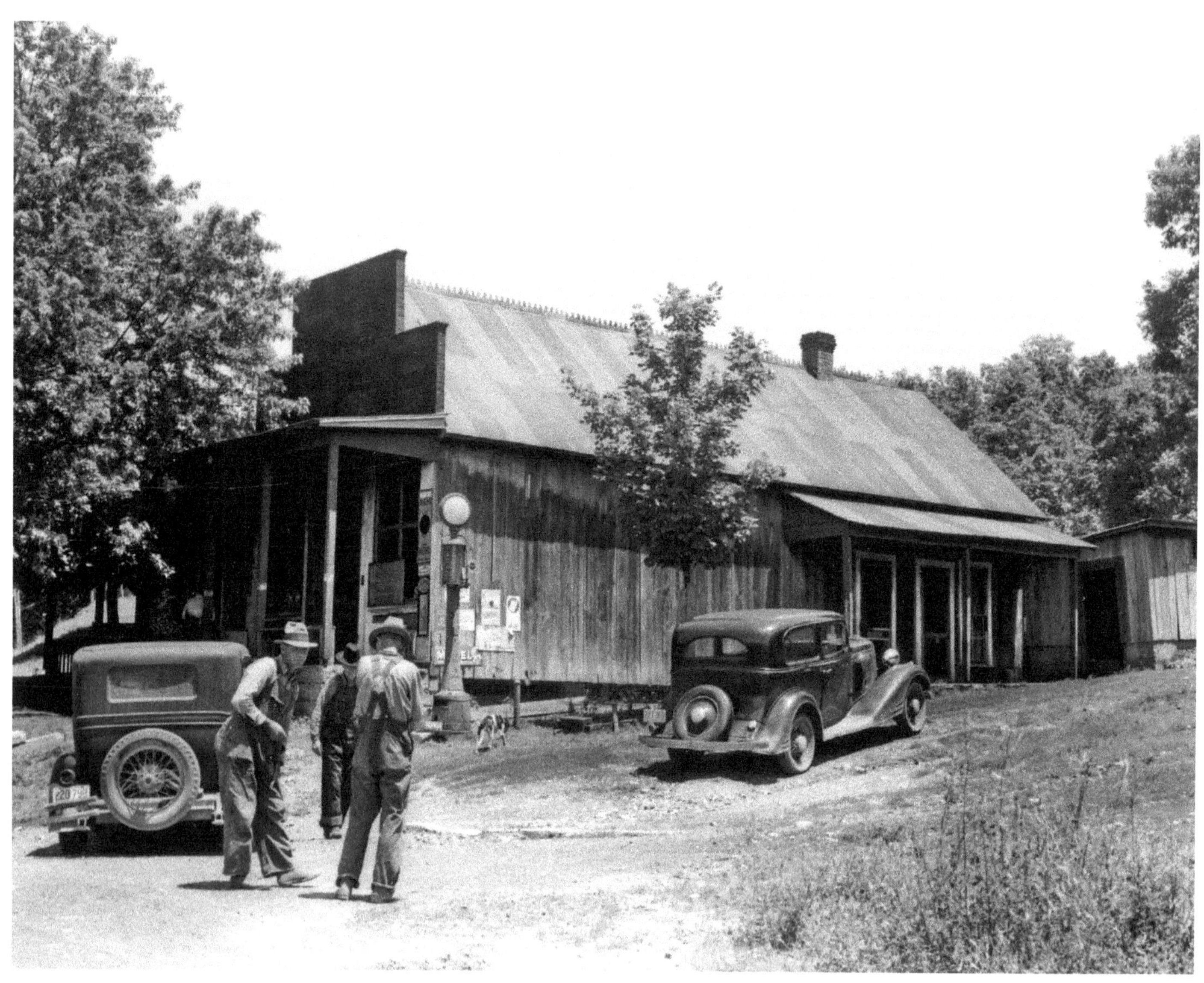

More than 44,000 acres of Martin County would become the Crane Naval Ammunition Depot for the production and storage of ordnance in 1940, resulting in the disappearance of settings like this one in Blankenship. At its height, the facility would employ nearly 10,000 workers, most of whom were women. The facility continues today as the Crane Naval Weapons Center.

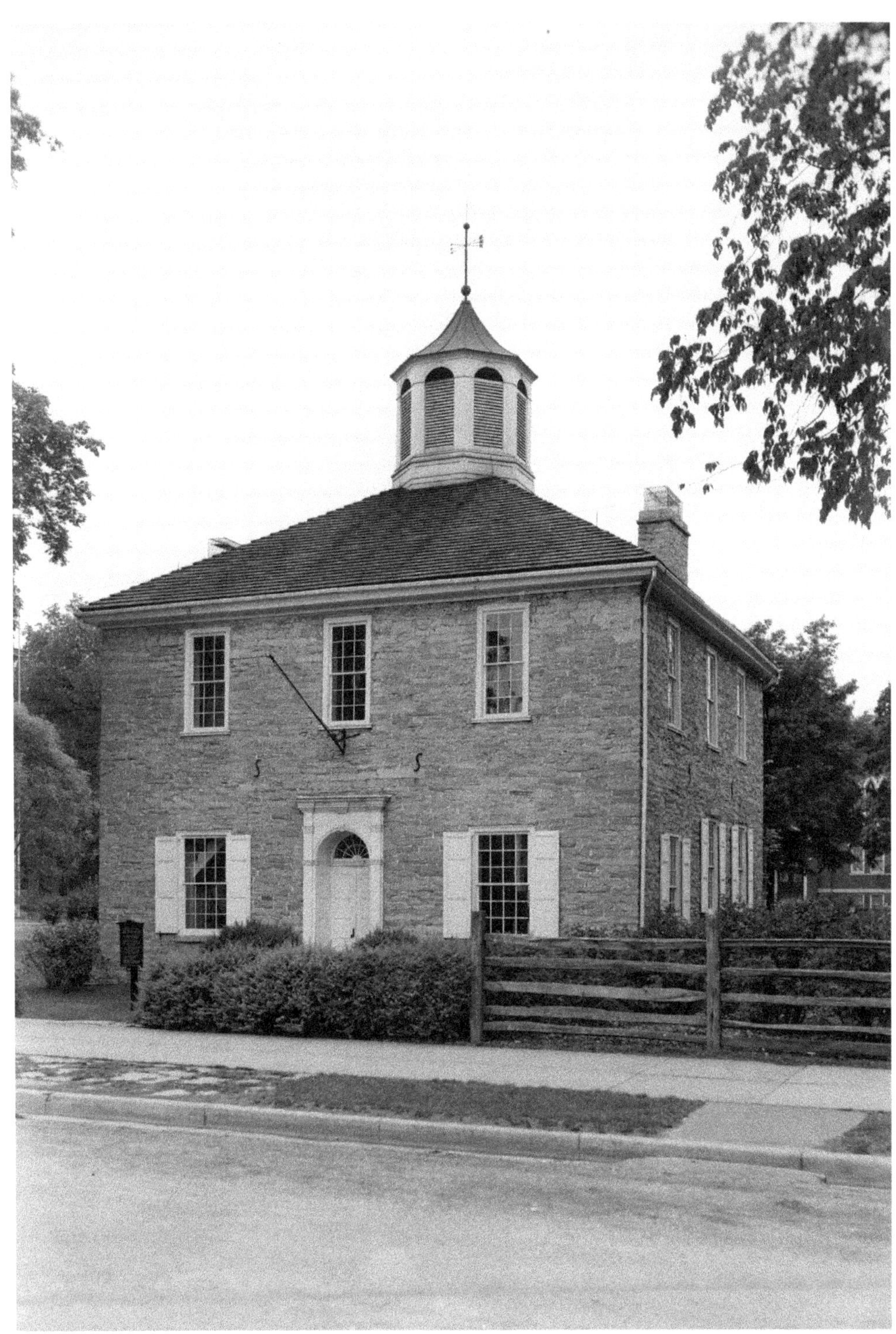

Corydon was considered the center of the inhabited portion of the Indiana Territory as early as 1810. So it was natural for Corydon to become the seat of government in 1813 and the capital when Indiana earned statehood in 1816. This was the state capitol building until 1825, when Indianapolis became the capital city.

A section foreman checks his watch as the Baltimore & Ohio freight arrives in Garrett. His son huddles beside him. Garrett is a true "railroad town." Created when the B&O built its southern line through Indiana, it was named in 1875 for John Garrett, president of the railroad. At its peak in 1913, the railroad employed more than 1,000 townspeople.

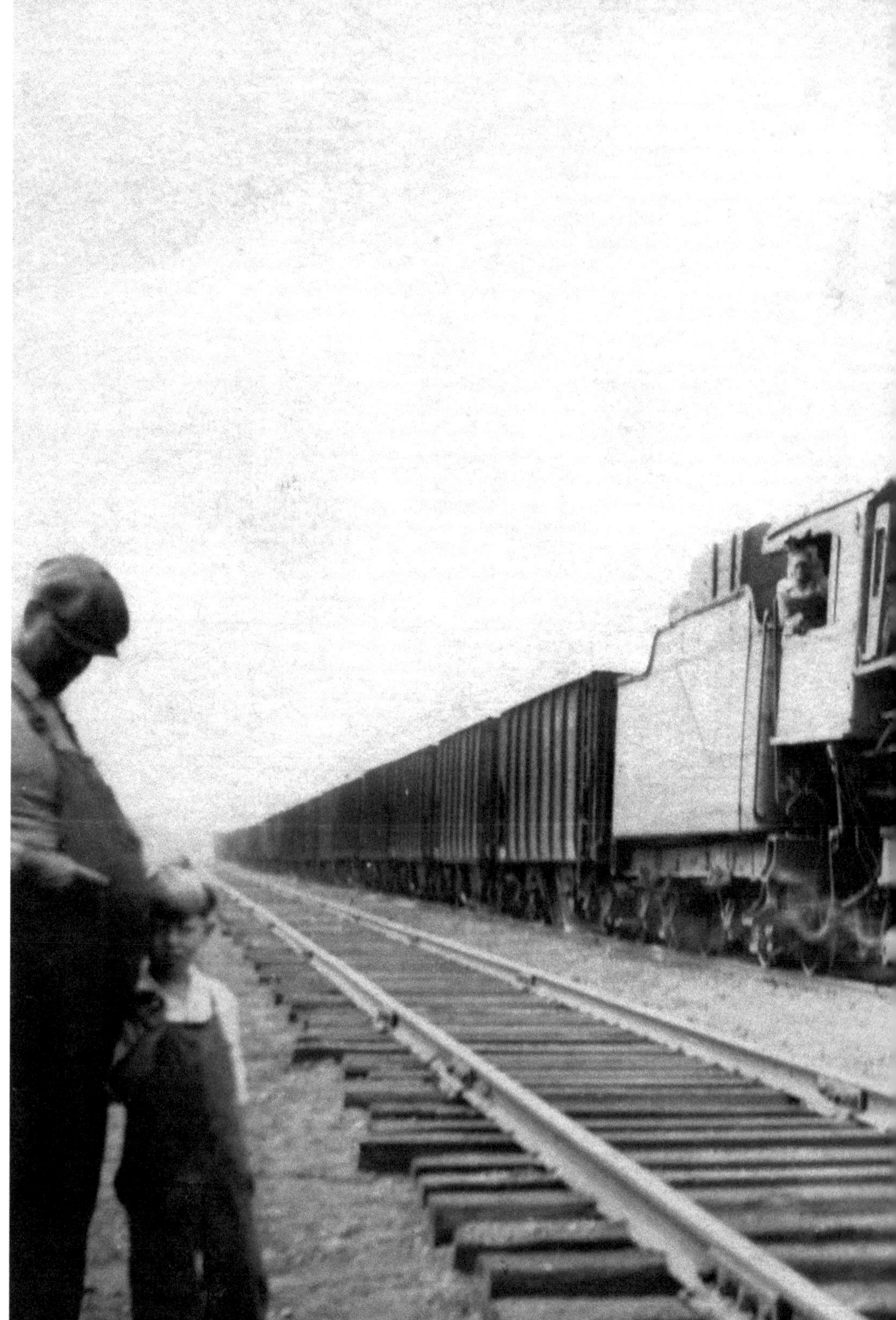

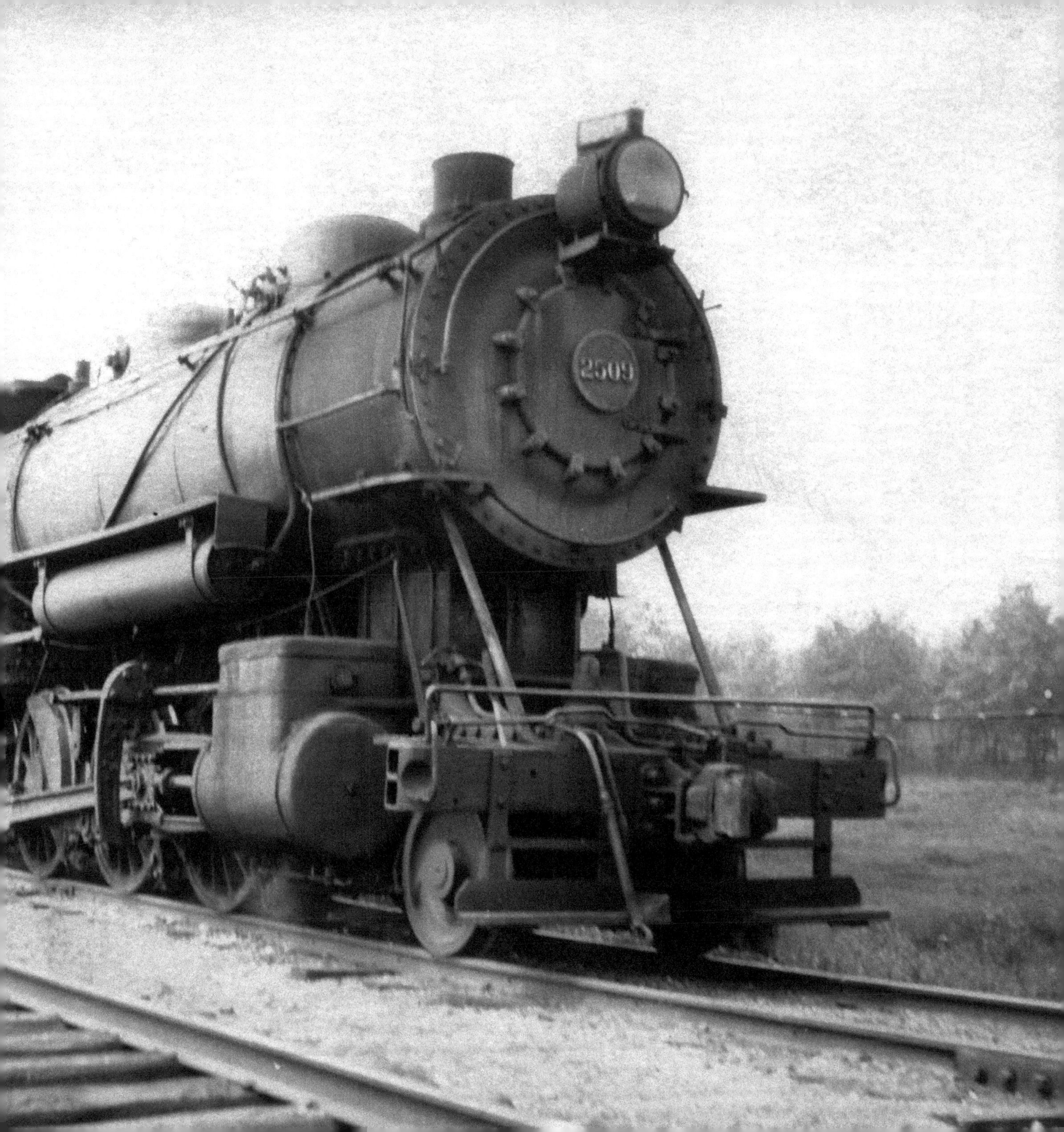
2509

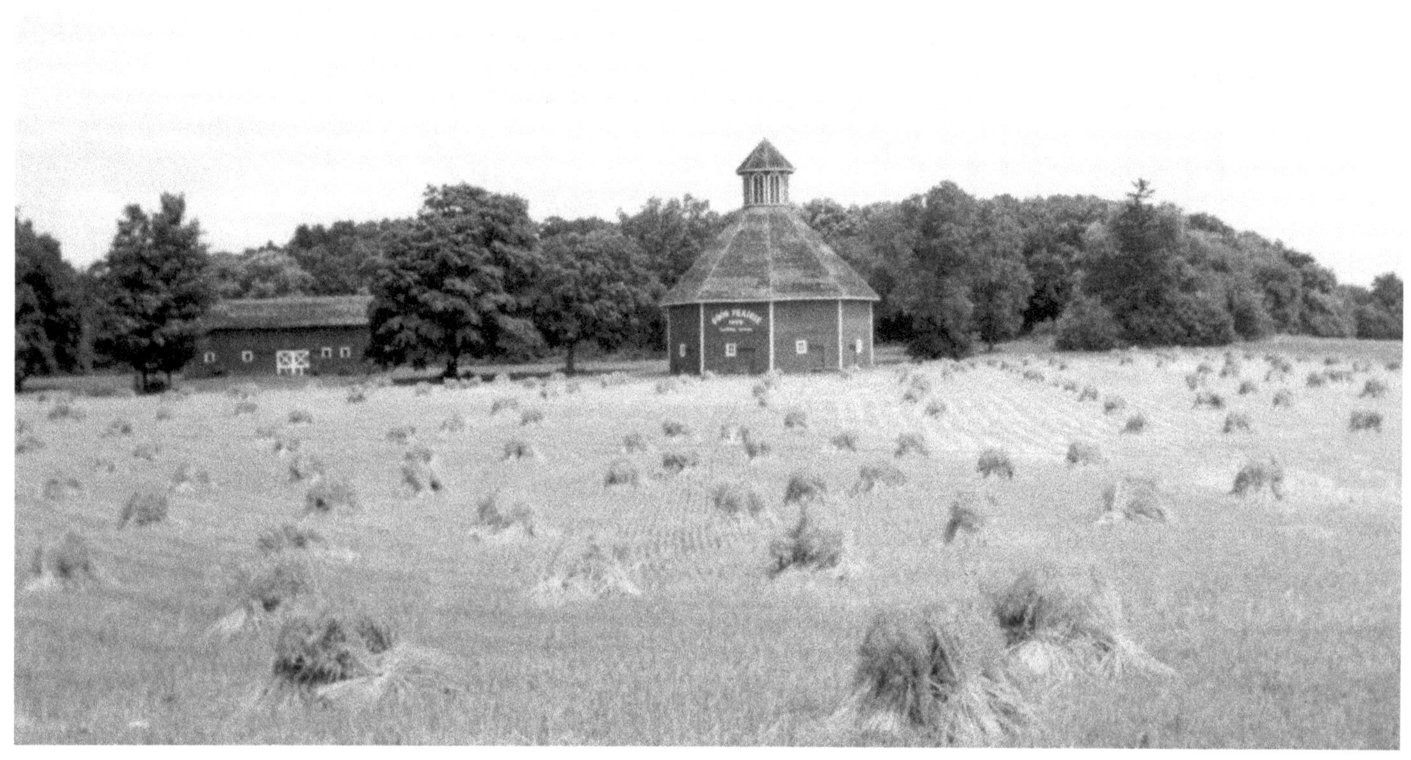

There are many round barns in Indiana, but the Door Prairie Barn in La Porte County is apparently the only nine-sided nineteenth-century barn in the nation. Built in 1882 for a horse and cattle breeder whose family settled the area half a century before, the barn's preservation through individuals and the La Porte County Historical Society is an example of Indiana's continuing efforts to preserve its heritage. Shocks of newly cut wheat fill the field surrounding the barn in this image.

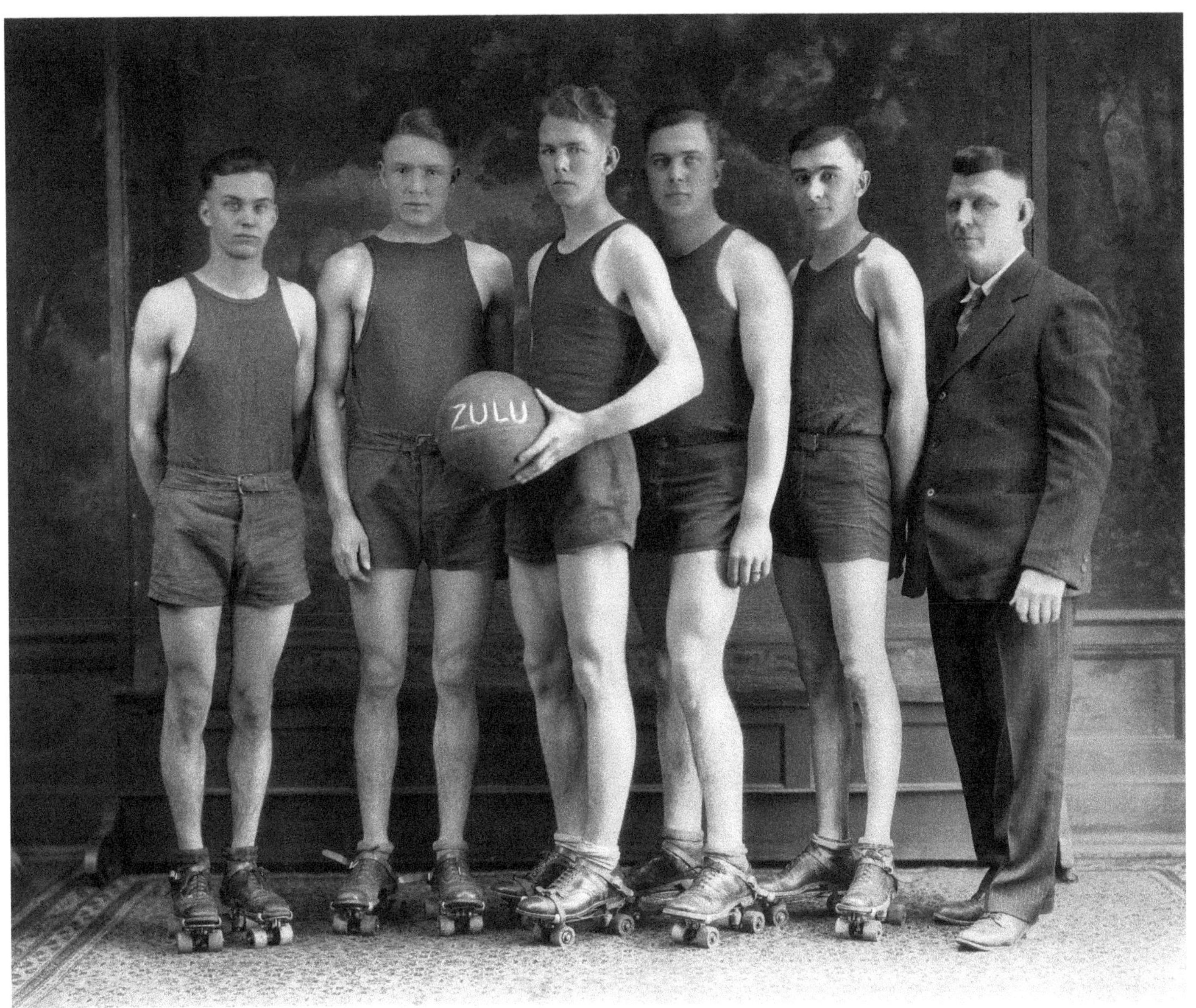

The Hoosier State enjoyed its zany moments in the 1930s. This basketball team on roller skates, shown here around 1934, played its games at the Zulu Tavern and Dance Hall owned by Henry Girardot, who stands on solid ground at far-right. Good thing this team was playing before the jump shot was invented.

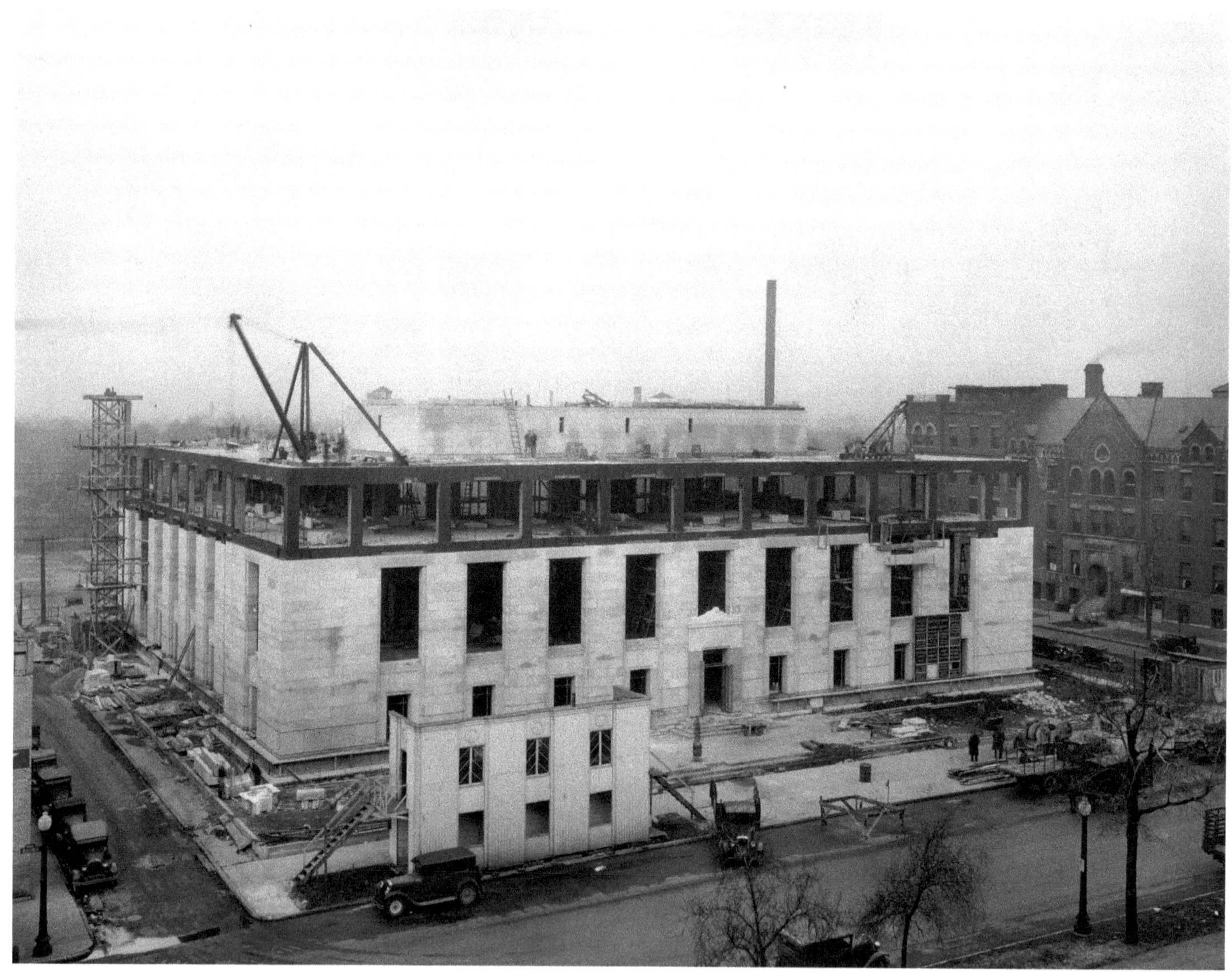

The Indiana State Library opened to the public about two years after this photograph was taken. The first library opened in February 1825, with the secretary of state acting as librarian. Until it opened in this building in 1934, use of the State Library was limited to state employees and government officials.

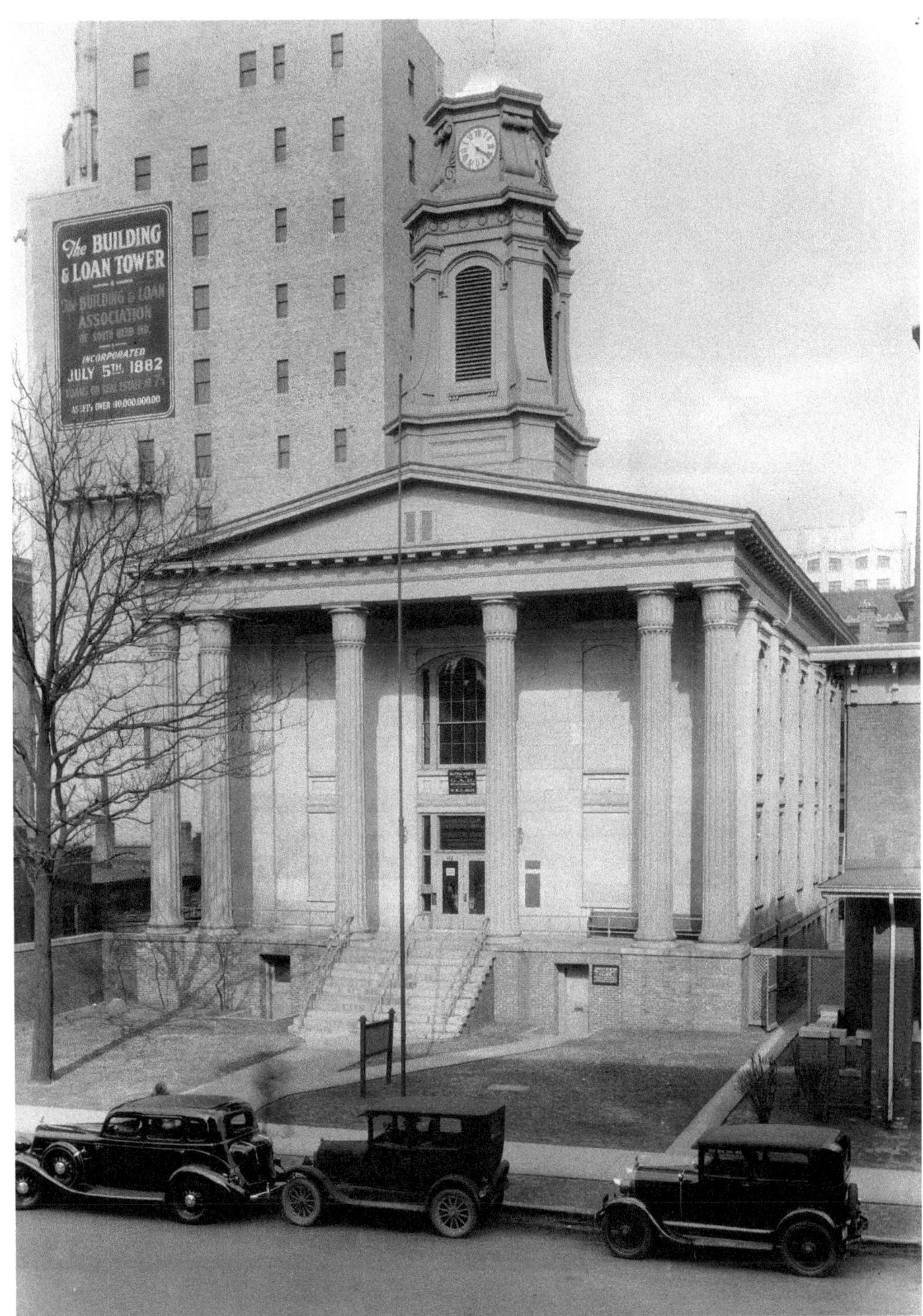

The old St. Joseph County Courthouse had weathered more than is evident in this 1934 image. It had been located on Main Street, in South Bend, for 40 years. According to historian Timothy Howard, when county officials decided to abandon it at the turn of the century, the building "was taken in hand by a house mover from Chicago, lifted up, turned halfway back to front on Lafayette, all without disturbing a stone or brick."

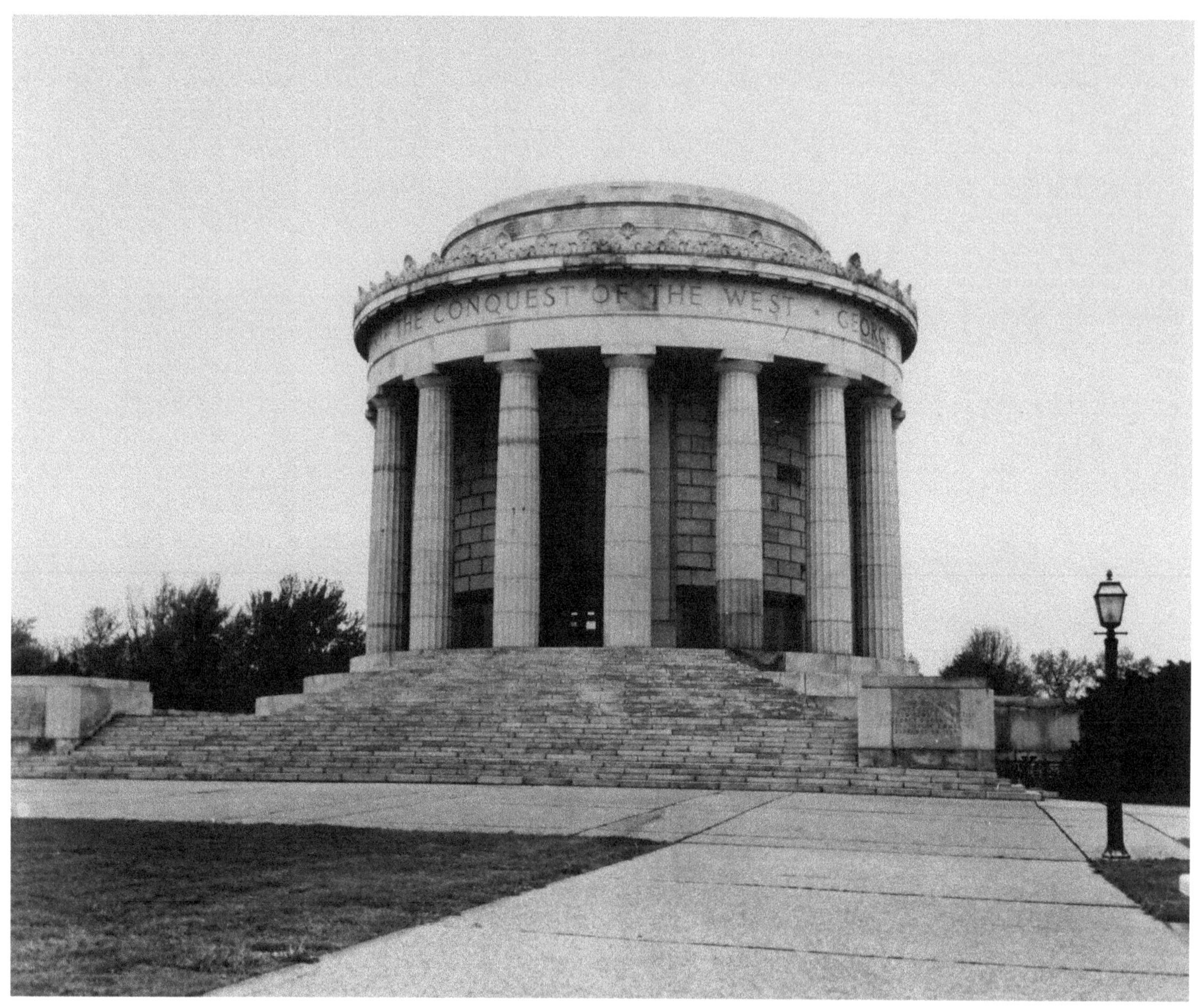

A groundswell of support for a memorial to Revolutionary War hero George Rogers Clark rose as the nation approached the 150th anniversary of its freedom. After prolonged debate, President Calvin Coolidge approved a memorial in Vincennes in 1928. Dedicated in 1936, the memorial stands on what was believed to be the site of Fort Sackville and is operated today by the National Park Service. A 2-cent stamp commemorating Clark's capture of Fort Sackville was issued by the U.S. Post Office in 1929.

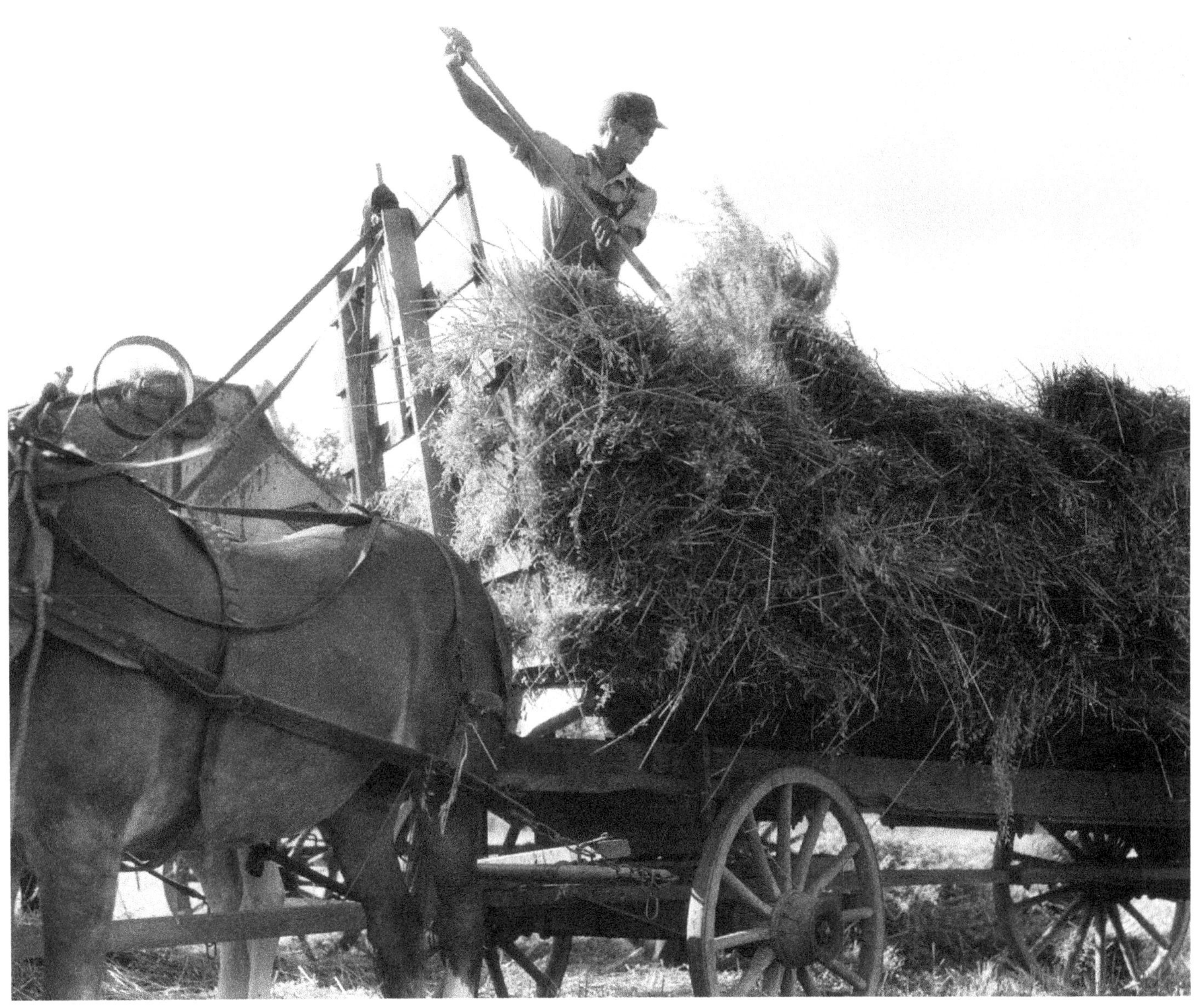

Dorothea Lange is renowned for her photographs for the Farm Security Administration during the Great Depression. Her most notable image was *Migrant Mother,* a study of a California woman taken in February 1936. Five months later Lange was in Indiana, where she photographed this young farmer threshing oats in Clayton.

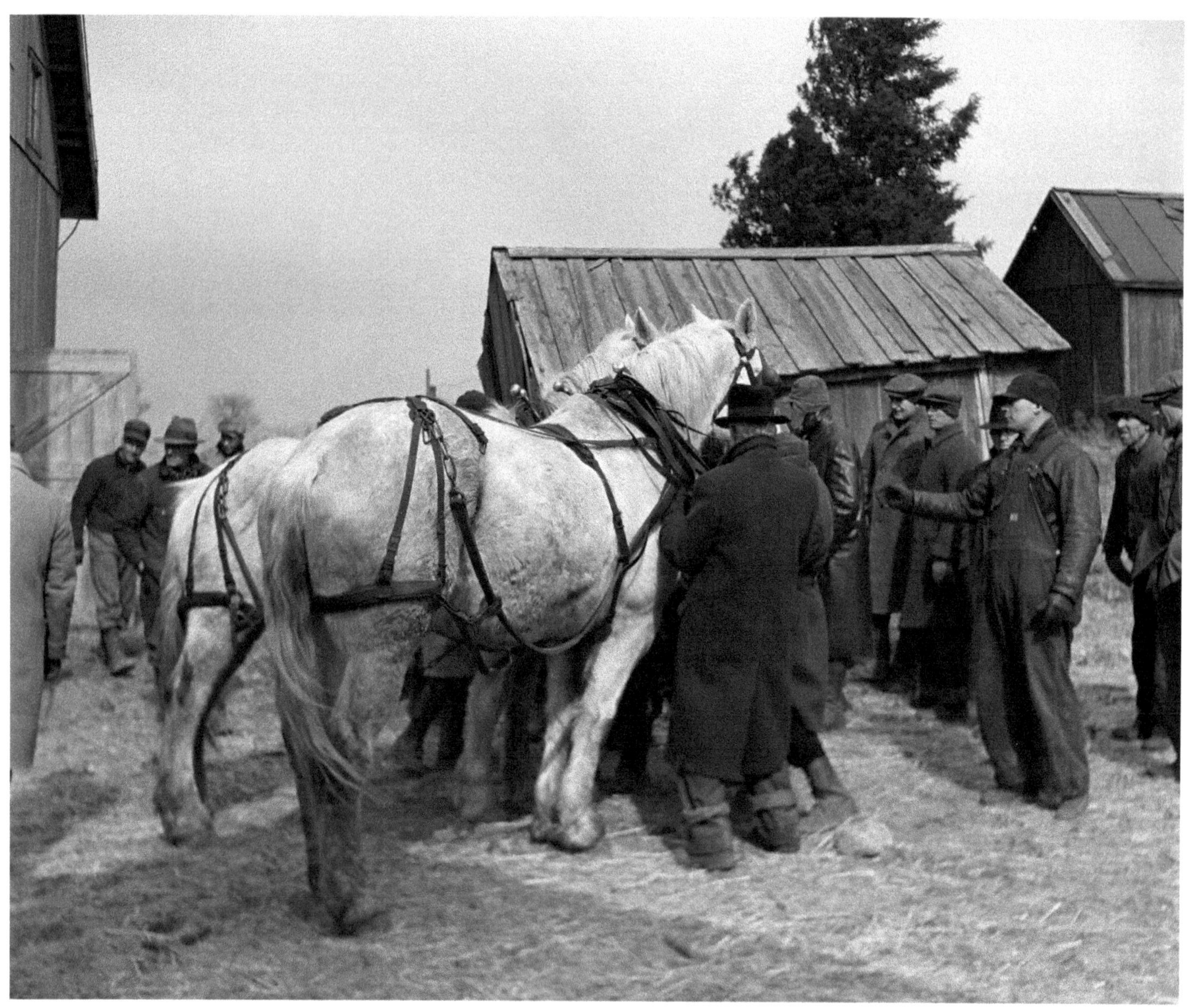

Bundled men and a breeze-whipped tree equal a cold, windy morning in February 1937 when Frank Sheroan's team of horses were auctioned as part of the closing-out sale for the tenant farmer near Montmorenci in Tippecanoe County. The depression's effect on Indiana farm prices during 1937 and 1938 was still giving rise to scenes like this one, and across the nation in 1938, unemployment still averaged 19 percent despite six years and a plethora of federal programs for farms and cities under President Roosevelt's New Deal.

On a farm near Normanda in Tipton County in the summer of 1937, it must have been difficult at times to know who was bossing whom around the yard. Selling chicken eggs, which might fetch a penny a piece, helped some farm families bring in spending money during the 1930s and 1940s in the rural areas of the Midwest.

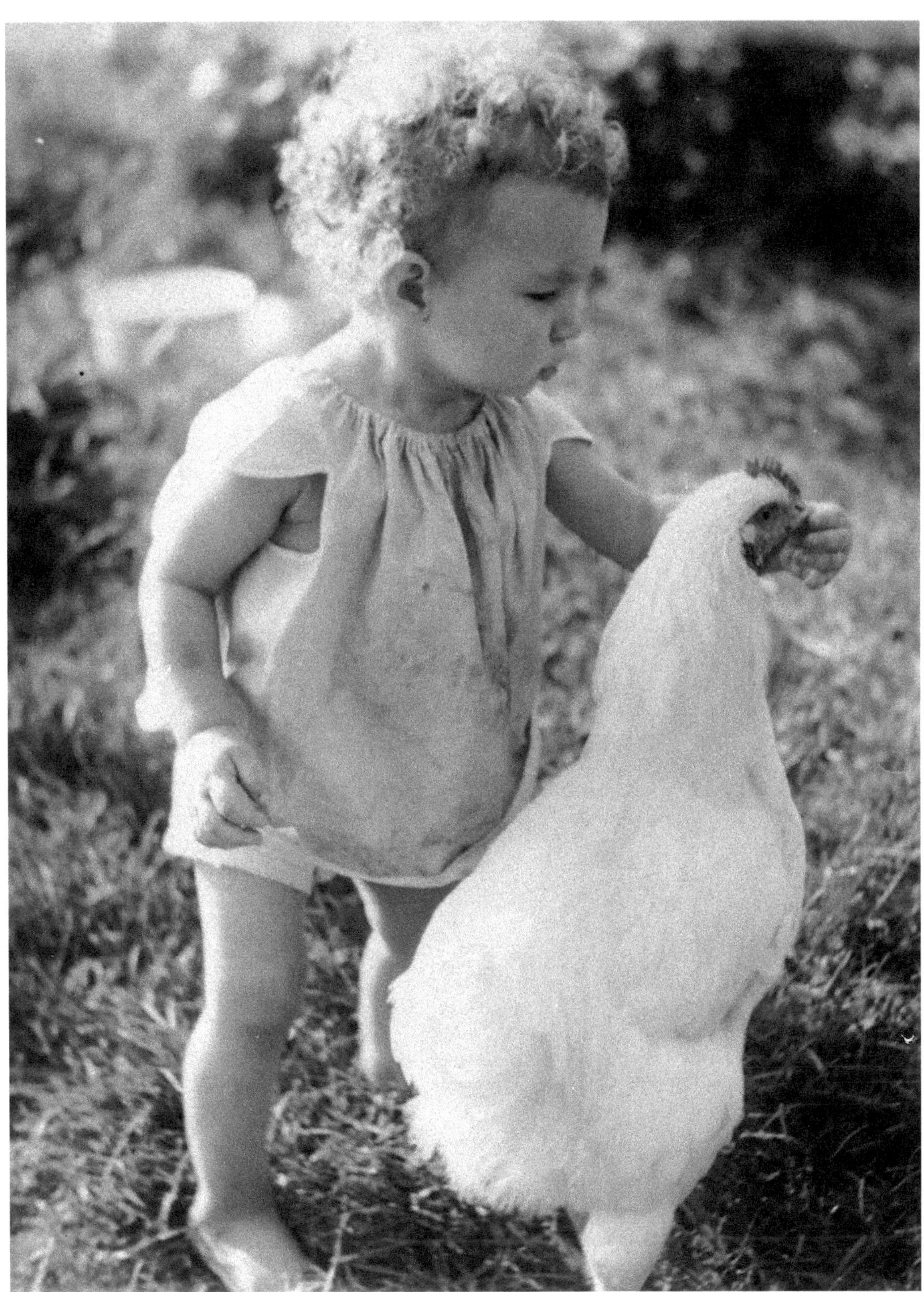

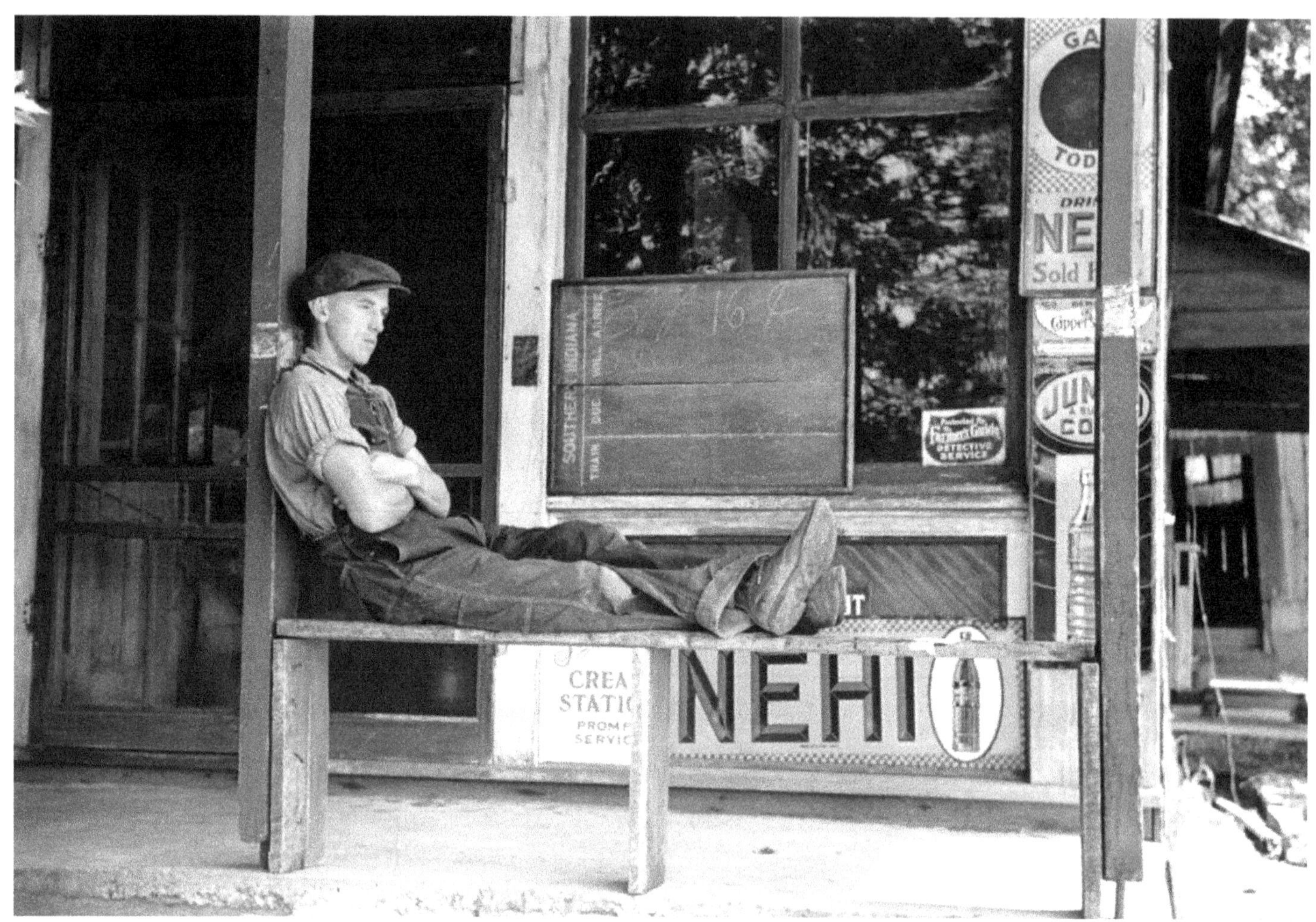

Arthur Rothstein photographed this man resting outside the general store in the southeastern Indiana town of Blankenship in May 1938. In a few years, the farms, homes, and businesses of this Martin County community would be gone, consumed by a massive military installation as the nation prepared for World War II.

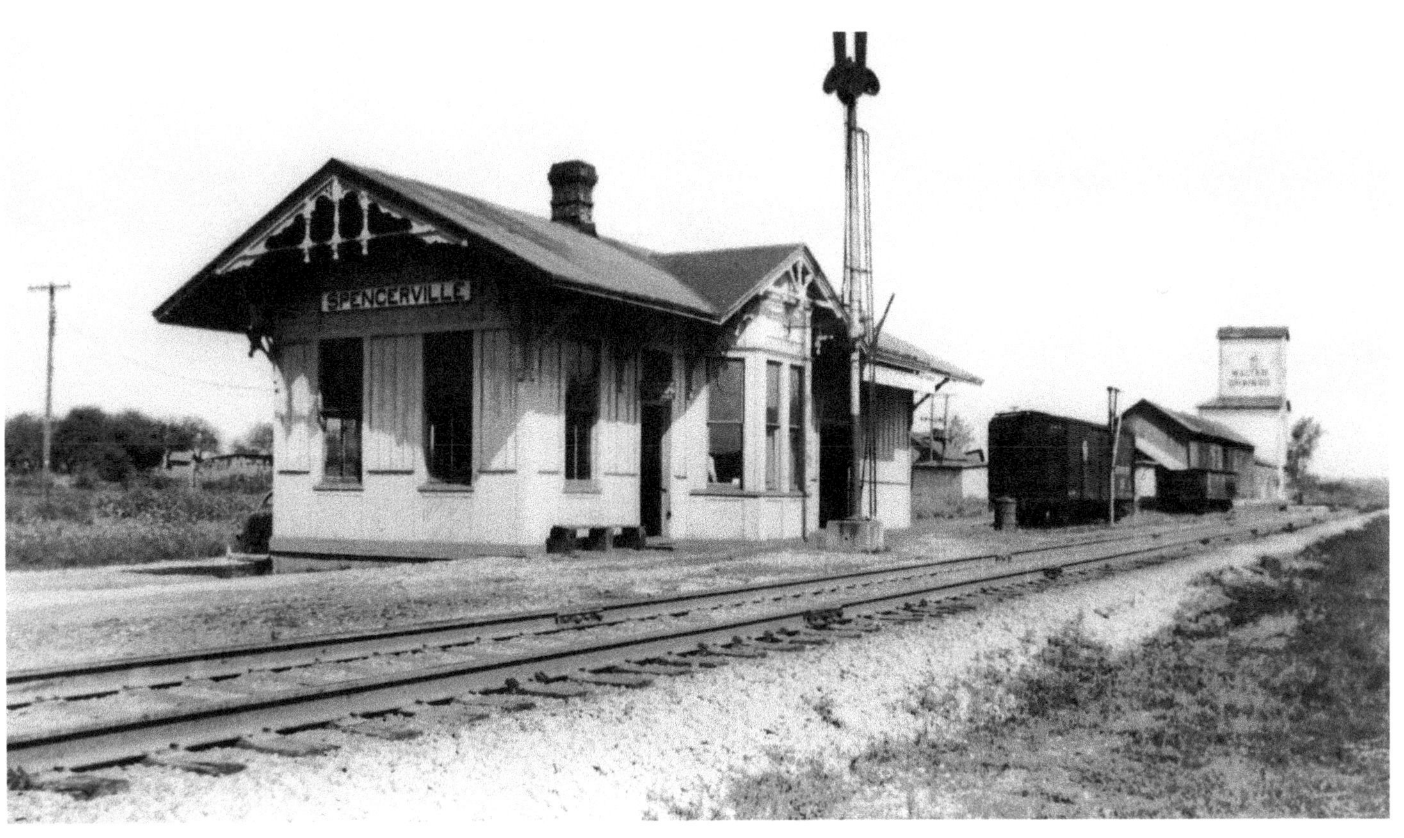

Small towns like Spencerville were not a regular stop on the Wabash Railroad in 1940. Instead, a semaphore placed atop the depot was used to signal that there was a passenger or freight waiting to be picked up. The town was the first community in DeKalb County, settled around 1828 and platted in 1842.

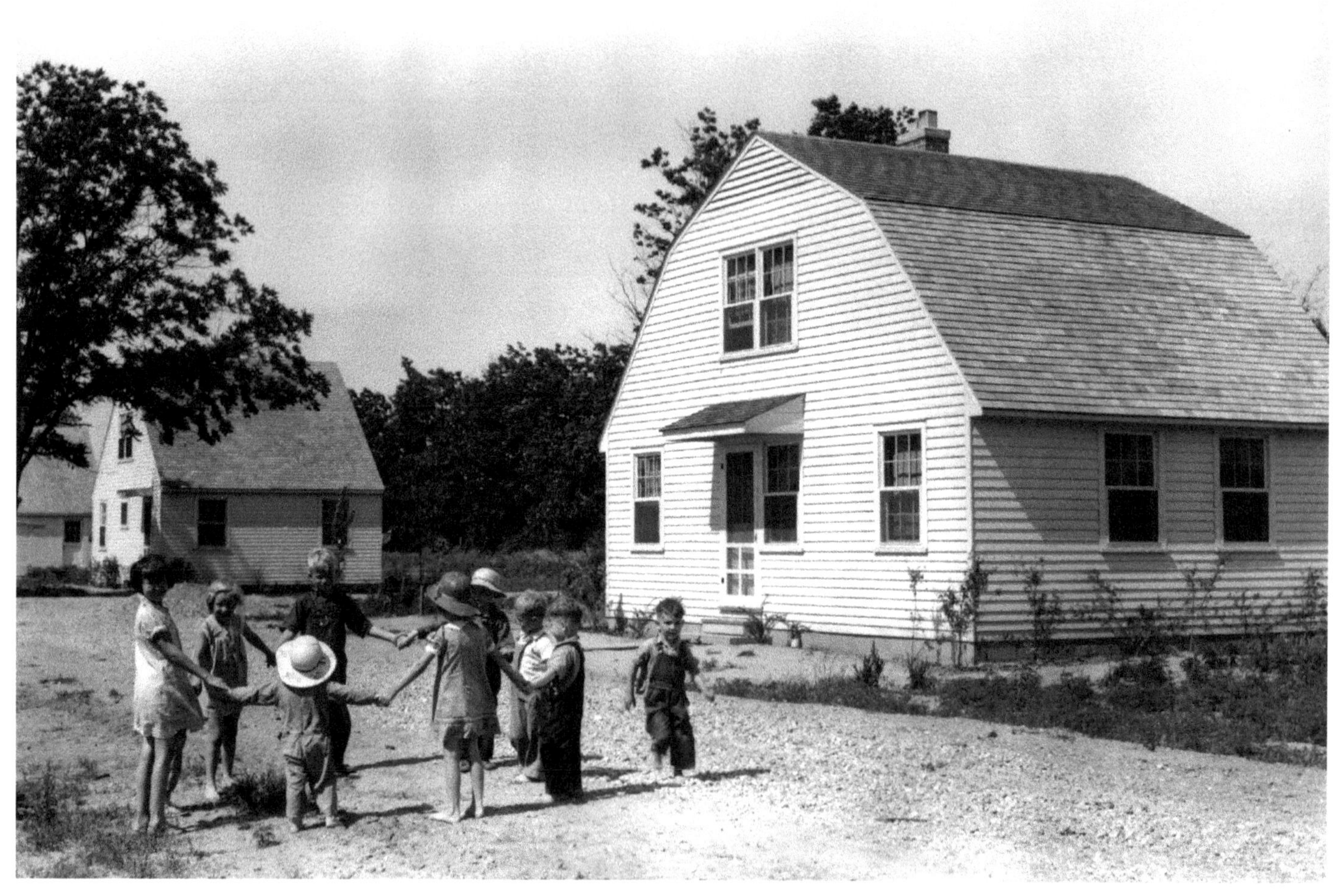

There is a timelessness about an Indiana summer and children at play on a farm. This July 1938 photograph from the Farm Security Administration describes the scene only as "Wabash Farms," where these children are perhaps enjoying Ring Around the Rosie. Traveling carnivals might entertain and have sometimes tested the innocence of older youth, where the unwitting might be enticed to try their marksmanship at booths offering double-or-nothing. And for adults in small towns or on the farm, there is always the camaraderie enjoyed at a community fish fry.

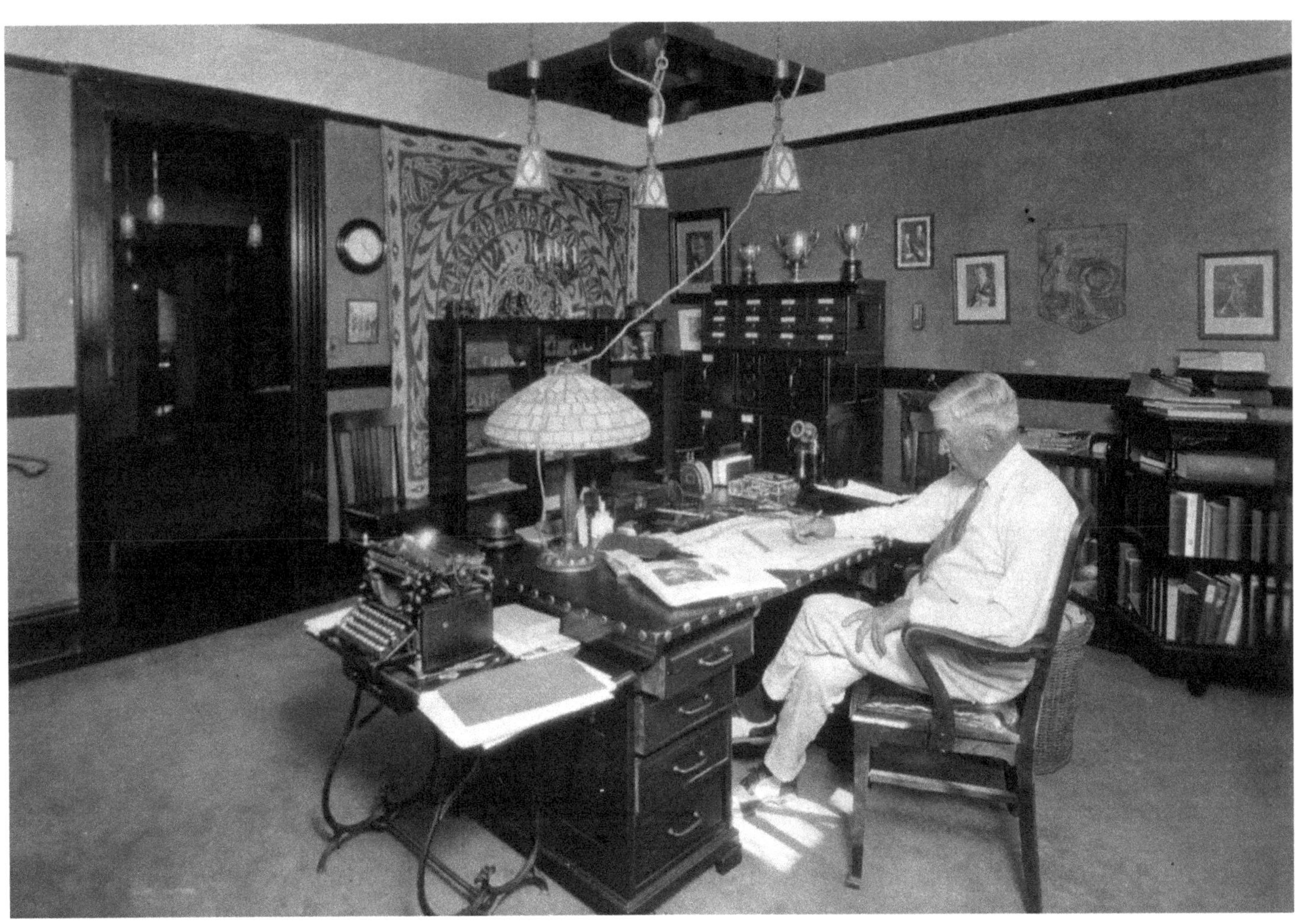

George Ade was a reporter, humor writer, and playwright whose early work was praised by such literary luminaries as Mark Twain and William Dean Howells. When his *Fables in Slang* sold 69,000 copies soon after publication in 1900, Ade was famous. In later life, he became wealthy enough to build an Elizabethan-style house with a study, in which he is shown, which included rooms for guests. Ade named the estate Hazelden, located in the community of Brook.

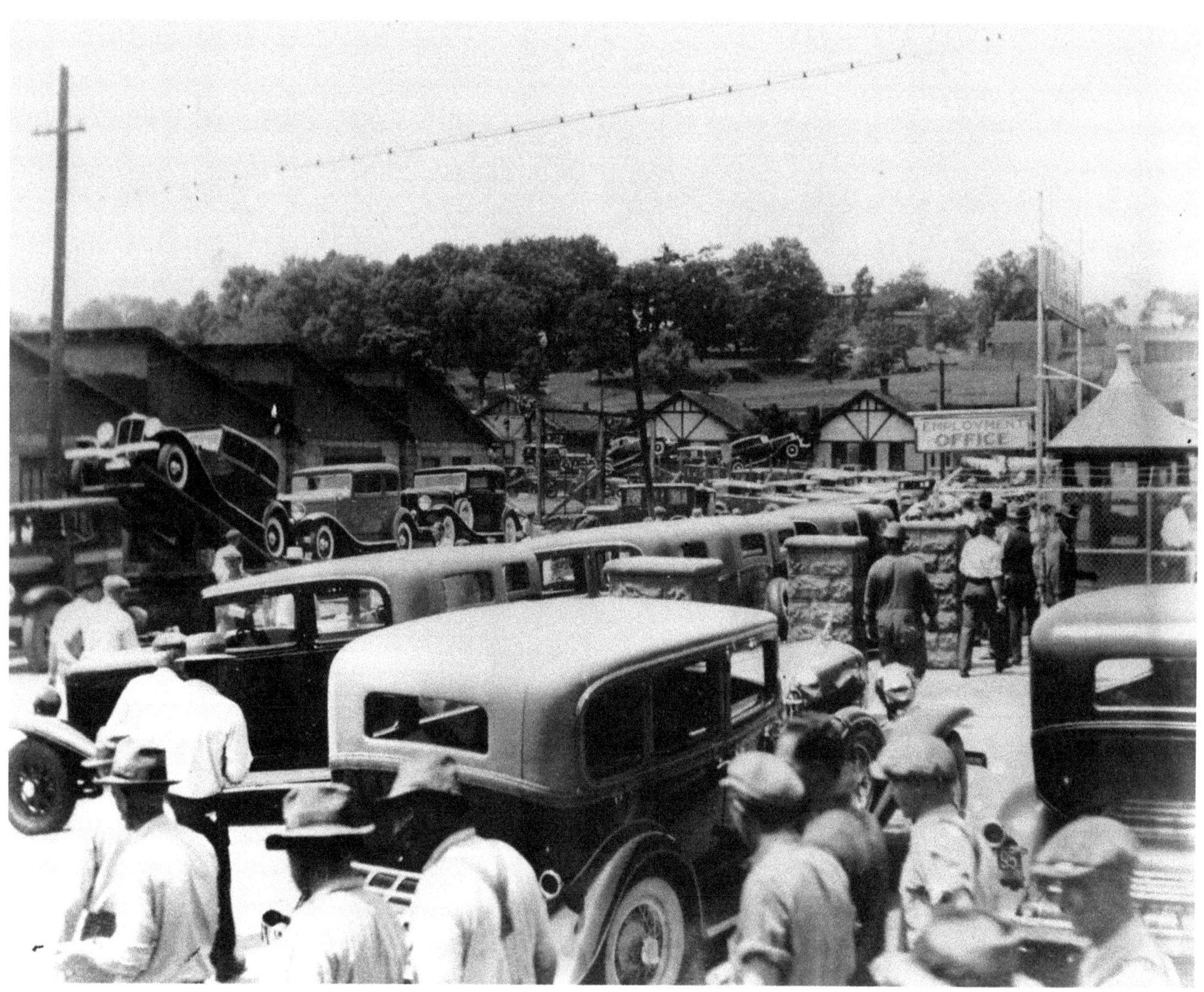

The activity outside the Auburn Automobile assembly plant in Connersville in 1931 was testimony to the achievement of entrepreneur E. L. Cord who had taken over the Auburn Automobile Company seven years earlier. Cord, who made Auburns one of the great success stories of the American automotive industry, expanded and modernized the company's production capability with this plant at 18th and Columbus streets.

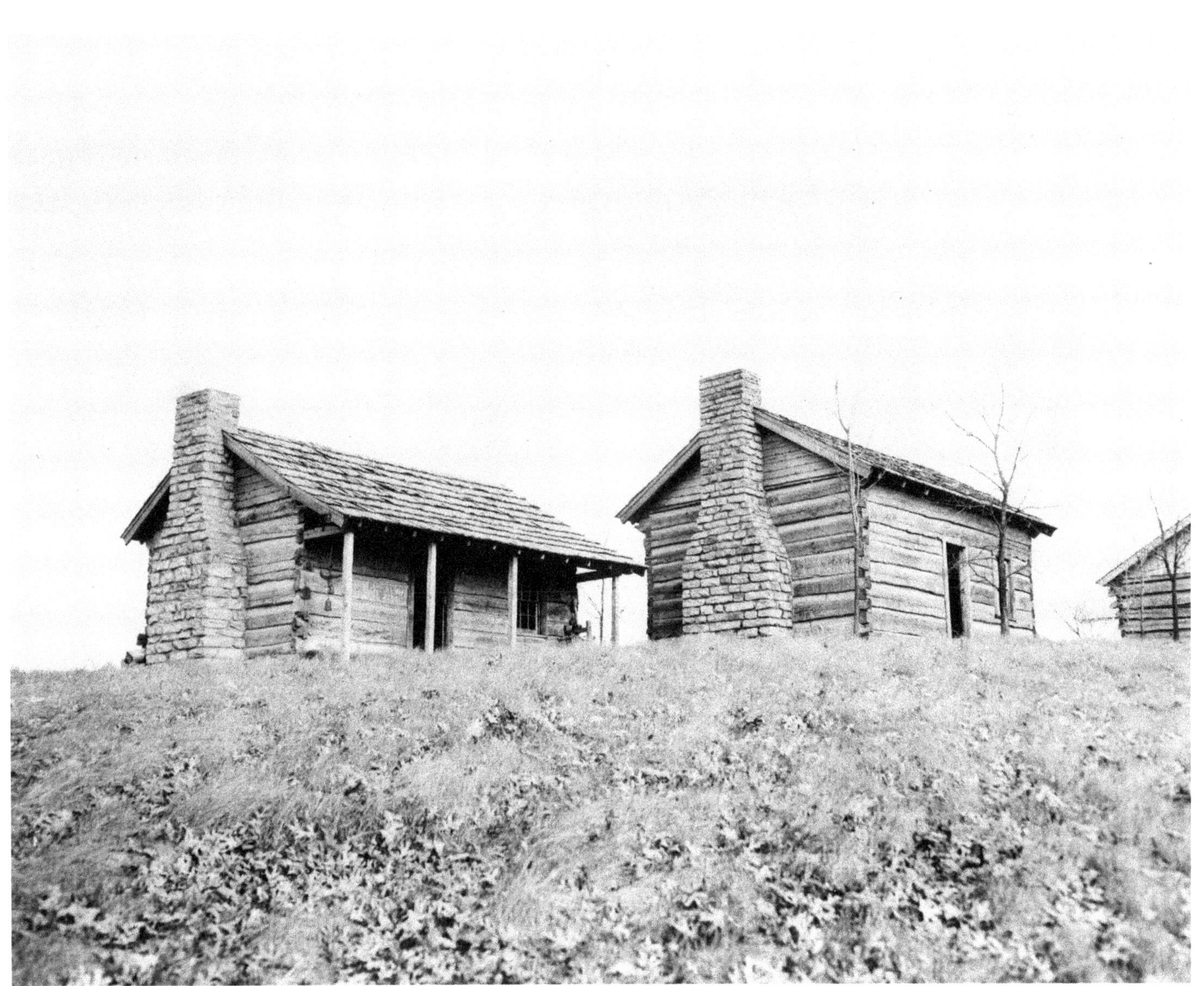

The Historic American Buildings Survey in the late 1930s was an effort to photograph the rapidly disappearing history of the nation. One such image shows a restored trading post, at left, and cabin, in the vicinity of Noblesville, said to have belonged to William Conner. Conner (1777–1855) was a pioneer settler, merchant, scout, interpreter, and state lawmaker whose trading post near the White River was the stopping place for many settlers making their way across the Indiana territory.

Some of the 25,000 workers at the $75 million power plant under construction in Charlestown in the late 1930s cross over the highway to work. The sleepy Clark County town was to experience exponential growth during the Second World War. In this photograph, however, the man with amputated limb and upturned hat in the foreground is evidence that the depression lingered on.

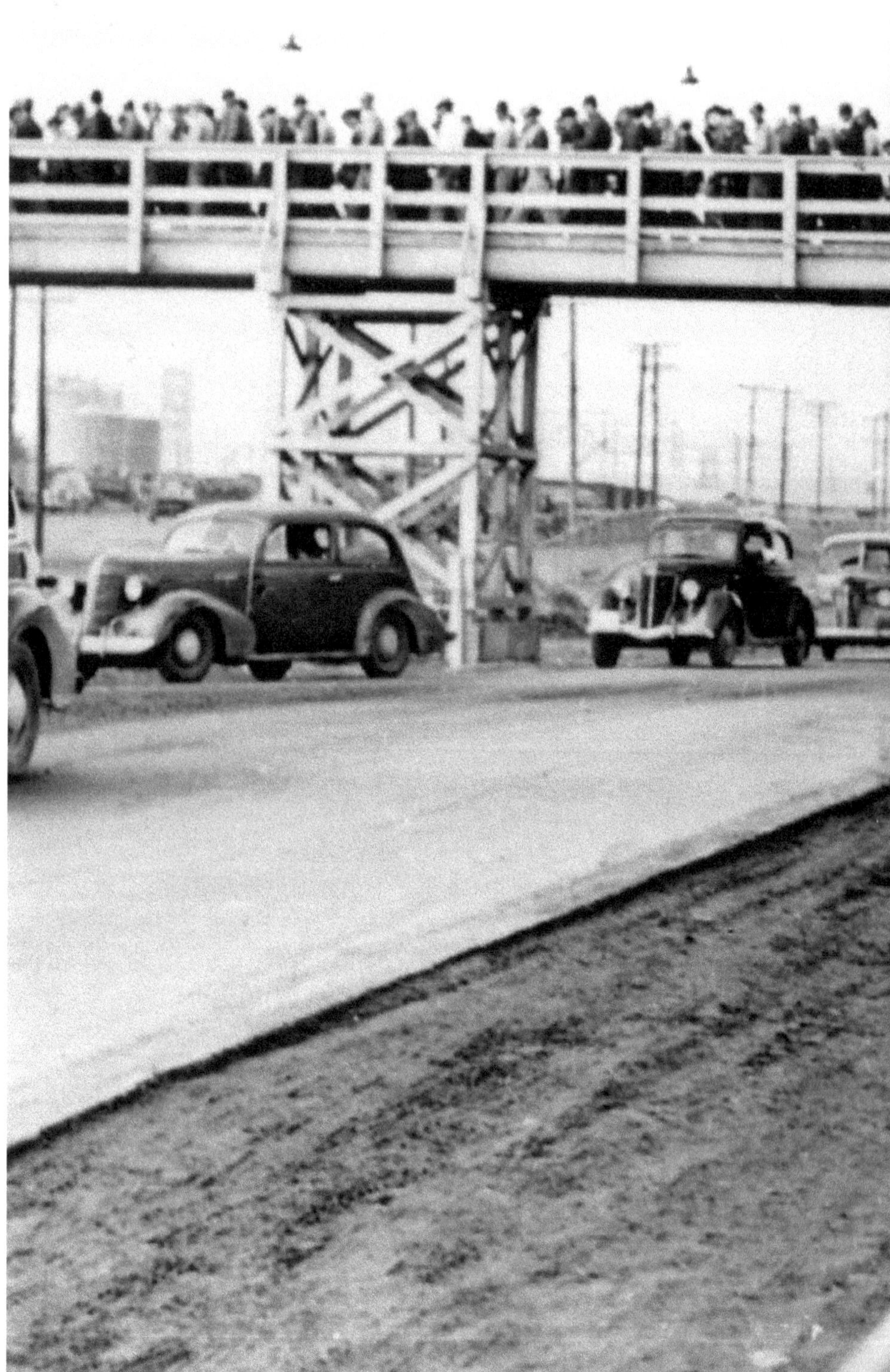

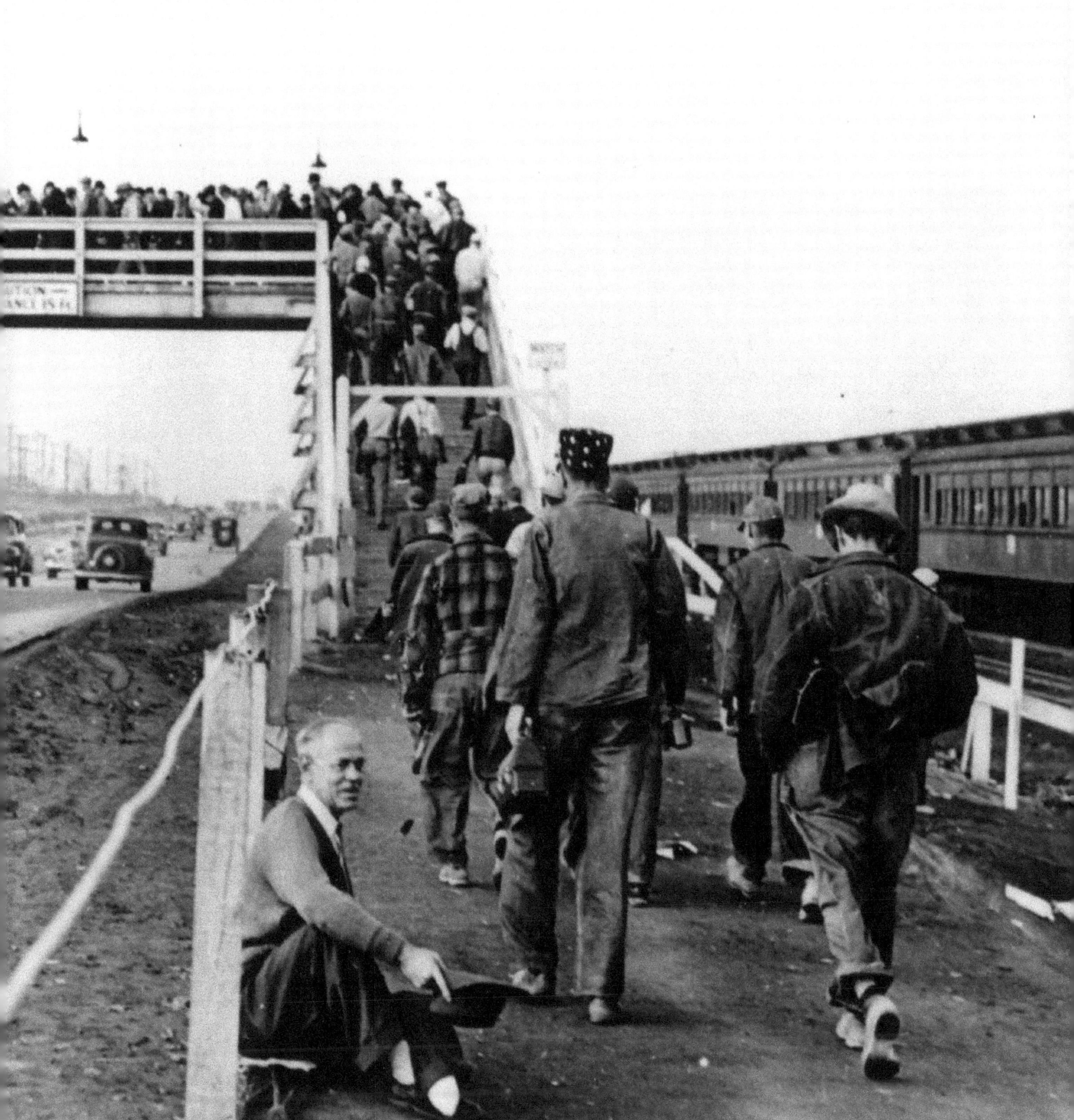

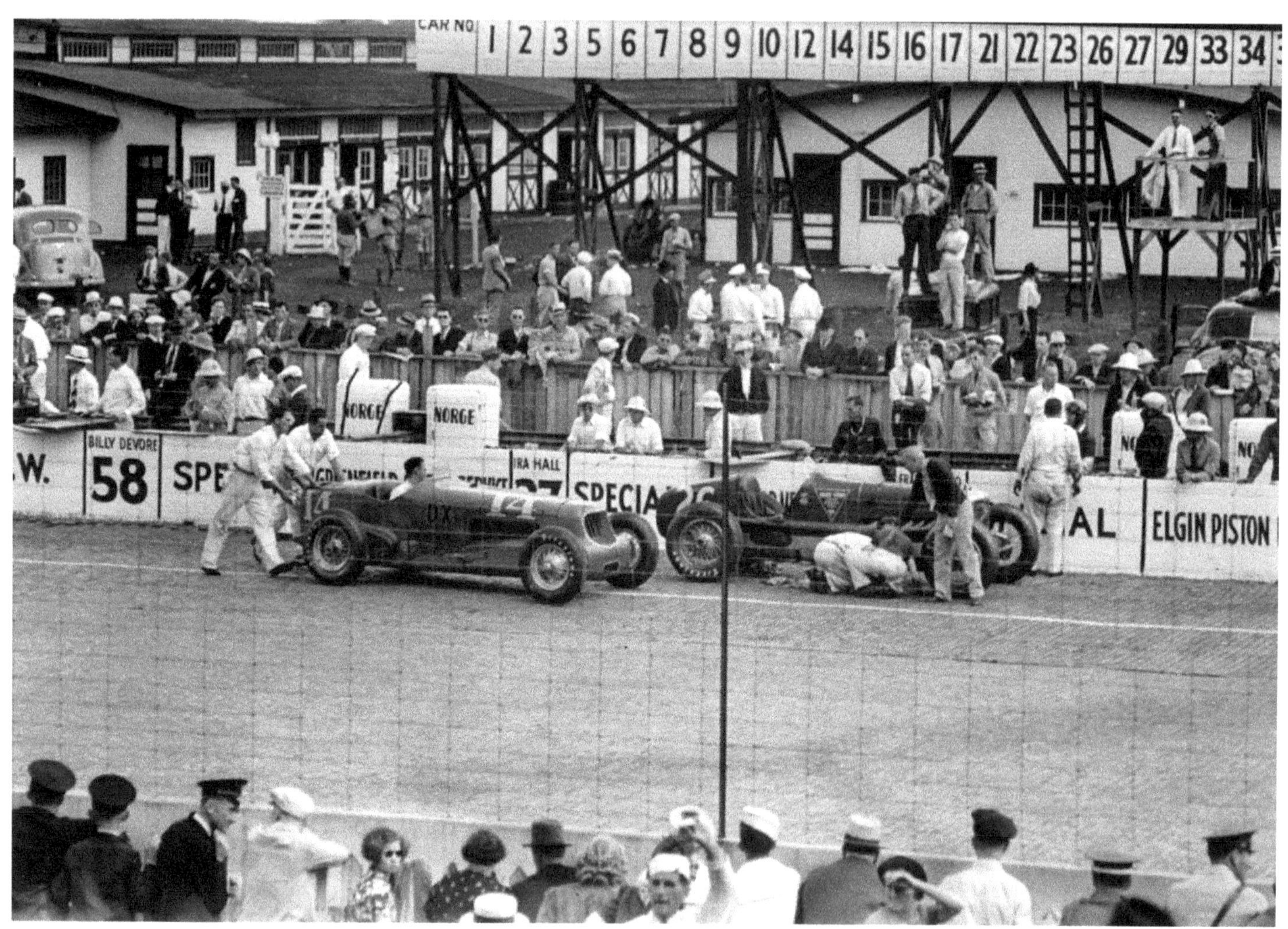

It was a disappointing day for the crews of the cars of Russ Snowberger (14) and Frank Brisko (26) at the 1938 Indianapolis 500. Snowberger had qualified with the second-fastest racer at a speed of more than 120 miles per hour, but a broken rod on the 56th lap ended his chance for victory and he finished 25th. Brisko's car, which started the race in 11th position, went out of the race on lap 39 and finished 31st.

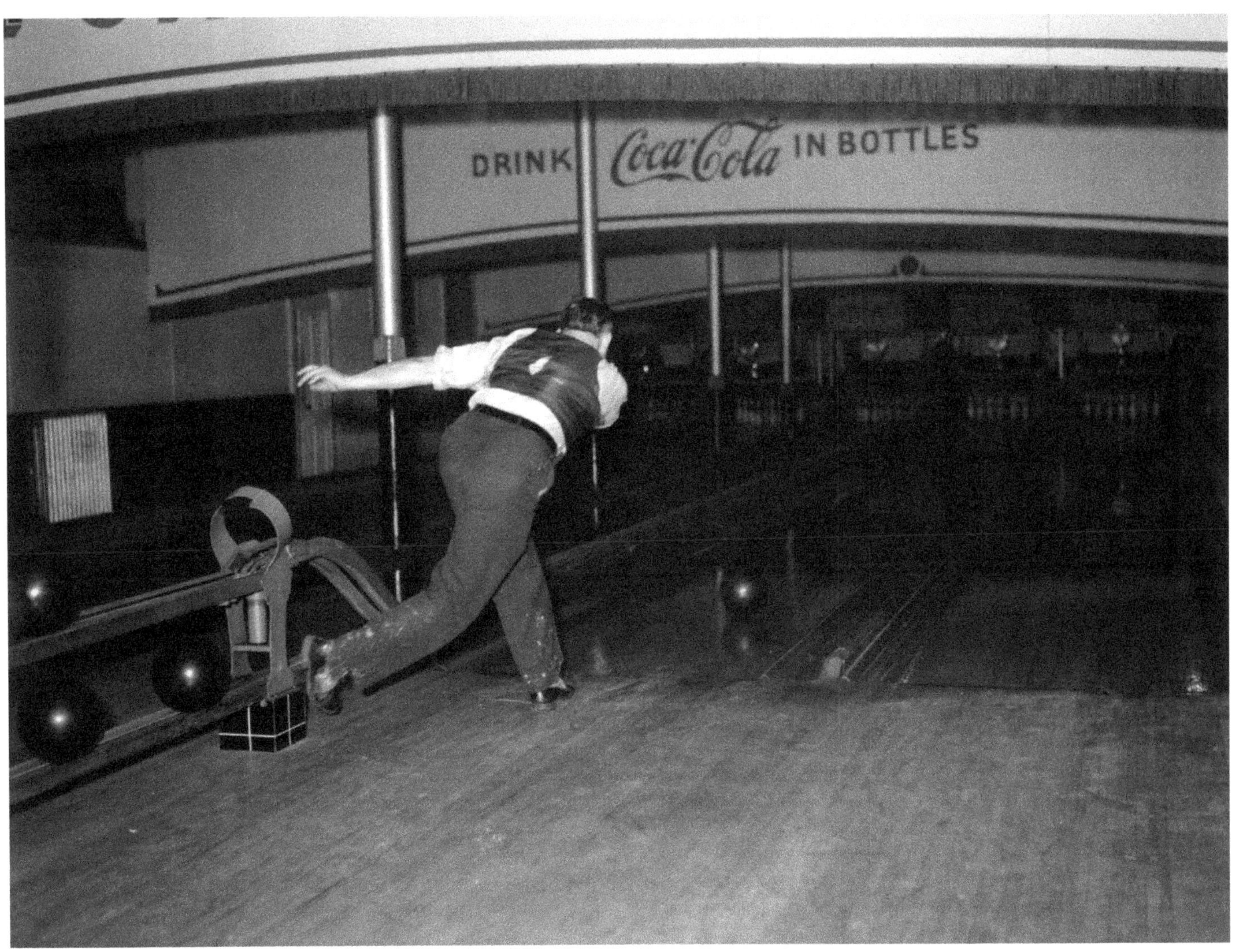

This lone bowler was photographed in Clinton, Indiana, in February 1940. Although his form is commendable, we can only guess whether his next score was a strike. The bowler's vest, dress shirt, and pants indicate that the modern bowling shirt was not de rigueur before the war.

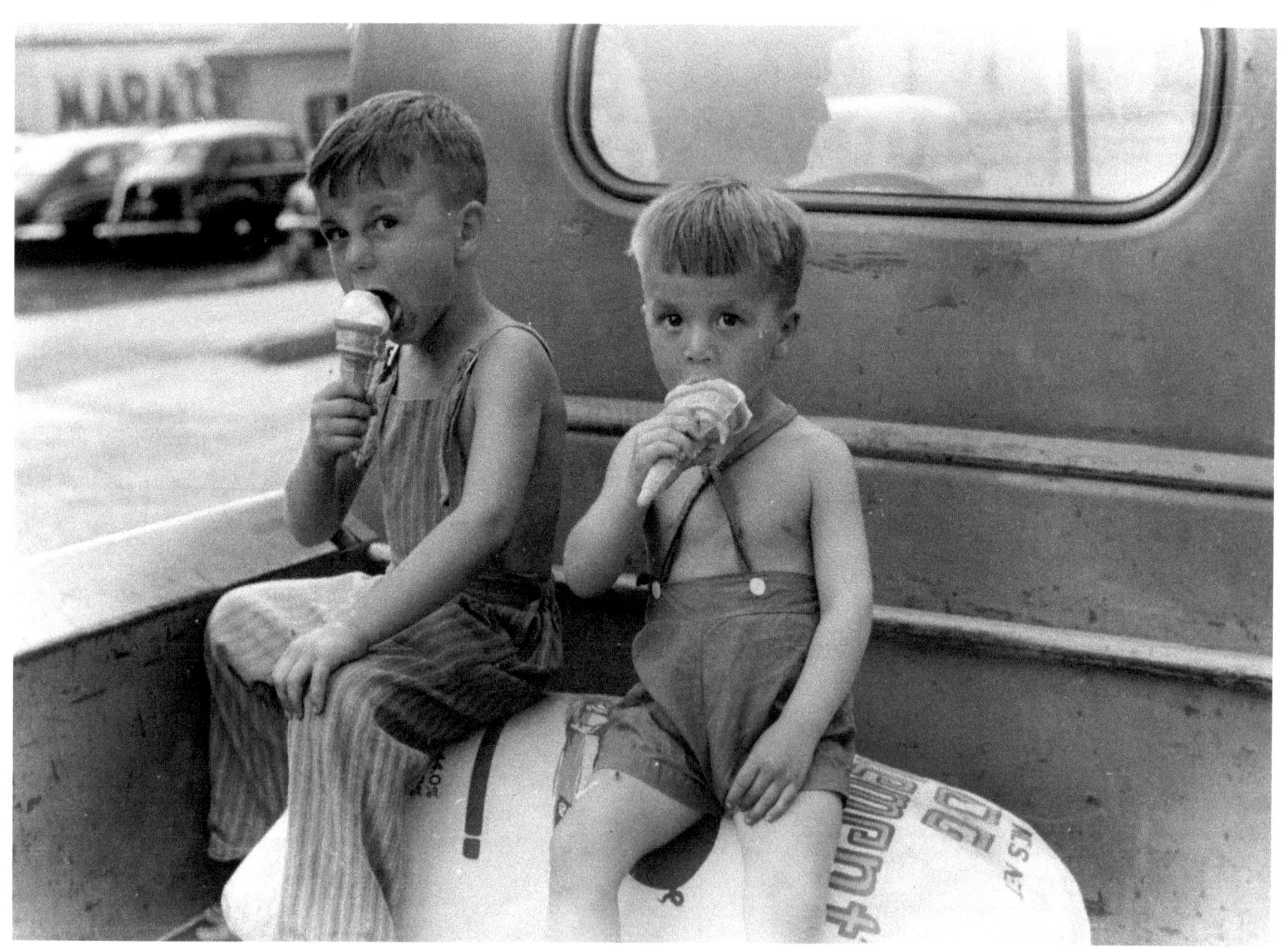

July 1941 was a simpler time. The U.S. wasn't at war yet and few things could be better than to sit on a bag of cement in the bed of your father's pickup truck and eat ice cream cones on a hot day. These two youngsters are enjoying ice cream in Washington, Indiana.

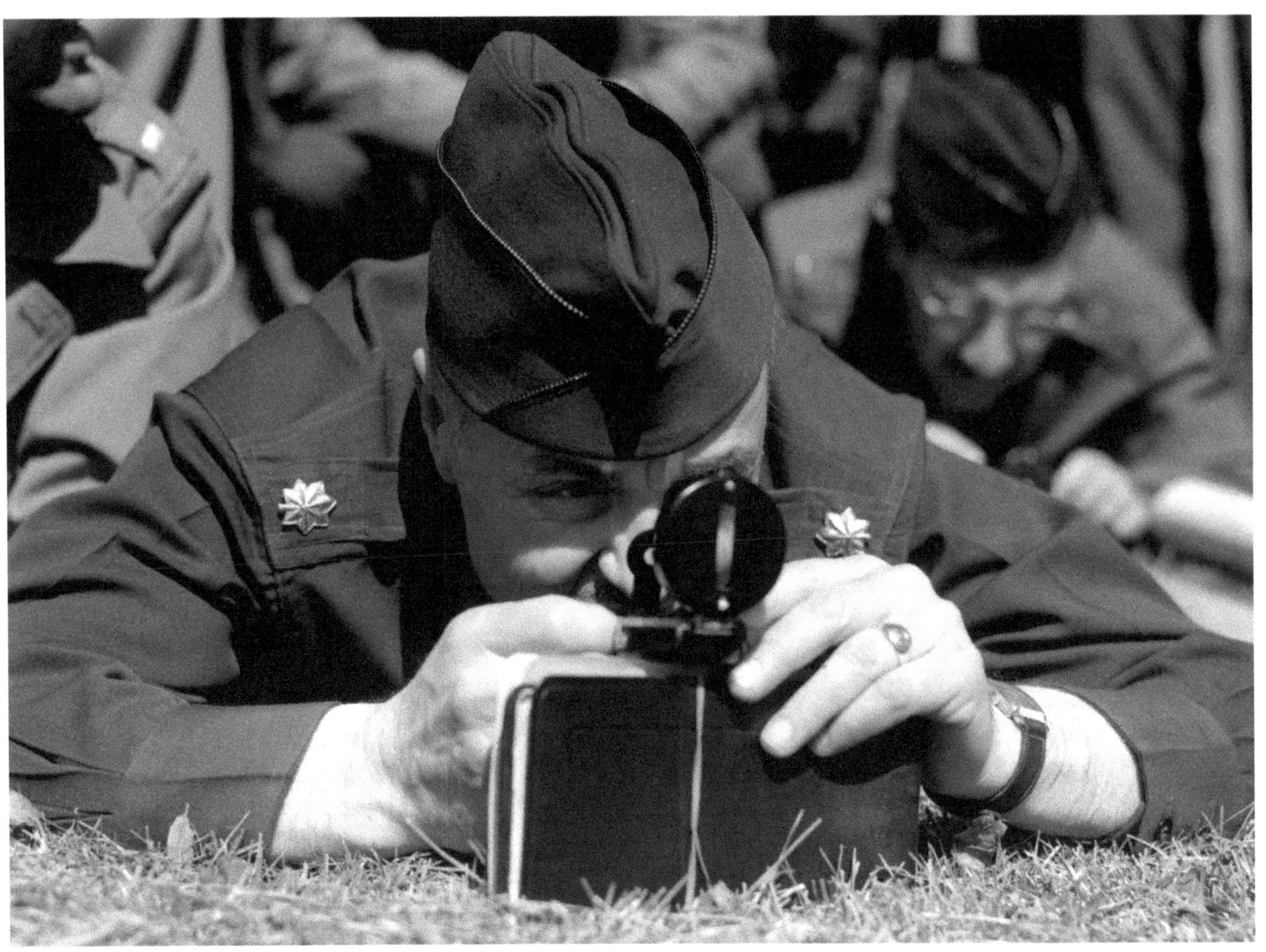

Major P. M. Hickox, a Methodist chaplain, learns to determine distances using a compass in a map-reading class at the U.S. Army Chaplain School at Fort Benjamin Harrison, Indiana, in April 1942. With the bombing of Pearl Harbor by the Japanese five months earlier, the United States was now involved in the Second World War and fighting to win. Losing to the Axis Powers would bring catastrophe to the free world, an understanding shared by nearly every American.

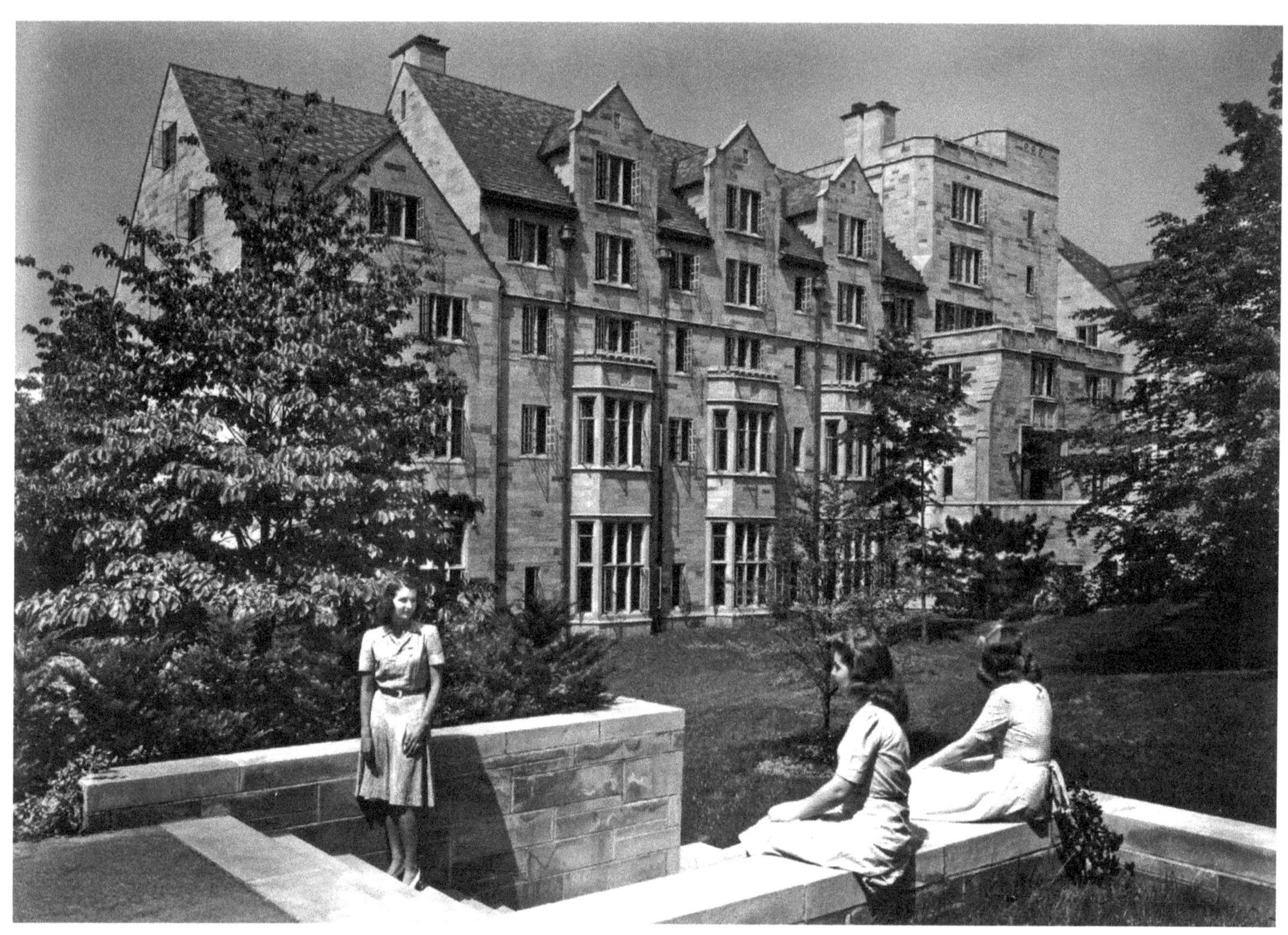

Three co-eds on the Indiana University campus in Bloomington pose at the Agnes E. Wells Quadrangle in 1942 where the former Beech Hall was renamed in honor of the university's first female graduate, Sarah Parke Morrison (1833–1916). Morrison completed her four-year degree in two years and went on to earn her master's degree. She became the first woman faculty member at IU when she was appointed adjunct professor of English literature in 1874.

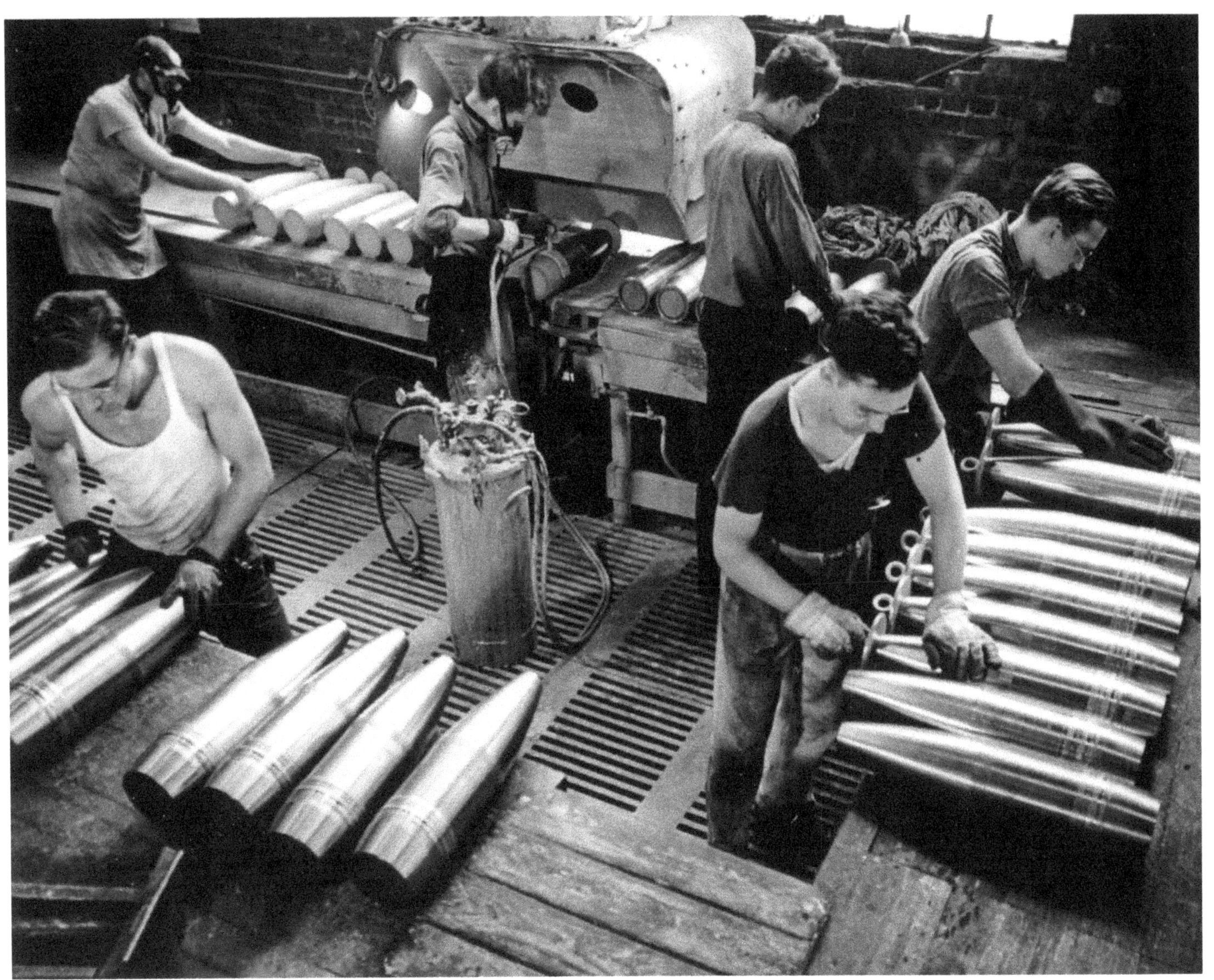

Six men inspect and paint ordnance at a plant in Hammond, retooled for the war effort from manufacturing railroad freight cars before the war. The disks being screwed onto the nose of each 155 mm shell (in the foreground at right) acted as wheels to keep the shells moving in a straight line along a production bench.

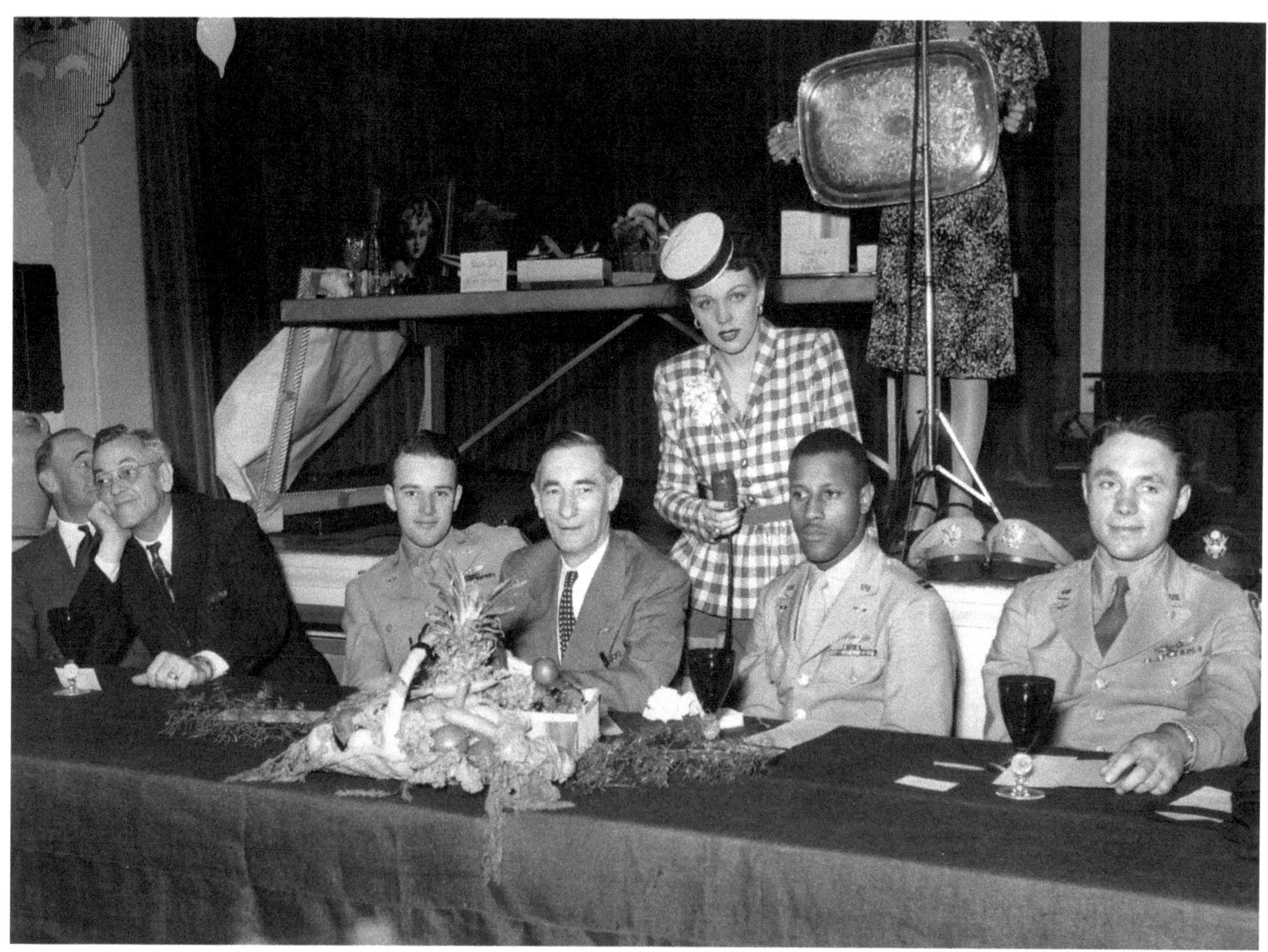

Mayor Harry Baals, center, is obviously pleased that this June 1944 War Bond drive has raised $1 million. Flanking the mayor are Major Walker Bud Mahurin of Fort Wayne, then America's top war ace, and Lieutenant Charles Hall, the first pilot among the Tuskegee Airmen to shoot down three Nazi fighter planes, who was visiting family in Fort Wayne.

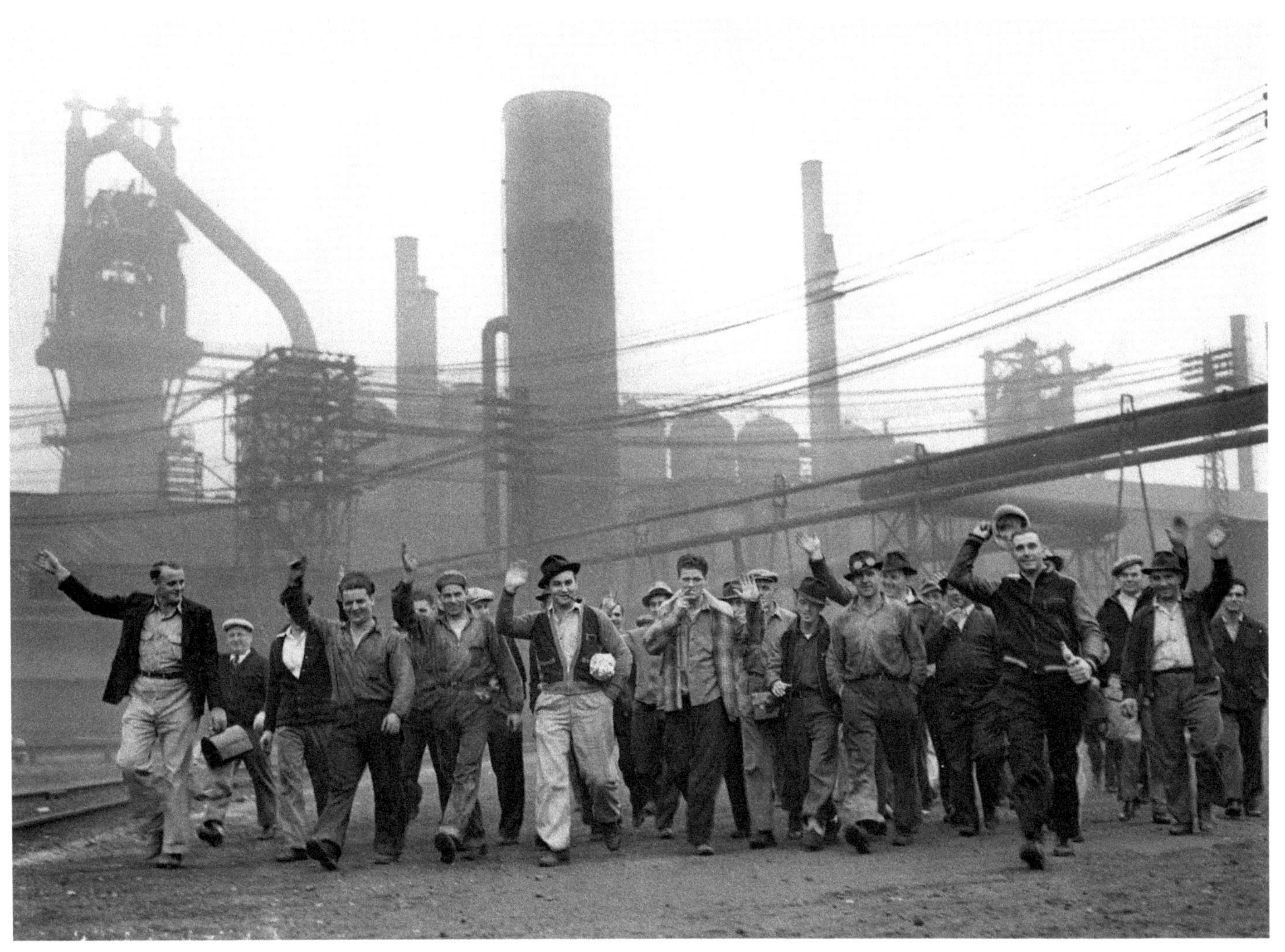

Wartime workers at Inland Steel wave to the camera, coming off their shift in Gary in October 1942. The photograph appeared in a company magazine with the heading, "Inland Men Answered America's Call for Millions of Man-Hours."

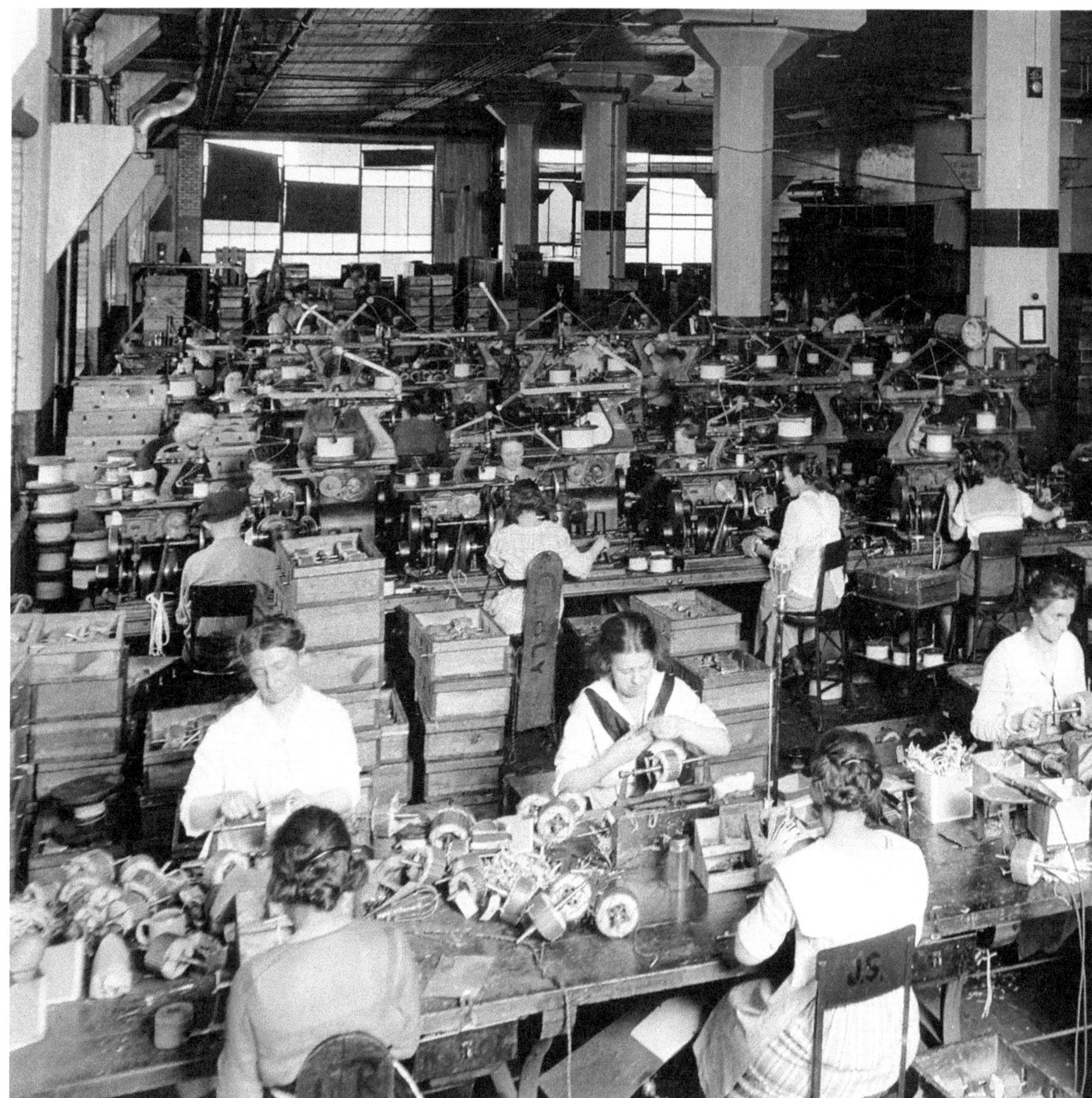
J.S.

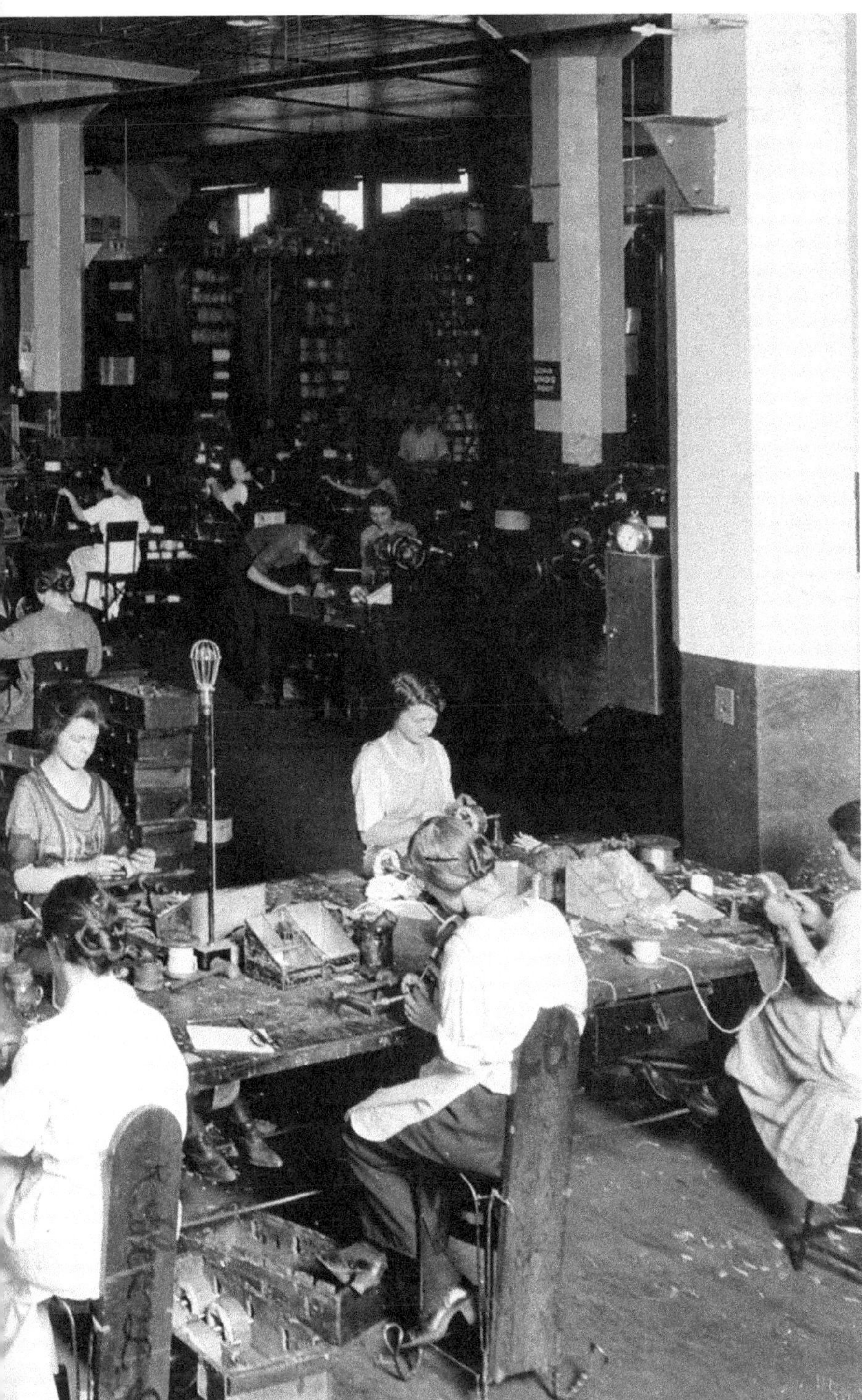

When World War II broke out, the General Electric factory in Fort Wayne suspended the manufacture of consumer goods to concentrate on war materiel. Women were hired in unprecedented numbers to replace the men entering service in the armed forces. Among the equipment they produced were small motors for aircraft.

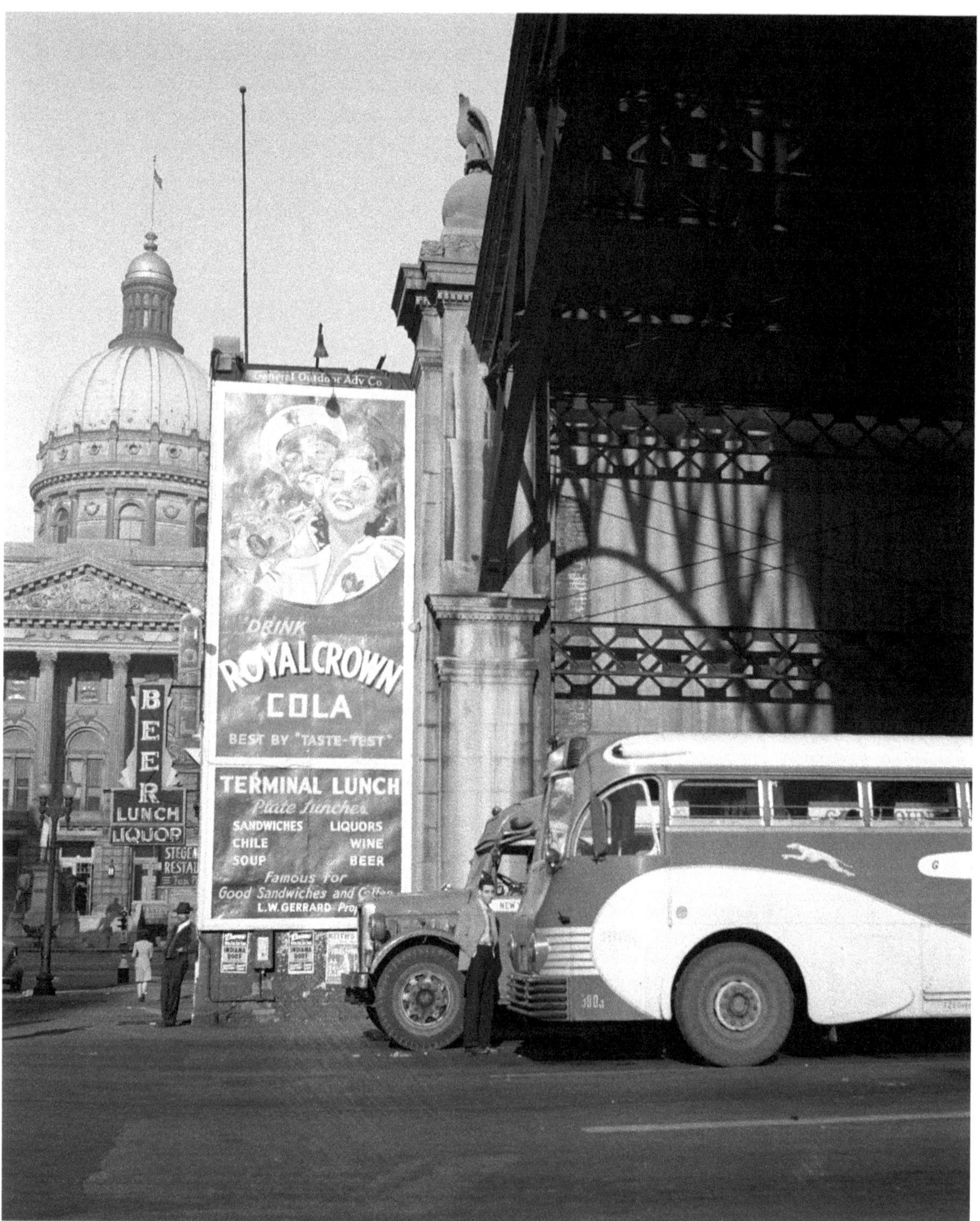

Advertising soft drinks, a billboard near the Indianapolis Capitol shows the happy countenance of an officer and his sweetheart in the fall of 1943. America was at war, and traveling often meant going by bus or train, since gasoline for automobiles was being rationed for use by the military.

A lone GI, a small suitcase in his hand, walks along Main Street in Richmond during the war. Statistics show that at least 250,000 Hoosiers served in World War II, and more than 10,000 gave their lives in defense of the nation.

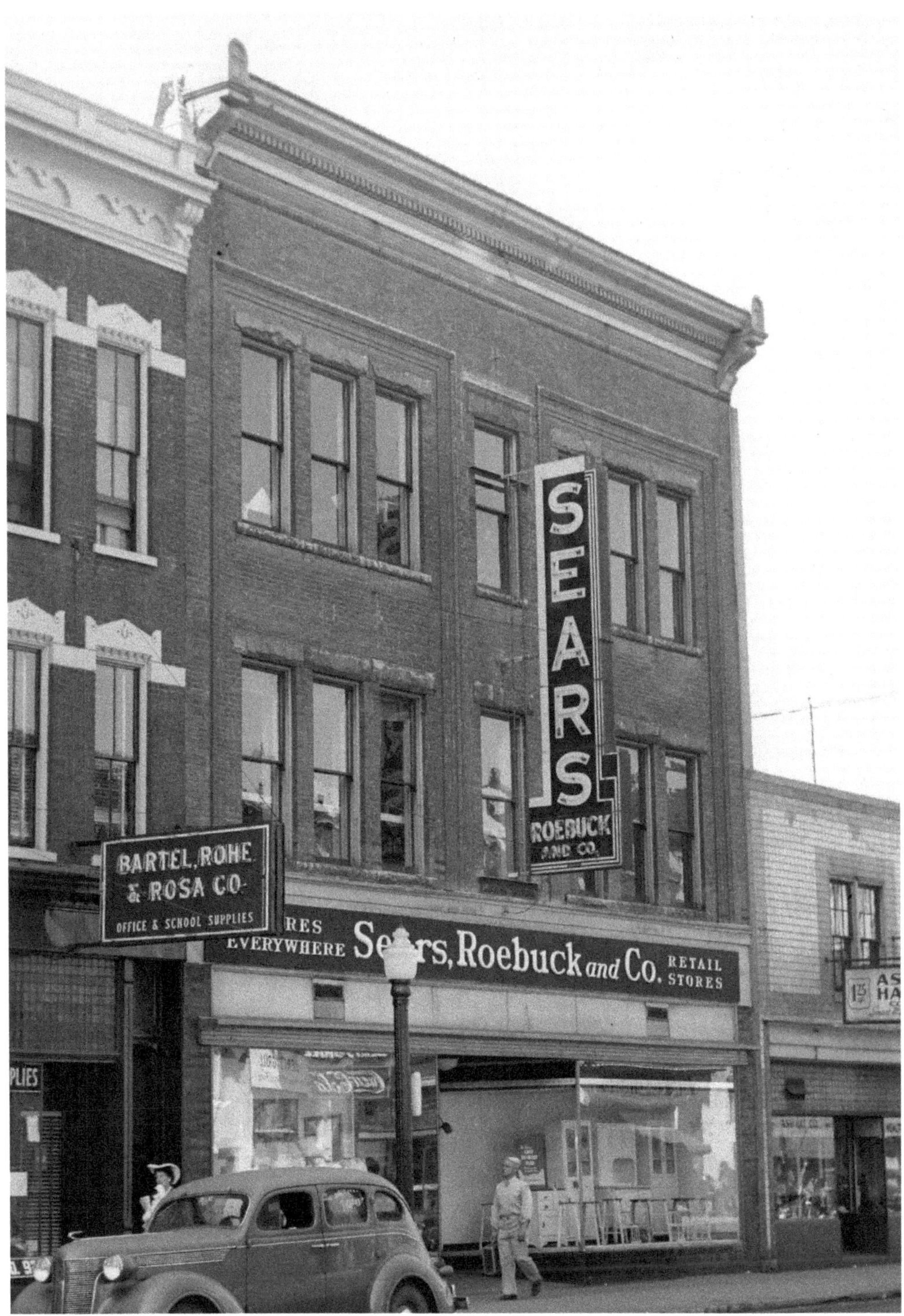

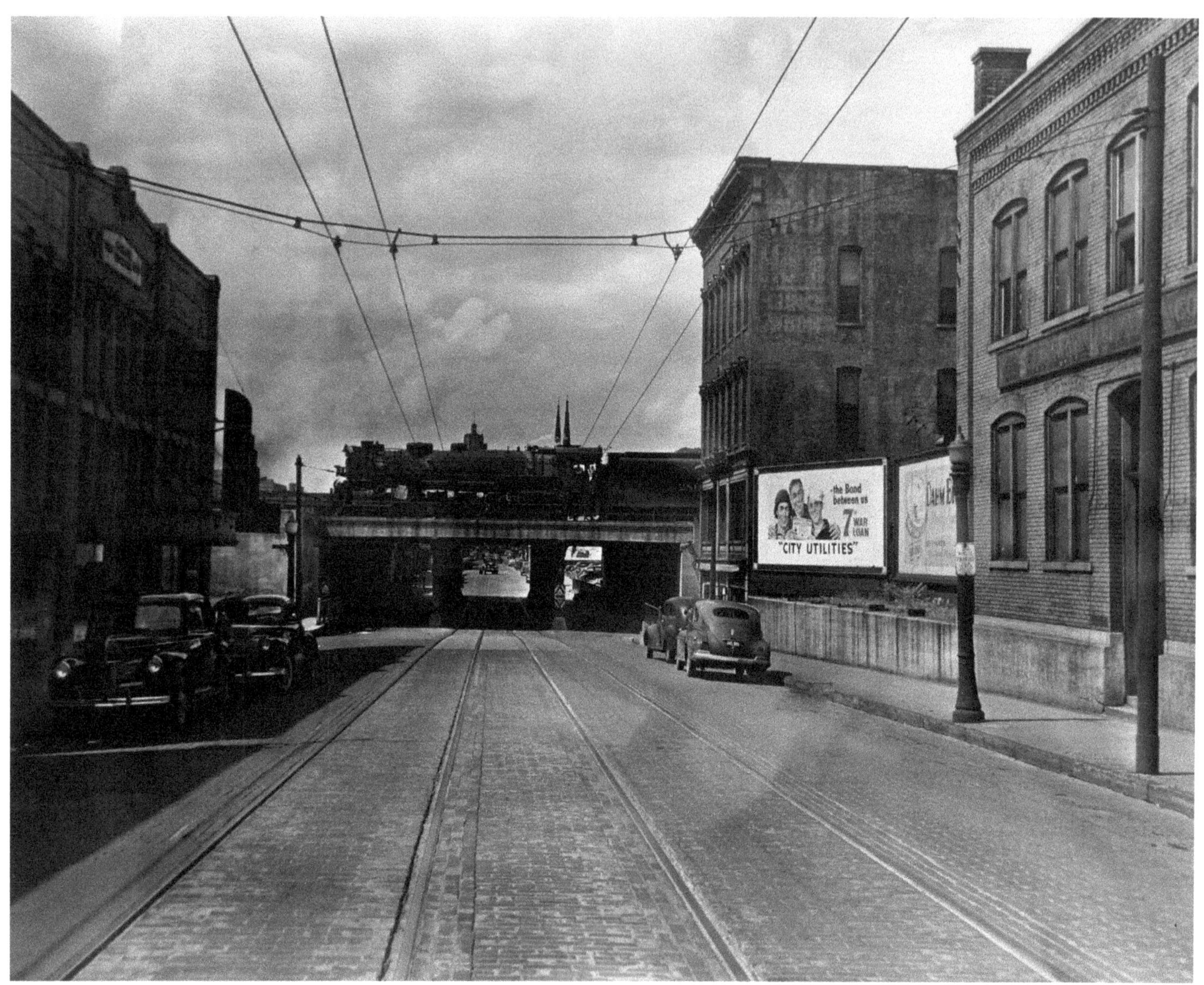

The end of the war in Europe was near when a photographer recorded this view of South Calhoun Street, a key thoroughfare in Fort Wayne. There was yet a war to win in the Pacific, however, and the billboard at right calls for united support of the 7th war bond drive. The drive, which began in mid-May 1945, raised a record $26 billion. The war would end with victory over Japan late that summer.

A Growing and Shifting Population (1946–1960s)

Most discussions of the post–World War II years initially revolve around the phenomenal growth in population known as "the baby boom." In numbers alone, the 1946–1960 growth is staggering. Indiana's population increased 18 percent from 3.9 million residents in 1950 to 4.6 million in 1960. Yet it was the demand that this additional population placed on Indiana's infrastructure that revised its historic assumptions.

The growth in population took place in the cities, while small towns in the state, and around the Midwest generally, dwindled. Towns with fewer than 5,000 residents had been home to 18 percent of the Midwest population in 1893, but this group represented only 10 percent of the population by 1952. Towns like St. Joe in northeastern Indiana remained self-sufficient after World War II and into the postwar years. The town enjoyed railroad service, a bank, grocery, post office, weekly newspaper, high school, and several businesses serving farmers. Today, only the post office remains. In contrast, Indianapolis was to become the third-largest midwestern city by 1980. Its population growth from 1950 to 1980 was a whopping 64 percent.

The advent of superhighways further isolated small towns and cities. President Dwight D. Eisenhower's Interstate Highway System achieved its goal of building a national network of limited access, high-speed roads. It removed traffic from small town Main Streets, however, contributing to their demise. The system also made cities like Indianapolis a maze of elevated roadways and ramps. Today, the state capital hosts four interstates in addition to another that rings the city and provides access to other highways.

A third aspect of the "baby boom" was the migration of families to the suburbs. Families who once shopped for large purchases in the cities could now spend most of their lives outside the central city from which their suburbs were born. As a result of demographic shifts, failed government programs, and other social forces, many inner cities would experience smaller tax bases, increased crime, and poorer schools.

On a brighter note, there has been a statewide movement to preserve Indiana's historical resources. Buildings have been preserved and artifacts saved. Photographs have been collected and now digitized for access by the public. It would seem that more people are agreeing with Theodore Dreiser, who wrote in 1915 that Indiana is a place where one finds "the soil more grateful."

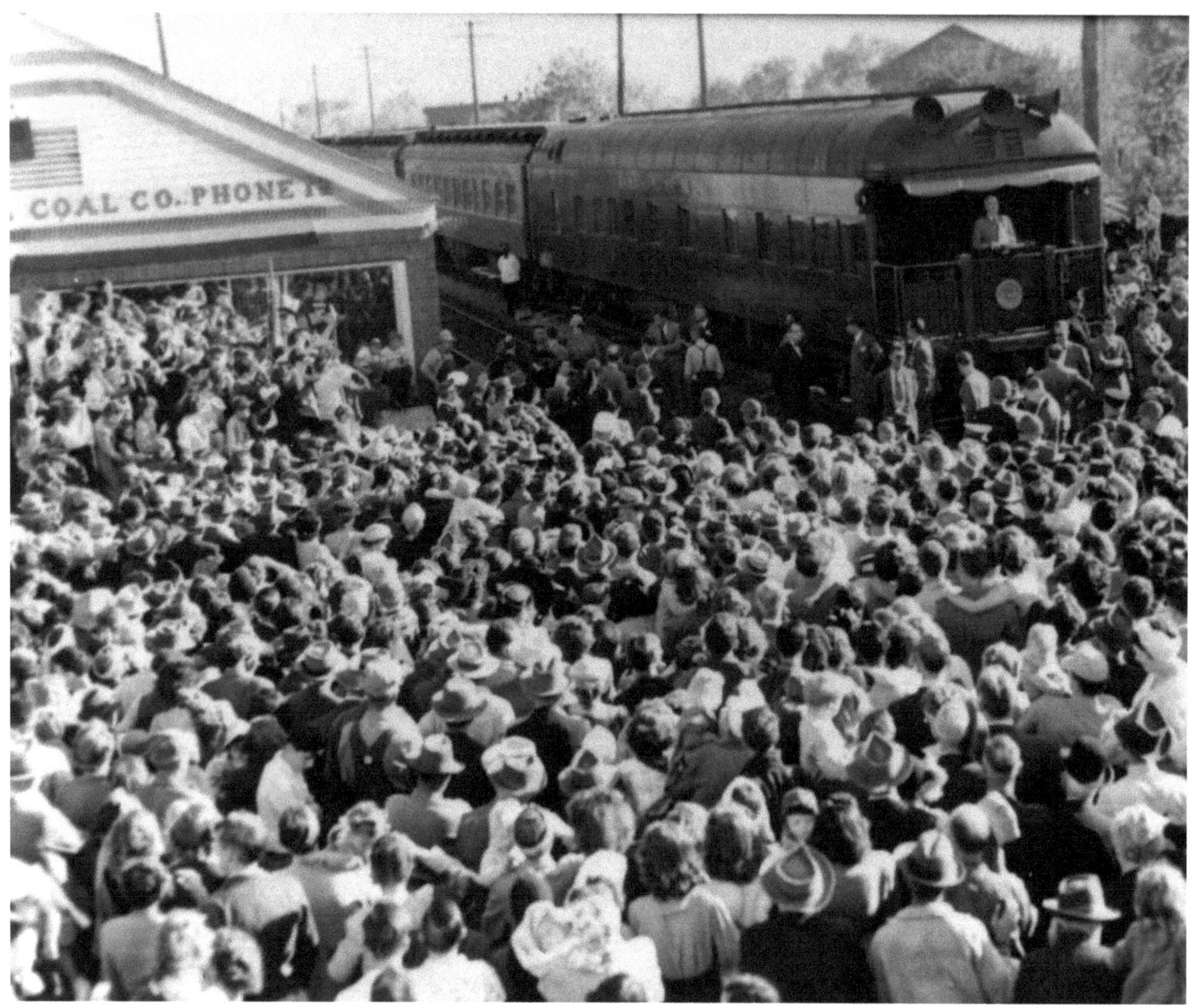

The crowd at Tipton engulfs the train from which President Harry Truman makes his address during his "whistlestop" campaign in the summer of 1948. Some thought the size of the crowd was attributable to just the curious wanting to see a president. But the November results in which Truman defeated Thomas Dewey demonstrated that voters liked "give-'em-hell-Harry."

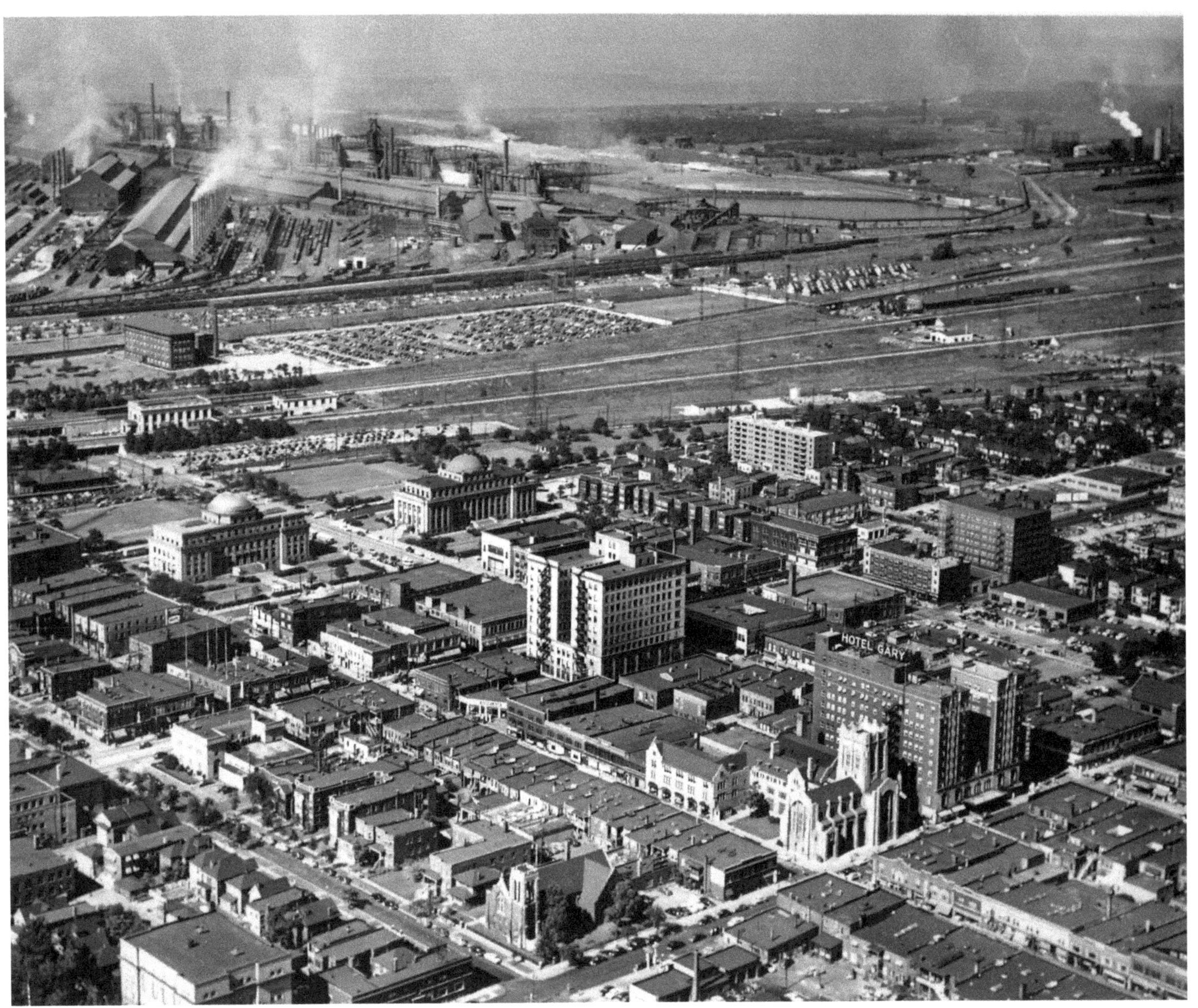

The 1950s were a period of continued growth and prosperity for Gary, evident in this aerial view of the city's downtown area and steel mills. The city's population grew by 33 percent to nearly 180,000 during the decade. Its renown even inspired a song, titled "Gary, Indiana," in the 1957 Broadway musical *The Music Man.*

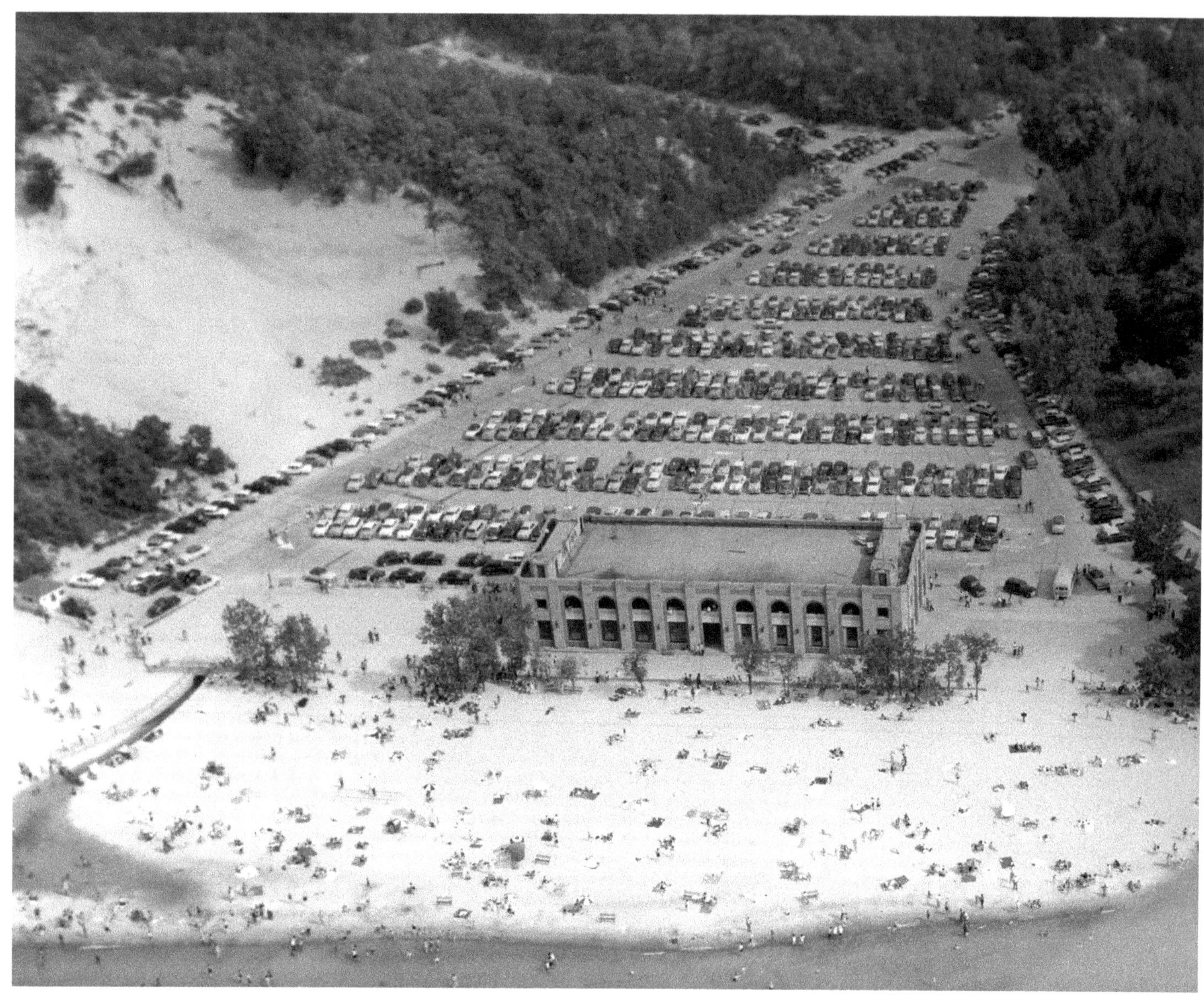

Efforts to promote a greater appreciation for Indiana Dunes State Park proved successful by 1955. The parking lot and bathhouse had been built by the Civilian Conservation Corps during the Great Depression, in anticipation of heavy use.

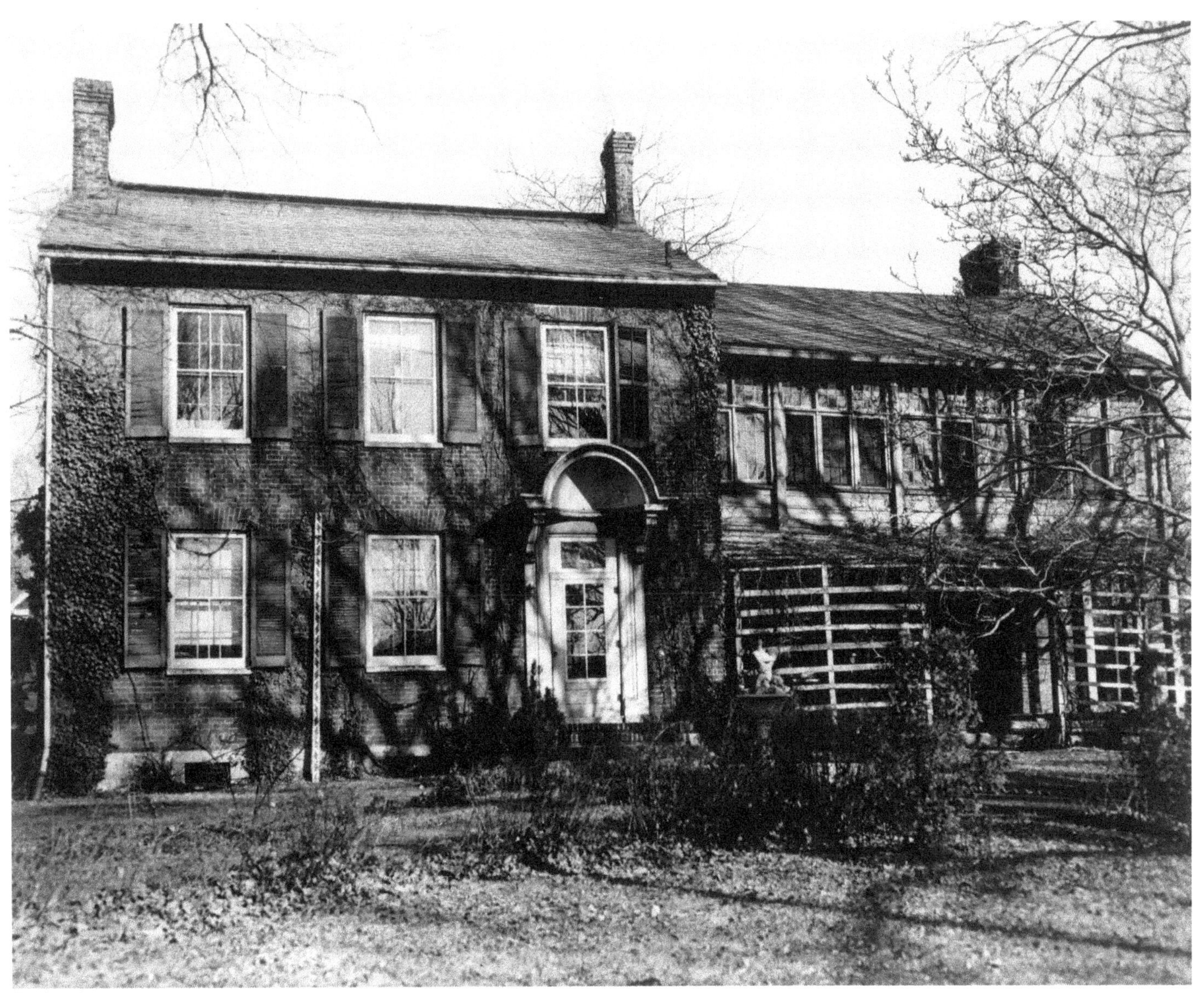

This large, brick house in Bloomington was built in 1835 as the home of Indiana University's first president, Andrew Wylie. Shortly after this photograph was taken in 1955, the university embarked on restoration of the structure. It is now a museum, re-creating the 1840s when Wylie lived there.

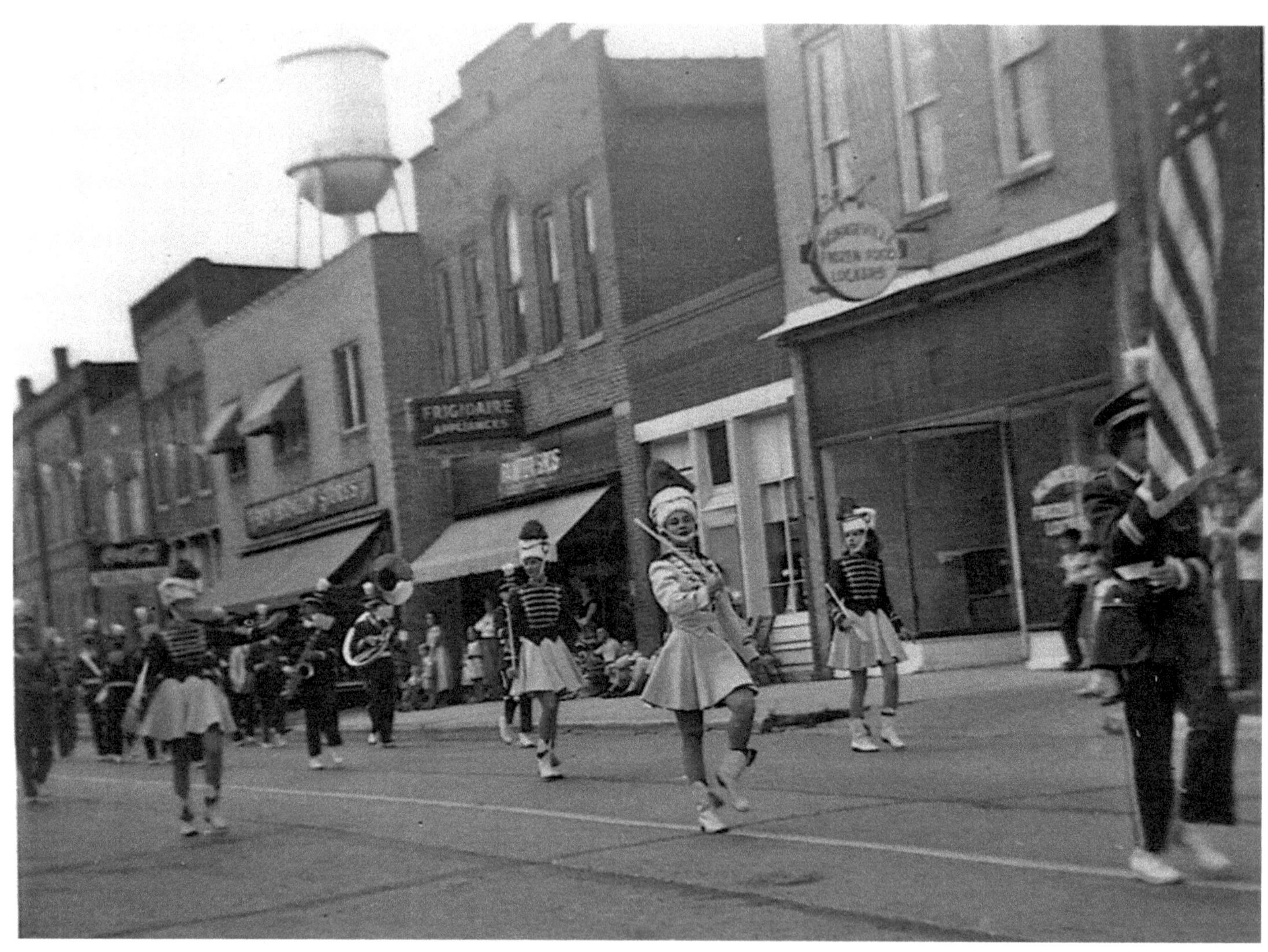

It makes little difference whether the location is an urban center or small town, whether the spectacle is high school bands or parade floats, Hoosiers love a parade. It has been that way since before the Civil War. From Memorial Day to Thanksgiving, Main Street Indiana has cheered soldiers and drum corps, floats and fire engines and farm tractors, cowboys, clowns, and politicians. Inspiring a lot of pride are the parades at county fairs, like this one in Monroeville in 1955.

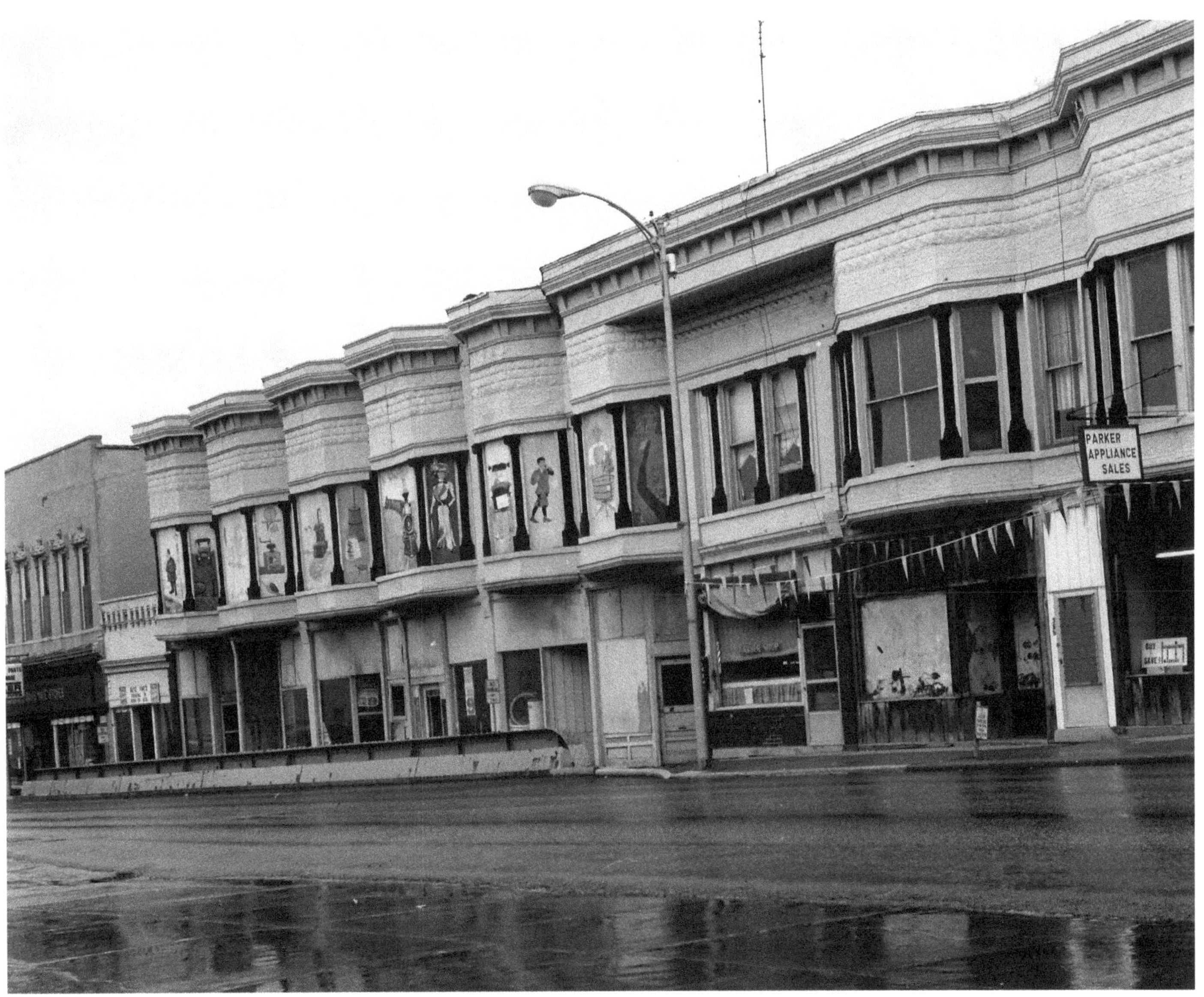

The buildings over the Little River in Huntington were like "castles in the air" from their inception in the early 1900s. They were built alongside two bridges in the center of the city, but separately suspended over the water, housing shops, offices, and dwellings before eventually deteriorating. Local artists painted murals to cover 18 second-story windows some years before the buildings were razed in 1977.

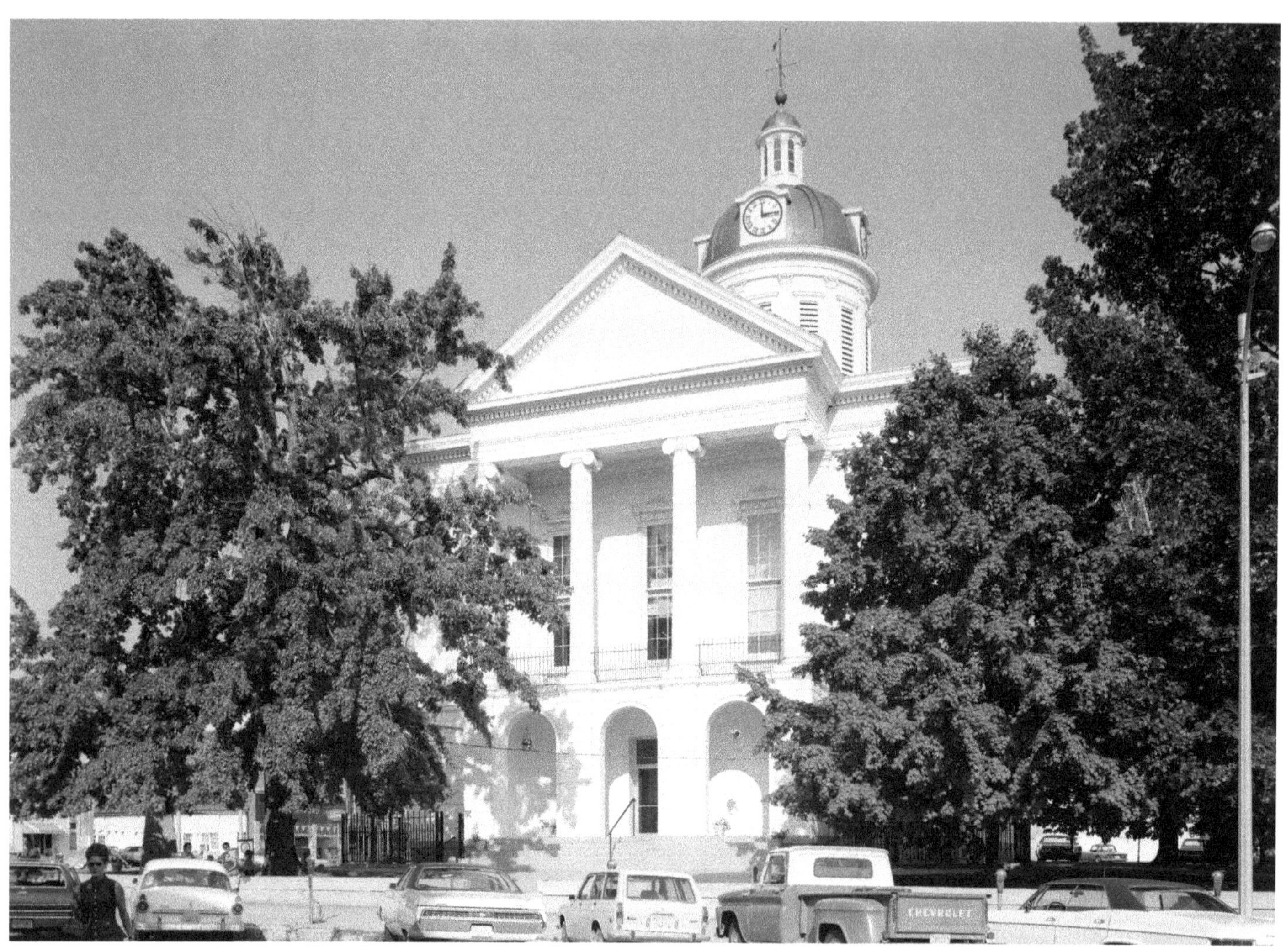

The Jefferson County Court House in Madison was built in 1855 when the Ohio River city was so prosperous that Indiana's first railroad connected it to Indianapolis. The courthouse sparkles in the sunlight in this photo taken not long after its centennial. But the courthouse burned in May 2009 when the dome and cupola caught fire during restoration work as Madison prepared for its bicentennial. City leaders stated that the courthouse would be rebuilt.

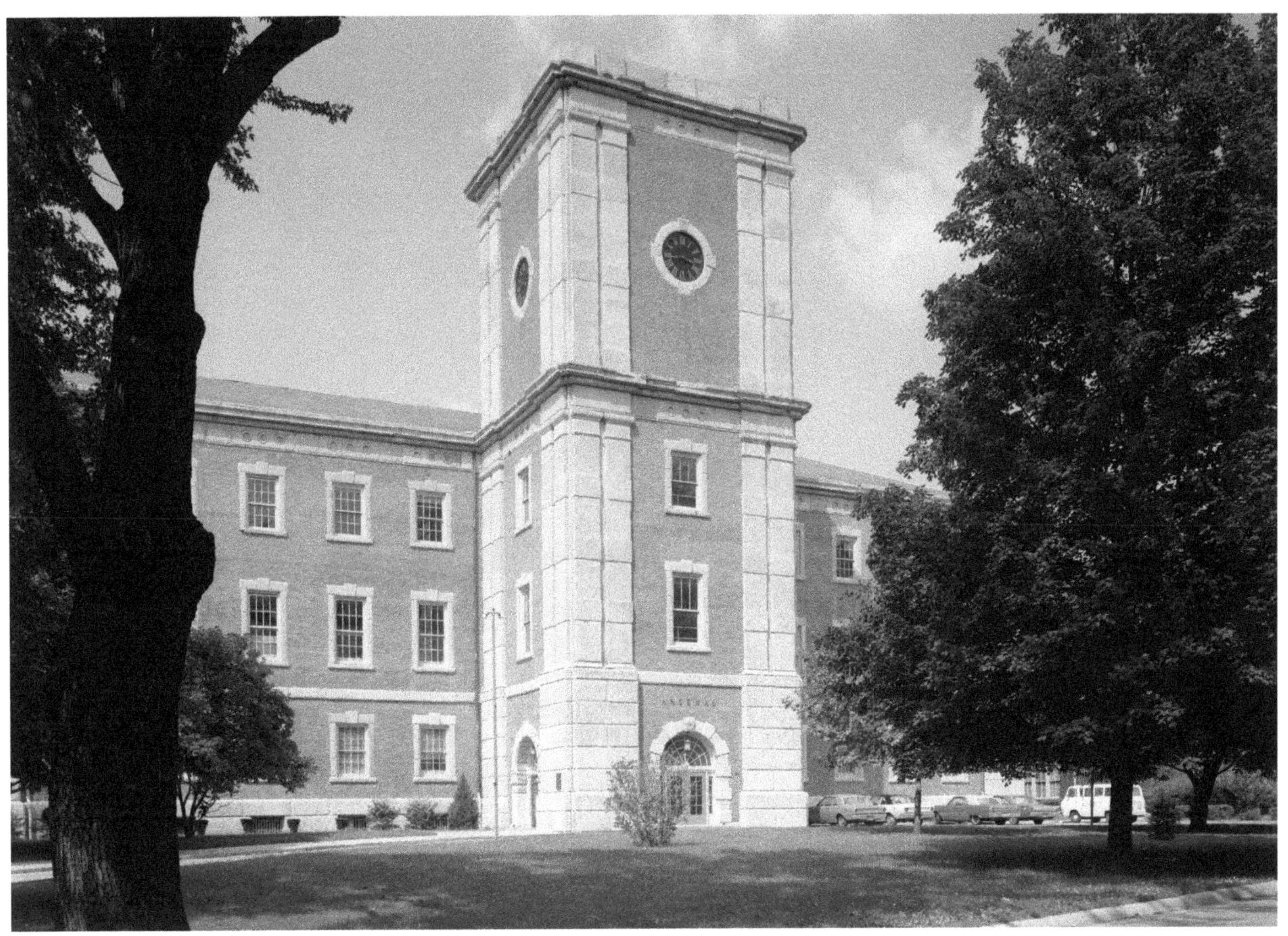

The U.S. Arsenal Building was built during the Civil War on the outskirts of Indianapolis as a safe storage facility for ammunition and gunpowder. The 1500 East Michigan Street complex was maintained by the government until 1903, when changes in ordnance made it unnecessary and new neighborhoods were growing nearby. It is now part of the Arsenal Technical High School operated by the Indianapolis Public School System.

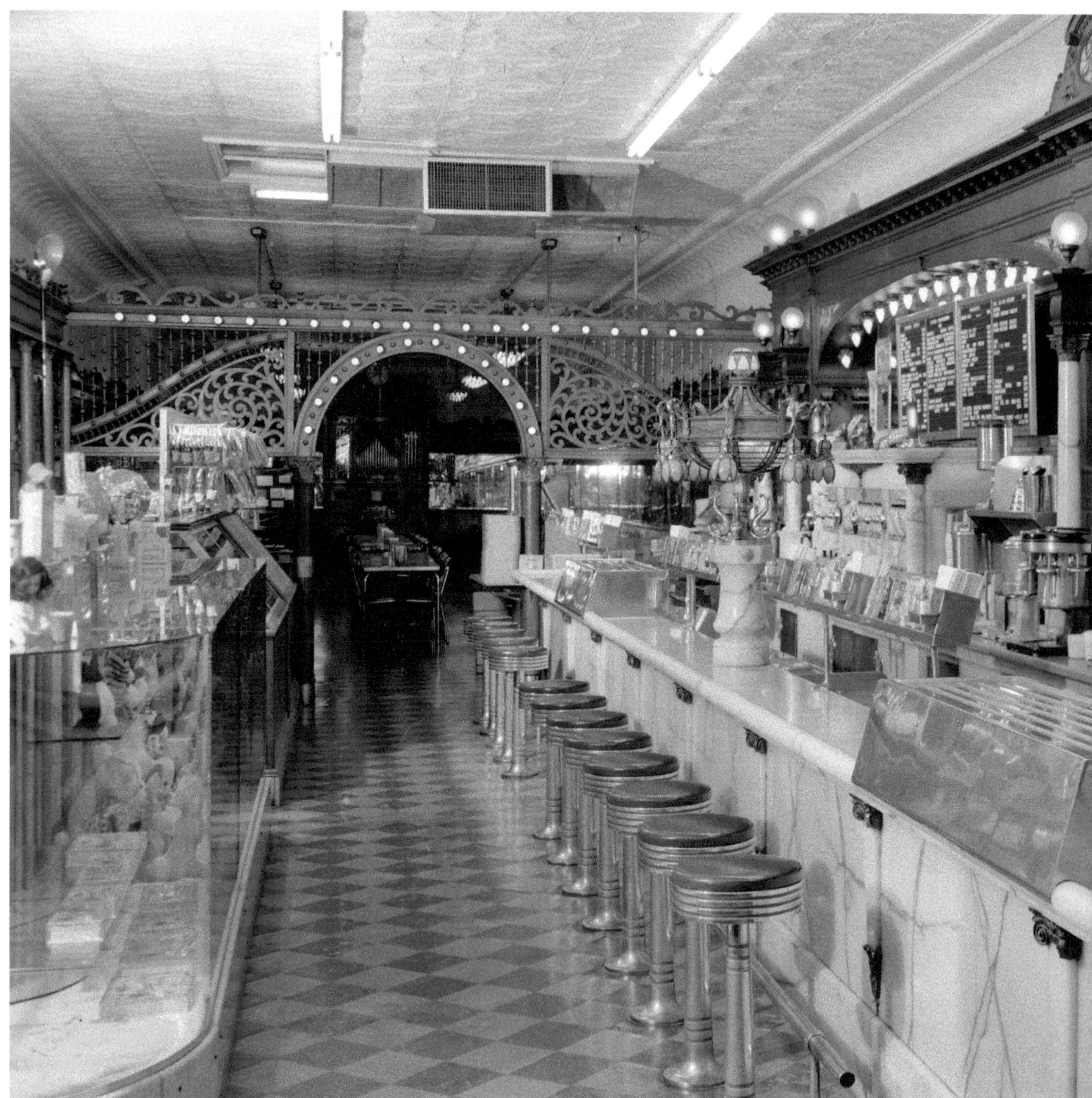

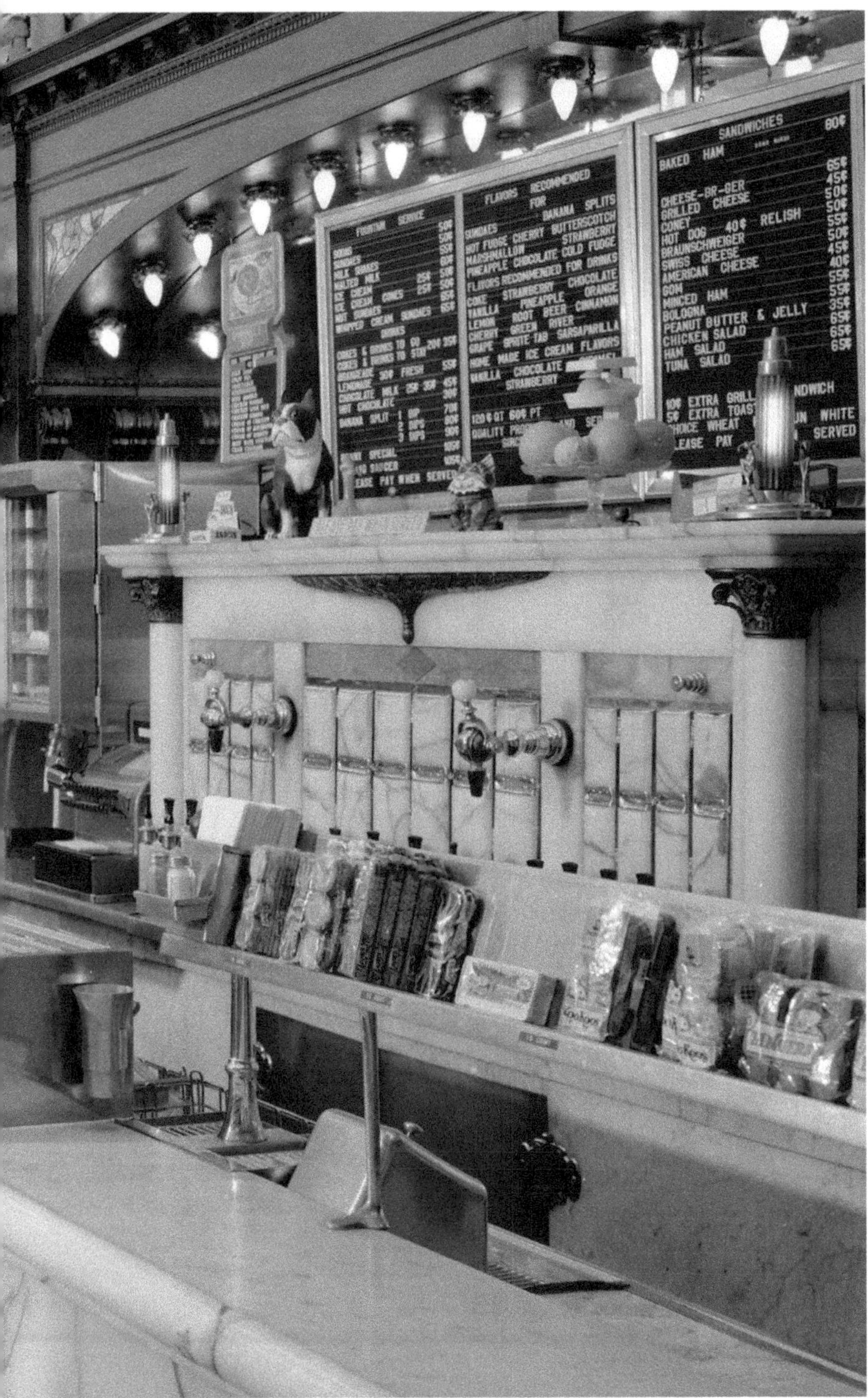

The elaborate interior of Zaharako's Ice Cream Parlor inspired its selection as a subject in the Historic American Buildings photographic survey. The soda fountain and confectionery served as a social center for the Columbus community from its founding in 1900 and still entices ice cream lovers everywhere to enjoy their favorite flavor inside its historic interior.

Senator Robert F. Kennedy began his campaign swing through Indiana for the Democratic presidential nomination in April 1968 with a rally at Gary airport. During an appearance later in the day in Indianapolis, Kennedy learned that Martin Luther King, Jr., had succumbed to an assassin's attack and shared the news with a large crowd. The brother of slain president John F. Kennedy was assassinated a few weeks later in California.

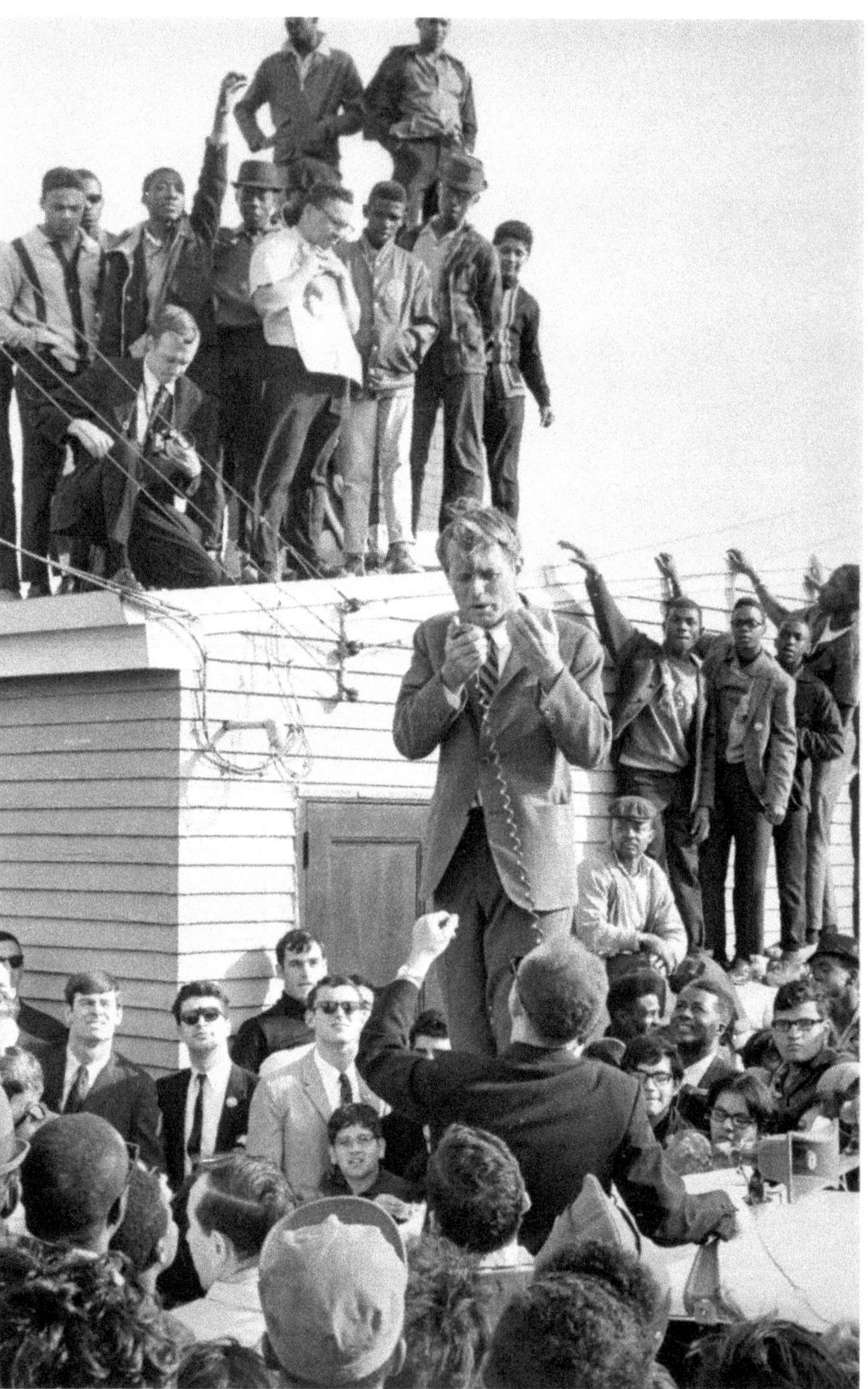

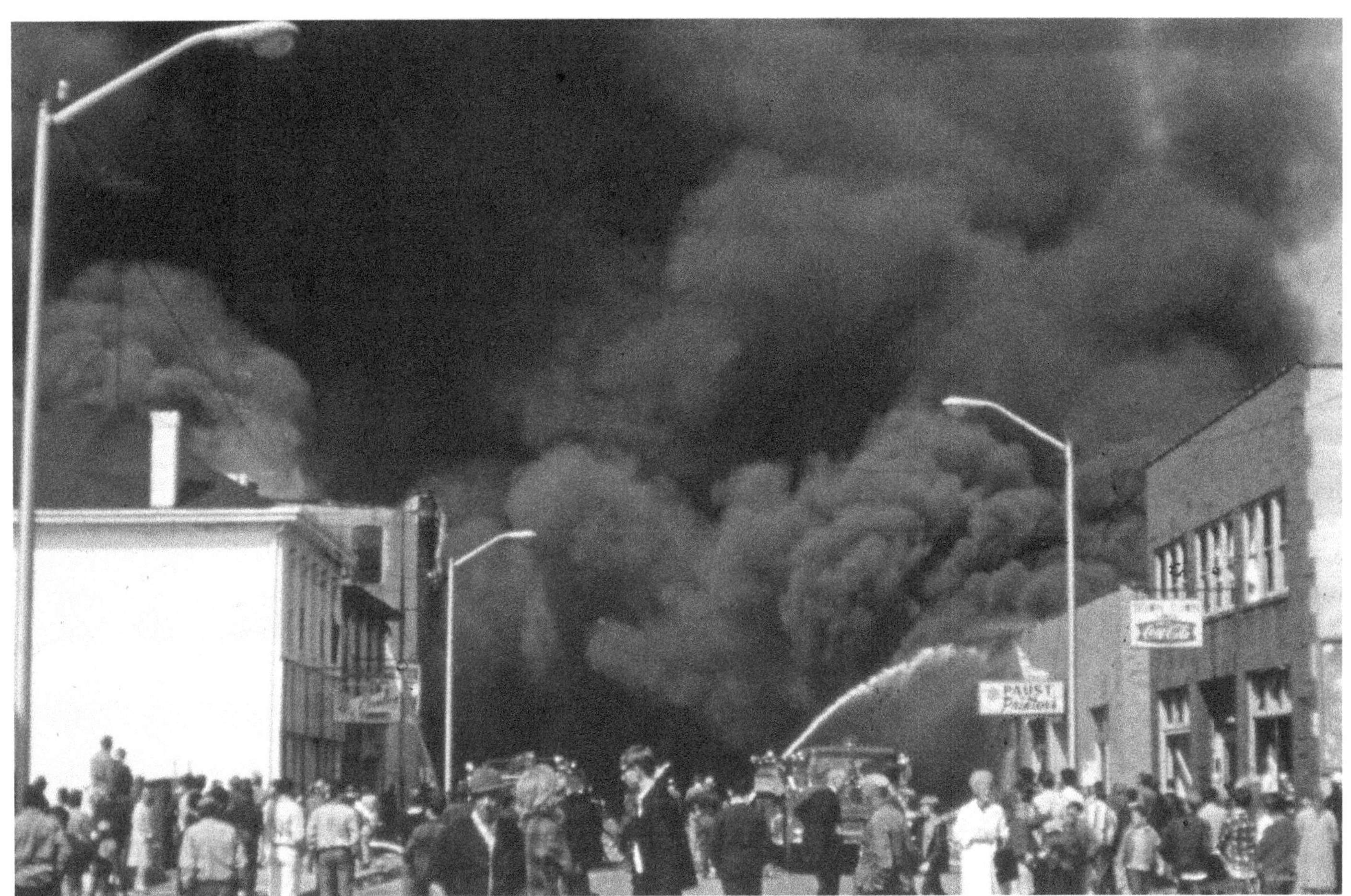

A gas leak on a Saturday morning in downtown Richmond led to an explosion and fire that left 41 persons dead and the business section of the city in shambles. An off-duty state trooper, Bob Cline, heard the explosion and caught the scene in a series of dramatic photographs that helped authorities determine the cause of the fire.

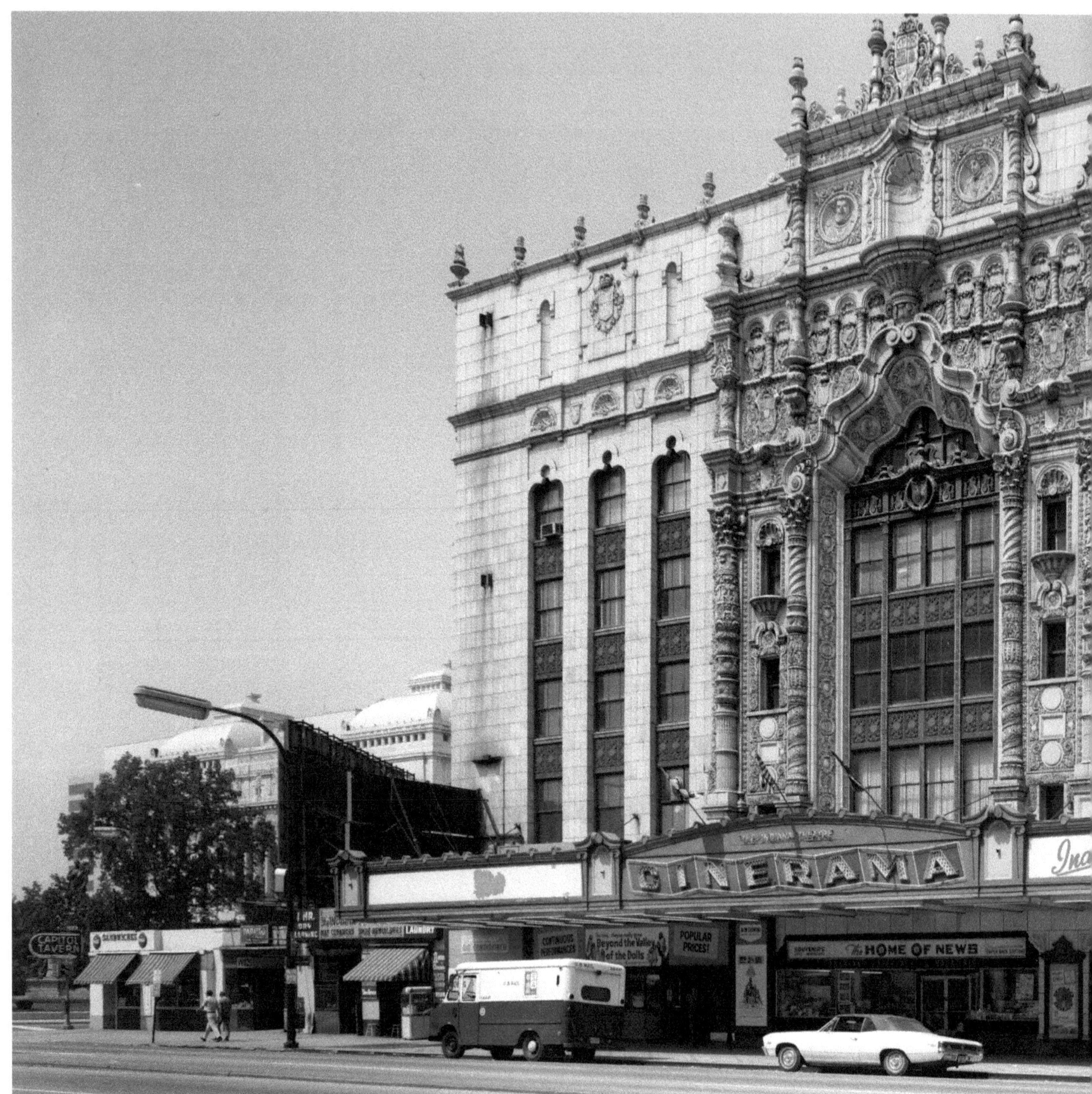
CINERAMA
CAPITOL TAVERN
SANDWICHES
1 HR.
LAUNDRY
CONTINUOUS PERFORMANCES
Beyond the Valley of the Dolls
POPULAR PRICES!
SOUVENIRS
The HOME OF NEWS

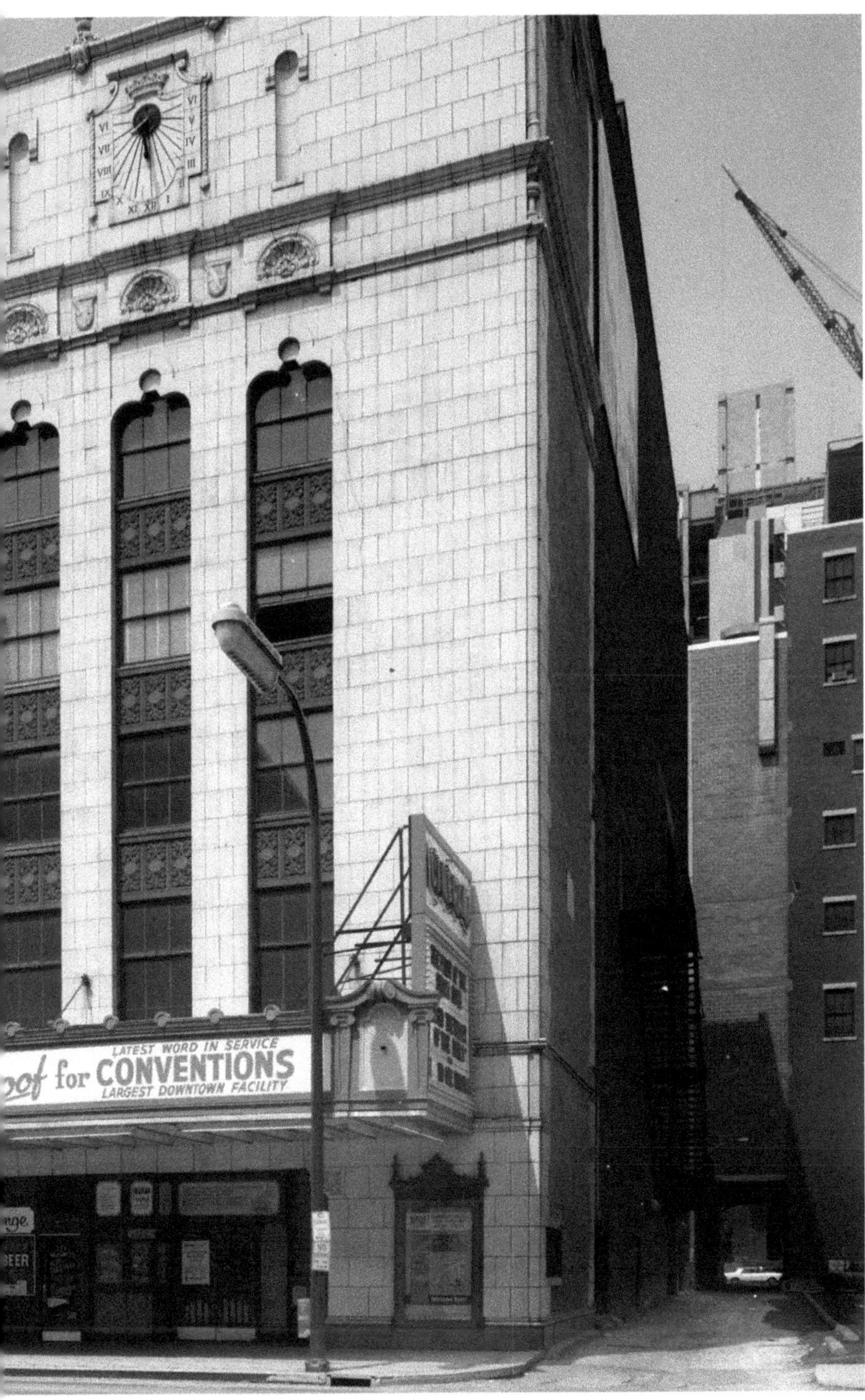

The Indiana Theatre on West Washington Street in Indianapolis was on the road to recovery in the 1960s, with efforts to save and restore the grand building under way. Built in 1926, the theater was an outstanding example of Spanish-style architecture then in vogue. The original marquee was saved and its terra cotta facade repaired. The theater includes a two-and-a-half-story lobby, 3,200-seat auditorium, and top-floor atmospheric ballroom designed to imitate a Spanish town plaza.

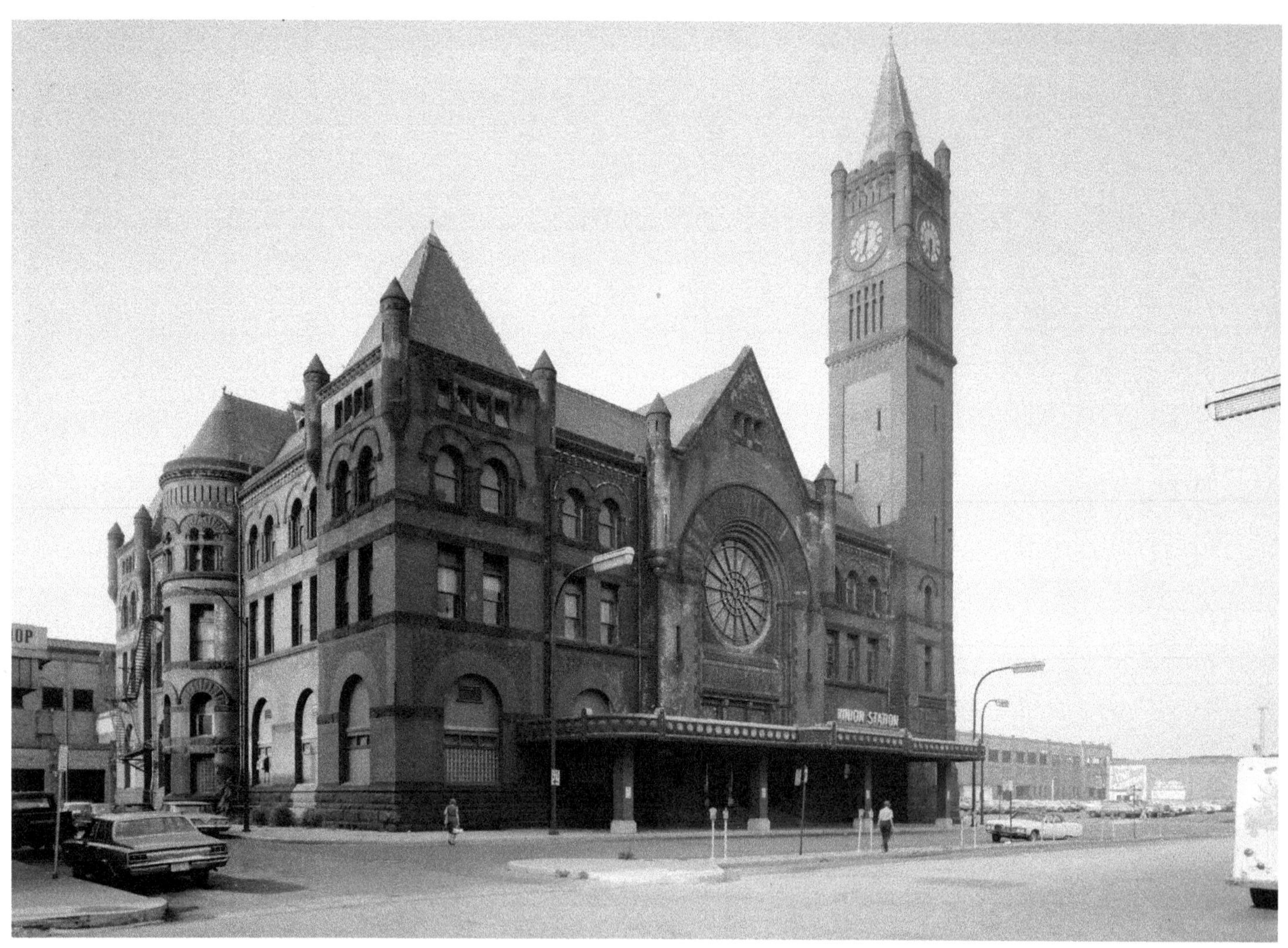

Union Station in Indianapolis is a classic example of American Romanesque Revival architecture, strongly influenced by the work of H. H. Richardson. The exterior is unusual in its skillful combination of brick and granite. The landmark's barrel-vaulted main waiting room is one of the finest large-scale spaces in Indianapolis and speaks to a time when mammoth steam engines brought people to the capital city. This image of the station was recorded in the 1960s.

Notes on the Photographs

These notes, listed by page number, attempt to include all aspects known of the photographs. Each of the photographs is identified by the page number, photograph's title or description, photographer and collection, archive, and call or box number when applicable. Although every attempt was made to collect all data, in some cases complete data may have been unavailable due to the age and condition of some of the photographs and records.

ii **Panorama of Madison, 1866**
Library of Congress
pan 6a04247

vi **Preparations for Balloon Race**
Library of Congress
03988u

x **Wabash and Erie Canal at Attica**
Thomas Castaldi, Allen County historian
Wedding Boat

2 **American Fort at Fort Wayne**
Allen County–Fort Wayne Historical Society
Fort Daguerreotype

3 **Huntington Business District, 1860**
Huntington City Township Public Library
Huntington Jefferson-Franklin Streets 1860

4 **Soldiers at Huntington Courthouse, 1861**
Huntington City Township Public Library
Huntington County Courthouse 1861

5 **Preparations at Indianapolis for Lincoln Funeral Train**
Indiana State Library
045 St House 1865

6 **St. Michael Church at Madison**
Library of Congress
HABS IND,39-MAD,8A-2

7 **Rooftop View of Huntington**
Huntington City Township Public Library
Huntington Jefferson St north to Canal abt 1900

8 **Main Building at Notre Dame**
Library of Congress
LC-USZ62-088441

9 **Kil-so-quah**
Indiana State Library
img897

10 **Four Trains Four Tracks**
Indiana State Library
img893

12 **Milligan Building**
Huntington City Township Public Library
Huntington Milligan Block 1887

13 **Morrisson Library at Richmond**
Wayne County Historical Museum, Richmond
0601_Richmond_Morrison-Reeves Library Exterior

14 **Depot at Atlanta**
Tipton Public Library, Tipton, Indiana
0211_Tipton_Interurban_Atlanta line

16 **The Pickett Family**
Cox Bunting Pickett Family Collection

17 **Covered Bridge at Richmond**
Wayne County Historical Museum, Richmond
0604_Richmond_Bridge & City

18 **Tipton County Courthouse**
Tipton Public Library, Tipton, Indiana
0207_Tipton_Court House Postcard

19 **Dill & McGuire Lawnmower Field Test, 1892**
Wayne County Historical Museum, Richmond
0608_Richmond_Mower Guys

20 **Horse Thief Detectives**
Miami County Historical Society, Peru, Indiana
0314_Peru_Horse Thief Detectives

21 **Richmond Coffin Works**
Wayne County Historical Museum, Richmond
0606_Richmond_Coffin Works_Composite

22 **Richmond Library Interior**
Wayne County Historical Museum, Richmond
0602_Richmond_Morrison-Reeves Library Interior

23 **Trestle Collapse at Otis**
La Porte Historical Society Museum, La Porte, Indiana
0415_La Porte_TrainWreckLaPorteCounty_bw

24 **Street Fair Days at Peru, 1894**
Miami County Historical Society, Peru, Indiana
0315_Peru_Street Fair Days

25 **Former President Benjamin Harrison and Well-wishers**
Miami County Historical Society, Peru, Indiana
0313_Peru_Harrison visit

26 **Brookside**
Allen County–Fort Wayne Historical Society
Bass Mansion (Schanz)

27 **Mayor Solomon Rouls at Work**
Tipton Public Library, Tipton, Indiana
0213_Tipton_Mayor's Office

28 **Canoeists in Bucolic Setting**
Library of Congress
3b44550u

29 **Brewery at Huntington**
Huntington City Township Public Library
Huntington Brewery Company

30 **Joseph Marshall Graham with Companions**
Cox Bunting Pickett Family Collection

31 **Sommerfield and Austin Studebakers**
La Porte Historical Society Museum, La Porte, Indiana
0410_La Porte_ SommerfieldLivery

32 **West Baden Springs Water Wagon**
John Martin Smith, DeKalb County Historian
0702_French Lick_Water Wagon

33 **Hotel at French Lick Springs**
John Martin Smith, DeKalb County Historian
0703A_French Lick_Golf_ rev1

34 **Downtown Peru**
Miami County Historical Society, Peru, Indiana
0317R_Peru_Downtown panorama Right

36 **The German House in Indianapolis**
Library of Congress
065077pu

37 **The Soldiers' and Sailors' Monument**
Library of Congress
3b44549u

38 **Cass County Train Wreck, 1901**
Miami County Historical Society, Peru, Indiana
0303_Peru_Cass National Wreck

39 **Veterans at National Military Home in Marion**
Library of Congress
3a48639u

40 **Indiana National Bank at Indianapolis**
Library of Congress
HABS IND,49-IND,17-2

41 **Indiana Union Traction Company Interurban**
Miami County Historical Society, Peru, Indiana
0312_Peru_Drayge

42 **Haynes Auto on Kokomo Street**
Library of Congress
LC-USZ62--099753

43 **Elkhart County Courthouse at Goshen**
Library of Congress
3c29032u

44 **Milwaukee Steamer Test Drive at Auburn**
Image courtesy of the William H. Willennar Genealogy Center, Auburn, Indiana
2003-001-1022

45 **Spencerville Ice Harvesters**
Lavon Hart Collection
ice

46 **William Jennings Bryan at Madison Chautauqua**
Library of Congress
3g04646u

47 **Pony Cigar Company at Fort Wayne**
Allen County–Fort Wayne Historical Society
Pony Cigar Factory (P157)

48 **Union Depot at Richmond**
Wayne County Historical Museum, Richmond
0610_Richmond_Penn Depot

49 **Miami County Officials and Assistants**
Miami County Historical Society, Peru, Indiana
0310_Peru_County Staff

50 **Cole Porter with Cousin Louis**
Miami County Historical Society, Peru, Indiana
0309_Peru_Cole Porter_ on left

51 **Gabriel Godfroy and Son George Godfroy**
Miami County Historical Society, Peru, Indiana
0304_Peru_Chief Godfroy & Son

52 **Downtown Lafayette**
Library of Congress
cph 3c05977

53 **Rappite Tavern in New Harmony**
Library of Congress
HABS IND,65-NEHAR,10-1

54 **Basket Factory in Peru**
Miami County Historical Society, Peru, Indiana
0302_Peru_Basket Factory

55 **Three Little Hoosier Maids**
Ellen England Collection
Three Little Maids

56 **Panorama of Purdue University**
Library of Congress
6a04356u

57 **North Delaware Street in Indianapolis**
Library of Congress
3b43801u

58 **South Street in Monroeville**
Allen County Public Library Ternet Collection
ACMV0023

59 **St. Meinrad Archabbey**
Library of Congress
3b41915u

60 **Homecoming Parade at Circus City**
Miami County Historical Society, Peru, Indiana
0307_Peru_Circus Parade Camels

61 **Homecoming Parade at Circus City no. 2**
Miami County Historical Society, Peru, Indiana
0308_Peru_Circus Parade

62 **Homecoming Parade at Circus City no. 3**
Miami County Historical Society, Peru, Indiana
0301_Peru_Baseball Parade

63 **Indiana Senate, 1905**
Library of Congress
6a34910u

64 **Grandest of All Memorials**
Library of Congress
HABS IND,49-IND,16-1

65 **Gandy Dancers of the New York Central**
Image courtesy of the William H. Willennar Genealogy Center, Auburn, Indiana
2002-09-03

66 **Princeton County Fair, 1907**
Library of Congress
6a27982u

67 **Mill Creek Threshing Party**
La Porte Historical Society Museum, La Porte, Indiana
0401_La Porte_Threshing

68 **DeKalb County Mint Still**
Indiana State Library
img903

69 **Sugar Beet Hoppers**
Allen County Public Library
ACWD0071

70 **Odd Fellows Home in Greensburg**
Library of Congress
6a04252u

72 **Steel Barrens**
Calumet Regional Archives, Indiana University Northwest, Gary, Indiana
0508_Gary_Building the Harbor

73 **Gary Under Construction**
Calumet Regional Archives, Indiana University Northwest, Gary, Indiana
0511_Gary_The Building of Gary

74 **Gary Under Construction no. 2**
Calumet Regional Archives, Indiana University Northwest, Gary, Indiana
0507_Gary_Furnace No.6

75 **Houdini in Indianapolis**
Library of Congress
LC-USZ62-079682

76 **The Evansville Waterfront, 1907**
Library of Congress
6a19269u

78 **Evans School in Tipton**
Tipton Public Library, Tipton, Indiana
0208_Tipton_Evans School with students

79 **Indiana State School for the Deaf**
Library of Congress
6a25523u

80 **Farm Produce Vendors, 1908**
Library of Congress
03213u

81 **Demolition of Miami County Courthouse**
Miami County Historical Society, Peru, Indiana
0311_Peru_Courthouse Demolition

82 **Messenger Boys**
Library of Congress
03227u

83 **Indianapolis Newsie**
Library of Congress
03220u

84 **At Frank S. Betz Company in Hammond**
Library of Congress
04466u

85 **Melon Basket Making**
Library of Congress
04483u

86 **GAR Reunion at Monroeville**
Allen County Public Library Ternet Collection
ACMV0500

87 **Meeting of the Ladies of the GAR, 1909**
Allen County Public Library Ternet Collection
ACMV0249

88 **Balloon Racing, 1909**
Library of Congress
065071pu

89 **Blue's Cigar Store Interior**
Miami County Historical Society, Peru, Indiana
0306_Peru_Cigar Shop Interior

90 **Rooftop View of Lebanon**
Library of Congress
3c05978u

91 **Wabash College at Crawfordsville**
Library of Congress
6a04260u

92 **Governor Marshall at Auburn Library Ceremony**
Image courtesy of the William H. Willennar Genealogy Center, Auburn, Indiana
2002-09-05-001

93 **First National Aviation Meet, 1910**
Library of Congress
LC-USZ62-123914

94 **Trouble at Mulberry**
Library of Congress
6a28884u

95 **New Albany's Rowe Fawcett Company**
Library of Congress
6a27724u

96 **Indiana University at Bloomington**
Library of Congress
6a04329u

98 **Bank Merger Celebration**
Library of Congress
LC-USZ62-046580

99 **Evansville's Municipal Market**
Library of Congress
LC-DIG-ppmsca-12682

100 **Indiana Literati**
Indiana State Library
img902

101 **Lafayette Powerhouse**
Library of Congress
HAER IND,79-LAFY,2A-3

102 **Judge Parker at Political Rally**
Library of Congress
10691u

103 **Great Flood of 1913 Devastation**
Library of Congress
3b22386u

104 **Confections of a Brakeman**
Huntington City Township Public Library
Huntington CBC engine in storefront 1913

105 **Steel City**
Library of Congress
6a19356u

106 **Indianapolis Model-T**
Indiana State Library
img909

107 **Purdue vs. Wabash at Stuart Field, 1913**
Library of Congress
6a29440u

108 **Early Indianapolis 500**
Library of Congress
LC-DIG-ggbain-13113

109 **Rooftop View of Terre Haute**
Library of Congress
pan 6aq04370

110 **Elkhart Hump Pusher Locomotive**
Library of Congress
19077u

111 **Gary Fire Department Group Portrait**
Library of Congress
pan 6a26193

112 **Indianapolis Skyline, 1914**
Library of Congress
pan 6a19301

113 **Bird's-eye View of La Crosse**
Library of Congress
pan 6a04222

114 **Mason Banquet**
Library of Congress
pan 6a27799

115 **Prairie Club at Indiana Dunes**
Calumet Regional Archives, Indiana University Northwest, Gary, Indiana
0503_Gary_Dune Hikers-neg

116 **Company B Leaving La Porte**
La Porte Historical Society Museum, La Porte, Indiana
0413_La PorteTrainLeavingComp BLaPorteCounty_bw

117 **Great Western Bicycle Factory Baseball Team, 1916**
La Porte Historical Society Museum, La Porte, Indiana
0411_La Porte_Sports GreatWstmCropped_bw

118 Ceremony for Greenfield's Riley Monument
Indiana State Library
img907

119 Christening of Open Hearth Furnace at Gary
Calumet Regional Archives, Indiana University Northwest, Gary, Indiana
0505_Gary_steel pour first heat

120 Axle-deep or Deeper
Tipton Public Library, Tipton, Indiana
0203_Tipton_Car in Mud

121 Carl Fisher at La Porte
La Porte Historical Society Museum, La Porte, Indiana
0407_La Porte_LincolnHwyParade_bw

122 Governor Goodrich for State Prohibition
Library of Congress
LC-USZ62-95896

123 Soldiers' Farewell Parade at Monument Circle
Library of Congress
pan 6a27804

124 Demolition at La Porte
La Porte Historical Society Museum, La Porte, Indiana
0404_La Porte_DemolishingBldg

126 Art Smith, Pioneer Aviator
Allen County–Fort Wayne Historical Society
Art Smith & Mechanic

127 Lexington Hill Climbers at Connersville
Library of Congress
HAER IND,21-CONVI,7-7

128 Parrot Petroleum of Fort Wayne
Allen County–Fort Wayne Historical Society
Parrot Petroleum

129 Aftermath of Townley Tornado, 1920
Allen County Public Library Ternet Collection
ACMV0536

130 Lebanon Interurban
Library of Congress
3c01741u

131 S. F. Bowser, Capitalist and Philanthropist
Allen County–Fort Wayne Historical Society
Bowser & Employee

132 Americanization Class at Gary
Calumet Regional Archives, Indiana University Northwest, Gary, Indiana
0509_Gary_Americanization Class

134 Picnickers at the Dunes
Calumet Regional Archives, Indiana University Northwest, Gary, Indiana
0502_Gary_Gypsy Hike Picnic

135 Earlham Hall at Richmond
Wayne County Historical Museum, Richmond
0603_Richmond_Earlham Hall

136 La Porte Theatre
La Porte Historical Society Museum, La Porte, Indiana
0408_La Porte_Lincolnway

137 Teacher with Young Scholars in Brazil
Cox Bunting Pickett Family Collection

138 Rumely Oil Pull Tractor
La Porte Historical Society Museum, La Porte, Indiana
0409_La Porte_RumelyOilPull_bw

139 William Jennings Bryan at Gennett Records
Wayne County Historical Museum, Richmond
0607A_Richmond_Gennett Records

140 Notre Dame Football Players at South Bend
Library of Congress
cph 3c28532

141 Windfall Twins
Tipton Public Library, Tipton, Indiana
0201_Tipton_2cars & 2guys

142 The LaFontaine Hotel
Huntington City Township Public Library
Huntington Hotel LaFontaine

143 Ku Klux Klan at Tipton
Tipton Public Library, Tipton, Indiana
0212_Tipton_KKK ritial

144 Peru Utility Crew
Miami County Historical Society, Peru, Indiana
0316_Peru_First Traffic Light Installation

146 Elkhart Music Men
Library of Congress
cph 3c21539

147 Grouseland in Vincennes
Library of Congress
HABS IND,42-VINC,2-2

148 President Coolidge at Hammond Dedication
Library of Congress
cph 3c02537

149 Scouts on Lincoln Highway at Zulu
Allen County Public Library Ternet Collection
ACMV0002

150 Oldest Church, at Vincennes
Library of Congress
HABS IND,42-VINC,1-1

151 Notre Dame Dedication Game, 1930
Library of Congress
LC-USZ62-057834

152 Scene at Blankenship
Library of Congress
LC-USF34-026545

153 The Corydon Capitol
Library of Congress
HABS IND,31-CORY,1-1

154 B&O Freight Train at Garrett
John Martin Smith, DeKalb County historian
0105_Garrett_train03_alt

156 Door Prairie Barn
La Porte Historical Society Museum, La Porte, Indiana
0405_La Porte_DoorPrairieBarn_bw

157 Zulu Rollerskate Basketball
Allen County Public Library Ternet Collection
ACMV0759

158 State Library Under Construction
Indiana State Library
img911

159 St. Joseph County Courthouse at South Bend
Library of Congress
HABS IND,71-SOUB,1-1

160 Vincennes Memorial to George Rogers Clark
Library of Congress
HABS IND,42-VINC,4-1

161 Threshing Oats
Library of Congress
LC-USF34-T01-9725

162 Farm Auction near Montmorenci
Library of Congress
LC-DIG-fsa-8b30203

163 Child with Hen at Normanda
Tipton Public Library, Tipton, Indiana
0204_Tipton_Child & Chicken

164 The Scene at Blankenship, 1938
Library of Congress
LC-USF33-T01-02751

165 Spencerville Depot
John Martin Smith, DeKalb County historian
0108_Spencerville Train Depot_alt

166 Farm Children at Play, 1938
Library of Congress
LC-USF34-026358

167 George Ade at Hazelden
Indiana State Library
img894

168 Auburn Automobile Employees at Connersville
Library of Congress
HAER IND,21-CONVI,7-10

169 Conner Cabins near Noblesville
Library of Congress
HABS IND,29-NOBL.V,2-1

170 Charlestown Power Plant Builders
Library of Congress
LC-USZ62-092914

172 Disappointed at the 1938 Indianapolis 500
Library of Congress
LC-USF33-T01-02750.tif

173 Bowler at Clinton
Library of Congress
LC-USF34-029491

174 To Washington for Ice Cream
Library of Congress
cph 3c29115

175 Major Hickox at Fort Benjamin Harrison, 1942
Library of Congress
LC-USW3-001741

176 Coeds at Bloomington Campus
Library of Congress
LC-G612-T-42440

177 Ordnance Makers at Hammond
Library of Congress
LC-USZ62-090357

178 Fort Wayne War Bond Drive
Allen County Public Library
00002794

179 Wartime Steel Workers at Gary
Calumet Regional Archives, Indiana University Northwest, Gary, Indiana
0510_Gary_WWII period steelworkers

181 The War Effort at Fort Wayne GE Plant
Allen County–Fort Wayne Historical Society
Women at GE c1920, Copy 1

182 Capitol Billboard
Library of Congress
LC-DIG-fsa-8d33263

183 On Leave in Richmond
Wayne County Historical Museum, Richmond
0609_Richmond_917 919 Main Sears

184 Fort Wayne near War's End
Allen County–Fort Wayne Historical Society
Calhoun St. Pennsylvania RR Elevation, June 1945 (P{1212)

186 Truman Campaign at Tipton
Tipton Public Library, Tipton, Indiana
0219_Tipton_Truman Rally

187 Aerial View of Gary
Calumet Regional Archives, Indiana University Northwest, Gary, Indiana
0506_Gary_Aerial

188 Indiana Dunes State Park
Calumet Regional Archives, Indiana University Northwest, Gary, Indiana
0504_Gary_Dunes Park

189 Wylie Home at Bloomington
Library of Congress
HABS IND,53-BLOOM,1-1

190 Monroeville County Fair Parade, 1955
Allen County Public Library Ternet Collection
ACMV0225

191 Huntington's Castles in the Air
Huntington City Township Public Library
Huntington Little River Twin Bridges buildings

192 Jefferson County Court House at Madison
Library of Congress
HABS IND,39-MAD,37-1

193 U.S. Arsenal at Indianapolis
Library of Congress
HABS IND,49-IND,21-1

195 Zaharako's Ice Cream Parlor in Columbus
Library of Congress
HABS IND,3-COLU,1-1

196 Robert Kennedy at Gary Airport
Calumet Regional Archives, Indiana University Northwest, Gary, Indiana
0501_Gary_Kennedy Rally_neg

197 Fire in Downtown Richmond
Wayne County Historical Museum, Richmond
0605B_Richmond_Explosion_B/W

199 The Indiana Theatre in Indianapolis
Library of Congress
HABS IND,49-IND,29-2

200 Indianapolis Union Station
Library of Congress
HABS IND,49-IND,20-3

Sources

Atherton, Lewis. *Main Street on the Middle Border.* New York: Quadrangle Books, 1974.

Baker, Ronald L. *From Needmore to Prosperity: Hoosier Place Names in Folklore and History.* Bloomington: Indiana University Press, 1995.

Cooper, Patricia A. *Once A Cigar Maker.* Urbana: University of Illinois Press, 1992.

Goebel, Dorothy Burne. *William Henry Harrison: A Political Biography.* Indianapolis: Historical Bureau of Indiana Library and Historical Department, 1926.

Goldberg, Vicki. *Lewis W. Hine: Children At Work.* New York: Prestel, 1999.

Horvath, Dennis E., and Terri Horvath. *Indiana Cars: A History of the Automobile in Indiana.* Indianapolis: Jackson Press, 2002.

Hudson, John C. *Making the Corn Belt: A Geographical History of Middle-Western Agriculture.* Bloomington: Indiana University Press, 1994.

Hyman, Max R., ed. *Hyman's Handbook of Indianapolis.* Indianapolis: Max R. Hyman Co., 1897.

Jakle, John. *My Kind of Midwest: Omaha to Ohio.* Chicago: Center for American Places, 2008.

Madison, James H. *Indiana Through Tradition and Change: A History of the Hoosier State and Its People, 1920–1945.* Indianapolis: Indiana Historical Society, 1982.

Nye, David E. *Electrifying America: Social Meanings of a New Technology.* Cambridge, Mass.: MIT Press, 1990.

Price, Nelson. *Indiana Legends: Famous Hoosiers from Johnny Appleseed to David Letterman.* Cincinnati: Emmis Books, 2005.

Shumaker, Arthur W. *A History of Indiana Literature.* Indianapolis: Indiana Historical Bureau, 1962.

Sievers, Harry J. *Benjamin Harrison: Hoosier President.* Indianapolis: Bobbs-Merrill Co., 1968.

Teaford, Jon C. *Cities of the Heartland: The Rise and Fall of the Industrial Midwest.* Bloomington: Indiana University Press, 1994.

Thornbrough, Emma Lou. *Indiana in the Civil War Era, 1850–1880.* Indianapolis: Indiana Historical Bureau and Indiana Historical Society, 1965.

HISTORIC PHOTOS OF INDIANA

This is the land of Hoosiers. Of George Rogers Clark's conquest at Vincennes, a key victory for the Revolution. Of covered bridges. A fledgling automobile industry. Notre Dame. The National Road and the Lincoln Highway and Carl Fisher. Cole Porter. The Milwaukee Steamer and the Rumely Oil Pull Tractor. Riverboats on the Wabash and the Ohio. The Wabash and Erie Canal. Interurbans. James Whitcomb Riley and George Ade. Small towns and big cities. Street Fair Days in Peru. The first state capitol at Corydon. Steel in Gary. Evansville's Municipal Market. Airmail by balloon. Union Station in Indianapolis and the Indy 500. Dunes along the Lake Michigan coast. Gandy dancers, circus parades, rollerskate basketball. Of sugar beets, sugar maples, and soybeans.

This is *Historic Photos of Indiana.* Filled with nearly 200 photographs reproduced in vivid black-and-white, with captions and introductions, showing the reader the places, people, and events that helped shape the lore and history of the Hoosier State.

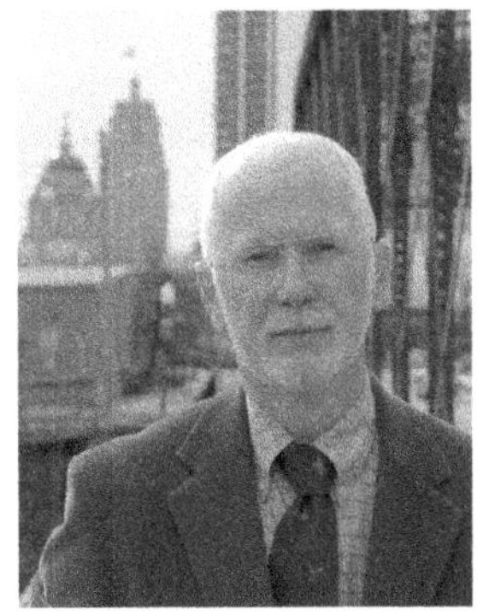

Scott M. Bushnell is the author of *Historic Photos of Fort Wayne* (Turner Publishing, 2007). He is a former reporter and editor for newspapers in New York and Connecticut and the Associated Press. Bushnell is also the author of *Hard News, Heartfelt Opinions: A History of the Fort Wayne Journal Gazette* and co-author of *Roanoke: The Renaissance of a Hoosier Village.* He and his wife, Barbara, reside in northeastern Indiana.

WWW.TURNERPUBLISHING.COM

www.ingramcontent.com/pod-product-compliance
Lightning Source LLC
LaVergne TN
LVHW060609110826
845154LV00003B/61
* 9 7 8 1 6 8 4 4 2 1 0 0 8 *